The Cry Was Unity

THE CRY
WAS UNITY

Communists and African Americans, 1917–36

Mark Solomon

UNIVERSITY PRESS OF MISSISSIPPI—*Jackson*

Manufactured in the United States of America

01   00   99   98   4   3   2   1

The paper in this book meets the guidelines for permanence and durability of the Committee on Production Guidelines for Book Longevity of the Council on Library Resources.

Library of Congress Cataloging-in-Publication Data

Solomon, Mark I.
The cry was unity : communists and African Americans, 1917–36 / Mark Solomon.
p.   cm.
Based in part on the author's doctoral dissertation.
Includes bibliographical references and index.
ISBN 1-57806-094-X (cloth : alk. paper). — ISBN 1-57806-095-8 (pbk. : alk. paper)
1. Communism — United States — History.   2. Afro-American communists — History.   3. Afro-Americans — Politics and government.   4. United States — Race relations.   I. Title.
HX83.S665   1998
335.43'089'96073 — dc21
98-16013
CIP

British Library Cataloging-in-Publication data available

To Pauline

Contents

Contents

Acknowledgments

All books, I suspect, are collective enterprises, encompassing the labor not only of the author but also of many colleagues, librarians, archivists, students, family members, friends, and acquaintances. This book is certainly that kind of venture. Many people responded to an endless list of requests, and I am happy to report that I cannot recall a single individual who refused to help.

First, I must acknowledge the late Frank Friedel who guided me through a doctoral dissertation that was both a germinal point and distant echo of this book. At a time when topics of this sort were not welcomed with open arms in academia, Frank took me on, guided me with wisdom and patience through rough waters, and asked only that I treat the subject fairly. I hope that I have not let him down. Daniel Aaron also extended to me in those early days the benefit of his erudition and insight.

Robin D. G. Kelley read an outrageously long first draft with patience, humor, and a remarkably probing, critical spirit. The book has been vastly improved by his creative, thoughtful reading. Robert A. Hill's indefatigable and thorough research, his brilliant work on Marcus Garvey and Cyril Briggs, his generous sharing of materials, and his valued friendship were essential to this project. Mark Naison and Nell Painter read early, partial incarnations of this book. Their trenchant criticisms were tough, justified, and welcome. The late Philip S. Foner read an early version and extended criticism leavened by encouragement. Milton Cantor offered excellent ideas on the scope and organization of the book and gave support beyond the call of duty. Aida Donald read an early draft and offered astute and very helpful suggestions.

I met Robert Kaufman in a musty reading room in New York City. We were drawn to the same archive because our work converged at important points. He was a carnivorous researcher, devouring everything in sight and dissecting his materials with both relish and sparkling intellect. Bob was felled tragically by cancer before his fortieth birthday. I wish to thank Anne Schneider for allowing me to cart off boxes of documents that Bob had accumulated. I hope that this book, in some measure, does justice to Bob's memory.

Harvey Klehr always responded promptly and generously to my requests for information on the Communist Party and on use of the Moscow archives. Arthur Kaledin, Elizabeth Wood, Katherine Bromberg, May Fisher, Rochelle Ruthchild, and Tatyana Kromchenko all facilitated the task of extracting and transmitting materials from the overworked staff at the Russian Center for Preservation and Study of Documents of Contemporary History. Roberta Manning of Boston College helped me with translations of the titles of various collections at the Russian Center and led me to J. Arch Getty who provided valuable information on the archive. Galina Khatoulary and Valery Klukov are two brilliant young Russian scholars at the start of what will be outstanding careers. Their translations of material in Russian were flawless. Most important, they offered incisive interpretations of the meaning of documents and helped me to a better understanding of the ways of the Communist International. Valery's insights into the Comintern debate on the Negro question virtually qualifies him to the title, if he would have it, of coauthor of the chapter on that subject.

Jonathan Scott Holloway generously allowed me to use materials from his excellent paper on John P. Davis and the new black activism of the 1930s. Theodore Draper led me to Samuel Adams Darcy, who answered my questions on the Comintern debate on the Negro question with alacrity and thoroughness. Mary Licht of the Research Center for Marxist Studies shared her knowledge of the pioneer black Communists and allowed me to have a copy of Hermina Huiswoud's priceless history of the life of Otto Huiswoud. The late Mimi Alexander in Los Angeles gave me valuable copies of Cyril Briggs's correspondence, most of which are now at the Southern California Research Library. Yasanouri Sano combed through reels of microfilm on government investigations of Communists with extraordinary patience and a sharp eye. Arthur

Zipser provided information based on his lifelong studies of American communism. The late Alice Citron provided rare pamphlets from the 1930s. William Weinstone wrote illuminating letters on Lenin's view of the national question. My old friend from our teenage days of agitating and advocating in Bedford-Stuyvesant, Marvin Borenstein, diligently searched the photo archive at the Schomburg Center for Research in Black Culture. Wendy Fisher helpfully edited an early draft. Kristin Small uncomplainingly read a lengthy early draft. There were many others who gave me tips on sources and helped in innumerable ways. My gratitude is extended to all of them.

The dozens of individuals who allowed me to interview them, who put up with my clumsy handling of recording equipment, and who tolerated my fumbling questions deserve a special note of thanks. I hope a degree of justice was done to their heroic and principled lives.

The staffs at Simmons College and Harvard University endured my repeated requests for interlibrary loan materials with warmth and efficiency. For their excellent assistance, I also wish to thank librarians at the Chicago Historical Society, Columbia University, Emory University, the Federal Bureau of Investigation, the Moorland-Springarn Research Center of Howard University, the Library of Congress, the New York Public Library, the Tamiment Institute of New York University, the Research Center for Marxist Studies, the Schomburg Center for Research in Black Culture, the Southern California Research Library, the University of Michigan, the Southern Historical Collection at the University of North Carolina, the Archives of Labor History and Urban Affairs at Wayne State University, and the Wisconsin State Historical Society.

My colleagues in the history department and in the administration at Simmons College provided unwavering encouragement and support. William Kahl, the former provost at Simmons, generously gave me time and space for travel and writing. Departmental colleagues John Hunter, Henry Halko, Richard Lyman, Laurie Crumpacker, Susan Porter, and Keith Gorman were veritable fortresses of collegiality, always willing to help ease the burden of work on the book. The department staff over the years assisted without a single complaint. The late Ruth Hirsch typed reams of copy in precomputer days. She would give me that "what, more?" look and then churn the work out with consummate skill. Student assistants Nancy Israel and Catriona Oakes collected hundreds of note cards culled from old newspapers and magazines. Marie McHugh and Mary White did all sorts of things to get the book on the way. Most important, they adopted the project as their own, and their enthusiasm helped fuel it to completion. Former students who went on to careers in teaching were a special source of advice and information. Ellen Slatkin often took time from work on her doctorate to give me valuable information on trends in historiography. My thanks to all of my Simmons friends.

I had heard from many in publishing that Seetha A-Srinivasan, the editor-in-chief at University Press of Mississippi, was one of the best in the business. My experience certainly confirmed that assessment. Her advice was always on target, her prodding was always well timed, and her marvelous blend of tough-mindedness and gentleness always struck the right chord. Most of all, her belief in the project was essential to its completion. Lys Ann Shore's editing culled out errors, polished the writing, had me clarify what needed clarification, and made the manuscript measurably better. She is terrific, and I deeply appreciate her help. Of course, whatever errors remain are entirely my responsibility.

Various agencies have given indispensable financial support for this project. The National Endowment for the Humanities awarded a generous fellowship in historical and cultural studies of U.S. ethnic minorities, which allowed for months of uninterrupted research. A grant from the Marion and Jasper Whiting Foundation permitted travel. The project received essential support through a series of grants from the Simmons College Fund for Research. My thanks go to all those agencies.

Pauline Solomon, my partner for decades, suffered uncomplainingly with the ups and downs of this project, helped in innumerable ways, and never lost faith that something of reasonable value would emerge. Important as all that is, it pales in comparison to the moral and political values she has held unwaveringly over all the years and which pervade this book. We met as kids who were imbued with a spirit of social activism. We aren't kids any more, but the fire of justice still burns within her. She holds a place along with the people in this book who dedicated their lives to a just world.

Abbreviations

AAA	Agricultural Adjustment Act
ABB	African Blood Brotherhood
ACLU	American Civil Liberties Union
AFL	American Federation of Labor
AFU	Alabama Farmers' Union
ANLC	American Negro Labor Congress
CBP	Claude Barnett Papers, Chicago Historical Society
CEC	Central Executive Committee (CP)
CFL	Chicago Federation of Labor
CFWU	Croppers' and Farm Workers' Union
CHS	Chicago Historical Society
CI	Communist International (Comintern or Third International)
CIC	Commission on Interracial Cooperation
CIO	Congress of Industrial Organizations
CMA	Colored Merchants Association
Comintern	Communist International (CI, or Third International)
CP	Communist Party, USA
CWA	Civil Works Administration
DJ-FBI	Department of Justice — Federal Bureau of Investigation

DW	*Daily Worker*
ECCI	Executive Committee Communist International
FLCFWU	Farm Laborers and Cotton Field Workers Union
HKP	Henry Kraus Papers, Archive of Labor History and Urban Affairs, WSU
HL	*Harlem Liberator*
ILA	International Longshoremen's Association
ILD	International Labor Defense
Inprecorr	*International Press Correspondence* (CI)
ITUCNW	International Trade Union Committee of Negro Workers
IWO	International Workers Order
IWW	Industrial Workers of the World
JCNR	Joint Committee on National Recovery
KKK	Ku Klux Klan
KUTV	University of the Toilers of the East, Moscow
LAI	League against Imperialism and for National Independence
LC	Library of Congress, Washington, D.C.
LD	*Labor Defender*
LSNR	League of Struggle for Negro Rights
LU	*Labor Unity*
MHVP	Mary Heaton Vorse Papers, Archive of Labor History and Urban Affairs, WSU
NA	National Archives, Washington, D.C.
NAACP	National Association for the Advancement of Colored People
NAACP Papers	Papers of the NAACP, LC
NERL	National Equal Rights League
NFU	National Farmers' Union
NIRA	National Industrial Recovery Act
NL	*Negro Liberator*
NM	*New Masses*
NMU	National Miners Union
NNC	National Negro Congress
NPT	Negro People's Theater
NR	*New Republic*
NRA	National Recovery Act

NTWIU	Needle Trades Workers' Industrial Union
NTWU	National Textile Workers Union
NUL	National Urban League
NYPL	New York Public Library
NYT	*New York Times*
NYU	New York University
OHAL	Oral History of the American Left, Tamiment Institute, Bobst Library, NYU
PolCom	Political Committee (Communist Party)
Profintern	Red International of Labor Unions (RILU)
RILU	Red International of Labor Unions (also called Profintern)
RKC	Robert Kaufman Collection, Tamiment Institute, Bobst Library, NYU
RMP	Robert Minor Papers, Butler Library, Columbia University, New York
RTsKhIDNI	Russian Center for the Preservation and Study of Documents of Contemporary History, Moscow
RTsKhIDNI 495	Fond for Executive Committee of the Communist International, RTsKhIDNI
RTsKhIDNI 515	Fond for the Communist Party USA, RTsKhIDNI
RTsKhIDNI 534	Fond for the Red International of Labor Unions (also Profintern), RTsKhIDNI
SACP	South African Communist Party
SCRL	Southern California Research Library, Los Angeles
SCU	Share Croppers' Union
SLC	Stockyards Labor Council
STFU	Southern Tenant Farmers' Union
STFU Papers	Papers of the STFU, Southern Historical Collection, University of North Carolina, Chapel Hill
SWOC	Steel Workers Organizing Committee
TC	*The Crusader*
TDC	Theodore Draper Collection, Woodruff Library, Emory University, Atlanta
TL	*The Liberator*
TUCONW	Trade Union Committee for Organizing Negro Workers
TUEL	Trade Union Educational League

TUUL	Trade Union Unity League
UCs	Unemployed Councils
UCAPAWA	United Cannery, Agricultural, Packing and Allied Workers of America
UCP	United Communist Party
UMW	United Mine Workers
UNIA	Universal Negro Improvement Association
WESL	Workers' Ex-Servicemen's League
WP	Workers Party (USA)
WPA	Works Progress Administration
WSU	Wayne State University, Detroit
YCI	Young Communist International
YCL	Young Communist League

Introduction

This is the completion of a project that began in the 1970s and was put aside when other interests took over. However, several factors converged to bring me back to the book. First, the archives of the Communist International were opened, making materials available that promised an enriched understanding of the encounter between African Americans and Communists. There was also the ever present responsibility to scores of people who had opened their hearts and minds at a time when it was still not easy to discuss Communist connections. My debt to them could only be repaid by producing this book.

Admittedly, I was also goaded by victorious ballot initiatives to eliminate affirmative action, legislative measures to reduce black representation, and court decisions to eradicate much of what remained. With that agenda dominating, much of today's discussion was about racial reconciliation without racial justice, the value of resegregation, the virtue of black capitalism, or the worth of an official apology for slavery. Academics brought forth weighty studies claiming that compensatory programs are no longer needed—either because of their success in nurturing the growth of the black middle class or because of their failure to end a miserable ghetto pathology. The contradictions didn't seem troubling to them.[1]

Whether it constituted "presentism" or not, I felt that an exploration of the relationship between blacks and reds in the 1920s and 1930s had a lot to say to

President Clinton's "conversation on race." In fact, that earlier experience had some ideological and moral aspects that ran deeper than today's discussion. The pivotal issues then were neither tactical nor sentimental; they involved the basic structure and character of American society. Capitalism's cornerstone was seen to have been laid by slavery and fortified by racism. Therefore, the achievement of equality implied the ultimate transformation of the nation's economic and social foundations. That concept reached far beyond the racial landscape, to the recasting of the economic and psychological lives of all working people. Indeed, black striving for freedom was welded to the fortunes of the working class — creating an inseparable link between the movement of workers to free themselves from capital and the movement of blacks of all classes to end oppression. In the long term, the attainment of equality meant at last the realization of the nation's democratic promise and the building of a new society.

In the Communist view, African Americans had withstood systematic and special oppression from which capitalism had derived a flow of superprofits and a constellation of other advantages gained through fostering racial division among the dispossessed. That oppression was "national" in character — enveloping race, class, and nationality. It was punctuated by myriad forms of physical and psychological violence and was grounded in vicious racism that contorted the whole society. At the same time, that subjugation had forged a dialectic of layered, many-sided resistance driven by a deepening national consciousness.

The fight for racial justice could not be perceived as charity, mawkishness, or an exorcism of guilt. The "Negro question" was certainly not the Myrdalian "dilemma" in the heart of tormented white society torn between its "American Creed" of "high national and Christian precepts" on the one hand, and, on the other, its inability to jettison prejudice rooted in community conformity and complex social interests.[2] Rather, the oppression of blacks was an essential element in preserving the system and had to be combated with unprecedented passion as an indispensable requirement for achieving social progress.

Communists dared not speak of "integration" (a term that came into vogue during the Cold War) into capitalism's proverbial "burning house." On the other hand, they believed that racial separation would sunder the working class and sustain the old order. The conception of the Negro question as a national question negated both sterile absorption into the dominant order and a narrow separatist outlook. While seriously flawed, the theoretical projection of a national question nevertheless suggested a way to resolve the historic tension between assimilationism and separatism. It pointed to a third road to liberation based on unqualified equality *and* self-determination, grounded in the distinct, historically evolved nationality of the Negro people.

The theoretical linkage of special oppression and black liberation with social struggle on a broader plane led to some propositions that had an influence upon the African American struggle: stress upon the depth, magnitude, and tenacity of "white chauvinism" and the need for whites to fight it with uncompromising vigor; the concept of multiracial "mass action" as an indispensable means of achieving justice in a polity that had become seriously deformed and deliberately inoperative in regard to the claims of the Negro people. Economic and legal justice, then, would require relentless pressure and mass protest.

The Communists advocated special measures to compensate for generations of special oppression. The concept of "super-seniority," pressed upon the emerging industrial union movement, was a forerunner of affirmative action. At the same time, such measures were linked inseparably to the need for economic reforms to assure employment for all—thus grounding support for special steps to end discrimination in the overarching interest of the entire working class. On the political front, the Communists pressed for black representation, arguing that efforts to advance black political power based upon principles of fair representation would inevitably propel the entire political dialogue to the left.

Inherent in the Communist position on the Negro question, in general, was the strategic concept of a Negro-labor alliance as the cornerstone of progress. Despite periodic strains and ruptures, that informal alliance has been a major element of left-of-center union activity and politics since the 1930s. Starting from nearly unimaginable ideological rigidity in the sectarian Third Period of the late 1920s and early 1930s, the Communists nevertheless contributed to sensitizing trade unions and broader segments of the society to the depths of discrimination and the pressing need to struggle for racial justice in the interests the vast majority.

Of course, the black-red relationship was never a perfect fusion. Especially in the formative 1920s, communism was perceived by many African Americans to be lightyears away from their history, politics, culture, and psychological makeup. In the early period, the Communist Party was largely foreign-born and nearly all white. The Communists' political language was alien; their internationalism sometimes appeared to undermine racial priorities; their efforts to supplant traditional middle-class black leaders with workers were often perceived as mindlessly meddlesome and arrogant; their bravado and self-absorption was abrasive to African Americans who were creating their own agenda and who did not necessarily seek support and advice from the outside. Also, many blacks viewed Communists as pariahs who would only add to their already substantial vulnerability.

Nevertheless, many barriers to a red-black relationship were overcome. In climbing seemingly insurmountable walls of historic estrangement between radicals and African Americans, the Communists learned and taught some important lessons. And sectors of the black community, in facing the reds, defined acceptable terms for a political relationship that accommodated their interests. The imperfections, successes, and failures of the attempted collaboration provide an expansive field for study of the problem of building political and cultural relationships between the races.

All that may seem ill timed in light of the present consignment of communism to the proverbial dustbin of history. But that cuts two ways. While some might consider that recent events have made communism irrelevant, those same events have also opened the door to more detached, objective assessments — on all sides — shorn of the ideological passions of the last half-century. There is at least a tinge of persuasiveness in the words of East German intelligence wizard Markus Wolf in his recent autobiography: "Any history worthy of the name cannot be written only by the winners."[3]

The old debate over the American Communist Party's ties to the Soviet Union — which was at the core of many studies undertaken during the Cold War — has abated but has not disappeared.[4] Theodore Draper's work remains the standard for the viewpoint that the American Party was ruled by Moscow, responded to the fluctuations of its policies, and obeyed no truly American need.[5]

Draper's conception was largely unchallenged until the 1970s, when a group of "new historians" (many veterans of the New Left) began to publish articles and books that sought to revise the Cold War view of American communism. More important than Comintern directives was the Party's life and work at the social and cultural grassroots where the material and spiritual realities of Communist lives were manifested in a thoroughly American context.[6]

The studies of the new historians captured American communism with far greater breadth than Draper's adroit but timeworn journey into the netherworld of foreign control. Their exploration of the many-sided nature of the American Communist experience was more informative than Draper's dismissal of Communist work for peace, for industrial unionism, for black liberation, as "sideshows" compared to primary service to Soviet interests.[7]

But many of the new historians had their own dogma: They conceded the external control of the Party, but granted a margin of freedom from foreign dictates in the spaces between leaders and lower level activists. In doing that, they at times succumbed to trendy anticommunism and produced incomplete, if not faulty, scholarship. Their portraits did not fully conform to the way the Party functioned and did not seriously examine the nature of external influences — reducing the issue to cancerous sores, best excised from the movement's relatively healthy tissue. At times, the formula became downright rigid and schematic. For example, one study maintained that "on issues where the Comintern spoke specifically, Harlem Communists ... changed their analysis at the drop of a hat ... and generally showed a lack of intellectual integrity and moral balance. But on issues which the Comintern neglected to provide guidelines, they fought for racial and economic justice with a voice that seemed powerful and authentic."[8]

The symbols and legends of American Communists and their allies were ignited and stoked by a distinct set of beliefs nurtured both in native soil and in a perception of being part of a vast international movement. That movement, in the view of many Communists, black and white, represented a powerful, indispensable factor in the battle on native grounds against oppression and inequality. Indeed, on the Negro question, at least, Comintern injunctions insisted on a "powerful and authentic" commitment by American Communists to fight for black liberation.

This book suggests another approach to studying American communism: to examine the interplay of national and international forces, of theory and practice, and of leadership and rank and file in the making and execution of policy. Of course, everyone in this political drama brought to his or her commitment a unique psychological makeup, emotional timbre, and quality of intellect and labor. There were many who hoisted their umbrellas at the first sign of rain in Moscow or New York. There were others whose political work did not await orders from Moscow or from U.S. Party headquarters. However, in acknowledging that all these people functioned within a coherent political culture that was both national and international in scope, one does not have to accept Draper's fatuous assertion that the "good Communist" was ipso facto a slave of Moscow.

The founders of American communism responded largely to the conduct of the socialist parties of the Second International, which supported their own countries in a perceived imperialist war. Socialist ranks all over the world were split — with the apostates filled with bitterness at the nationalism that they believed had corrupted socialists and had made a mockery of Marx's proletarian internationalism. A renewed internationalism was the dream of the left-wing groups that sought to create new communist parties to obliterate the material and psychic borders that buttressed imperialism and nurtured betrayal.

The left wing of the Socialist Party of the United States in 1919 reflected that desire. It also drew sustenance from the October Revolution in Russia, which had taken that country out of the war and had embarked on an uncharted journey to build the first socialist state in history. The left-wing Socialists who formed the Communist Party (initially in two groups) believed that the world had entered a new epoch. Capitalism was now faced with an alternative system spanning one-sixth of the Earth's surface and had thus presumably entered general — and terminal — crisis. While that notion was to bring grief to Communists the world over, it had a dizzying resonance for those who embraced the Third International. Politics, local and global, now flowed from the confrontation of two world systems, and the fate of the class struggle in each nation was now inseparable from the struggle for survival of the first workers' and peasants' state.

Many of the women and men who came to Moscow for Comintern meetings were experienced revolutionaries who commanded considerable respect. Especially in the formative period, debates were vigorous and freewheeling, with conclusions often in doubt. Even Lenin's views were not immune from examination. His "Colonial Theses" at the Second Congress in July 1920 were subjected to heated debate and accepted only after revision. The debate on the Negro question at the pivotal Sixth Congress in 1928 was a complex affair — at times rich in theoretical and historical exploration and at other times hobbled by pettiness, infighting, and faltering grasp of the African American experience. Its outcome was not necessarily guaranteed by hovering Russians. The interplay between Soviet desires and factional maneuvering among the American delegates ultimately tipped the scales for national self-determination. But black Communists in particular, who looked to Moscow for succor from the racism that infected white American comrades, did not consider the debate and its outcome to be wholly lacking in intellectual honor and ethical constancy.

The Americans who embraced communism were neither mindless dupes of the Soviet-dominated Comintern nor the new historians' wily, independent radicals cleverly sidestepping external directives. And for that matter, their ties to the Soviets and the Comintern were neither automatically self-destructive nor magically beneficial.

Most Comintern directives sought to impose "correct" Marxist-Leninist canons aimed at theoretical purity, militant devotion to self-defined working-class principles, and uncompromising revolutionary work. Some mandates were reminiscent of a parent's tough love for an errant child. Others probably provided a needed sense of distance and perspective to straighten out muddles in national parties.

Examination of the Comintern's files on the American Communist Party, its Anglo-American secretariat files, and the documents of the Red International of Labor Unions does not reveal a "secret world of American communism" — at least in terms of proposals and directives on the Negro question in the United States. Those papers do reveal Comintern imperiousness, personal squabbles, political differences, Communist control of supposedly independent groups, and self-serving maneuvers that rarely, if ever, got onto the public record. But more often than not, the documents are a mirror of the ideological and political intensity that drove the public activities of American Communists.

In some respects the Party's international ties endowed it with the "franchise" — privileged association with the first purportedly socialist state and "fraternal relations" with parties in the developed and developing world that played major political roles. It provided the Party with "importance" beyond its numbers because communism, not the myriad factions of the left, had become at least half of the political equation that virtually defined the politics of the twentieth century.

But unlike the Chinese and Italian communists, who waited a few years after the Bolshevik Revolution before founding their parties, the U.S. Communists rushed headlong into a break with the Socialist Party, into formation of new parties, and into the Comintern — not allowing precious time to deepen their national roots before entering the global arena. The delicate balance between an "international perspective" and the need to respond to conditions at home was thus hard to maintain. A confusion of Soviet state interests with a loftier internationalism often led American Communists into murky channels. Looking homeward and looking to Moscow at the same time created a perpetual duality. This sometimes produced tensions but more often than not led to willing acquiescence to foreign-made decisions that were often applied reflexively in the United States.

Even that compelling proposition cannot be advanced without qualification. For example, the ultra-leftist Third Period line, promulgated at the Sixth Congress, declared an end of capitalist stabilization, the onset of wars of all kinds, and "gigantic class battles." In that context, social democracy and reform were characterized as the last lines of defense of capitalism — while Communists were enjoined to concentrate their political fire on liberals. The Americans complied with characteristic fidelity and excess. Yet, despite the mind-bending nastiness and sectarianism of the Third Period from 1928 to 1934, some of the most daring, uncompromising, and ground-breaking battles were waged, especially for African American rights.

The Comintern connection was never static, but was an ever changing process involving human beings who often accepted external hegemony without hesitation, but who also strove mightily to come to grips with national realities. The relationship, and the accommodations and conflicts inherent within it, has to be evaluated in terms of specific historic circumstances and the handling of concrete political issues. On that basis, perhaps, the relationship can be demystified and the ability of American Communists to make some gains despite their supposedly deadly obedience to external forces can be better understood.

This book looks at the Comintern and Soviet dimensions in relation to the evolution of the U.S. Communist position on the Negro question. The Comintern pressed the issue of Negro rights as a matter to be treated with utmost seriousness; it was not to be considered a marginal "field," but one essential to the overriding goals of the international communist movement. That pressure was decisive in forcing the U.S. Party to depart from the pattern of neglect and hostility to African Americans that had often characterized its radical predecessors. But the application of the theoretical precepts shaped in Moscow soon was influenced by American realities. The Comintern did not order the imprisonment and death sentences of the Scottsboro boys. That cause and others — not orders from Moscow — became the most influential factors in drawing Communists and their allies into a vortex of political struggle.

I have chosen to cover in this volume the period from the founding of Cyril Briggs's *Crusader* in 1917 to the launching of the National Negro Congress in 1936. This time span encompasses the evolution of Communist policy on African American liberation from a traditional "colorblind" class outlook to a deeper conception of the Negro question as a national question — and finally, to the achievement of a broad-based Negro-labor alliance. In the nearly two decades covered by this study, one can analyze the evolution of a policy and observe how a movement broke free from isolation and ideological abstractions to achieve a significant place in the battle for racial justice. A future volume will look at the black-radical relationship from the late 1930s through the Cold War years.

It has become fashionable in studies such as this to stress cultural and social context in general and "oppositional culture" in particular. In the hands of sensitive and well-grounded historians (such as Robin Kelley and George Lipsitz, for example), the latter concept has produced brilliant insights. But cultural history and oppositional culture have often propagated impenetrable abstractions that locate motivations in vague longings and social habits derived from memory and accumulated spiritual goods. Intentional or not, such concepts have at times obfuscated concrete power relationships grounded in class, race, and nationality. The main figures in this book, black and white, were, of course, influenced by their cultural and social backgrounds (noted in this study). Those were important — but often secondary. The dominant influences were the effects of the crushing burdens of the economic crisis and a consequent consciousness of social injustice, racial and national oppression, and class partisanship. That consciousness is the principal focus of this book.

This study also provides an overview of the black-red relationship that may stimulate scholars to undertake needed regional studies, epitomized by the outstanding work done by Robin Kelley on Alabama and Mark Naison on Harlem. There is much to be mined from studies of the Southwest and West in particular, where the claims of radical Mexican Americans both intersected with and rivaled the concerns of African Americans.

This brings up the issue of the vast multiracial character of the nation's social life and political conflicts — far more manifest today than in the period explored in this book. In the 1920s and 1930s, of course, people of Latino, Asian, Native American, and other backgrounds felt the lash of discrimination along with blacks. However, what befell blacks, both historically and contemporaneously, established the precedents for the discrimination suffered by other groups. The black-white dimension was the central concern of the players in this story and is consequently the central concern of this book. Where appropriate, I have used the racial designations for African Americans that were extant in the period under study.

It has become something of a tradition in studies of this sort for the author to explain his or her generational experience and its impact upon the book. Generational experience is, of course, only one aspect of the intellectual and spiritual equipment that an author brings to his or her work. There is no such thing as generational consensus on matters of historical interpretation. But the knowledge and feelings of historians are shaped largely by their personal circumstances.

I was a white kid who went to a nearly all-black public school in the Bedford-Stuyvesant section of Brooklyn during the wartime and postwar years. Many of the teachers, black and white, were radicals, and some were Communists. (Virtually all were driven from the school system in the McCarthy period, tragically eliminating a group of teachers committed to genuine equality in learning.) Mine was reputedly a "problem school," and teachers received some kind of bounty for teaching there. Those teachers, however, were not motivated by bounties, but by a consuming respect for the children and for their heritage. We celebrated the birthdays of Frederick Douglass and Paul Robeson; we marveled at Harriet Tubman and Sojourner Truth; we saluted the scientific achievements of Charles Drew; and we sang James Weldon Johnson's "Lift Every Voice" at assembly. (Most of us knew its stirring lyrics better than those of the "Star Spangled Banner.") It's safe to say that such things rarely, if ever, went on anywhere else—and the decency and sensitivity of those teachers impressed me deeply.

I was also drawn to the radical speakers who periodically parked their sound-trucks with their brightly painted slogans by the subway near our apartment, and who spoke with passion for democracy and racial justice. I soon found myself on street corners soliciting signatures for the freedom of Rosa Lee Ingram, a Georgia mother and sharecropper who had been sentenced to death for killing a landlord while resisting sexual assault—and eventually mounting stepladders (to my parents' chagrin) to imitate the passions of those elder activists.

Many who grew up in the 1940s and matured in the 1950s lived in a political milieu that was still strongly influenced by the Communist Party and its allies. The intellectual and political ferment in much of the movement for black liberation reflected that influence. I grew up when such towering figures as Robeson, W.E.B. Du Bois and other lesser known but inspiring figures of the African American left were on the scene. I tried not to miss any public gathering where either Robeson or Du Bois was scheduled to appear. I clung to Du Bois's words and dogged him through the corridors of the radical Jefferson School where he lectured in the early 1950s. With friends, I hovered over Robeson's recording of his classic *Othello,* wore out my album of his "Songs of Free Men," and tremblingly sought his support in my sophomoric quarrel with administrators of the left-wing summer camp that he visited annually. I admired the insights of Dr. William Alpheus Hunton of the Council on African Affairs, who awakened an awareness of the rising anticolonial tide in Africa. William L. Patterson was in and out of jail in those days, but never seemed distracted or short of patience with those around him. The courtly but distant James Ford was in Brooklyn, and Benjamin J. Davis Jr., always eloquent and impeccable, was making fiery speeches to "fellow workers" all over the city. There was Adam Clayton Powell Jr., arriving late and breathlessly at a public meeting—who enraptured his audience nevertheless and justified the near filibuster of his legendary fellow member of Congress from Harlem, Vito Marcantonio, who had stalled until Powell's arrival. Among my contemporaries were young people of enormous talent who were molded by the likes of Robeson, Du Bois, and the others—the remarkable playwright Lorraine Hansberry; the founder of the Negro Ensemble Company, Douglass Turner Ward; the novelist John O. Killens; as well as many others who refused to be ground down by the McCarthy years and went on to productive work in unions, shops, universities, law, and politics.

The environment we knew was one of spirited demonstrations to save the lives of Rosa Ingram, Willie McGhee, the Martinsville Seven, and other victims of a racist legal system. It included attending vibrant interracial dances at Rockland Palace in Harlem, sitting in awe in the back of Birdland to ask Charlie Parker to support Du Bois for the Senate, and listening to Miles Davis, engaged by the unhip Marxist Labor Youth League, which somehow thought that Davis's brilliant, elliptical bebop was right for dancing. All of that had nearly disappeared by the mid-1950s. But that defiant interracialism, grounded in the unity of cultural traditions, of shared support for all who labored for an end to oppression at home and abroad never died. Its special commitment to, and admiration for, black culture, history, and community life survived and fused with a pervasive sense that the liberation of one group was essential to the spiritual and physical freedom of all. I believe that had the force of that experience flowed more strongly into the 1960s and into the present, a far greater degree of black-white unity could have been achieved.

That experience and legacy, for better or worse, informs this work and shapes the author's point of view.

West Newton, Massachusetts
February 1998

PART I

The Early Years, 1917–28

CHAPTER ONE

The Pioneer Black Communists:
Cyril Briggs and the
African Blood Brotherhood

T hey came to communism by ones and twos. The first African American to enter the emerging Communist Party in 1919 was Otto Huiswoud who was from Surinam (formerly the Dutch West Indies). He had been active in the Harlem 21st Assembly District club of the Socialist Party, where he met Arthur P. Hendricks from British Guiana. Coming from similar colonial backgrounds, they became close friends and together joined the Socialist left wing, which was destined to be expelled from the Socialist Party and propel the party's left toward communism. Hendricks was a theology student with a powerful, persuasive intellect and a strong interest in Marxist theory. However, he died of tuberculosis before the expulsion of the left wing in the spring of 1919. Huiswoud attended the National Left Wing Conference in June 1919 and was among the group that met to found the Communist Party on September 1, 1919.[1]

The roots of communism among African Americans are entangled in complex and contradictory political thought and practice. Nineteenth-century African American thinkers overwhelmingly embraced a capitalist ethos as a pathway to freedom and independence. But the entrepreneurial spirit was accompanied by a sense of sharing that was inherent in African roots and in the notion of "the land" as a repository of collective values. Also, blacks threw themselves unhesitatingly into the struggle to overthrow the property rights inherent in slavery. They did this with full awareness that they were engaging in revolutionary action.

Radical and socialist antecedents to American communism, in regard to race, were no less complex. The early, pre–Civil War Marxists certainly had a sense of the urgency of the slavery issue and its portentous implications for white labor. Post–Civil War pioneer labor leaders, such as William Sylvis, sought to reach out to black workers. But typically, Sylvis could not breach the prejudices of the members of his own molders' union. At the dawning of the twentieth century the Socialist Party had adopted a "pure" class outlook, in which the liberation of wage labor through socialism would automatically solve the problems of race and racism. Eugene Debs, the seminal Socialist, only promised that the Negro would rise as the working class rose. The distinctive dimensions of the black experience were not understood; the special needs and demands of African Americans were ignored.[2]

Yet in twentieth-century Harlem a socialist current emerged. Its foundation was laid by West Indian immigrants and native African Americans. The West Indians carried into Harlem a sensitivity to the social stratification of their Caribbean homelands. This had engendered a sharp class awareness and assertive psychological makeup, heightened by their majority racial status in the islands and their relatively extensive colonial schooling. Those colonial roots made them fiercely anti-imperialist and hostile to capitalism.[3]

The West Indians converged with the African American Socialists Hubert Harrison, A. Philip Randolph, and Chandler Owen. Harrison, a pioneer Socialist ideologist, was active in the Party from 1911 to his departure in 1920. At street-corner meetings and in public forums, this brilliant speaker electrified crowds by excoriating capitalism as the source of racial oppression, urging blacks to embrace socialism even though the Socialists had not yet embraced blacks. In a tide of rising radicalism, punctuated by the Bolshevik Revolution in Russia, the Harlem Socialists organized the interracial 21st AD Socialist Party club in the summer of 1918 and also launched the Peoples Educational Forum, which offered discussion and debate grounded in socialist analysis. The club and the forum attracted Huiswoud, Hendricks, the spellbinding orator Richard B. Moore, the aspiring actor and writer Lovett Fort-Whiteman, and the teacher and organizer Grace B. Campbell—all of whom found their way to the Communist Party when the Socialists continued to be unresponsive to the problems of African Americans. Wilfred A. Domingo of the 21st AD club became active on the periphery of American communism, but did not join the Party.

Frank Crosswaith, Randolph, and Owen continued their activities within the Socialist Party.[4]

Cyril Briggs did not come to communism from the Socialist Party. He took pride in his refusal to affiliate with a movement that failed to come to grips with the Negro question. Briggs considered himself a "race man." He was born on May 28, 1888, on the tiny island of Nevis in the eastern Caribbean, the illegitimate son of a woman of color and a white overseer. His light complexion earned him in later life the description, "Angry Blond Negro." He chose not to cross the island's rigid color line into the insular white segment of Nevis's stratified social order and instead, lived his life as a proud, assertive black man.[5]

After an utterly colonial education, Briggs knew that the island could not absorb his restless intelligence. Shortly after his seventeenth birthday, on the Fourth of July, 1905, he landed in New York City to join Harlem's growing West Indian community. His congenital stutter foreclosed any prospect of mass leadership and left him, for the most part, writing and organizing away from a public platform.[6] After learning the ropes within the burgeoning black immigrant population, Briggs in 1912 nailed a writing job with the community's *New York Amsterdam News*. In those early years, Briggs signaled the core of his emerging radical beliefs: an inseparable linkage among "race pride," "manhood rights," racial solidarity, and working-class partisanship.

For Briggs, President Woodrow Wilson's call for war on Germany and support for the right of subject peoples to "have a voice in their own government" sparked optimism about the right to self-determination. But the execution of thirteen black soldiers who had mutinied against their white officers in Houston, Texas, undermined Briggs's hopes for Wilson as liberator.[7]

For the time being, Briggs abandoned hope in Wilson, but his belief in self-determination remained and deepened. It was fanned by the lingering impact of the Irish Easter Rising, which had fired the imagination of the "New Negro" radicals. The Irish rebellion exemplified a revolutionary nationalism that found its way into the rhetoric voiced on street corners and in the emerging radical press of rapidly urbanizing African American life. It inspired Briggs's oft-cited editorial, "Security of Life for Poles and Serbs, Why Not for Colored Nations?" in which he advocated a separate black state within the borders of the United States.[8] Pointing to the outnumbered black community, denied opportunity and recompense for centuries of unrequited toil, Briggs called for the ceding of one-tenth of U.S. territory for the "pursuit of happiness" under black self-government.

In January 1918 the president unveiled his Fourteen Points, which called for the "impartial adjustment of all colonial claims." Briggs's hope in Wilson revived, quickening a dream of "Africa for the Africans," which appeared to be more feasible than self-determination in an undefined region of the United States. From that point on, Briggs was nearly obsessed with the potential for decolonized Africa as he embraced self-determination rooted in "Africa for the Africans." African American self-rule, however defined, was now linked to a primary emphasis on African liberation.[9]

So powerful was the lure of African freedom in the wake of the impending postwar settlement that Briggs, with financial support from the West Indian merchant Anthony Crawford, began the *Crusader* in September 1918. Crawford hoped for a journal of "racial patriotism" drawing upon the example of Jewish efforts to forge a Zionist state in Palestine. Wartime migrations from the South had expanded the nation's ghettoes; tens of thousands of black men were returning from Europe, many of whom would no longer countenance submission to racial attack. A growing urban intelligentsia had coalesced into the New Negro Crowd of militant writers, ideologists, and organizers, who had launched a small barrage of radical publications. New Negro radicals perceived a possible new ally and pressure point in the Russian Revolution. Something was going the black man's way—something useful to add to the growing discomfort of his enemies.[10]

Briggs's *Crusader* soon settled on a credo: dedicating the magazine to "Africa for the Africans" and to "a renaissance of Negro power and culture throughout the world." The first issue excoriated "alien education" that taught black and white children about the glories of Rome, but nothing about the great African kingdoms of antiquity. "Race patriotism" embodied in a "Race Catechism" was spread in stories of black achievement in commerce and the arts. Declaring that he was "pro-Negro" first, Briggs supported the local Socialist candidacies of Randolph and Owen without supporting their party. On national issues, he called for an end to "twaddling" in the face of lynching and peonage: It was time to demand "nothing more or less than an independent, separate existence." The flame of a national separation was now an ill-defined but lingering flicker.[11]

By December 1918 the *Crusader* had become the "Publicity Organ of the Hamitic League of the World." This league was the brainchild of George Wells Parker, a businessman, naturopath, and Afrocentric from Omaha. Responding to Briggs's offer to publish expressions of race patriotism, Parker submitted articles claiming that Africa was the cradle of civilization and that Africans constituted the greatest of races. A relationship developed, and in exchange for financial support, Briggs's journal affiliated with Parker's Hamitic League, which developed a program that echoed Briggs's influence.[12]

By February 1919 the *Crusader* had concluded that the aim of the emerging League of Nations was not to prevent wars, "but to suppress revolutions on the part of the oppressed and the dissatisfied." Far from being a vehicle for ending colonialism, it was a cover for "thieves and tyrants" to maintain a grip on their empires. By April Briggs had begun to ferociously denounce Woodrow Wilson, who had promised self-determination but had delivered "damnable and hypocritical" mandates, a system that differed from colonialism only in name.[13]

Something else appeared in the same issue: the first clear evidence of a Marxist sense of social class as a root category. Commenting on the deportation mania that was then gripping the nation, Briggs drew a parallel between the forced removal of black workers from a Pennsylvania steel town (where they had migrated during wartime labor shortages) and the deportation of white foreign radicals. In both instances, he claimed, "the mailed fist of capitalism" came down on working people. Sadly, blacks were not interested in the fortunes of foreign-born whites, and the racial prejudices of white workers blinded them to the fate of black labor. Capital, however, was not divided by prejudice or by nationality, but was united in pursuing its own interests at the expense of workers of both races. By May and June Briggs's *Crusader* was repeatedly forging links between capitalism and colonialism — and projecting a shared proletarian identity between black and white workers as the counterweight to the dominant system. Months before the founding of the Communist Party (in September 1919) Briggs had been open to the ideas and policies of the Socialist left wing, which was about to split from the Socialist Party to launch American communism.[14]

Cyril Briggs had begun a long journey on an uncharted road. Unlike the other New Negro radicals, he merged black nationalism with revolutionary socialism and introduced the twentieth-century global revolutionary tide to black America. The formation of the Third International in March 1919 was a defining event. Its hostility to the veiled colonialism of the League of Nations paralleled Briggs's "League of Thieves" editorial in the March 12, 1919, *New York Amsterdam News,* which brought the wrath of postal authorities down upon the paper. Lenin's International marked a dramatic contrast with the

Second International's ambivalence over the colonial question. In contrast to Wilson's bogus self-determination, the Comintern's manifesto called for the overthrow of colonial exploitation and ended with a plea: "Colonial slaves of Africa and Asia! the hour of triumph of proletarian dictatorship of Europe will also be the hour of your triumph."[15]

During and after the 1919 Red Summer of antiblack rioting, Briggs forged an ideological link among national, race, and class consciousness that provided a basis for blacks to join the communist movement. Reaffirming his racial consciousness, Briggs declared that he was "first, last, and all the time" a Negro whose true native land was "glorious Africa." In the midst of rising antiradical deportation hysteria, he would not disdain his own removal from American soil, as long as it was to a free Africa. Irish, Jews, and Poles all sought a national existence, so "why should not the Negro seek such ends?" Yet "the Negro's place is with labor." Although the trade unions were racist, the vast majority of African Americans were of the working class. There was, Briggs claimed, a growing realization that no force on earth could permanently hold apart black and white labor, "these two most powerful sections of the world proletariat." Resolution of the contradiction between a separate black national destiny and unity with white labor seemed to be at hand: Blacks would win the most from "the triumph of Labor and the destruction of parasitic Capital Civilization with its Imperialism incubus that is squeezing the life-blood out of millions of our race."[16]

The summer of 1919 was pivotal for the fusion of black radicals and Communists. Race riots were sweeping the country; the press was facing growing censorship; the socialist left was in the throes of factional turmoil and realignment. Briggs was in the midst of all this, decrying assaults on press freedom, denouncing attacks on black communities, and looking away from Wilson for new allies in the struggle for a free Africa. He had become an integral part of Harlem's activism, forging friendships with Otto Huiswoud, Grace Campbell, W. A. Domingo, Hubert Harrison, Claude McKay, and other Harlem radicals. Having ended his ties with the *New York Amsterdam News,* Briggs now routinely characterized the Soviets as allies of black global racial aspirations. Conversely, antibolshevism was seen as a hypocritical cover for perpetuating racism and attacking black radicalism. There was no point to Negro conservatism because blacks had nothing to conserve. What better company for Negroes than radicals who stood up for blacks as the abolitionists had once done? In October, as the Communist Party was in its second month of existence, he compared black resistance to white mobs with Bolshevik resistance to czarist oppression. "Bolshevist!!!" was the brazen headline of an editorial claiming that the epithet was hurled at those who thought for themselves. Such a slur held no terror for Briggs and his friends. "If to fight for one's rights is to be bolshevists," Briggs said, "then we are Bolshevists!" At the same time, he was absorbing Marxism's major theoretical postulates and urging his readers to discover that "labor-power applied to the natural resource is all wealth."[17]

In the first months of American communism, Briggs drew closer to Huiswoud and McKay, who were both members of the underground Communist movement. McKay introduced Briggs to Robert Minor and Rose Pastor Stokes, native-born white Communists who showed strong interest in the Negro question. Briggs became friends with both. There is little doubt that Briggs joined the Party in mid-1921, affiliating with Stokes and Minor's Goose Caucus faction, which advocated parallel legal and underground parties. The approximate date of Briggs's formal entry into the Party is verified in a letter written by McKay to a Comintern official in December 1922. McKay complained that although he had introduced Briggs to the Communists, he himself had higher regard for the political and intellectual gifts of the editors of W. A. Domingo's defunct *Emancipator,* whom he had wished to draw into the Party. But the Communists had shown more interest in Briggs "because he had a magazine." Briggs, according to McKay, was recruited "a few months" before the demise of the *Crusader* in February 1922.[18]

In later years Briggs insisted that his decision to join the Party was based primarily on concern with the national question rather than with the issues of class or socialism per se. His interest in Marxism-Leninism "was sparked by its hostility to imperialism and specifically by the Soviet solution to the national question, its recognition . . . of the right of self determination of nations formerly oppressed by Tsarist Russia."[19]

Those early connections with Communists influenced the evolving political character of Briggs's African Blood Brotherhood and the degree to which blacks themselves influenced Communist involvement in African American life. A small notice in the October 1919 *Crusader* (the same issue in which Briggs defiantly refused to reject the "Bolshevist" label) informed the magazine's readers that "Mr. Cyril V. Briggs announces the organization of the African Blood Brotherhood for African Liberation and Redemption. . . . Those only need apply who are willing to go the limit." With the ABB, Briggs sought to draw together the themes of race patriotism, anticapitalism, anticolonialism, and organized defense against racist assault. The organization projected fraternity and benevolence, and even offered a program of calisthenics. Richard B. Moore, a Barbadian Socialist who accepted Briggs's invitation to join the ABB, noted that the Brotherhood was driven initially not by its notorious quarrel with Marcus Garvey (which came later), but by the need for self-protection and by a vision of black liberation on a global scale.[20]

In the beginning the ABB was not a "black auxiliary" of the Communist Party. Although the Brotherhood's founders were increasingly influenced by communism, it is unlikely that in 1919 the embryonic Communist Party was able or willing to be a progenitor or founding patron of the Brotherhood. The Party as yet had no particular sensitivity to the Negro question. Its attention in any case was distracted by competing factions vying for Comintern recognition. The ABB's blend of lingering Hamitic Ethiopianism and class consciousness was probably, at this point, beyond the imaginative reach and understanding of Communists. Although Briggs's interest in communism had been manifest at the founding of ABB, the event was independent of direct Communist influence. By 1921, however, Briggs was prepared to join the CP, and the Party was anxious to make the Brotherhood the arena of "mass work" for its small African American cadre. The ABB was not "taken over" by the Communists, but Briggs and some other leaders were amenable to an ever deepening relationship.[21]

Another long-term linkage between the ABB and the Party was provided by Otto Eduard Geradus Majelia Huiswoud. Huiswoud was born in Paramaribo, Dutch West Indies (now Surinam), on October 28, 1893, son of a man who had been a slave until the age of eleven. His early education was Roman Catholic. He was apprenticed as a printer, but shipped out on a Dutch banana boat bound for Holland in January 1910. On January 17 he jumped ship in Brooklyn due to horrendous conditions on board, and worked at various times as a printer, waiter, cook, dishwasher and janitor.

Huiswoud began to listen to socialist speakers in New York's Union Square and devoured socialist literature. By 1916 he had joined the Socialist Party. He went on to Cornell University to study agriculture and became involved in socialist groups on campus. In 1918 Huiswoud took a summer job on a pleasure boat on the Fall River Line. The International Seamen's Union was not interested in either unionizing or protecting the ship's black crew members who, under Huiswoud's leadership, walked off the vessel at Boston and stood with folded arms on the pier — until the fully booked shipping company was pressured to negotiate for higher pay and better working conditions.

At the end of summer Huiswoud did not return to Cornell. The Socialists had heard about his strike leadership and were impressed. They offered, and Huiswoud accepted, a one-year scholarship to the Rand School in New York. There he encountered the future Comintern official Sen Katayama, who became a life-long friend. Assigned by the Socialists to Harlem's 21st Assembly District, he met Randolph and Owen, and joined the editorial board of the *Messenger*. He also met the influential, bookish Hendricks and the group destined to become Communist activists: Richard B. Moore, Lovett Fort-Whiteman, Edward Welsh, and Grace Campbell. Some in the branch joined the Party's left wing, embracing policies against war and in favor of industrial unions, and rankling at racism in the Party's southern regions. Huiswoud and Hendricks were among that small group. Thus, Huiswoud took part in the left-wing bolt to communism, while Hendricks died before the founding of the Communist Party.[22]

Huiswoud was the first black charter member of the Party. At the founding convention of the aboveground Workers Party in December 1921, he was elected to chair its Negro Commission. With the Brotherhood's approval, Huiswoud was assigned by the Party to work in the ABB. He soon became a member of the Brotherhood's Supreme Council and was named national organizing secretary of the ABB after his return from the Fourth Comintern Congress in 1922. During the early 1920s his activities veered between organizing tours for the ABB and participating in the deliberations of the Comintern. That intersection would allow him to play a pivotal role in the early black-Communist relationship.[23]

Along with emerging international communism, the Irish Sinn Fein inspired the ABB. Sinn Fein's secrecy, paramilitary aura, and embrace of national self-determination influenced the ABB even more than Lenin's "party of a new type." After all, the Irish and the Negroes were both oppressed in both the Old and New Worlds. In his catechism on strategy and tactics, Briggs argued that the Irish-American example of standing up for a free Ireland was a model for how blacks should stand up for an independent Africa. He also borrowed the mystical and organizational accouterments of a hierarchical order dominated by a Supreme Council, secrecy, passwords, ritual, and a clandestine oath swearing loyalty and obedience to the council and its officers (including "the death if necessary in the fight for the liberation of the Father-land").[24]

In January 1920 the African Blood Brotherhood called for an amalgamation of African Americans on a "race first" principle. With that accomplished, an alliance with liberal, radical, and labor movements should next be forged. Later, racial unity itself would be refined into an alliance based on black working-class leadership. Among blacks, only class divisions were tolerable — not schisms based on skin color or place of birth. The linked concept of multiracial alliance was pruned to a core principle of a labor-led alliance of African Americans with "advanced" white workers. That was proclaimed at an early stage of the *Crusader* and was reiterated with mounting passion throughout the life of the African Blood Brotherhood.[25]

The Brotherhood's first political program, promulgated at its 1920 convention, drew together several strands: traditional racial self-reliance, moral and financial support for African liberation, resistance to the Ku Klux Klan, a united front of black organizations, higher wages and better conditions for black labor, cooperatives, and a convergence of racial and class consciousness. It started with a plea for "racial self respect" and concluded with a call for "co-operation with other darker races and with the class-conscious white workers." Contrary to later claims by Briggs, there was no mention of African American self-determination.[26]

Nationalistic prejudices were becoming less digestible as Briggs drew closer to the Communists. As "publicity organ" of the Hamitic League of the World, the *Crusader* carried a few articles whose Hamitic passions seemed, when not taken in context, to suggest anti-Semitic and other ethnic hostilities. On one occasion, Hamitic League propagandist James N. Lowe, writing on the "bogus values" of "Hebrew Politicians and Pagan Greek Philosophers," commented that "the first nature of a Jew was himself, and the second the abuse of other men."[27]

By the end of 1920 the Hamitic League had disappeared from the *Crusader's* masthead. As Briggs's Communist associations matured, he appeared to compensate for past Hamitic broadsides by attacking anti-Semitism and noting that while the oppression of blacks was most severe, Negroes and Jews shared a historic experience of persecution. He noted approvingly that the Bolsheviks were assaulting the anti-Semitism that had scarred czarist Russia; radical Jewish workers were a significant factor in the Third International, and the national aspirations of Jews were part of the arc of struggle against empire that ran from Ireland to Africa to the Far East.[28]

Increasingly, Briggs sought to fuse his own sense of African identity and national culture with Leninist internationalism. He found in African antiquity the primitive communism that provided an Afrocentric root to the vision advanced by the Third International. He declared that "Africa for the Africans" did not connote capitalist development (which was implicit in Garvey's program): "Socialism and Communism [were] in practical application in Africa for centuries before they were even advanced as theories in the European world."[29]

This viewpoint was synthesized and expanded in April 1921 in a seminal editorial entitled "The Salvation of the Negro," in which Briggs confronted fundamental strategies for survival. The destruction of capitalism, he said, and the creation of a "Socialist Cooperative Commonwealth" (made probable by the Bolshevik Revolution) was "along the lines of our own race genius as evidenced by the existence of Communist States in Central Africa and our leaning towards Communism wherever the race genius has had free play." But how could peoples of African descent reclaim their distinct political and cultural heritage? Could they reject black statehood and accept the "point of view of 'humanity'" that it would be most preferable to achieve liberation under the Socialist Cooperative Commonwealth? Perhaps this would be preferable, he averred, "but the Negro has been treated so brutally in the past by the rest of humanity that he may be pardoned for now looking at the matter from the viewpoint of the Negro than from that of a humanity that is not humane." How could the deepest racial and national stirring of black people be satisfied in the face of hostile white societies that had already once destroyed the "African Communist System"? How to find genuine self-determination in a postwar world where the rebirth of African freedom was still a distant dream and where the creation of a separate black state in North America was not on the horizon?

Briggs offered a strategy that charted a new path to freedom: The best and surest way to salvation was through "the establishment of a strong, stable, independent Negro state (along the lines of our race genius) in Africa or elsewhere; and salvation for all Negroes (as well as other oppressed peoples) through the establishment of a Universal Socialist Cooperative Commonwealth. To us it seems that one working for the first proposition would also be working for the second proposition." The socialist commonwealth would be the protective framework for black national independence. A black embrace of socialism would not be based on the desires of a generalized humanity or a communist movement, but upon the national aspirations of people of African descent themselves. And that embrace would not be a matter of total absorption into a Marxist ethos; for Briggs and the ABB the relationship should be an *alliance,* in which a distinct black agenda would never disappear.[30]

Briggs had welded black liberation to revolutionary socialism. He had broken new ground and in so doing had redefined the traditional ideal of self-determination and racial sovereignty. Those goals now ran through the transforming vision of anti-imperialist alliance with the working class and a socialist future. African freedom would come only through the "substitution of the Socialist Cooperative Commonwealth for the vicious Capitalist system." With the time not yet ripe to free Africa from white control, organization and propaganda at the ramparts of the dominant system were on the present agenda.[31]

The African Blood Brotherhood never exceeded more than about 3,500 members. Its complex program, its secrecy, its lack of charismatic leadership (unlike the Garvey movement), its risky radical opposition to the dominant society at a time of political repression: all these factors undermined any possibility of its becoming a large organization. The ABB's leadership was dominated by emigrants from the Caribbean; its membership appears to have been drawn significantly from veterans of the Great War, from a segment of the new intelligentsia, and from stable sectors of the working class. Many were recruited from reading the *Crusader,* and some posts were formed in response to exposure to that journal. A small group of adherents in the Harlem Menelik Post constituted the core leadership. Chicago's Pushkin Post was stabilized in the early 1920s by the involvement of pioneer midwestern black Communists. Other posts arose in response to specific conditions, such as in the coal-mining region of West Virginia, where aggrieved and militant black miners formed an ABB affiliate. For all its blood oaths, secrecy, and hints of paramilitary training, the Brotherhood was a poorly financed educational and propaganda organization built largely around disseminating the *Crusader* and promoting discussion of its views.[32]

The ABB gained notoriety in the early summer of 1921 when a shadowy link was forged in the white press between the Brotherhood and the riot that virtually destroyed the black community of Tulsa, Oklahoma. Three days after the burning and pillaging of black Tulsa, the *New York Times* ran a front-page report that caricatured the resistance of a deeply rooted community as a conspiracy hatched by ABB organizers. Yet, aside from the *Times* report, "no further information was located regarding the Tulsa chapter of the African Blood Brotherhood."[33]

The ABB's association with the heroic acts of twenty-five men who fought off a much larger group of armed whites was widely admired by blacks. The Brotherhood reveled in its linkage with Tulsa, but shrouded its alleged role in ambiguity. The "commander of the Tulsa Post" said, "Whether we directed Negroes in their fight in self-defense is certainly no crime in Negro eyes, and is left for the white Oklahoma authorities to prove. For ourselves, we neither deny or confirm it."[34]

The Tulsa riot brought a surge of support and energy to the Brotherhood, nudging it away from its coveted secrecy. Two thousand people turned out for a mass meeting at Harlem's Palace Casino on June 12, 1921; Briggs claimed that scores of applications to join were flooding the national office. The convoluted seven-degree process for membership in the ABB was softened. A "first degree" would now automatically be granted to "every person of high intelligence." Replying to accusations of Negro conspiracy leveled by a Tulsa minister, Briggs wrote that "the African Blood Brotherhood is not a 'secret order of revolutionists,' but simply a Negro protective organization pledged to mobilize Negro thought, and organize Negro manpower to a defense of Negro rights wherever and by whomsoever attacked." The June 1921 issue of the *Crusader* for the first time identified the magazine as the official organ of the ABB, signifying a changeover of the Brotherhood to an aboveground status. The same issue presented the "constitution of the African Blood Brotherhood," which defined the ABB as "essentially a propaganda organization." Membership was now open to anyone of African descent; posts could be formed at the grassroots by a minimum of seven persons. Perhaps not coincidentally, these steps paralleled the actions taken by the Communists to establish an aboveground legal party.[35]

The Brotherhood was being drawn irresistibly into Marxism's field. The *Crusader* eagerly echoed (and perhaps inspired) the Communist *Toiler's* assertion that the underlying motive of whites in the Tulsa carnage was to grab African American oil lands. Tulsa was now within the vortex of Marxism's assault on capitalism and on those who supported the system — white or black. There was no justice in capitalist America, the *Crusader* asserted. How many more Tulsas would it take before Negroes rejected their treacherous bourgeois allies and joined with "the radical forces of the world that are working for the overthrow of capitalism and the dawn of a new day, a new heaven on earth"?[36]

Briggs and the New Negro radicals who gravitated into the Communist orbit were staking out new ideological grounds on the black political landscape. Shortly after the "Salvation" article, Briggs joined the Communist Party and resolved some of the article's ambiguities, softening (but not renouncing) the nationalist temperament. He and his ABB comrades now clearly advocated a historic shift in the objectives of the black freedom struggle from assimilation into the bourgeois order to a socialist transformation; in the class composition of black leadership from middle class to proletarian; and in the class character of African American alliances with whites, from bourgeois liberal to the working-class left. The difficulty of the task was acknowledged in a *Crusader* editorial that grappled with the pervasive suspicion among blacks about the reliability of white labor as an ally. It said that those blacks who saw only white hostility had been soured by false protestations of friendship in the past. It was futile to deny that the white working-class majority was racist. At present, it said, "every white worker is a *potential* enemy of the Negro," but not the *actual* enemy. Racism existed in the working class; it had to be rooted out so that blacks could willingly join in an alliance arising from common interests and common ground. This view had a powerful impact on the racial policies of American communism.[37]

The embrace of communism carried with it a promising connection with Soviet power as indispensable ally, patron, and spiritual guide. For the new black Communists the Soviets were an exhilarating source of strength, pride, hope, and respect for black interests. Heretofore anonymous men and women would now have an international stage where they would be taken seriously and where power was manifest and at the disposal of the black liberation struggle. The greatness of Bolshevik power — as anti-imperialist force, as liberator of labor, as cleanser and avenger of racism, as faithful ally — became an ardent belief and defining point of the African Blood Brotherhood.[38]

Briggs came to a class consciousness through a primary race consciousness that never suggested simple absorption into working-class ranks. This led him to a unique strategic concept: Black-white working-class unity would be a decisive aspect of black efforts to drive a wedge between white labor and capital. Thus, blacks should do nothing to encourage the solidification of whites on racial lines. Ultimately, self-interest grounded in the harsh realities of struggle would force white labor to recognize the commonality of the interests of all workers. Blacks should work to obliterate white workers' misconceptions about

African Americans, which were cooked up "by vicious anti-Negro capitalist propaganda." On the other hand, the "acid test of white friendship" would be white acceptance of black self-defense — even the killing of whites in such defense. That test was just beginning, but the blacks who chose communism were willing to cast their racial and national aspirations with the class struggle. That was the way to secure the fragmentation of white society and destroy the sources of racial oppression. "Join hands with the Workers' Republic," Briggs proclaimed, "IT IS CAPITALISM THAT IS RESPONSIBLE FOR YOUR DEGRADED POSITION AND FOR YOUR EXPLOITATION AS WORKERS."[39]

THE COMMUNISTS

The adoption of revolutionary socialism by the African Blood Brotherhood deeply affected and ultimately transformed the racial views of the emerging communist movement, divided from the start into two groups. The Communist Labor Party said nothing about the Negro. The program of the Communist Party of America (largely composed of foreign-born members) barely departed from the traditional Socialist refusal to treat race as distinct in any meaningful way from class: Racial oppression was simply a reflection of economic bondage. The Negro question was complicated by race, but its proletarian character was dominant. The Communist Party declared that it would agitate among blacks to unite "with all class conscious workers."[40]

Such acknowledgment that racial oppression at least "complicates" the problems of African Americans could have opened the door to new thinking and imaginative work for Negro rights. But the Party's inability to overcome its largely mechanical lumping of race and class was only a part of the strangling political narrowness that marked the birth of American communism. Both parties were so mired in sectarianism, so disdainful of reforms and of partial, immediate demands, so scarred and debilitated by the Palmer raids, and so isolated by their underground modus operandi that they were not yet able to produce creative theory or become a magnet for blacks or whites.[41]

In May 1920 a convention was called at Bridgman, Michigan, to merge the underground factions. The United Communist Party joined a segment of the CPA to the CLP. Meanwhile, thirty-four delegates held yet another underground convention in New York City in July 1920 to continue the Communist Party without contamination by the "centrist" Communist Laborites. That gathering criticized the United Communist Party for giving *too much* prominence to the Negro question by treating it as a separate issue. The Communist

Party, more deeply grounded in foreign-language federations, believed that its large European base represented a purer and more compelling radical commitment than the native and foreign-born hybrid that constituted the UCP. It is not surprising that the CP had little patience for an "American" concern such as the Negro question. Yet the UCP assigned, however briefly, Joseph Zack Kornfeder to contact black radicals in Harlem. Kornfeder later claimed that the assignment came as a result of a letter to the American Communists from V. I. Lenin "in the late fall of 1920." However, a search of the Lenin archive failed to produce the letter. Lenin scholars in Moscow had never heard of it. Nevertheless, its existence became enshrined in Cold War hagiography, and it has been cited often as the springboard to American Communist interest in the Negro question.[42]

Black Communists were inclined, at this period of bruising factional struggle, to edge toward the UCP, which showed greater sensitivity to African American issues and was pushing harder to get at least part of its political corpus aboveground. The language and political content of UCP positions on the Negro question resonated with the views of the African Blood Brotherhood. At that juncture in early 1921 the Communists were acutely aware of Briggs's magazine and were echoing what had been said repeatedly in the *Crusader*. The convention of the United Communist Party at Kingston, New York in January 1921 counseled party activists to tear down the barriers of race prejudice that separated black and white workers and to tie both to "a union of revolutionary forces for the overthrow of their common enemy." The UCP program also said that "Negro Communists must enter lodges, unions, clubs, and churches" to spread "revolutionary ideas" and must organize "direct-action" bodies among blacks to resist lynching and mob rule. Missing from the statement was a clear commitment to fight racism within the Party. That issue would fester for nearly two years until the complaints of black Communists would be brought to the floor of the Fourth Comintern Congress.[43]

That first strategic directive for work in the African American mainstream reflected the united front projected in the first program of the African Blood Brotherhood. The UCP program put a seal of approval upon what Briggs and his comrades in the ABB were already saying and doing. The program even echoed the paramilitary rumblings that were the ABB's early stock in trade. While the Brotherhood limited its military aspirations to aiding African liberation, the Communists had dreams of recruiting black ex-servicemen to provide military training among blacks for the "inevitable revolutionary outbreak."[44]

Under Comintern prodding and rank-and-file pressure, the two parties met in another "unity convention" at Woodstock, New York, in May 1921. In the frenzy of reconciliation after nearly two years of bruising factional battle, the Negro question was again on the back burner. No specific Negro demands were listed in the unified party's program, though there was a reference to blacks as victims of political disfranchisement. There is also no evidence of a black presence at the long, secret convention that was limited to thirty delegates. At that point, the Communist movement had not yet developed the passion for inclusiveness that marked its later history.[45]

Nevertheless, the unified Communist Party opened a new phase of engagement with black issues and concerns. The first discussion of blacks to appear in the consolidated Communist press, written under the noms de plume of John Bruce and J. P. Collins, had a feel for black life that could only have come from consultation with the black Communists. "The Negro Problem" would not be solved by simply calling for the abolition of capitalism. From the racial foundations of enslavement, lynch terror, and white labor's contempt and scorn, the Negro had adopted an insular and fervent racial ideology. Black "opportunist leaders" exploited "anti-white feeling," while white radicals faced among blacks "a stone wall of closed mentality because of organized labor's attitude toward the Negro." To win the Negro, the Party had to yoke class to race and correlate its objectives "with their [black] ideology and their immediate wants and sufferings." Blacks should be met with clear language and special consideration for their point of view. The Party needed to put the "human factor" into its Negro work: "The desire for enjoyment, dances, exercises, song, music, games, displays, parades, etc., must be met." Blacks yearned for equality and recognition of their human dignity. Flowing from that, they wanted a free Africa that would inescapably bring them to the struggle against imperialism. They wanted more food and better working conditions. That would lead them to unions and closer contact with white workers. Their struggles for political equality, especially in the South, would facilitate the right to organize; attainment of the right to vote would democratize political rule and advance freedom of speech — which would rock the foundations of the lingering system of peonage.[46]

The Party's job was to fight for those reforms — and also to place the blame for black suffering at the feet of the capitalists. When the Negro recognizes his enemy, "he will be the most embittered, consistent and tireless opponent of capitalism" and will face his tormentors "with a fierce hatred." To give organized, effective expression to that sentiment, "Negro militants" should be united into a "center capable of organizing the Negro masses." Garvey's UNIA was hobbled by opportunism; Du Bois's NAACP was smothered by white liberalism. That left the African Blood Brotherhood.[47]

By the summer of 1921 Briggs had formally committed himself to a Communist movement riven by disappointment and marginality. Still underground, a putatively united party was dazed by the collapse of the revolutionary tide in Europe and disoriented by the economic stabilization and conservatism that were beginning to appear in the United States. This led to a rancorous debate over party organization that degenerated into another factional dispute. The new Central Executive Committee, an amalgam of the CP and UCP leadership, took seriously the Woodstock convention's call for greater and more effective use of legal channels. But it also clung to the notion of maintaining a parallel underground organization. That constituted a victorious middle ground, advocated by the Goose Caucus, between those who wanted a strictly underground party and those who wanted only a broader legal party. The middle position satisfied Briggs and was consistent with his own cautious steps to bring the Brotherhood into political daylight. Claude McKay noted that while Briggs and Huiswoud were members of the Goose Caucus, and he and other, unnamed blacks were in favor of a unitary legal party, the pioneer black Communists "are all a unit on the purely Negro problem." In the late summer or fall of 1921 the CEC claimed that it had made headway through "the Negro organization"—a reference to the ABB, which it now treated as a Party auxiliary. By the end of 1921 Briggs was emboldened to appear as one of two "fraternal" delegates from the Brotherhood to the founding convention of the aboveground Workers Party of America at the Labor Temple in New York City from December 21 to 24, 1921.[48]

The Workers Party program took a step toward recognizing the struggles and aspirations of blacks as important to the working-class movement. One could hear Briggs's voice in the document's recital of the role of slavery and lynch terror in the nation's accumulation of capital, of northern capital's betrayal of the freedmen, of the use of racial prejudice to subject blacks to extreme exploitation and to divide the working class. The program offered support to blacks "in their struggle for liberation" and for full economic, political, and social equality. It challenged labor's discriminatory policies and blamed the unions for the compulsion among blacks "to develop purely racial organizations which seek purely racial aims." This statement aligned the Workers Party with Briggs's criticism of organized labor and reflected a will to stand with radical blacks against trade-union racism. Finally, the Workers Party promised "to destroy altogether the barrier of race prejudice that had been used to keep apart the black and white workers, and bind them into a solid union of revolutionary forces."[49]

For Communists, these words took on the weight of Talmudic instruction. By stating that blacks were fighting for their "liberation," the new Party breached a simplistic class analysis; in stressing the issue of discrimination, the WP was edging toward accepting the special dimensions of the assault on blacks; by blaming the labor movement for black hostility, the Party was attempting to distinguish victims and victimizers in a way that had never before been done by a radical group in relation to unions. Finally, by establishing a Negro Commission under Huiswoud, the Party appeared to be giving organizational substance to its ideological claims. The ABB delegates could feel that they had had an impact. But a residue of racial antagonism, neglect, and a patronizing attitude toward blacks remained. A long road, leading inevitably through Moscow, had to be traversed to achieve a significant degree of consciousness and commitment to black and white working-class unity.

CHAPTER TWO

Looking for the Black United Front

The presence of ABB delegates at the Workers Party convention in December 1921 was a bruising point of contention between the ABB and Marcus Garvey. Garvey had arrived in New York in 1916 from his native Jamaica, where two years earlier he had founded the Universal Negro Improvement Association. Nurtured in the racially stratified West Indies, Garvey brought to those blacks in the United States who bore the stress of new urban living a message of racial nobility, strength, and beauty. As for whites, Garvey insisted that their racial prejudice was congenital; appeals to white society's sense of justice and to its vaunted democratic principles were useless. Ultimately, the only hope was self-determination for all African peoples on African soil. As for the Communists, they might be worthy of sympathy, but they were white pariahs who could do nothing for their own cause, much less for Negroes who had to be for themselves.

Cyril Briggs, however, took issue with Garvey's growl about "colored radicals" making common cause with "Bolsheviki." He thought that Garvey was being numbingly superficial. The ABB's open alliance with the Workers Party brought international connections and a place for radical African Americans on the world revolutionary stage. It brought links with two hundred thousand souls in groups tied to the Workers Party, as well as access to an undisclosed amount of property. Compare that, Briggs argued, with Garvey's pathetic and useless groveling before presidents and monarchs who had perennially ridiculed, raped, and slaughtered black folks.[1]

The dispute over the Workers Party capped the growing alienation between Garvey and Briggs. In its formative days, the Brotherhood had seen itself as an elite unit of committed fighters, a vanguard of sorts, influencing the mass-based Universal Negro Improvement Association. Garvey's movement, Briggs had declared, was the greatest development in modern racial organization. Whatever puffery and self-aggrandizement afflicted Garvey, whatever the deleterious influence of the "intellectual nincompoops" who surrounded him, Briggs believed that the UNIA, with the ABB to guide it, could become a radical mass movement and a foundation for global racial unity.[2]

The growing size and significance of the postwar ghetto sharply raised the stakes in the contest for leadership. Garvey's increasing prominence, his attacks on assimilationist leaders, his ability to win the hearts and minds of newly proletarianized blacks, his utopian African hegira, which seemed to divert attention from the struggle for survival in the here and now: all this provoked jealousy on the part of those who believed themselves senior to the upstart Jamaican. Briggs shared that social and political mood. But his ideological disagreements with Garvey were earnest and pivotal; they reflected sharply differing class allegiances.[3]

Briggs worried about Garvey's narcissism and questioned the UNIA leader's intention of anointing himself, without a global mandate, as the race's "Supreme Highness." That was hardly helpful to achieving broad-based consensus and unity in the struggles against imperialism and domestic racial oppression. At the 1920 convention of the UNIA, Briggs pleaded that Garvey appoint a pan-Negro galaxy of radical activists to his "cabinet," but the plea fell on deaf ears. Briggs began to perceive an approaching racial calamity. The convention ground on, bereft of probing discussion of strategy or finances. Like others, Briggs was becoming convinced that Garvey was a lousy businessman who would not be subjected to "careful planning" and to constraints upon questionable business practices.[4]

Briggs's attacks on the black bourgeoisie escalated in the summer of 1921. Racism was now seen less as an endemic trait in all whites than as a vile and unrelenting outgrowth of capitalism aimed at dividing the workers of both races. Why support leaders and propagandists who kowtow to capitalists? The Negro race was a race of workers, and the "true Negro" resisted the white man's system. Alluding to Garvey, Briggs pleaded, "Let us, then, stop supporting the enemies of the workers, and the servile lickspittle tools of White Capitalism."[5] Would it be revolutionary socialism or obeisance to capitalism for the black masses? The ideological course of black liberation became the decisive issue.

Garvey bowed magnanimously to Briggs's request to allow Rose Pastor Stokes to address the UNIA convention in August 1921. With passionate voice she greeted the delegates as fellow workers and called for a Communist-black alliance to destroy capitalism "root and branch." In the name of freedom for all, she begged for cooperation "with the revolutionary working class of the world." Directing herself to the soul of Garveyism, she continued, "Friends... you want Africa. Africa should be yours (great cheering)... You want a free Africa; you don't want an enslaved Africa, do you? (cries of no, no!).... Go East and you will find the red armies of Russia are marching shoulder to shoulder with black men." Garvey responded coyly that Stokes was merely a "Soviet professor," one of many "professors" espousing varying viewpoints before the congress. After hearing them all — Democrats, Republicans, Irish nationalists — the congress would decide on its policies.[6]

Facing intensified government surveillance and an impending indictment, Garvey was about at the end of his tolerance for Briggs and his reds. Near the end of the convention, the Brotherhood distributed the third number of a deceptively official-looking bulletin whose headline proclaimed, "Negro Congress at a Standstill — Many Delegates Dissatisfied with Failure to Produce Results." At that point, the ABB was expelled from the body and retreated from the UNIA in a spate of derisive laughter and intense mutual recrimination.[7]

In a speech on September 21, 1921, Garvey savaged Briggs, saying that "the little boy who runs the 'Crusader' " was really a white man who allegedly traveled as a white in the South and "trie[d] to be a Negro" in New York. Briggs, he charged, was sponsored by the Communists and wanted the UNIA to become "iconoclastic" destroyers of capital. The Black Star Line operated on capitalist principles, which were despised by "lazy, good-for-nothing Negro men" being paid off by white Bolsheviks who sought to undermine black enterprise. Unlike those Negroes awash in white Communist money, the UNIA was a Negro organization from top to bottom, financed by Negroes alone. "Socialist idiots," he added, advocated the obliteration of governments, mocking the intelligence of black men: "keep far away from those Socialistic parasites who are receiving money from the Soviet and Communists to... bring about universal chaos and destruction."[8]

Briggs denied that ABB was controlled by Communists or that it wished to smash government and destroy capital. Garvey had confused capital with capitalism. The former was wealth, while the latter was control of that wealth by the few over the many. The ABB did not oppose government in principle, it simply opposed imperialist government. Briggs added that Garvey had repudiated social equality; he had told Negroes to be loyal to their respective national flags; he had refused to denounce murders committed by the United States in Haiti; he had been guilty of shameless compromises and servile surrender of the rights of blacks. The "Negro Moses" was charged with nothing less than treason. For the first time, Briggs attacked Garvey's "Back to Africa" standard, claiming that a free Africa did not require a mass exodus of African Americans.[9]

Briggs's denial of Communist auspices glossed over the complex relationship between the Party and the ABB. He needed no urging from the Party to attack Garvey. The Communists, in fact, were pressing their black recruits to isolate Garvey and win the UNIA's rank-and-file to a revolutionary outlook. Briggs helped forge that strategy; he also took Party money to fund his weekly convention bulletin. But he had an independent streak that showed itself in his seeking not to oust Garvey, but to induce him to lead a broad movement for global black unity.[10]

Shortly after the convention débâcle, the Supreme Council of the ABB again pleaded with the UNIA for unity and cooperation in building the worldwide federation. Race-proud Negroes were invited to join both organizations. The UNIA responded by accusing Briggs and the ABB of being unable to muster the intelligence and skill to build their own movement, thus trading upon the alleged defects of the UNIA to gain their own adherents.[11]

That exchange turned out to be a last gasp; the fragile relationship between the ABB and the UNIA was sundered. The Communist Party noted the split and considered it a signal for an all-out effort to win the UNIA rank-and-file to the ABB's banners. Briggs dropped his campaign to induce Garvey to lead a worldwide anti-imperialist movement and announced that he was taking his case to the masses with pamphlets, leaflets, and public meetings.[12]

At the end of 1921 and into 1922 the conflict between Garvey and Briggs became increasingly bitter and personal. The *Crusader* escalated its attacks on the UNIA leader to a point where the magazine appeared to consist of little more than anti-Garvey invective. Garvey was accused of collaborating with the Ku Klux Klan, committing financial blunders, and lying about Briggs's relationship with the Communists. At the same time, the UNIA head displayed a talent for poking maliciously at Briggs. The *Negro World* ran its oft-cited "notice" telling Harlemites to beware of a white man passing as "A Negro for Convenience." Briggs responded with a libel action. At the trial Garvey countered that Briggs had invited him in writing to join in overthrowing the government. (J. Edgar Hoover agreed with that interpretation of a letter Briggs had written.) The magistrate found no sedition and also had trouble understanding what was libelous about calling someone white. But he found for Briggs and instructed Garvey to publish an apology in the *Negro World*.[13]

Briggs's belief that undermining Garvey was a precondition for advancing black liberation became a near obsession that led to an uncharacteristic plea for government action. Goaded and manipulated by the confidential informant known as Agent 800, Briggs became a marginal source for the government's effort to nail Garvey. The outcome did not enhance the standing of the two men and the movements they led.[14]

Briggs's dealings with federal agents began with information provided by businessman and supporter Anthony Crawford, who disclosed the "extravagantly excessive price" that Garvey had paid for his first Black Star Line ship, the nearly unseaworthy *Yarmouth*. As the ideological struggle between Briggs and Garvey intensified, it became entangled with Briggs's escalating indictment of injudicious financial practices by the UNIA. Echoing Briggs, the Party accused Garvey of using funds raised from the dreams and pocketbooks of workers "to pay the salaries and 'traveling expenses' of the adventurers and jokers who are misusing an ideal cause in behalf of their own selfish ends." Three days before Garvey's indictment, Briggs met with a federal postal inspector to ask when action would be taken. He was accompanied by a "legal advisor," Murray Bernays, a left-wing lawyer associated with the defense of Communists. Bernays's presence led the Justice Department's special agent Mortimer J. Davis, who dealt with Briggs, to speculate that the Communists were interested in eliminating Garvey as a "stumbling block" to their own ambition to win a large following among blacks.[15]

The Brotherhood enjoyed a burst of good fortune in the fall of 1921 when three UNIA leaders — Bishop George Alexander McGuire, James D. Brooks, and Cyril A. Crichlow — bolted to the ABB. What turned out to be the last two issues of the *Crusader* bristled with optimism and with plans for a weekly paper, the *Liberator*, to challenge Garvey's *Negro World*. But despite alleged support from "153 Negro organizations and churches," Briggs was not able to raise the money. He was also undermined by the querulous Claude McKay at the CI Congress. McKay had heard from Otto Huiswoud that the Comintern was going to subsidize "a propaganda Negro paper in America." Briggs was still a Goose, and McKay was livid with anyone who did not support a solely open Party. He wrote the Comintern that Briggs was "not a capable editor" and lacked the ability of those who produced the *Crisis* and the *Messenger*— not to speak of Domingo's *Emancipator*. The best black talent, McKay insisted, was still outside the Party because of the CP's internal factional feuds and "underground tactics." McKay derided the *Crusader* as "more of a Negro family journal" and urged that a subsidy be postponed until an effort was made to recruit *Emancipator's* editors to create a black Communist weekly.[16]

The defections of prominent UNIA members hardly spurred the Brotherhood to widen its ideological appeal. In October 1921 the ABB's Supreme Council issued a program that conceded only that broader political forces need not endorse the entire Brotherhood program in order to make common cause and need not embrace Soviet rule, only recognize the Soviets as implacable foes of imperialism. But the ABB called for creation of a secret pan-African army. Weapons would be smuggled into Africa by men "in the guise of missionaries, etc." as a prelude to gradual liberation of the continent, culminating in the establishment of the "world-wide Negro federation." Domestically, a national federation of black organizations would be created and would enfold "a secret protective organization." That would be "the real Power," admitting only the best and most courageous of the race to its essentially military order. Ancillary black labor organizations would develop cooperative enterprises run on a democratic, participatory basis. A compelling proposal ended the program: "The revolutionary element which is undermining the imperialist powers that oppress us must be given every encouragement by Negroes who really seek liberation. . . . We should immediately establish contact with the Third Internationale and its followers in all countries of the world."[17]

But that clarion call for blacks to join Lenin's International was unacceptable to the new ABB recruits from the UNIA. There is no evidence of their active participation in the Brotherhood other than writing articles for the *Crusader*. Before the validity of a revolutionary commitment could be proved to black communities, the revolutionary tide began to ebb in Central Europe with the collapse of uprisings in Germany and Hungary, and with the consolidation of world capitalism in the aftermath of the Great War. At home, the dominant political trend was a conservative stabilization under Republican rule. The black communities of the North, formed by migration, provided a degree of insularity from a hostile white society, which the mass of new black proletarians did not wish to engage unless forced to do so. To a considerable extent, Marcus Garvey's UNIA resonated for African American working people as Briggs's ABB could not, because the former vibrantly expressed outrage at the dominant white society without directly and dangerously confronting the bourgeois order.[18]

The black Communists had other problems. The Party apparently would not — and did not — staunch the ABB's financial hemorrhage, despite the internal struggle waged by Briggs and his black comrades to elevate the Negro question within CP ranks. Failure to raise funds for the *Liberator* actually signaled the demise of the *Crusader*. The final issue heralded Garvey's arrest, treating his incarceration in the Tombs as the capstone of the magazine's half-year campaign of exposure and vituperation. The issue offered no hint of the magazine's impending demise, and many observers among the New Negro radicals claimed to be mystified by its disappearance. But the enervating battle against Garvey had exhausted the *Crusader*. The journal's collapse and the weak finances of the ABB forced Briggs to seek new employment. In March 1922 he secured work in the national office of the Friends of Soviet Russia, and in November he became organizer for the Yorkville branch of the Workers Party. With the assistance of Grace Campbell, Briggs launched the twice weekly Crusader News Service, which fed news items and opinion pieces to the Negro press. Otto Huiswoud, who had returned from the Fourth Comintern Congress in Moscow, took over the remaining potential for recruiting to the ABB, touring several cities in the summer of 1923. At that time, Post Menelik officially selected Huiswoud as a delegate from the ABB to the Workers Party. The Harlem Post was now the representative body of what remained of the ABB. In June 1922 the West Side Harlem Branch of the Workers Party was formed with the following provisional officers: Huiswoud as organizer, Briggs as recording and financial secretary, and Richard B. Moore, Grace Campbell and Claude McKay as members of "the Propaganda and Educational Committee." The absorption of the ABB into the Party had accelerated.[19]

The battle between Garvey and his enemies left no last man standing. Garvey could awaken rage, hope, and pride in an uprooted, oppressed population. But he had no effective response to Briggs's claim that racial consciousness alone was not enough to win freedom in the modern world, where power was based partially on race but centrally on corporate, class, national, and military forces. Without the progressive alliances that were ruled out by his African nationalism, Garvey sought to mollify the very elements attacking him, such as the government, or barter with those racists who approved of racial apartheid for their own reasons (like the KKK). That, of course, grievously subverted Garvey's moral authority. Conversely, Briggs's efforts to turn the UNIA ranks to revolutionary socialism was in shambles; his ideological fusion of racial consciousness and the Third International had not illuminated for the masses the path to liberation. But both men ushered in variants of radicalism that were to clash in rich and suggestive ways and have a deep and lasting impact on black life and on the nation.

As the ABB declined, Briggs returned to a long postponed campaign for cooperative stores and an insurance plan for Brotherhood members. Perhaps the conservative ascendancy returned him to a scheme with dim promise of bringing financial viability to the ABB. In July 1923 Briggs sought funds to establish twenty-five cooperative stores for ABB members in various cities. The endeavor would insulate black workers against capitalist exploitation and promote "unity with all blacks and truly class conscious white workers." Briggs also proposed that ABB offer sickness and death benefit insurance. But the dream of a cooperative store network and an insurance fund was dashed by the reality of the Brotherhood's financial insolvency.[20]

By about this time the ABB had absorbed the Harlem Educational Forum, successor to the Peoples Educational Forum of the 21st AD Socialist Party club. But there was trouble raising rent money for meeting halls, and the ABB turned to the year-old Harlem Branch of the Workers Party for help. By the fall of 1923 government agents reported that bad weather or a single member's illness was enough to force cancellation of meetings of the Supreme Council. The Brotherhood appeared to be in the grip of "lethargy and poor organization." Shortly thereafter, the ABB was integrated into the Workers Party; it was virtually dissolved in early 1924, although some individuals appeared as Brotherhood representatives to the founding of the American Negro Labor Congress in 1925. The African Blood Brotherhood was virtually interred with the founding of the ANLC. As the ABB declined, Briggs and his black comrades explored other avenues to ideological and organizational influence.[21]

THE SANHEDRIN

In late 1922 William Monroe Trotter, the publisher of the *Boston Guardian*, secretary and guiding light of the National Equal Rights League, called for the formation of a council of Negro leaders. At Trotter's urging, Dr. Matthew A.N. Shaw, a Boston physician and president of the NERL, wrote to the

NAACP, declaring that the defeat of an antilynch bill underscored both the importance and the urgency for the NAACP, the ABB, the NERL, the International Uplift League, and the National Race Congress to come together to issue an even more inclusive call to "unify our forces."[22]

The ABB immediately came on board as initiating sponsor of a United Negro Front Conference (scheduled for March 1923 in New York City), with Cyril Briggs as organizer. Kelly Miller, the Howard University dean and head of the National Race Congress, jumped the gun and announced that the conference was a prelude to a "Negro Sanhedrin," a term inspired by the Hebrew name for a Supreme Council or assembly of Jews during Maccabean times. The New York meeting produced a concordat that reflected a mild thaw in relations among ideologically diverse black groups. The document called for unity of action while allowing full autonomy of participating organizations.[23]

International communism's "second period" of "partial capitalist stabilization" was dawning, and assumptions about impending revolution were waning. The new period suggested a more defensive, alliance-oriented posture in which cooperation across ideological lines became part of the Communist agenda. Briggs willingly muted the Brotherhood's revolutionary rhetoric, but Kelly Miller was less accommodating. He called for a "sane, temperate" conference and warned that "wild demands which the demandant has no means of enforcing, are but vain vociferations whose echo returns to torment his own ears."[24]

Miller was appointed chair of a Committee on Arrangements to operate from Washington. Briggs became secretary of the United Front's principal committee in New York, which believed that it was empowered to issue invitations and draw up an agenda for Miller's committee to follow. But the vagaries of the lines of authority, as well geographical separation, gave Miller an opportunity to take control. He simply declared that the United Front Conference (or "Race Front" conference, as he preferred to call it) had ceased to function with the appointment of a Committee on Arrangements. The Briggs-Trotter conference, he said, "has no headquarters, or achievement, or money, or other agencies to foster such a movement." The center of gravity for planning the Sanhedrin shifted to Washington. As Miller drew mainstream civic, fraternal, professional, and religious groups into the Sanhedrin, he reminded Briggs "with all due modesty" that "the All-Race Congress is inseparable from my name."[25]

The Sanhedrin convened in Chicago from February 11 to 15, 1924, with 250 delegates from 20 states, representing 61 national organizations. Despite the listing of the nearly moribund African Blood Brotherhood and a smattering of black labor unions, the conference was dominated by entrenched middle-class leadership. Briggs, Huiswoud, Domingo, Moore, Randolph, Trotter (and the deceased Shaw) were listed as members of the Committee on Arrangements, but were conspicuously absent from the speakers' list. Also missing was any meaningful sign of the United Front Conference's agenda, which included racism, legal discrimination, economic exploitation, intraracial cooperation, "industrial betterment" (higher wages and shorter hours), and action to combat lynching, segregation, disenfranchisement, and peonage. The Sanhedrin's agenda under Miller's sway was dominated by uplift and self-help issues. Its breadth did not extend to the unified "broad working class" participation envisioned by the Brotherhood and the Communists. Miller never intended to breach the ideological confines of his own class and cultural milieu. Nor did the Sanhedrin have a clear plan for continuing its explorations. The United Front Conference, which Briggs had hoped would continue as an umbrella for a coalition of black organizations, did not survive beyond the spring of 1924.[26]

The Sanhedrin did mark the debut of the Workers Party in the broader black community. The ABB's role in the planning process had excited the Party's Negro Commission, now under Robert Minor's direction. The Sanhedrin's nominally open door made it possible for the Workers Party to participate and to offer a series of resolutions that reflected the political mindset of the Communists in the mid-1920s.[27]

With enthusiasm quickened by a new sense of acceptance, the Party's Negro Commission viewed the presence of the WP group as evidence that Sanhedrin participants—from the Odd Fellows to the National Negro Funeral Directors Association—were ready to give sympathetic consideration to "the labor issue." After all, Miller had written about the overwhelming working-class composition of the black community and had speculated that a united black working class could be a pathway to freedom. The Communists also were showing some appreciation that the social distance between classes in the black community was far less than among whites. The *Daily Worker* suggested that the oppression of African Americans was the nation's equivalent of the multi-class subjugation of colonialized people under European imperialism.[28]

But the Party's blissful disregard of the Sanhedrin's political and cultural persona locked it in a sectarian chamber. The Communists called upon the gathering not only to fully embrace the class character of the Negro question, but also to unite with labor's left "and give added strength to the revolutionary forces" to overthrow capitalism, the "common enemy of white and colored workers."[29] The Sanhedrin was not about to buy that.

Yet the resolutions offered by the WP contingent illuminated both the Party's rising sensitivity to the Negro question and the extent to which it was politically out of touch with black America. At the top of the list was the labor union question — framed with extraordinary urgency rising from the vulnerability of the new, largely unskilled migrant black proletariat. The labor resolution begged the Sanhedrin to launch a union organizing drive among blacks and to mobilize the black press behind such a drive. A resolution on sharecroppers and tenant farmers pointed to the poverty and terror facing rural blacks and advocated all-black sharecropper unions should whites resist interracial organization. Segregated housing and the clustering of African Americans into exploitative residential "black belts" were condemned. Segregated education was excoriated as a bedrock of oppression. Jim Crow transportation, restaurants, and theaters kept up vicious caste distinctions that nourished growing disenfranchisement at the ballot box. Armed resistance to lynching was commended, and a constitutional amendment to bar that barbaric practice was advocated. Resolutions on international issues condemned the League of Nations as an imperialist conspiracy, demanded self-determination for U.S. colonies, appealed for the independence of Africa, pleaded for the Sanhedrin to convene the All-World Race Congress, proposed a delegation to visit Soviet Russia, and called upon the Sanhedrin to "endorse for the Negro's song of freedom, the anthem known as 'The Internationale.'"[30]

In spite of such sectarian fervor, the WP and ABB resolutions submitted to the Sanhedrin were important contributions to the ongoing quest for equality. Some of the proposals — such as desegregating schools, ending bars to intermarriage, promoting industrial unionism, implementing rent control, and others — eventually became law. The resolutions, and the spirited debate they provoked, suggested that Marxism could play a positive, creative role in the black community — baring the class relationships that underlay the oppression of blacks, offering an uncompromising and progressive agenda for liberation, stressing the international aspects of the Negro question, and laying the groundwork for a shift in African American leadership to an emerging working class. For all its excesses, the WP resolutions sought to walk the difficult path that welded present-day reforms to a long-term vision of transforming change.

For the Party and for the handful of black Communists, the Sanhedrin was a figurative baptism. African Americans entered an arena of discussion and debate representing a movement whose roots were in Europe and in predominantly white native radicalism. Unlike the other delegates, they represented a force that appeared to be external to the black community. But they were confident that their radicalism was true to the core of black needs and aspirations. And they were heard, as they took the floor repeatedly to press their program.[31]

At the final session, recommendations on labor, education, and other issues were shunted to a Commission on Permanent Results for future consideration. In the Party's view, that group was controlled by ghetto profiteers and "professional men who cater to white capitalists." Otto Huiswoud rose to demand a hearing on working-class issues on behalf of the 95 percent of the race who were workers. Miller capitulated in the face of protests by Communists scattered throughout the hall. A watered-down labor resolution was passed, which retained the WP's appeal to unions to end discrimination and to promote unionism among blacks. All direct references to organized labor's color line and the need for industrial unions were eliminated. The rest of the Workers Party program was watered down or rejected. Nevertheless, the Party's Gordon Owens declared that "Radical Negro Labor" was not discouraged in the face of the dominating presence of "obnoxious" petty capitalists. Previous signs of sensitivity about the social position of the black bourgeoisie dissipated. In the months following the Sanhedrin, the Party's attacks on the black middle class escalated. One year later, Israel Amter ruminated in the Soviet press about how only the sixteen delegates from the WP and ABB and a handful of "low clergy suffering under the yoke of the princes of the church" dared to struggle for the Negro against the tools of the enslavers.[32]

There was a subsequent meeting of the Sanhedrin in Washington. The conservatives were prepared; the Communists were not. The Workers Party was barred from the meeting, despite an angry, bitter correspondence between Briggs and Miller. That was the last meeting of the Sanhedrin.[33]

GARVEY AGAIN

Despite the wreckage of the ABB-Garvey encounter in 1921, the Communists still desired to win Garvey's constituency. At the Fourth Comintern Congress in 1922, Otto Huiswoud noted that "the rebel rank-and-file element" in the UNIA was disposed to an anti-imperialist outlook. Any movement that impeded imperialism, the Comintern responded, ought to be supported. At Garvey's 1924 convention, the situation was different from what it had been in the clash of 1921. Garvey now stood convicted of mail fraud; his movement had sustained steady losses of membership and income; his vulnerability was manifest.[34]

Robert Minor had become responsible to the Party's Central Committee for Negro Work. Although the Communists had not yet accepted the need for black leadership in that position, Minor was at least the most knowledgeable white for that assignment. Born in San Antonio, Texas, in 1884, he had gone from odd jobs to editorial cartoonist, winding up at the Socialist *Call* during the Great War after resigning from the New York *World* rather than support its prowar position. After the Russian Revolution, he broke with his anarcho-syndicalist ideas and remained a devout Communist until his death in 1951. Minor despised his southern racist roots and spent a lifetime studying the legacy of slavery and the neglected history of slave rebellions, and stressing both the special oppression and revolutionary potential of the black masses.[35]

Minor reasoned that the U.S. government, egged on by Garvey's opponents, had targeted him as a means of destroying the UNIA, establishing a deportation threat against black noncitizens, and silencing the black radical impulse. While critical of Garvey's "hat-in-hand diplomacy," Minor was far less subjective than Briggs about the UNIA leader and was inclined to connect the effort to influence UNIA's following with defense of Garvey.[36]

With all that in mind, the Workers Party approached Garvey's 1924 convention in a friendly and supportive spirit. In two letters addressed to the convention, the Party commended black anticolonial struggles around the world, gently contrasting them with Garvey's comparatively submissive behavior. The Communists again extended an invitation to UNIA to join the Soviets and the emerging nonwhite movements of India and China in worldwide coordination of liberation struggles. The second letter, written in response to reports of Garvey's tenders to the Ku Klux Klan, offered an alternative black-labor alliance to destroy all manifestations of Jim Crow as the only way for UNIA to realize its ultimate aspiration of freedom for peoples of African descent.[37]

The friendly spirit began to evaporate when a lone Workers Party delegate, Olivia Whiteman, rose to challenge the notion that racial conflict in the South, a topic for debate, could be solved "to the satisfaction of all concerned." No self-respecting Negro, she declared, would ever accept a solution that would satisfy the white ruling class. That was a prelude to the final rupture; mutual expressions of sympathy and respect collapsed into an abyss of irreconcilable ideological differences. The issue was, in Minor's words, Garvey's "pretended 'diplomatic' dicker" with the Ku Klux Klan.[38]

The WP's disappointed, scolding second letter asked how the masses could believe that a movement willing to surrender to the Klan would stand up to the combined forces of imperialist states vying for control of Africa. By fomenting race hatred, it said, the Klan splits the working class into warring camps. Beware of the lyncher who calls the black man a baboon and monkey, and bemoans the end of slavery. Such a creature would leave Negroes all the more degraded, terrorized, and tortured — without a home in Africa or anywhere else.[39]

Garvey waved aside a motion to table the letter. Such a long and concerned message deserved consideration. The UNIA had sympathy for the Workers Party; like the UNIA, it was an underdog. But the UNIA was a "peculiar underdog" that suffered prejudice, even from other underdogs. Whether a white man was a worker or a capitalist, if he claimed not to feel different from a Negro, he was a liar. The UNIA belonged to "the Negro party, first, last, and all the time."[40]

As for the Communists, Garvey continued, they had a long way to go to gain some effectiveness and power for themselves, "but in the meantime we are for ourselves." The white worker was crushed by the white capitalist, but that was brutality between brothers. In a crisis the white worker and the white boss would join hands — "and I think that the white communist is a brother to them if anything happens."[41]

The Workers Party's approach to such a profoundly racial deconstruction of power in America was articulated before the letters were sent, and it never deviated: Garvey's dicker with the KKK would demoralize the worldwide freedom struggle of subject peoples. The UNIA's chimerical separatism reflected sharpening class differentiation in the black community, whereby growing numbers of petty bourgeois businessmen and politicians were using racial solidarity to exploit their own people — fomenting a crackpot allegiance of "the Negro masses to Negro leaders who betray them to the ruling class."[42]

That line could not resonate with the workers, small shopkeepers, businessmen, and intellectuals who embraced Garvey's cry of "up you mighty race." The powerlessness of the Communists, the questionable egalitarian credentials of white labor, and the strength of the nation's repressive apparatus together had directed the latent militancy (which the Communists shrewdly recognized) of Garvey's social base away from confrontation with the larger society and toward a racial insularity and a dreamed-of African hegira. For the time being, that militancy would be restricted to a nonconfrontational posture and program. A merged racial and class consciousness would have to await new circumstances.[43]

Minor sat at the press table, pondering the "strange light" cast by the convention upon the "vast chasm" of misconception, hatred, pain, and danger that the division of the working class on racial lines had caused. Speech after speech insisted that 99 out of 100 white men in America accepted the Klan's racist doctrine—inwardly, if not outwardly. That, Minor mused, was the basis "of this peculiar nationalistic philosophy of this anticlerical, anti-imperialist organization of Negro working people which drives it to the incredible stand against fighting the Klan murder organization which kills, tortures, and burns their black brothers."[44]

Shortly after the convention, the Communists launched a series of bitter attacks on Garvey. The WP convention of 1925 called for the imposition of "working-class hegemony" on the UNIA and resolved to form a Party "fraction" within Garvey's organization to conduct "open battle" against its petty-bourgeois leaders. But that call for factional warfare within UNIA was futile; it actually turned out to be a step toward abandonment of the organization. The *Daily Worker* began to downgrade the size of Garvey's meetings and now claimed that his strength was vastly overrated. But the decline of the UNIA brought no joy to Robert Minor. With Garvey in jail and the association's numbers dropping, Minor, who always expressed intense sympathy for the yearning of Garvey's followers, saw only calamity for the Negro people and for the working class as a whole.[45]

With the dissolution of the underground party in April 1923, the Workers Party was now the sole Communist organization. It next turned to the fledgling Farmer-Labor Party. This step was reinforced by the belief that the black vote, in the face of the temporizing of both major parties on the KKK, was moving to political independence. Staking out its claim that industrial unionism and independent politics could not advance without an assault on racism, Minor's Negro Commission wrote a "Negro Equality" proposal for submission to the founding Farmer-Labor convention in 1924. The proposal demanded the new party's support for full political and social equality through nondiscriminatory union membership, constitutional measures to assure equality at the ballot box, and an end to segregation.[46]

On the convention floor, all references to social equality and an end to seg-regation were eliminated. After a bitter fight, in which much of the original language was reinstated, the entire proposal was resubmitted to the platform committee. An innocuous plank emerged, entitled "Negro," which recognized the "particularly vicious" victimization of blacks and pledged to include them in Farmer-Labor efforts to free all toilers. All references to black recruitment to unions, black voting rights, and "equality" were again expunged.[47]

Minor pointed out that although a lone Communist (though not identi-fied as such) defended the "Negro Equality" proposal, the Workers Party did not rise in its own name to support it. The Party was in the midst of a vicious factional battle between William Z. Foster and Party secretary Charles E. Ruthenberg. Minor, a member of the Ruthenberg faction, implied that Party leaders under the sway of the Foster group went along with those concessions in the hope of mollifying antiblack southern farmers and AFL leaders with an eye toward future cooperation. Worse, in Minor's view, Communists were guilty of serious backsliding when called upon to challenge the hardened racial prejudices of fellow white workers and would-be political allies.[48]

Whatever the truth of the factional tangle, events at the Farmer-Labor con-vention demonstrated that the Party had by no means adopted an uncompro-mising, consistent antiracist posture. Its efforts to build a base in the black mainstream had yielded little. But its own small cadre of black activists de-manded that the Party push on. Pressure also came from the ultimate arbiter of legitimacy and ideological direction: the Comintern. After the experiences with Garvey and the Sanhedrin, the Party turned to building its own organization dedicated to black-labor unity: the American Negro Labor Congress. That de-cision was inseparably linked to the inner life and experience of the Party in its first six years and to its ties to the international communist movement.

CHAPTER THREE

The Comintern's Vision

LENIN'S VIEW

The last quarter of the nineteenth century and the beginning of the twentieth beheld the rise of modern imperialism. That phenomenon sparked a debate among Marxists about the importance of the "colonial question" to the interests of the laboring masses of the industrial nations. It preoccupied the Seventh Congress of the Second (Socialist) International, held at Stuttgart, Germany, in 1907.[1]

V. I. Lenin, in attendance at that congress, had begun to attack proponents of "pure revolution," based solely on the working class. He sensed that turn-of-the-century czarist Russia was weakened by the presence of oppressed nationalities and by a peasantry beset by feudal survivals. These groups, alienated from the czarist empire, were vital potential allies of Russia's small proletariat. His policy, already formulated for the Bolshevik faction of the Russian Social Democratic Party during the revolution of 1905, called for an alliance between the working class and the peasantry.[2]

Lenin's vision of such an alliance extended to the modern world as a whole, where he perceived an indissoluble link between the proletarian movements of the West and the largely peasant-based national revolutionary movements of the East. Oppressed national minorities and subject nations were powerful players in the modern revolutionary process — potential "reserves of the proletariat" — whose struggles to free themselves from imperial domination would hasten the end of capitalism. Denial of the rewards of colonial exploitation to the imperialists was also denial of "the main field from which imperialism draws its reserve forces." Ultimately, national democratic revolutions to overthrow dependency would come under the leadership of workers and would take a socialist direction, thus linking national democratic and anticolonial movements with socialism. Therefore, Lenin maintained, working-class movements in advanced countries and national movements for liberation were *both* revolutionary movements — two aspects of a linked social process.[3]

Scattered references to African Americans also occur in Lenin's voluminous writings. In *Capitalism in Agriculture* he referred to the American South as "segregated, hidebound, a stifling atmosphere, a sort of prison for 'emancipated' Negroes" and pointed out the similarity of the Russian *otrabotki* system ("our survival of feudalism") of rent payment through work for the landlord and the sharecropping system that trapped blacks in the United States.[4]

On February 25, 1919, John Reed wrote to Gregori Zinoviev, soon to be president of the Third International, which was founded a few days later. He inaugurated the Comintern's discussion of African Americans with an acute sense of black suffering and resistance — and a blissfully confused and overdrawn portrait of the revolutionary impulse among African Americans. Reed was offering "some facts" about American Negroes to help Zinoviev "in composing your appeal." After reviewing the terror in the South, Reed noted that the Great War had instilled in blacks a new spirit of resistance to lynching and racist violence. With Wilson's hint of a better life (in exchange for support for the war) now shattered, Negroes in the North were meeting the attacks upon them "with surprising resistance." Their battle cry: "for every Negro killed, two whites shall die." The most important agitation among blacks was being done by "Randolph and Mason [sic]," who were preaching revolutionary socialism and armed resistance to massacres. Their newspaper, the *Messenger*, was "semi-nationalist, semi-communist." Finally, most Negroes preferred being called "colored people."[5]

At the first three Comintern congresses, the African American question was debated in terms of its possible relationship to the national and colonial questions. The Manifesto of the First Comintern Congress, which affected Cyril Briggs so strongly, called upon the colonies to unite with the metropolitan working class. Responding to Lenin's call at the Second Congress for critical discussion, Reed said that the striving of American Negroes was expressed in a "strong racial and social movement" rapidly gaining in class consciousness. Blacks did not seek a "separate national existence," as demonstrated by their weak response to Garvey: "They consider themselves first of all Americans at home in the United States." (Ironically, those words were uttered on the eve of UNIA's spectacular growth.) The Negro should be considered a vital part of the working class and brought into the labor movement. Communists should seek relationships with Negro movements for equality and argue the futility of bourgeois rights and the necessity of revolution to lift the burden of racial oppression and free all workers. That was, at best, a small step beyond the Socialists' color-blind economism.[6]

Lenin's "Preliminary Draft Theses on the National and Colonial Questions" at the Second Congress went further. He urged Communist parties to "support . . . revolutionary movements among the dependent nations and those without equal rights (e.g., in Ireland, among the American Negroes, etc.)." Whether he intended to include African Americans under the rubric of an "oppressed nation" or among "those without equal rights" meant little to the unfolding Comintern debate on the American Negro question. Lenin had drawn a wide arc of special oppression from Africa through Asia to black America. Blacks would inevitably become part of the linkage of national oppression and social revolution.[7]

At the Third Congress in 1921 the South African delegation proposed that the CI's Executive Committee should study the Negro question. Nothing came of this immediately beyond routine acceptance. The South African Communist Party, at that time composed largely of white European immigrants, was actually trying to deflect attention from national self-determination for South Africa's black majority by talking about "the proletarian movement among the Negroes."[8]

The Fourth Congress in 1922 undertook the first extensive discussion of the American Negro question in which African Americans were prominent, stressing the special dimensions of racial prejudice (in general and in the Party). Claude McKay was there. The brilliant, mercurial poet and writer had recently resigned from the socialist *Liberator* after an extended conflict with his equally prickly and zealous co-editor, Michael Gold. The thirty-three-year-old, Jamaican-born McKay yearned to see the cradle of proletarian revolution and wanted to witness the deliberations of the Fourth Comintern Congress. His opportunity to get to Russia came with support from members of the Harlem intelligentsia, such as James Weldon Johnson, Richard B. Moore, and Arthur Schomburg, who wanted him to go and were ready to help. With a credential from the African Blood Brotherhood, McKay made it to Moscow.⁹

There McKay was confronted by a suspicious, resentful U.S. delegation, which (if McKay is to be believed) sought to bar his entry to the congress. He blamed his problems largely upon the delegation's Goose majority, which favored maintaining an underground party. Refusing to bend, he earned their enmity and was treated as an interloper. McKay also complained to the Comintern that "comrade Sasha" (Pastor Stokes) objected to his presence in Moscow because of his charges that the American comrades had neglected work with blacks and had allowed some to drift away from the Party. Never one to downplay his own achievements, McKay wrote a Comintern official that Pastor Stokes knew "of my work more than anyone else," including the fact that he had "got[ten] the best Negro group in New York to get in touch with the C.P." But Moscow was the place to tell the truth about the formative Party's abysmally weak consciousness on the Negro question. The American Communists had squandered valuable time in petty squabbles while the capitalists were trying to turn blacks into strikebreakers. It was time to call a "Negro Congress," McKay wrote, "and the Third International will be amazed at the fine material for Communist work there is in the Negro Race."¹⁰

Sen Katayama, head of the Eastern Section of the Comintern, came to the rescue. Katayama, a Japanese revolutionary with a reputation for bulldog tenacity, had gone to a small Christian college near Nashville, Tennessee. There he had developed an interest in the Negro question and a strong feeling that distinct black voices needed to be heard by the Comintern. He made sure that McKay got a pass to the Fourth Congress.¹¹

McKay had spurned Zinoviev's invitation to speak at the opening session at the Bolshoi Theater on November 5. But weeks later, after a triumphal round of speeches to local soviets, soldiers, factory workers, and students, McKay overcame his earlier reticence and agreed to speak. He attributed his success to his "authentic" dark complexion (compared to the light-skinned Huiswoud, whom he despised). He claimed to have no stomach for bombast and delusion. He was not about to paint a false portrait of the black masses poised at the revolutionary ramparts. Neither would he exaggerate the work of Communists. In self-proclaimed sadness and candor, he said that bourgeois reformers had fought harder for the rights of blacks than Socialists and Communists had done. Among the left in the United States he found repeated manifestations of racial prejudice. The Party, at all levels, was guilty of inattention to Negro work. American Communists would have to purge themselves of chauvinism before they could influence Negroes with radical propaganda. Blending Wobbly syndicalism and racial consciousness, McKay concluded that racial conflict within the working class was a looming disaster. The Negro question was the central problem of the class struggle; the fight for racial justice was a matter of self-preservation for American labor.[12]

Otto Huiswoud also addressed the Fourth Congress. He argued that the Negro question was basically an economic problem exacerbated by racism. Huiswoud too stressed the dangers of explosive working-class divisions inherent in organized labor's racist policies, which made it hard to argue black workers out of strikebreaking. He described the murderous racism facing blacks in the South. At the same time the emergence of Negro mass organizations along with newspapers and magazines suggested social diversity and cultural attainment that could place American blacks in the vanguard of the liberation movements of colored peoples. The UNIA's anti-imperialist temper ran through Negro life, and its organization stretched from an American base into the heart of Africa. It was time to give serious attention to the Negro question.[13]

The congress responded. It established a Negro Commission, whose members were drawn from both industrial and colonial countries. Huiswoud was installed as chairman, and McKay was invited to attend its meetings. Comintern leader Karl Radek proposed that an initial draft of the commission's theses be rewritten because it was "too Marxian in its phraseology." The passion for plain language was becoming contagious. The resulting "Theses on the Negro Question" placed all peoples of African descent ever more firmly within the global struggle against imperialism, declaring that it was "the special duty of Communists to apply Lenin's 'Theses on the Colonial Question' to the Negro problem." The final document stated that the American Negro, who stood at the "center of Negro culture and the crystallization of Negro protest," had a history that "fits him for an important role in the liberation struggle of the entire African race." The world Communist movement had a duty to fight for racial equality globally, to support every black movement that undermined capitalism and imperialism, to win blacks to unionism, and to organize a "general Negro Conference or Congress in Moscow." A report to the Presidium of the Congress, described as "more private in its nature," suggested that African Americans be recruited to study at the KUTV (University of the Toilers of the East) in Moscow, which had been established the previous year to train revolutionaries from colonial and dependent nations. Some of the Negro graduates would be used as organizers in Africa until an African cadre could be developed. A wedge now existed for the later claim that the Fourth Congress had linked the American blacks to colonial and national liberation and had thus opened the door to the adoption (in 1928) of the slogan of self-determination in the Black Belt of the American South.[14]

At the Fourth Congress Huiswoud, an imposing intellectual, sailed confidently through the shoals of international communism, buoyed by his charter membership in the Party. He returned to the United States at a peak of influence (but soon to be eclipsed by Fort-Whiteman), armed with the CI's injunction to elevate the Party's Negro work. In 1923 he became the first black member of the Central Executive Committee and made a final effort to inject new life into the African Blood Brotherhood, as its national organizer. In contrast, McKay's individualistic, poetic temperament did not suit the Party. Antagonism grew between the writer and the organization, and McKay began his long journey to anticommunism and Catholicism.[15]

BACK HOME

The Communist underground phase ended in April 1923, when the submerged and legal groups were fused into a sole aboveground organization called the Workers Party. At its December 1923 convention, the Party reported twenty-five thousand members.[16] But the African American segment was minuscule, concentrated in New York and Chicago, and tussling with the Party's complex and often alienating social texture. Most of the white rank and file did not speak English, and the English that was spoken was so jargon-ridden that one member reported years later that he, an American-born teenager and a product of Chicago's schools, needed a translator — for English words. Imagine what that experience must have been like, he reflected, for rural African Americans who had recently emigrated from the Deep South?[17] On the other hand, Harry Haywood described warm and caring relations within the Young Communist League and the Party among those who reached out to each other across the racial divide. In the Party's contradictory gestation, both reports were probably valid.[18]

Five years after the defeat of William Z. Foster's great steel and packing-house strikes, the Party sought sporadically to attack Jim Crow unions and establish a degree of moral authority in the black community, principally in Chicago, which was the site of the Communists' national office. One ground-breaking battle involved black women, many of whom did double duty as wives and workers, trying to hold families together with far less than a minimum standard of living. A strike of those women against Chicago's garment shops broke out in 1924 when the International Ladies' Garment Workers Union launched an organizing drive. The Party moved in. A storefront was turned into a makeshift command post as Party activists, most of them women, spread out among the strikers to win them permanently to trade unionism. The small, vulnerable garment shops began to capitulate. A beachhead of unionism was thus established among black women. But the AFL's resistance to nondiscriminatory unionism remained an enormous obstacle to additional gains.[19]

The persistence of deplorable ghetto housing during supposedly flush times led the Party into organizing a tenants' movement on Chicago's South Side. By the mid-1920s the rate of southern rural migration to urban areas had accelerated, and the consequent threat to the health and safety of a race hemmed in by segregation had become alarming. On the last day of March in 1924 the Party organized the Negro Tenants Protective League. At its first modest storefront meeting, the top Communists in Negro work—Robert Minor, Lovett Fort-Whiteman, and Otto Huiswoud—spoke, calling for rent strikes. But the scattershot growth and instability of the ghetto made organization difficult. The rent party, rather than the rent strike, seemed a more effective way to deal with the "rent hogs." For the time being, the tenants' movement foundered, only to rise once again under different conditions at the end of the decade.[20]

FOSTER'S IMPACT

In 1920 William Z. Foster had founded the Trade Union Educational League as a "left-progressive" catalyst within the labor movement. By 1923 the TUEL was firmly in the grip of the Workers Party and had begun to carry the Party's "Negro program" for equality and an end to Jim Crow unions into scores of central labor bodies and local labor organizations.[21]

For some time Foster had anguished over the consequences of labor's color line for the packinghouse and steel strikes he had led in 1918 and 1919. While some black workers from the South had experience with labor organizing on the docks, in the sawmills, and among tenant farmers, many more either were unfamiliar with unions or recoiled from their racist policies. When Foster led various packinghouse unions into the Stockyards Labor Council, he attempted to draw in black meat packers through white-and-black, community-based locals. The SLC achieved a precarious biracial unity. Countering the formation of an all-black company union, the SLC elected a Negro worker to a vice-presidency and hired seven paid Negro agents, but growing racial tension in 1919 threatened the tenuous solidarity. In response, Jack Johnstone, Foster's long-time colleague and then head of the Labor Council, organized street-corner meetings in the South Side ghetto and a parade of black and white packers through the community. The SLC passed a resolution expelling from the council all affiliates that refused to accept blacks on an equal basis. During the Red Summer riots that July, the SLC organized black-white solidarity meetings and issued a pamphlet whose emphatic call for interracial cooperation as a matter of survival was a model of clarity and passion. Nonetheless, a near civil war raged for two weeks as six thousand police officers and soldiers smothered the black community. Thirty thousand white stockyard workers and four thousand blacks voted for a strike to force withdrawal of armed forces from the area and for the return of terrorized Negroes to the yards under union protection. When the riots ended and troops were withdrawn, the packinghouse workers returned to their jobs.[22]

Foster had witnessed the widespread use of strikebreakers in both his strikes. Negro workers held such deep animus toward discriminatory unions that many of them delighted in taking jobs from whites and breaking strikes. The need for action to obliterate the union color bar was urgent. At the same time, influential black leaders who counseled strikebreaking had to be confronted. Foster viewed the problem of unity between blacks and the labor movement as a battle against both organized labor's racist policies and anti-union sentiment in the black community. The hint of ambivalence in Foster's thinking gave rise to factional whispers that he was willing to sacrifice black workers to solidify the left in the labor movement. Such rumors hung over his head from the derailing of the social equality plank at the 1924 Farmer-Labor Convention to the crucial debate on the Negro question at the Sixth Comintern Congress in 1928, where a confidential memo with no date or signature charged that Foster "typifies [the] spirit" of the old Socialist Party in its "half-hearted work among Negroes."[23]

Foster's alleged doubts did not deter his TUEL from staking out an unequivocal position on racial equality in labor's ranks. Ex-Wobbly William F. Dunne had joined Foster in forming the TUEL and in later years would make forays into the deep South to demand racial equality. He was the author of articles in TUEL's *Workers Monthly* that went beyond Foster in making a distinction between white racism and black distrust of whites. Dunne argued that black suspicion was justified based on historic oppression and contemporary misery. He disputed a notion that Negroes were "natural" strikebreakers and insisted that white workers had the primary responsibility for winning blacks to the labor movement. Dunne was willing to face down taboos, and he challenged the myth of the black rapist—which had even gained currency on the left. Dunne, Foster, Minor, and Pastor Stokes, though from different factions, extended important support for the handful of black Communists in establishing the first Party-inspired Negro labor organization in 1925. Such were the slivers that kept Comintern injunctions alive and kept the Party, though unsteadily, on a path to engagement with black Americans and with the legacy of racial oppression.[24]

A Failed World Congress and an American Negro Labor Congress

The Comintern's promise to organize a World Negro Congress ran into trouble. After the CI's Fourth Congress, its Executive Committee admitted that no progress had been made. Reaching 140 million black Africans who were under imperialism's heel, lived in inaccessible areas, and spoke many different languages was a daunting task. Getting people to Moscow, especially from the African interior, was also difficult, especially in light of sure resistance from the imperialist states. Prospects were better for the United States and the Caribbean, but still it was hard to find "suitable organizers" who would work with necessary caution. But with sufficient energy and an awareness of its significance, a Negro congress could materialize that would improve the Comintern's image as emancipator of blacks. A permanent Negro commission of the Comintern had to be appointed at once, and the various sections of the CI had to carry out their roles under its direction.[25]

A communication to the Workers Party from the Comintern in the winter of 1923, however, informed the Party that the CI's Presidium had discussed the formation of a World Negro Congress and decided that the project was "too unprepared." The Party was asked to ready the ground for the promised congress by handling "the propaganda for the development of [the] negro movement."[26]

Progress in both Chicago and Moscow could be gauged in an angry letter written by Fort-Whiteman to Zinoviev from Moscow's Lux Hotel on October 21, 1924.[27] Fort-Whiteman was in Moscow for a crash course in organization and was a delegate to the Fifth Congress. He had become more visible than Briggs, Moore, or Huiswoud in the Party hierarchy, though he had drawn re-

sentment for his flamboyant, self-possessed manner and his close relationship with Minor. His political experience extended back to the IWW and the
Harlem Socialists, and he had had training as a writer and speaker. He was a
native-born, Tuskegee-schooled American, and this may have been a factor in
his rapid advance. Fort-Whiteman's black peers grumbled that he had become "Minor's Man Friday," but he was capable of independent thought and
action, as his letter to Zinoviev reveals. Writing as "James Jackson, American
Negro," Fort-Whiteman reminded Zinoviev of the Fourth Congress's promise
to convene a World Negro Congress in Moscow. Perhaps alluding to the CI
having passed the ball to the Workers Party, he said that the WP had made
"no serious or worthwhile efforts to carry Communist teaching to the great
mass of American black workers." He complained that although he was a full-
fledged delegate to the Fifth Congress, the Party's Central Executive had refused to pay his expenses. His trip was financed instead "by individual Negro
Communists, inspired by the belief that by sending one of their group to
Moscow, he might be successful in getting the Comintern to take some practical steps helpful to our work among Negroes both in America and on a world
scale." A process begun tentatively in 1922 now revealed a pattern: African
American Communists would look to Moscow for succor and for settlement
of their grievances with the Workers Party.

Negro Communists, Fort-Whiteman continued, were seeking to undermine
the influence of petty-bourgeois black leaders. But the Party had given little
or no cooperation. A catalyst was needed to achieve working-class hegemony
among black Americans; it could not wait for the languishing world congress.
He himself had "recently submitted a statement of suggestions to the Far Eastern Section of the Comintern in respect to the practicability... of calling an
American-Negro Labor Congress at Chicago, composed of delegates of the
various Negro industrial and trade unions." The matter was in the hands of
the Far Eastern Section and hopefully would come before the ECCI. Thus the
American Negro Labor Congress had been born in the minds of African American Communists. They now turned to the Comintern for support in bringing it to life.[28]

Fort-Whiteman wished to be practical. The Negro question had unique
psychological dimensions. Blacks experienced and understood their suffering
as rooted primarily in their race, not their class. Even wealthy blacks faced
persecution. Out of that reality a "peculiar" racial psychology had developed.
Marx's ideas had spread slowly among blacks because Communists had failed

"to approach the negro on his own mental grounds." The Negro was revolutionary "in a racial sense and it devolves upon the American Communist Party to manipulate this racial revolutionary sentiment to the advantage of the class struggle." Work must begin in the South; the Party had to quicken its response to the ghetto housing crisis and other afflictions arising out of the great migration.[29]

Comintern authorities felt obliged to respond to this "emigrant of the oppressed Negro race" in the pages of their *Communist International*. The Party in the United States must not evade "the ticklish question" of race antagonism; it had to expose "its class basis." Racial persecution appeared with the dawn of class society, but "negroes were not born with saddles on their backs; neither were whites born with spurs on their feet." Racism among white workers did not disprove the class character of the Negro question, it merely demonstrated how far white workers had been contaminated by bourgeois ideology. However, the American Communists' failure to come to grips with racism dulled the class consciousness of black workers as well and played into the hands of petty-bourgeois nationalists. This was one of the first of many cautionary messages from the CI to the American Communists about the dangers inherent in "white chauvinism," the ideology and practice of race hatred.[30]

At the Fifth Congress (1924) the American Negro question was fully subsumed under the national and colonial questions. The Comintern was rapidly drawing the African Americans into that framework. Yet the congress hesitated to state flatly that American Negroes were an oppressed nationality that required self-determination. For colonized and dependent nations, such a demand was mandatory; for the United States, self-determination could not solve all national problems, especially where "an extraordinarily mixed population" existed. The Fifth Congress appeared to edge beyond a one-dimensional class analysis to grant that the American Negro question was at least a problem of racial oppression that transcended class in critical ways. A hint of a new direction in Comintern thinking was underscored in the instructions sent to the Workers Party by the ECCI's Negro Commission regarding the founding of the ANLC. Buried in the "confidential" communiqué, the following sentence leaps out: "Our chief slogan: 'The Right of Self-Determination even to Separation' must be complemented for America by the demands of absolute social equality." Was the "complement" to be added to self-determination, or did it negate the concept? The issue was unclear.[31]

In December 1924 the CI Secretariat sent a "strictly confidential" letter to the Workers Party Executive demanding action on the black comrades' call for a Negro Labor Congress in the form of an immediate reply setting forth "the Party's attitude." But the Workers Party did not have time to respond. Early in 1925 the CI Secretariat set up the long-delayed permanent Negro Commission headed by John Pepper (Joseph Pogany), the Hungarian-born veteran of the Bela Kun uprising who had been a virtual leader of the WP as Comintern representative. Fort-Whiteman was at the first joint meeting of the ECCI Secretariat and Negro Commission (on January 12, 1925), along with an assortment of Russians, Germans, and others. The commission (with the ECCI Secretariat) sent a memo to the Workers Party on January 16 detailing the Negro Labor Congress's composition, program, leadership (Fort-Whiteman to be chief organizer), and objectives (including the creation of a Communist "fraction" that "should conduct the Congress not officially but indirectly"). The ANLC was instructed to stand for integrated unions, all-black unions where necessary, and organization of agricultural workers and tenant farmers. But a waffling injunction stated that the Congress need not take up "social demands." Mainstream and left-wing unions were to be invited to send delegates; at-large delegates were to be elected at "large mass meetings" in major black communities. Finally, the Chicago meeting of black unionists and white supporters should call for the elusive World Negro Congress.[32]

After Fort-Whiteman's return to the United States, he received a "top secret" message (with a copy to the Workers Party) from Dombal, Orlov, and Voznesensky, leaders of the Kresintern, the Comintern's peasant organization. The message asked for a thorough airing of the situation of Negro farmers and agricultural laborers at the ANLC congress. It urged that the role of the church be dealt with, criticizing "'spiritual'" leaders but trying to avoid "hurting any religious feelings." The Kresintern anticipated the attendance of delegates from Africa and the Caribbean, and hoped that the congress would form a "peasant section," linking it with South Africa, Liberia, Angola, Kenya, the West Indies, the Philippines, and Brazil. The CI dreamed of using the ANLC as a catalyst for a global "Negrotern" — a mighty big order for a new, small, and relatively isolated federation.[33]

In the meantime the American Communists were again locked in a factional struggle, which virtually split the Workers Party into two organizations. Neither faction was immune to charges of neglect and chauvinism. A "parity commission," fashioned by the Comintern, was established with equal numbers from each faction. Under the chairmanship of CI representative S. I. Gusev, who cast the deciding vote, the commission formulated the most comprehensive program to date regarding black liberation. It broke no new ground, but its recognition of the importance and transforming potential of the new Negro working class flowed into an unambiguous demand for the destruction of Jim Crow unionism. For the first time the Party, echoing the Comintern, advocated the separate "organization of Negro workers" wherever bars to existing unions were insurmountable. "Social equality," the phrase whose absence had angered McKay in 1922 and had recently chilled the CI, was now part of the resolution.[34]

The Parity Commission gave a farewell salute to the remnants of the African Blood Brotherhood, suggesting that its "local organizations" merge with the forthcoming American Negro Labor Congress. This was also a temporary farewell to the influence of Cyril Briggs's revolutionary nationalism. With emphasis now on the labor movement, Briggs began to drift further into the background, eventually reemerging in 1929 as an influential African American leader of the Party.[35]

The Comintern's intervention in 1925, with its contradictory brew of ideological cleansing and political unreality, did not end with the Parity Commission. The CI also pressed Bolshevization upon the Workers Party: This required the dissolution of virtually autonomous foreign-language federations within the Party, the consolidation of the entire membership into either neighborhood or shop units, a campaign to spread the English language, and pressure to nudge Communists into cooperative relations with a mix of national, ethnic, and racial groups. On the racial front, Bolshevization implied an organizational meshing of blacks and whites inside the Party. Before Bolshevization, the main sphere of "mass" activity for black Communists had been within the ABB, which at least had some ties to the larger black community. After Bolshevization, the sphere of non-Party work shifted largely to the American Negro Labor Congress. The ANLC had few community ties and was also presumably open to white membership. Within the Party, some blacks had already connected with the white rank-and-file through the daily grind of newspaper distribution, tenants' activities, and the like. There, they experienced both friendship and estrangement, concern and neglect, respect and racism. But the new political-organizational scheme pulled some blacks further away from community roots and into widening relationships among white Communists whose views on race did not depart significantly from those of a larger society saturated with racism.[36]

Perhaps the greatest long-term impact of Bolshevization upon black Communists was evolution toward a centralization of political line and structure that eventually became "democratic centralism" and squeezed out much of the pluralism among the black Communists. In the mid-1920s there was an unstated policy of coexistence between quasi-nationalist currents, represented mainly by Briggs and Richard B. Moore, and a nuanced assimilationism, represented by Fort-Whiteman and Huiswoud. The failure to embrace pluralism within a shared political program (the problem, of course, existed in different forms among white Communists) robbed the Party of insight, energy, and the unity that came from intellectual diversity. Marxism was reduced to formula and caricature, which left a trail of tension and expulsions for various "deviations." Ideological conformity embedded in democratic centralism would ultimately choke democracy and often force black Communists to make dubious formal choices between "nationalism" and "class struggle."

Lovett Fort-Whiteman was "centralizing" his own role and influence from Moscow as chief organizer of the Party's work among blacks. He was also taking charge of implementation, at last, of a program that had been agreed upon at the Fourth Comintern Congress in 1922: the sending of African American students for study at the KUTV in Moscow. In mid-1925 Fort-Whiteman informed the director of KUTV that ten students (including three women), all in their twenties, were being selected with great care for KUTV. Through schooling in Moscow, young African Americans would soon be thrust into the center of the politics and ideology of international communism — a remarkable development for a group fresh out of the ghettoes of American cities and new to the cause of revolution.[37]

CHAPTER FOUR

The American Negro Labor Congress

The American Negro Labor Congress was supposed to transform the entire American racial and social landscape. It would be a centralized movement of black protest led by labor; it would cleanse organized labor of racial prejudice and heal its crippling inner divisions; it would help lay the groundwork for industrial unionism; it would turn the black masses away from bourgeois misleaders and advance the "hegemony" of the working class; it would be black America's contribution to training and leadership of the worldwide anti-imperialist movement. This was a tall order.[1]

ANLC's organizers hoped that union and nonunion black workers, as well as farmers, intellectuals, and militants of all races would descend on Chicago. But months before the founding convention, Otto Huiswoud, Richard B. Moore, and other black Communists were worried about a "fiasco." They pleaded with the Party's leaders not to "place the stamp of our Party conspicuously upon the Congress," thus playing into the hands of conservative union officialdom and "killing the movement from its very start." White Communists should not be in the forefront of preliminary organizational work; black comrades should be on all Party committees responsible for the ANLC; propaganda should be "simply written and adjusted to the psychology and status of Negro workers." As things turned out, that critical advice was not heeded.[2]

The Comintern's injunction to organize mass meetings to promote the congress got the Party into the streets of Chicago. By early May 1925 the South Side was hearing about everything from the battles of the Moroccan Riff people against Europeans to this new Labor Congress; the "Reds" and their talk of class struggle were becoming a local fixture. There were other hopeful signs. In Pittsburgh the TUEL got C. W. Fulp, the black president of a United Mine Workers local, and various members of the Mine and Hod-Carriers unions to commit to the Congress. Cleveland building-trades workers were coming; Henry Lee Moon of Cleveland's sympathetic black paper, the *Herald,* would be attending. So would the pro-Red maverick Episcopalian bishop William Montgomery Brown and Briggs's old colleague George Wells Parker. Speakers from colonial and dependent countries, such as C. T. Chi of the Chinese Students' Alliance, would appear at the Congress's "anti-imperialist night." Telegrams of support mandated by the Comintern (which were not helpful, to say the least, in building a broad movement) were coming in from Communist parties and unions associated with the Comintern.[3]

Huiswoud and Moore were right. The specter of a radical organization seeking to harness a new black proletariat was not greeted kindly by the AFL. William Green, AFL president, warned Negro workers about Moscow gold being dangled before them and the awful consequences of thinking that their grievances could be solved by overturning the government and establishing "a Soviet republic." The Chicago *Daily News* warned its readers that government investigators had found that behind the Congress were Communist agitators seeking to stir up a "revolutionary awakening" among Negroes. The *Literary Digest* rounded up white press reaction to the Congress and noted that most papers either saw the Congress as a nightmarish Moscow plot to Bolshevize blacks or ridiculed it as a futile venture.[4]

Most of the Negro press either ignored the congress or else, according to Robert Minor, was "honest, sincere, and fair" in its coverage. Black newspapers that took notice were inclined to see the "Communist threat" posed by the congress as a firebell that tolled a warning to the nation to end racial oppression or face a growth of Bolshevik influence among blacks. The Urban League's *Opportunity* said that blacks would agree with the ANLC's list of racial grievances, but would reject its underlying Communist agenda. However, the Urban League magazine responded acidly to William Green's attack on the congress, asking how the AFL leader could tell blacks to stay away from the

ANLC's welcoming embrace, when the federation itself spurned blacks. The *Chicago Defender,* like much of the African American press, talked about the destructive force of Jim Crow that seeded the ground for such a congress (calling the AFL "the largest Jim Crow organization in the world"); it was not about to blindly join the AFL's white-orchestrated chorus, which, however indirectly, denigrated the Negro's grievances. The Baltimore *Afro-American* greeted the congress as a legitimate expression of the needs and aspirations of black workers. W.E.B. Du Bois would not submit to the *New York Times's* efforts to draw black leaders into a fearful condemnation of the ANLC. Noting that Communists had shown sympathy and support for blacks around the world, he defended their right to explore "industrial reform" in Russia, China, or anywhere else. Howard University economist Abram L. Harris noted that a revolutionary meeting of blacks confounded the image of a conservative polity. The congress challenged black leaders to deal with the connection between capitalism and race — and the creation of "a highly exploitable substratum" of black labor. The Communists were sincere, Harris concluded; their radicalism flowed not from Moscow gold, but from the reality of oppression. Yet Harris doubted that their appeals to class interest would resonate with the racially charged black public. At least the ANLC was a healthy revolt against the color barriers built by organized labor.[5]

A. Philip Randolph and Chandler Owen were the most persistent black critics of the ANLC. Randolph and Owen offered the pages of the *Messenger* to support the Trade Union Committee for Organizing Negro Workers and its social-democratic, anticommunist outlook as a counterweight to the ANLC. The TUCONW, launched by the Urban League with financial help from the Garland Fund, dispatched black applicants to various unions, with modest success. But the TUCONW, with its generally nonconfrontational outlook and partial dependence on the unions themselves, fell apart after a year, when those very unions failed to provide promised financial support.[6]

But Randolph and Owens's social democracy and deep animus toward the Communists survived as they became more impressed by the strength and durability of capitalism. Care in building alliances within an accepted political norm became their watchword. Cooperation with the existing labor movement, they believed, was the only realistic hope for black workers. Their caution was nourished by the government's hostility to communism and the suspicion of Moscow-inspired subversion, which they believed threatened to crush blacks who flirted with it. Randolph told the *New York Times* that Negroes needed industrial unionism and economic justice, but not at the price of Moscow pulling the ANLC's strings.[7]

Such doubt and outright opposition among black leaders was not the only problem for ANLC. These were the "lean years" for the labor movement in general. In the black community class consciousness seemed to be growing slowly at best in the face of white working-class hostility; the situation was complicated by the rural background of the new proletariat. Since blacks were always vulnerable to being the first fired, fear of job loss and repression from radical association was another constraint. Then there was the Party's myopia. Most of the black Communists were determined to meet the Negro worker on his "own mental grounds." But the Party ignored the social and cultural roots of the ANLC's proposed constituency.[8]

After the Party's and TUEL's hard work, only thirty-three accredited delegates were seated. They came mainly from the large eastern states, the industrial centers of Ohio and Pennsylvania, and the host city of Chicago. Only two were from the South: an express handler from Lake Charles, Louisiana, and an ANLC "local committee" member (probably from the Workers Party) from Galveston, Texas. They *were*, on the whole, working men and women—janitors, hod carriers, cooks, plumbers, laborers. A. Rodriguez, of the "Unorganized Mexican Workers, Brownsville, Pa." (ANLC had a small group of miners in this coal community), was the only Latino worker at the congress. It was hardly the "large mass affair" proclaimed by Minor in the pages of *Workers Monthly.*[9]

Despite warnings from African American activists in the Party to avoid large-scale white involvement, a predominantly white audience filled the hall under a banner that proclaimed, "Organization is the first step to freedom." The strange duality in the gestation of communism in the black community was underscored by two vastly differing presentations. On the one hand, Richard B. Moore, an electrifying speaker, challenged the audience to match his own five-dollar contribution (from the paltry wages of an elevator operator) and ended with a soaring recitation of McKay's "If We Must Die." On the other hand, Russian ballet and theater groups appeared to provide entertainment. No black artists were on the program. Bishop William Montgomery Brown, in one of the more curious presentations, attacked religious superstition and ended by shouting "Down with Capitalism! Long Live Communism!...Long live the AMERICAN NEGRO LABOR CONGRESS on a footing with AMERICAN CAUCASIANS." Lovett Fort-Whiteman also engaged in some impolitic braggadocio, announcing the departure of the black students for training in Moscow.[10]

The congress cobbled together a program that echoed the Party's 1924 resolutions before the Sanhedrin. At the core was a typical compound of incisive thinking and sectarianism anchored in the culpability of capitalism in racial discrimination and the consequent need for black-white working-class solidarity. The ANLC bowed to the Comintern proposal that black unions be formed where blacks met a wall of resistance to white unions. But it did plead with the AFL for cooperation. Racial consciousness among the delegates was manifested when the notion of "caste" over class as the cause of racial oppression found expression in the resolutions adopted by the congress. The ANLC would also convene that long-coveted World Race Congress and lay the basis for a world organization to liberate all people of color from imperialism and colonialism.[11]

The congress aspired to create local councils with representatives from black and interracial unions and farm organizations, as well as with individual black workers seeking union membership. The ANLC envisioned the councils joining with local labor organizations and community groups to form broadly based "interracial labor committees." A national committee of nine was led by Fort-Whiteman and H. V. Phillips, along with six workers (including a miner, a steelworker, a hod carrier, and a street sweeper) and the head of the Howard University students' organization. The congress adjourned after singing "The Internationale."[12]

Life was hard for the ANLC from the start, and despite some accomplishments, it never got better. Dues payments for November and December 1925 did not reach a hundred dollars. The ANLC strove to keep its paper, the *Negro Champion*, alive despite periodic shutdowns due to lack of funds. But subscriptions never exceeded four hundred. Local activities were hobbled by heartlessness, sloppiness, and unreliability. In 1926 the comrade left in charge of the national office apparently locked the doors and disappeared for months. The congress struggled on, sending Fort-Whiteman on an organizing tour, issuing the occasional manifesto, bewailing the torpor and racism in the house of labor, and dreaming of organizing the South. It ran forums, principally in New York and Chicago. For example, in Chicago it responded to the upsurge of black culture with a discussion on "the Negro and Art," concluding that only the end of capitalism would open black art to "originality and freedom." Here and there, the congress gained new recruits, such as James W. Ford and

George Padmore (Malcolm Meredith Nurse), who went on to play major roles in the Communist movement.[13]

The ANLC had no success in building broadly based community interracial councils or putting a dent in the AFL's exclusionary policies. But it was on the scene in the fall of 1926 when one hundred black women, facing pay cuts and assembly-line speedup, walked off their jobs at a stuffed-date factory on Chicago's South Side. When police attacked their picket lines, the ANLC plunged in, pressing the AFL for backing, calling upon the International Labor Defense to help arrested strikers, and setting up support groups. William Fitzpatrick, president of the Chicago Federation of Labor, invited Fort-Whiteman and Mrs. Fannie Warnettas, the strike leader, to address the CFL. But violence and strikebreakers finally broke the strike, and the CFL never gave the women the union charter that was promised.[14]

When white mobs drove blacks from their homes in Carteret, New Jersey, in the spring of 1926, the ANLC joined in protest with local civic leaders, black and white. In New York City the ANLC local supported black motion-picture projectionists in their long strike against the white-owned Lafayette Theater. Despite the threat of a court injunction (which had already silenced Frank Crosswaith), Moore took to a soapbox at the request of the projectionists. Police immediately arrested him. The sight of a police car driving recklessly into the crowd of people listening to Moore provoked community organizations to protest against the arrest. The American Civil Liberties Union defended Moore, who was found guilty of obstructing traffic and given a suspended sentence. The projectionists eventually won their demands.[15]

Decades later, Harold Cruse in his *Crisis of the Negro Intellectual* charged that Moore and the Harlem Communists were blind to the cultural implications of the projectionists' quarrel with the Lafayette Theater — fighting on "ultra remote terms involving capital and labor" and ignoring the need for black hegemony over Harlem's cultural institutions. Moore and his comrades saw the battle of the projectionists against discrimination as representative of the larger social realities confronting the new urban black proletariat. Without a primary effort to advance the interest of the black workers, an autonomous community of culture could not be established. Perhaps that is what Moore had in mind when, at a mass rally for the projectionists, he commented that Harlem could not be the Mecca of the New Negro because it had come to be governed by a bunch of exploiting politicians and businessmen who were determined to keep the working masses in thrall.[16]

But the battles were sporadic and inconsistent. In the spring of 1927 the ANLC's overall lethargy and ineffectiveness gravely concerned the Party. The CP's Central Executive Committee issued "directions" for the Party fraction that was preparing for a critical meeting of the ANLC's National Committee. The Party demanded frank, critical discussion by the ANLC leadership, which had to face the organization's failure to act on pressing issues, such as segregation and lynching. ANLC had done no work in the South, and it had no plan for increasing membership and finances or for building the *Negro Champion*. With unintended irony, the Party noted that the congress was "operating on too narrow a basis. The Communist Party direction was pressed too much to the forefront." The CP's Negro Commission added that the prominence of whites in the Chicago Council "has become an issue" and proposed to virtually screen the involvement of white Communists. Party fraction members of the ANLC were enjoined to press for a major reorganization.[17]

The CEC directive, pushed by some black comrades, marked the end of Fort-Whiteman's career in the ANLC. The Party fraction was instructed to propose that Moore replace him and his "leftist sectarian policies and incompetent direction" of the Congress. Fort-Whiteman had a passion for Soviet Russia and expended a good deal of energy writing Comintern officials seeking, at various times, invitations to Moscow to study farm organizing or to write a book on the national question. He was on the Party's ticket in New York in 1928 and 1929. But his last public appearance for the Party was at its 1928 convention mass rally in New York. That same year Fort-Whiteman was a delegate to the Sixth Comintern Congress, and he remained in Soviet Russia where he taught political science at the Cercerin Institute near Moscow. He never returned to the United States and died shortly before World War II.[18]

The fraction agreed that it was handicapped from the start by overbearing direction from the Party (even as it again responded to that direction). It blamed Robert Minor for failing to stop Fort-Whiteman from plunging the ANLC into "severe isolation." The ANLC black comrades had their own demands, which signaled a push for greater black input and control over issues affecting blacks: participation in the highest level Political Committee (PolCom) when the Negro question was to be discussed; placement of a Negro comrade on the CEC; the sending of several more students to Moscow. The fraction expressed hope for "more realism" and a better application of the united front policy. Yet it proposed that "Negro work be replenished" by an appeal for financial help from the Comintern, as well as by a special drive by the Party and the ANLC to fund Negro work.[19]

THE WORLD STAGE

Fort-Whiteman's departure from the ANLC was part of the growing turmoil affecting black Communists. In 1927 Cyril Briggs was dispatched to the Caribbean. In response to the demands of the ANLC fraction, Otto Huiswoud was returned to the Central Committee. A short time before taking over leadership of the ANLC, Moore got his opportunity to appear on a world stage. In February 1927 he represented the ANLC in Brussels at the International Congress against Colonial Oppression and Imperialism. This was not the holistic gathering of all peoples of African descent envisaged by Briggs and later by the Comintern, but the congress and its 174 delegates from 21 countries represented a sizable constellation of prominent radicals and opponents of colonialism, including Albert Einstein, the French writer Henri Barbusse, Madam Sun Yat-sen, and Jawaharlal Nehru.[20]

Moore was the rapporteur of the committee on the Negro question and had a major hand in drafting its resolution.[21] His participation in the Brussels congress was at least a partial fulfillment of the ANLC's aspiration to inspire and organize the building of a worldwide Negro movement. The congress ended with the formation of a permanent organization, the League against Imperialism and for National Independence (LAI). This helped encourage the global involvement of African American and Caribbean American Communists in building labor organizations in colonial and dependent areas. Internationalism became contagious: Huiswoud, like Briggs, extended his activities to the Caribbean and as an ANLC organizer helped found the Jamaican Trades and Labor Union.[22]

A year after the Brussels meeting, the Fourth Congress of the CI's Red International of Labor Unions (also called the Profintern) met in Moscow in a troubled mood over the pitiable weaknesses of the trade union movement among native populations in Africa and the Caribbean, and among blacks in the United States. Vast areas of Africa lacked trade unions or peasant organizations; in other places weak unions without international ties barely existed. The RILU congress set up an International Bureau of Negro Workers, led by James W. Ford, with instructions to "prepare and convene an International Conference of Negro workers at the end of 1929." RILU's Executive Committee met in Moscow in July 1928 in conjunction with the Sixth Comintern Congress. Black American Communists William Patterson, Otto Hall, Harry Haywood, H. V. Phillips ("Carleton"), and Ford attended. That meeting resolved to establish an International Trade Union Committee of Negro Workers, sponsored by the RILU, to rapidly draw black workers around the world into trade unions and prepare for a global conference in 1929.[23]

Handicapped by scant funds and staff, and having difficulty in reaching unionists (and potential unionists) in the colonies, the global conference did not materialize in 1929. However, the Second World Congress of the League against Imperialism did meet at Frankfurt, Germany, in July 1929. Ford was a delegate representing the essentially fictitious ITUCNW of the RILU. He organized a couple of meetings of black unionists and revolutionaries who were attending the congress, including several Americans: Patterson, Mary Burroughs, Henry Rosemond, a black leader of the furriers' union in New York, and William Pickens from the NAACP.[24] Also present were Jomo Kenyatta from East Africa and Garan Kouyaté from West Africa. Those meetings resulted in a decision to proceed with the project for a world conference, and a provisional international committee on arrangements was elected, with Ford as chairman.[25]

After the British government of Ramsay MacDonald refused to allow the First International Conference of Negro Trade Union Workers to meet in London, it finally convened in Hamburg, Germany, from July 7 to 9, 1930. Most colonial activists were denied passports, but seventeen delegates managed to get to the radical German port city from Jamaica, Trinidad, Nigeria, Gambia, Sierra Leone, Gold Coast, Cameroon, and the United States. A program was adopted, and an international commission was set up to expand contacts with unions and individuals in the colonial world, to issue a newsletter, and to establish headquarters in Hamburg. Ford, coalminer Isaiah Hawkins, and George Padmore were the U.S. representatives on the commission.[26]

Padmore, from Trinidad, had been recruited from the ANLC to the Party as a law student at New York University in 1927. Deeply race-conscious, a hard worker, and a prolific writer, he was anointed by Foster as a coming leader and was taken to Moscow in 1929 to report to the Comintern on the founding convention of the Trade Union Unity League. He stayed in Moscow, where he became head of the RILU's Negro Bureau and was even elected to the Moscow City Soviet. Padmore succeeded Ford in 1931 as editor of the ITUCNW's *Negro Worker*.[27] Although the world race congress led by Americans never materialized, American and West Indian blacks played a continuous role in the painful process of building a base for revolutionary unions in the colonial world.

A New Start

After a stay in Europe following the Brussels congress in 1927, Richard Moore plunged into the battle to give new energy and direction to the ANLC. In 1928 the organization's headquarters had relocated to New York, where Moore and a handful of local activists sought to build community alliances around specific injustices faced by black working people. Under Moore's leadership, the ANLC in early 1928 organized the Harlem Tenants League. Victimized by inflated rents and inhumane conditions, Harlem residents responded to the newly founded league and to Moore's argument that only organized pressure would bring relief. The demand for an extension of rent laws spurred letters, petitions, demonstrations, and rent strikes. Confrontation with landlords and politicians, at that point, struck a more responsive chord than the battle for trade union equality. Hermina Huiswoud and Grace Campbell emerged as important women leaders; W. A. Domingo and George Padmore used their writing talent to craft a call for a rent strike. From the winter of 1928 the Tenants League, though still small, met regularly; by the summer of 1929, with the expiration of an emergency rent law, it was able to rally local unions and community organizations to engage in protest in Harlem's streets.[28]

On another front, the ANLC mobilized in support of a group of black seamen who came under attack after the S.S. *Vestris* sank in stormy seas in November 1928. Black firemen on board had worked feverishly for twenty-four hours to maintain steam and pump the bilges; when told to take to lifeboats, they nevertheless sought to help passengers first. Although some crew members and passengers perished, the firemen clung to each other in floating wreckage until they were rescued. News of an investigation by the U.S. attorney alleging cowardice brought the ANLC to the side of the assailed seamen. Joining with the left-wing Marine Workers Progressive League and community groups, the New York ANLC organized a rally that attracted twelve hundred people to St. Luke's Hall in Harlem. Otto Huiswoud said that if the seamen did indeed forsake "parasitic" white passengers to save fellow workers, they acted "correctly." While that rhetoric strained the dream of interracial unity, it got a strong reaction from the crowd. On that night, at least, the ANLC had correctly gauged the mood of the community.[29]

The ANLC was hardly visible in basic industry, but it did have a small group of coalminers in the Pennsylvania fields. Charles Fulp, a cofounder of the ANLC, was the leader of United Mine Workers Local 1773 in Primrose, Pennsylvania. In January 1928 the tall, brawny Fulp came to New York to raise funds for miners who had struck the bituminous mines of Washington County. John L. Lewis's machine had little patience for rank-and-file initiatives in a difficult strike and tried to drive a wedge between black and white miners by conjuring up the image of Negro strikebreakers. But every pit committee in the county was headed by a black miner, and the bonds between the races remained strong. Fulp had been appointed with four Slavic workers to head the relief committee that journeyed to New York after the UMW refused to help. He not only sought help for hungry mine families, but also worked tirelessly to persuade strikebreakers to abandon struck mines.[30]

With a foundering strike, Communists and other left-wingers took over the growing relief burden. Fulp, Isaiah Hawkins, and other black miners formed the Negro Miners' Relief Committee. Their efforts led them to Pittsburgh on April 1, 1928, where they helped found the Save-the-Union Committee under Communist and left-wing leadership. Five blacks were elected to a national executive committee, and one black miner from Indiana declared that after twenty-eight years in the UMW, this was the first time he had been permitted to speak. A broader strike to bolster the existing stoppage was called for mid-April. Hawkins and other ANLC blacks plunged into the Save-the-Union Committee and the widened strike. Hawkins was expelled from his local by the UMW brass, but he continued to work under the committee's banners.[31]

By July the strike was dying. Coal operators were able to place the burden of a sick industry during flush times on the backs of the miners—by outlasting them, starving them, beating them with pools of strikebreakers. Yet that small group of black miners nurtured by the Communist Party and the ANLC continued to believe in and work for the cause of unionism and interracial solidarity. Driven from the United Mine Workers, they carried their valuable experience (in the coming Third Period) into the Communist-led National Miners Union, which grew out of the Save-the-Union Committee. They played important roles in the large, violent strikes that engulfed the coal regions of Kentucky, West Virginia, and Pennsylvania in the 1930s. And in those strikes, a significant degree of black-white solidarity was achieved due to the work and influence of that nearly forgotten group of black miners.[32]

Solidarity was not the watchword in ANLC's approach to A. Philip Randolph's Brotherhood of Sleeping Car Porters. When Randolph in June 1928 called off a strike against the Pullman Company at the last minute, he earned the ANLC's bitter enmity. Three hours before the scheduled walkout, Randolph had received a telegram from AFL head William Green advising him that "conditions were not favorable" for a strike. With hopes for compulsory arbitration in shambles, Randolph seized upon Green's message to bail out of the strike. The ANLC accused Randolph of selling out to the AFL, choking the workers' militant spirit, and depending on phony bourgeois laws. Randolph responded that Communist charges were the "sorriest nonsense and silliest tommyrot which could only emanate from crack-brained fanatics or low grade morons."[33]

Nurturing a union in an atmosphere of economic stabilization and conservatism, Randolph by the late 1920s had become well versed in the art of not exceeding the system's capacity for toleration. He could combine the seemingly irreconcilable qualities of militancy and circumspection; he could stiffen the porters' backbones and wheedle the bosses at the same time. For him, sensitivity to power (union and business) was more than accommodation, it was essential to wrest concessions. The Communists, in his view, recklessly breached the system's limits, incautiously offended institutions, and would inevitably bring ruin upon the best hopes of those who had been deprived of the benefits bestowed by the larger society.[34]

Even someone as facile as Randolph could not easily walk that fine line between tactical accommodation and violation of principle. There were times to duck and times to fight; Randolph occasionally had trouble making that distinction. Sometimes he kept faith with the faithless and trusted the government and the AFL bureaucracy far more than was warranted. But the Communist-ANLC response to Randolph's phantom strike of 1928 betrayed its own fatal weaknesses. The base among the porters to which Randolph clung was more than was possessed by the ANLC, which was largely isolated from organized labor and just beginning to find a voice in the black community. Outwardly the ANLC-Communist attack on Randolph was self-assured; inwardly the Communists were beginning to sense that their relentless stress on interracial working-class unity was insufficient to build bridges to the black masses.

In the late 1920s, as the hope for a fusion of black workers and organized labor remained unfulfilled, a perceptible, though muddled, shift in Communist thinking could be detected. The broader racial aspect of the Negro question began to receive greater attention, though it soon became entangled in the Party's ongoing factional struggle.

In 1927 Jay Lovestone had replaced the deceased Charles E. Ruthenberg as the factional foe of William Z. Foster and Alexander Bittelman. Lovestone, now general secretary, had written disdainfully of the prospects for organizing in the near feudal rural South. He advised that the only hope for the radicalization of black America lay in continued migration to the North and in industrialization of the South. Bittelman, now secretary of the Negro Commission, answered that the South remained a particularly brutal domicile for the vast majority of Negroes. To simply welcome migration as a basis for welding Negroes to unions ignored the many-sided character of the suffering of blacks. The Negro question transcended trade union solutions. That debate would not be settled in Party journals; it would be propelled to Moscow and become part of the Sixth Comintern Congress's reexamination of the Negro question.[35]

Throughout the spring and summer of 1928 the Party struggled with the ANLC's weak condition. In advance of a meeting of the Central Executive Committee, "Negro Comrades of New York City" submitted a "thesis for a new Negro policy," which attacked the ANLC from curiously leftist assumptions combined with a whiff of Lovestone's disdain for a holistic approach to the Negro question. Its principal authors were two followers of Lovestone, Lovett Fort-Whiteman and H. V. Phillips. The group claimed that the ANLC had been formed as a recruiting ground for the Party and that it had failed miserably. The ANLC's emerging stress on opposing lynching, Jim Crow, and political disenfranchisement was ill advised and misdirected. Lynching was an "occasional practice" that was confined to the South and affected "an exceedingly small number" of blacks. Jim Crow had engendered a distinct Negro commercial bourgeoisie and had formed the basis of Negro cultural, intellectual, and social life: "The Negro has come to regard [Jim Crow] as possessing certain unique advantages." Disenfranchisement, the thesis went on, was of little interest to the black bourgeoisie and little use to black workers who had no one to vote for. The thesis concluded that the ANLC was a dumping ground for black Communists who were considered only "appendages" to the Party. By being shunted to the ANLC, blacks were "Jim Crowed" and robbed of "the larger opportunities of revolutionary development, which is to be derived from a direct struggle through the Party in behalf of all the workers independent of race." The New York group's proposals were stark and unrelenting: liquidate the ANLC which obviated class solidarity; develop a program of northern-oriented economic demands, which would wean blacks from racial to class consciousness; organize a campaign to recruit blacks directly to the Party.[36]

That document was destined to become a convenient whipping-post in the factional wars that raged into the Sixth Comintern Congress. It became a favorite target of those pushing self-determination. For them, the thesis was a vile example of what happened when the Negro question was again reduced to the old reformist notion that black liberation was a barely significant aspect of the class question.[37]

The Party's Political Committee met on April 30, 1928, and adopted one element of the New York letter: the need to recruit more blacks to the Party and its leadership and to decompartmentalize Negro work, making it the task of all Communists. The PolCom stated flatly that the Negro question, "in the spirit of all Comintern decisions," was a "RACE QUESTION" that demanded that Communists "fight for Negroes as an oppressed race." It added, however, that neither race nor class should be deemphasized; that the Party had a special duty to champion and organize black workers to lead the race movement; and that the fight to bring blacks into existing unions would continue. As for the ANLC versus "purely Party work," the PolCom came out in favor of both: the ANLC to unite Party and non-Party elements, and also a drive to recruit, develop, and educate "a cadre of Negro Communist workers." With the latter goal in mind, Fort-Whiteman was added to the editorial staff of the *Daily Worker* (though he soon left for Moscow and never returned); Huiswoud became a full-time Party organizer; and Briggs (having returned from the West Indies) became editor of the *Negro Champion*. To further enhance the Party's visibility, black Communists in non-Communist organizations were told to declare their Party membership openly; Moore was singled out for that directive. The old warning by Huiswoud and Moore about narrowing the ANLC through open association with the Party was buried in the growing scrap heap of ignored proposals. The CEC accepted the committee's proposals, adding an injunction to strengthen the Party's Negro Department.[38]

The Party's Negro work flowed increasingly away from the ANLC as a broader vision of the Negro question dictated work on concerns such as lynching and ghetto housing. The International Labor Defense and tenants' rights groups were specifically geared for such multiclass issues. The ANLC was left with little more than the elusive dream of breaking the AFL color bar. In 1929 the ANLC appeared to be reduced to activities in New York City, which had become home to its national office. There, it organized support for an unauthorized strike of sand hogs and picketed the Tip Top Restaurant in downtown Manhattan to protest its discriminatory policies.[39]

At the Communists' Sixth National Convention in March 1929, Huiswoud could account for only five active ANLC chapters with a total of 180 members. The ANLC functioned not as a mass movement of industrial workers, but as "a propaganda sect." But there was no mention of the Party's responsibility for the narrowness that made the ANLC a shadowy presence at best in the black community.[40]

Something was happening that would crush any lingering chance for the ANLC to shed its sectarianism. In the previous summer the Sixth Comintern Congress had pronounced a coming end to the Second Period of "partial capitalist stabilization." The world appeared to be entering a Third Period of growing general crisis, intensified imperialist competition leading to war, anti-imperialist revolutions in the colonial world, and heightened "class against class" conflict in the industrial world. The CI mandated that a new period marked by economic crisis and a growing war threat required a drastic change of line: Liberal reformers, social democrats, and union leaders now represented various gradations of "social fascism," a reformist last line of defense against transforming change. A clean break had to be made with reform through the building of a "united front from below" in unions and mass organizations, as well as the creation of new militant leftist organizations to challenge liberal and reformist influence.[41]

The ANLC's post–Sixth Congress revised program dropped its call for broad cooperation of all Negro organizations and substituted a dissertation on the sharpening class struggle. By 1930 the theory of the Negro question as a national question was in place, and it was time to inter the ANLC and create a "League of Struggle for Negro Rights," whose program would reflect the "national" aspirations of African Americans.[42]

The ANLC was probably doomed in any case. The anti-labor climate of the 1920s, the AFL's hostility to black workers, black labor's skepticism about unions, the gnawing problem of racism among white workers put an end even to more mainstream efforts, such as the Trade Union Committee for Organizing Negro Workers. But a genuine effort to create a programmatically diverse organization not under Party control, to encourage flexibility, to build genuine cooperation across class and cultural lines, and to undertake a broader range of activities might have given the pioneer ANLC a longer lease on life and a considerably greater influence in the black community.

The ANLC has been an easy target, but its dismissal does an injustice to a pioneer effort to recognize and harness the potential of a new African American working class to bring about radical change. However small, however isolated, that group of black militants nonetheless touched the lives of coalminers, women date workers, angry tenants, opponents of U.S. troops in Haiti, and more. They gained valuable experience that flowed into the struggles of the early 1930s and influenced the formation of the labor-oriented National Negro Congress in the popular front of the mid-1930s. History is made through big events and the accumulation of small doings that contribute to those big events. The ANLC's fundamental belief in the importance of black workers to the cause of unionism and social progress reemerged in the left-wing National Negro Labor Council under Coleman Young in the 1950s, in Randolph's black labor coalition in the 1960s, and in the present-day Coalition of Black Trade Unionists.[43]

CHAPTER FIVE

A Nation within a Nation

In 1928 a battle raged in the Soviet Communist Party over whether capitalism was entering a period of acute economic and social crisis that would foretell sharpened class struggle and revolutionary ferment. This was the outward manifestation of a conflict, orchestrated by Stalin and ultimately drenched in Soviet blood, for dominance over the Soviet Communist Party and the Comintern. For American Communists, an assessment that capitalism was entering an acute crisis would provide theoretical artillery for the faction led by Alexander Bittelman and William Z. Foster in its brawl with Jay Lovestone and John Pepper, who had become his factional ally and who shared his "exceptionalist" view of the system's staying power. Furthermore, if the period of "partial capitalist stabilization" was ending, a far more transforming analysis of the Negro question was in order. With regard to the Negro question, in its nine years of existence the American Communist Party had never come close to achieving its goal of becoming a recognized and respected champion of "the oppressed Negro people." On the eve of the Sixth Comintern Congress the Negro question in the United States was ready for a full airing within the framework of the larger conflict; a major effort to settle theoretical issues regarding the Negro question was at hand.

Before the start of the meeting, James Ford, who was in Moscow as a member of the RILU secretariat, received a cable from Richard B. Moore complaining about the Party's selection of H. V. Phillips and Lovett Fort-Whiteman to attend. Moore proposed to add himself, C. W. Fulp (now in the CP) from the Miners Relief Committee, veteran Chicago Communist Edward Doty, and Ford. Moore believed that he had been excluded for "supporting your [Ford's] criticisms" of the CP's inaction on the Negro question and for his own criticism of the Party's narrow approach to blacks.[1] Moore had been under counterattack for his friendly relations with "bourgeois" Negroes — his first brush with allegations of "petty-bourgeois nationalism." Ford forwarded the cable to Petrovsky, the secretary of the Anglo-American Secretariat, recommending Moore's list but also including Fort-Whiteman as a veteran ANLC organizer. Moore never got to the Sixth Congress, and neither did Fulp and Doty. Otto Huiswoud and Cyril Briggs likewise remained at home. Phillips was there as a youth delegate, and Fort-Whiteman was present but did not participate in the discussion of the national question. Ford took part, and so did KUTV students, as well as a student from the Lenin School — Heywood Hall, who had now become Harry Haywood. The veterans of the Party's painful early years — Huiswoud, Briggs, Moore — were absent, while the thirty-year-old Haywood was to emerge as the Party's leading theoretician on the Negro question.

THE SIXTH CONGRESS AND THE HAYWOOD-NASANOV THESIS

Heywood Hall was born in 1898 in Omaha, Nebraska, the grandson of a former slave and son of a packinghouse worker. The family, including Heywood, his older brother Otto, and his sister Eppa, later moved to Minneapolis and then to Chicago. In Minneapolis Otto listened to IWW street speakers and became a Wobbly sympathizer. Both brothers served in the Great War and came home bitter at the betrayal of the egalitarian promise for which they had served. Heywood got a job as a waiter on the Michigan Central and in July 1919 was swept from a returning run into the teeth of the Red Summer race riot in Chicago. Otto was attracted to the Garvey movement, but when he read his first copy of the *Crusader* in 1919, he joined the new African Blood Brotherhood. In 1921 he followed Briggs into the Workers Party. In 1922 Heywood asked to join Otto in the Party. Otto at that time was angered by racism in the local branch and urged Heywood instead to join the ABB until local problems could be resolved at the district or national levels — or by the Comintern. The global dimension impressed the younger brother. After a short time in the ABB, Heywood joined the Young Communist League. In the spring of 1925 he was recruited into the Party by Robert Minor. That summer Otto was on his way to schooling in Moscow as a member of Fort-Whiteman's first group. In early 1926 he was joined at KUTV by his younger brother. By 1927 the ideologically rigid Heywood had gone on to the more prestigious Lenin School. He had metamorphosed into Harry Haywood.[2]

In the same year, Charles Nasanov returned to Moscow from a sojourn in the United States for the Young Communist International. Haywood had known the young Siberian slightly in Chicago and now renewed contact. Nasanov had a strong interest in the national and colonial questions and had reached the conclusion that blacks in the American South constituted an oppressed nation for whom the right to self-determination should apply.[3]

Haywood claimed that he was dubious when Nasanov first raised the issue. Gradually, he began to perceive suppressed national yearning among black Americans. Haywood drew together the threads of a theory: Separated from the emerging bourgeois democratic society by their chains, enslaved blacks looked to liberation with abolition and the victory of bourgeois democracy in the Civil War. But Reconstruction was betrayed by the rising northern corporate order; the Thirteenth, Fourteenth, and Fifteenth Amendments were trampled as abandoned freedmen faced heightened racism and violence, the emergence of "Redeemer" governments, and the collapse of their hope for land. Share-cropping, peonage, and tenantry became their fate. The rise of modern imperialism froze blacks further into their landless and semi-slave condition, blocked the fusion of blacks and whites into a single nation, and sealed the special oppression of blacks. Equality through assimilation was foreclosed. Set apart by their common historical experience, blacks took on a distinct cultural and psychological makeup. They had become "a nation within a nation," whose equality could only be assured through self-determination. The Garvey movement was not a foreign transplant, but the voice of blacks longing for their own nation. Garveyism was dead, but black national feeling would rise again in times of stress. The next time, Communists must not allow that nationalism to fall into the hands of quacks and utopians; they must advance the right to self-determination in the Deep South as the "slogan for black rebellion."[4]

The theory's attractiveness lay in its implied departure from traditional dogma, which relegated blacks to a subsidiary role in the class struggle. By defining the Negro question as a national striving for self-determination, the theory elevated the black movement to an exalted position in the Leninist pantheon: as an indispensable ally of proletarian revolution and, moreover, as a movement that was revolutionary in itself. Racism was "a device of national

oppression, a smoke screen thrown up by the class enemy, to hide the underlying economic and social conditions involved in black oppression and to maintain the division of the working class." Consequently, racial chauvinism was
not a problem of prejudice alone, but an instrument of national oppression
that denied the revolutionary movement its most precious ally.[5]

Haywood and Nasanov were ready for battle at the Sixth Congress. The
first arena was the Anglo-American Secretariat's makeshift Negro Commission under the chairmanship of "Petrovsky." This individual, who was also
known as Bennett, was actually Dr. Max Goldfarb, an old Menshevik from the
Jewish Bund who had emigrated to the United States before the Great War
and returned to Russia after the revolution as a convert from social democracy
to communism. When the meeting opened, Haywood presented the Haywood-
Nasanov thesis for discussion. J. Louis Engdahl, leader of the International
Labor Defense, objected. He asked why discussion was based on a document
drawn up by "two self-appointed comrades" and not by the Negro Commission
as a whole. Petrovsky finessed Engdahl by proposing that "all documents" be
passed on to the Sixth Congress's larger Negro subcommission under the authority of the Colonial Commission, but that deliberations begin there and
then with the Haywood-Nasanov thesis presented as a draft resolution.[6]

The resolution was tentative and conditional, breaking less new ground than
Haywood later claimed. It began with a traditional emphasis on the growth of
a new urban black proletariat and the need for working-class leadership of
the black liberation struggle; it castigated the Fort-Whiteman–Phillips notion
that it was impossible to build a mass movement by fighting Jim Crow, lynching,
and disenfranchisement; it attacked Lovestone's characterization of southern
Negroes as "a reserve of capitalist reaction"; and it chided Moore for allegedly
stressing work in petty-bourgeois organizations and among the intelligentsia.[7]

Nowhere in the document does the term *self-determination* appear. References to southern blacks are scattered and vague, and there is a back-door
mention of the national question: "Although there some peculiarities in the
Negro question in the United states which distinguish it from most OTHER
NATIONAL PROBLEMS, nevertheless the sum total of the economic, social
and political relations existing between the Negroes and the white population
make this question one of an oppressed national (or racial) minority." The
parenthetical phrase "or racial" was a huge obfuscation, which created a wedge
for the new line. Haywood and Nasanov in fact maintained that "the central
slogan in all our Negro work both in the North and South must be 'Full social

and political equality.'" They asserted even more cautiously that in the South "there are some prerequisites which MAY lead to the future development of a national (racial) revolutionary movement among the Negroes."[8]

A major feature of the Haywood-Nasanov resolution was its unrelenting attack on "white chauvinism" in the Party. It cited specific instances of "open antagonism to Negro comrades," failure of white comrades to combat societal racism in major cities, and problems of paternalism and "pampering" of black comrades that "prevented their political development." This marked Haywood's debut as a crusader against white chauvinism in the Party. Supplementary remarks continued to refer cautiously to "the prerequisites of a nationalist movement exist[ing] in the United States." But Haywood added that the Party's slogan "must be social equality and self-determination." That mention of self-determination was enough to set off a bruising debate.[9]

Samuel Adams Darcy, the Communist youth leader, said that Haywood and Nasanov showed no understanding of the difference between a national minority and a racial minority. The solution to the Negro question lay not in establishing "a separate independent republic," but in winning equality. Otto Hall rejected the claim of a black national minority and also insisted that the Party should stress full social and political equality. That was the start of a personal estrangement between the Hall brothers. Phillips argued that the resolution emphasized the black peasantry to the detriment of workers. Ever the Lovestone man, he insisted that Negroes rejected political separation, adding that industrialization was breaking down black geographical unity in any case. Midwest Party leader William Kruse said that a national movement would inevitably be captured by racial separatists. Bertram Wolfe, a Party founder, specialist in agitation and propaganda, and perhaps the sharpest mind in Lovestone's camp, detected the ambiguity in the thesis — its "refusal to take a stand on the conception of the Negro problem in America as a national or a racial question."[10]

Alexander Bittelman, the Foster faction's theoretician, was the first participant, black or white, to support Haywood and Nasanov. He said 9 million blacks remained in the South, 70 percent of whom were impoverished farmers. It made no difference whether Negroes in America were a racial or national minority because either way they were "fighting for national liberation" and thus were allies of the working class. In a faint endorsement of self-determination, Bittelman said that it "is not so terrible" and could be "put forth in the future." At the end of the day, every black Communist opposed the thesis. Every white Communist, save Bittelman, was also opposed.[11]

Harry Wicks, a veteran of the old "left opposition" to the legal Workers Party, opened the discussion on August 3. He said the document had been drawn up for factional purposes—to undermine the Lovestone group. Manuel Gomez, the Party's anti-imperialist specialist, echoed Bittelman that there was little difference between race and nation. Historical circumstances were welding blacks into "one group on the basis of oppression" with an emerging community of territory and culture that validated self-determination. William Dunne called the thesis "a contribution," especially in its stress on a "new question" of white chauvinism in the Party. He characterized Negroes as a "national racial minority" and suggested that self-determination was part of a "revolutionary program," not an immediate demand. John Pepper, who had a reputation for turning on a dime, washed his hands of Fort-Whiteman's case against opposition to lynching and disenfranchisement. While characterizing the Negro question as a race question, he covered his left flank by arguing that blacks were developing toward nationhood in terms of a growing integration of land, culture, language, and economic life. His most audacious gambit was to propose that the Party should press for complete social equality, but in "4–5 states [where] Negroes are in a majority... [he had] no objection to raising [the] issue of [a] Negro Soviet Republic in certain parts of [the] U.S."[12]

William Z. Foster said the Haywood-Nasanov thesis marked a "step forward." Trying to suppress his own doubts, he added that self-determination was not segregation; rather, it was a response to discrimination in the same vein as the Party's advocacy of separate black unions where blacks were barred from white unions. Conceding that self-determination had no mass support among blacks, Foster maintained that the demand would grow as Negroes "became more politically conscious." In the meantime there was no conflict with the present demand for full equality. He added that the Party "systematically underestimated" the importance of Negro work. That was a manifestation of white chauvinism, which formed the underlying basis for the Party's neglect.

Petrovsky scolded the American comrades for not being helpful in preparing a thesis for the Congress's Negro subcommission. Some overpraised the Haywood-Nasanov document, while others considered it "a devil's device." He agreed with those who said it contained mistakes but was "a contribution."

Summoning the CI's authority, Petrovsky claimed that the Comintern had already spoken in the Second and Fourth Congresses: The Negro question was both a national and a racial problem. It was also international—a world question. The old Menshevik then took a swipe at Darcy and Wolfe, noting that their positions were "pure reformist." (He chose not to attack the black participants, all of whom, save Haywood, attacked the thesis no less fervently then Darcy and Wolfe.) Petrovsky concluded by noting that the thesis said nothing about self-determination and added that there was little reason to become paralyzed over that issue. Now was not the time for the slogan, he concluded. But whatever bits of change in position on the Negro question remained from the thesis, Petrovsky endorsed them. His voice was the Comintern's. The die was cast. Self-determination in the Black Belt was on the way to becoming the line.

The meeting then heard a message from James W. Ford, who was tied up with Profintern businesss. He was rising rapidly in international Communist ranks. Born in Pratt City, Alabama, in 1893, Ford was the son of Lymon Forsch, who had migrated to Alabama from Gainsville, Georgia, in the 1890s to work in the coal mines and steel mills. Ford worked his way through Fisk University. After service in the Great War, he migrated to Chicago, where he worked in the post office and became a union activist. He joined the ANLC and was recruited to the Communist Party in 1926. With his union background, the Party made him a delegate to the Profintern Congress in 1928. He became a member of the RILU Executive Committee and remained in Moscow for nine months. In the Party for only two years, Ford nevertheless possessed Olympian self-assurance; he was polished, austere, impeccably dressed, ambitious, and meticulously organized. He also had little patience with scholastic theorizing— and that was the thrust of his message.[13]

Ford dismissed the issue of an oppressed nation or an oppressed race as an "academic question." It would be important if the Party had any serious contact with the black masses. But fifty Negro members of the Party out of a black population of 12 million was "practically nothing." In the face of the ANLC's pitiful state, and the Party's failure to fight chauvinism in its ranks, the discussion about slogans was a waste of time. Ford went on to accuse the Bittelman-Foster majority in the Central Executive Committee of using the debate over race or nation as a factional football. Not only was Haywood wrong about the national character of the Negro question, Ford said, Haywood could not "produce a single fact" to validate his claims about the national tendencies of black workers and peasants. He then challenged the participants to make connections with the aspirations of the Negro masses. Theoretical discussions, sociological studies, and new resolutions that diverted the Party from those tasks were "sabotage of real Negro work."[14]

On the final day of deliberations at the House of Trade Unions, a subtle but palpable change was in the air. A consensus based on a compromise of sorts was in the making. But that compromise was less a genuine splitting of differences than an opening to give the Comintern what it wanted: a significant change of line on the Negro question in the American Communist Party.

Opposition to Haywood-Nasanov lingered. Communist youth leader Herbert Zam reminded the meeting that the Party's Political Bureau had defined the Negro question as a race question, with the full support of the Foster-Bittelman faction. Lovestone spoke. He was against the Haywood-Nasanov thesis because it had no foundation for its proposed policies, no analysis of the social composition of black America, and no sense of the relationship of that composition to the class conflict. Lovestone granted that the Party was afflicted with chauvinism, but said it had made "real efforts to fight this menace." He defended his viewpoint on "Southern Negroes as reserves of capitalist reaction" by quoting his quasi-mentor Bukharin to the effect that counterrevolution seeks its reserves "in the direction of the village." Lovestone also conceded that it would be wrong for the Party to declare itself against self-determination. Theoretically, at least, it might become an issue in the future. He asserted vaguely that Comrade Petrovsky had "laid down the proper basis" for an undisclosed conclusion. He ended by defending the Party's "race question" viewpoint, its progress in fighting white chauvinism, and its upgrading of Negro work.[15]

Like all the other African American participants except Haywood, "Farmer" (Roy Mahoney), a KUTV student and Lovestone supporter from the Midwest, rejected self-determination. The Party failed to influence blacks, he said, because it approached the subject from the outside with no understanding of what goes on among the mass of blacks in the United States. And that, he said, was the problem with this question of a nation. Negroes were not even "a pure race"; in the deepest recesses of the Black Belt, the effects of assimilation could be seen in the varied hues of the people. The white rulers, Mahoney claimed, understood the forces of assimilation and pressed their antimiscegenation laws to curb them. Blacks, in fact, were losing their "common territory" through migration to the North and to the cities of the South. Self-determination would find no response among the black public, Mahoney said. In an all-male debate, Mahoney was the only one to point out that the millions of working Negro women had been neglected in the Haywood thesis and in the whole discussion.

Nasanov noted that Lovestone agreed with Petrovsky and that Petrovsky agreed with the Haywood-Nasanov position—using the Comintern official as a bridge. This was a shrewd and significant observation. Lovestone was indeed retreating. Nasanov denied that Bukharin had ever said what Lovestone attributed to him and accused his own critics of overestimating the industrialization of the South. The black peasantry was a long way from becoming an industrial proletariat. But he agreed with Lovestone that the Party could not say that it was opposed to self-determination: "at the present time it is not a burning issue."

Sen Katayama (who had seen to it that Claude McKay received a pass to the Fourth Congress in 1922) was the custodian of memory. He insisted that the fundamental character of the Negro question had been settled at the Second Congress with Lenin's parenthetical reference to American Negroes. While regretting the factional influences in the discussion, he sought to bring about conciliation and consensus: The struggle against lynching and Jim Crow, he said, was both a racial and national issue. The fight for equal rights in the labor movement was both a class and racial question. Thus, the Negro question, in its different aspects, was racial, class-related, and national in character.[16]

Like Ford, William L. Patterson launched a blistering attack on the weakness and lack of "sincerity" in the Party's approach to blacks over the nine years of its existence. A student at KUTV, Patterson was a graduate of the University of California and the Hastings Law School. He had become one of Harlem's promising young lawyers who often represented landlords and businessmen. A politically restless young man, Patterson had balanced a law practice with a troubled, driven involvement in the movement to free Sacco and Vanzetti. In Harlem he had met Briggs, Moore, Huiswoud, and Grace Campbell, and had joined the Party. Shortly thereafter he was invited to study in Moscow.[17]

Patterson thought the Haywood-Nasanov document was "splendid" in its approach to the Party's everyday work. But the issue of whether the Negro question was racial or national "had no practical application." There was a vast agenda challenging the Party: to fight racial chauvinism, to study the Negro question in American Party schools (not just in Moscow), to strengthen the Party's Negro "auxiliary" organizations, to breathe new life into the *Negro Champion,* to reach Negro youth and students. Finally, Patterson warned that the mandate to build black unions must not be used to deflect the struggle for equality and against chauvinism in the old trade unions.[18]

There the debate ended. A picture emerges of how the change of line was maneuvered through the Sixth Congress. Petrovsky offered a motion to use the sixteen-point Haywood-Nasanov resolution as a basis for a redraft to be submitted to the Congress's Negro subcommission. The motion carried by a vote of six to four. The transcript did not record individual votes, but it can be assumed that the most outspoken African Americans voted against, the core of the Bittelman-Foster faction voted for, and—critical to the outcome—the Lovestone group abstained.[19]

Petrovsky then offered a six-point proposal to be attached to the Haywood-Nasanov resolution. It called for greater emphasis on Negro work in light of growing proletarianization of the black population, while also noting that most blacks still resided in the South and that the majority remained "peasant[s]" who constituted "the root of the Negro racial (national) problem." These masses had to be transferred into "reserves of the revolutionary movement." The proposal repeated the Comintern's standard perception of American Negroes as potential organizers and "champions of the international Negro movement against imperialism." Petrovsky pressed the need to mount a self-critical "courageous campaign" against white chauvinism in the Party. He then insisted on adding, one more time, that "there are certain prerequisites which lead to the future development of a national revolutionary movement among the Negroes."[20]

The hyperkinetic Pepper assaulted the meeting with amendments. His only winner was a proposal to struggle against the "Negro bourgeoisie as a class enemy." His biggest loss was an amendment to make self-determination "a propaganda slogan" in black-majority areas. His "Negro Soviet Republic" also lost. Bertram Wolfe wanted the word "may" inserted between "which lead" ("prerequisites which lead to...a national revolutionary movement"). That lost. An ostensible middle ground was emerging based on the concept of a racial *and* national question—with *national* switching places with *racial* in parentheses.[21]

The consensus was consolidated by the election of a five-member committee to draw up the document for submission to the Negro subcommission. With a symmetry that rekindled memories of Gusev's old Parity Commission, the elected group was composed of Haywood, Nasanov, Ford, Patterson, and

Petrovsky. The latter's vote, of course, would be decisive in an anticipated stalemate among the other four members. The Nasanov-Haywood-Petrovsky document became the basis for the extensive twenty-five-point resolution that was published by the Executive Committee of the Comintern on October 26, 1928, and the second resolution of October 1930.[22]

The full Negro subcommission of the Sixth Congress's Colonial Commission convened on August 8. Petrovsky, in the chair, had again become "Bennett." He summarized his six points and said that the expanded commission would have to discuss self-determination in the Black Belt of the United States. The debate was nearly a repetition of previous days — with two exceptions. First, the American Party's Negro work was yoked to the CI's demand that the South African Communist Party adopt the slogan of an "Independent Native Black Republic." Second, there was a tense debate over how to organize Negro unions without abandoning the fight for integrated unions. For the Fosterites, the concept of all-black unions, separated from labor's mainstream, was hard to swallow. Ford countered that the Comintern's new dual "revolutionary" union policy had opened the door to new unions for Negro workers. Once they were organized, he said, they would have a lever to pressure whites to unite with them. William Dunne offered a slogan to salve his integrationist conscience: "We should organize Negro Unions and then amalgamate [them] with White Unions." Bennett worried that the American comrades might use all-black unions to retreat from the fight for integration of existing AFL unions. He insisted that the Party had to stress the importance of organizing "joint white and Negro unions," even as it recognized the need to build black unions in some cases.[23]

Bittelman offered an amendment to the resolution: "The Communist Party of America shall include in its program a provision calling for the right of self-determination of the Negro masses in the United States." Bennett "fully accept[ed]" Bittelman's amendment. Among other things, it would be a blow against white chauvinism. However, he conceded that Otto Hall was "fully entitled to make propaganda among the Negroes against self-determination." Hall granted that the concept need not mean discrimination or segregation, but said that black Americans would interpret it in that way and the black petty bourgeoisie would seize it and "utilize this against us." His brother, Harry Haywood, insisted that the Party "recognize nationalist tendencies among the Negroes, although they are not a nation."[24]

Bennett proposed two votes: (1) adding the right of self-determination to the Party program; (2) emphasizing the fight for integrated unions while organizing black unions under special circumstances. Otto Hall objected to voting on self-determination with no opportunity for full rebuttal. He won a postponement of that vote pending submission of a report by opponents. The vote on trade union work was also delayed.[25]

Bennett then revealed that a "small bureau" existed to report on Negro issues in countries other than the United States and South Africa. It was composed exclusively of CI officials: Otto Kuusinen, head of the Colonial Commission, Mikhailov (Williams), and himself. The Ukrainian Comintern official, Scripnyk, perhaps sensing the awkwardness of that revelation, moved that the "small bureau" be expanded, implying that its charge would cover South Africa and the United States. Haywood and Ford were added to it, as well as Bunting from South Africa and Cardenas from Latin America.[26] Bennett withdrew. This altered process brought black American Communists into direct intervention in the South African Communist Party. It also brought to an end the work of the committee of five from the Anglo-American Secretariat's rump commission. A far more authoritative group led by high-level Comintern figures would prepare a draft for the full Colonial Commission on the American Negro question. The meeting adjourned with agreement that the concluding session would take up in order South Africa, British and French colonies in Africa, and the resolution on the Negro question in the United States.

The subcommission reconvened on August 11 with the recommendations of the Kuusinen group in hand. Petrovsky (the minutes returned to that designation) reported that something was terribly wrong in the South African Communist Party. The SACP had been formed in 1921, principally by Eastern European Jewish immigrants. Claiming black backwardness and white prejudice, the Party resisted Comintern pressure to work among blacks until the mid-1920s, when it recruited an able group of about a hundred black members who made an impact on unions and mass organizations. By 1927 the Party had increased its work in a rejuvenated African National Congress, and in 1928 the SACP had begun a struggle against the hated Pass Laws. Its native membership climbed to 1,750. But charges persisted that it failed to work vigorously among the native population. Petrovsky now announced that after "careful study" by Kuusinen's group, the SACP did not sufficiently stand as the champion of the black majority. The struggle in South Africa was for national self-determination through "an independent Native South African Republic." The SACP had to accept that. A committee was appointed to incorporate that view into a resolution. It was composed of Bittelman as chair, Haywood, and Mikhailov, with the addition of Roux and Bunting from South Africa. With the Americans (and Mikhailov) in control of shaping the new line for the SACP, the outcome of the American situation was not in doubt.[27]

The resolution on the Negro question in the United States was ready for consideration. Still working essentially from the original Haywood-Nasanov draft, the group agreed to the first two points (on the growing importance of black workers and the Black Belt rural majority) as read. Hall objected to point 3, which castigated Lovestone's view of black southerners as "reserves of capitalist reaction." He chose that moment to reiterate his view that blacks were not developing the characteristics of a national minority and instead desired to be part of the American nation. Petrovsky demanded an immediate vote on the general principle of self-determination. The vote was ten to two in favor. Having started with a majority, those who insisted that blacks sought assimilation into the larger nation had lapsed into silence (save Hall and one or two others) on self-determination. The weight of the Comintern, abetted by Haywood and the Bittelman-Foster faction, had created an untenable situation for those who opposed the concept. Bittelman, smelling blood, jumped in with an echo of Russian prerevolutionary battles. He wanted the Lovestone view of the South condemned as "a menshevik deviation from the correct Marxist-Leninist point of view." His motion was not accepted.[28]

Otto Hall scored a partial victory by a scant six-to-five vote on the crucial point 5, which declared that the "Party must come out openly and unreservedly for the right of Negroes to national self-determination in the Southern states where the Negroes form a majority." He moved that "the slogan of 'social equality' remain the central slogan of our party for work among the masses." That formulation survived editing and made it into the final resolution.[29]

Bittelman offered a reformulated amendment on all-black unions, which was accepted after heated debate. It stressed "a merciless struggle against the AFL bureaucracy which prevents the Negro workers from joining the white workers' unions." That wording was in the final draft, but preceded by a call for "special unions" for black workers barred from white unions.

Point 10 called for the strengthening of the American Negro Labor Congress. Hall, believing that the ANLC was moribund, objected. He was voted down. Point 12 dealt with white chauvinism in the American Party and called for "penetrating self-criticism." Pepper wanted confirmation that the Party had issued strong statements against lynching and that its election platform had condemned all forms of racial oppression. That was not accepted.[30]

Petrovsky then offered a long motion (which became point 15) enjoining the Party to always be aware of a "two fold task": to fight every vestige of chauvinism among white workers and to combat "bourgeois segregation tendencies of the oppressed nationality." He proposed that an "editorial committee" finish revision of the document (including seven additional points). Haywood, Bittelman and Mikhailov were elected to perform that task. The Comintern-Fosterite coalition was in complete control. For the time being, it had beaten back attempts to undercut self-determination and had also defeated "leftist" proposals for a "Soviet Republic" or organization of a separate black state. Discussion of the American Negro question ended there. The new line called for full racial equality, for the Party to draw closer to black proletarians, for a fresh organizing start in the South. It committed the Party to a slogan of self-determination "in those regions of the South in which compact Negro masses are living." The belief that Black Belt agrarian Negroes constituted the germ of a "national revolutionary movement" was now official policy. Yet it was incumbent upon the Party to explain to Negro workers and peasants that only unity with white workers and a "victorious proletarian revolution" would permanently resolve the agrarian and national questions.[31]

The New Line: Winning Hearts and Minds

Far from Moscow, most Communists in the ranks who paid any attention must have wondered what this issue of self-determination for the Black Belt was all about. The *Daily Worker* in November 1928 dutifully took a stab at the issue, in an editorial headlined "The Communists Are For a Black Republic." But most of the editorial was about a black republic for South Africa, while self-determination in the United States was projected as entirely dependent on a proletarian revolution. The Party itself remained virtually silent on the new line for over a year. As late as February 1930 Otto Huiswoud was still saying that blacks in the United States were an oppressed racial minority whose progress was bound up with migration and the building of race organizations under working-class leadership.[32]

The only early discussion of the issue appeared in CI's *Communist International,* and was conducted mainly in German. Before the conclusion of the Sixth Congress, Pepper leaped into print with his "Negro Soviet Republic." Later, James Ford and William Patterson rehashed their view that there was no national sentiment developing in the black community—only a yearning for equality in the American nation. Harry Haywood located the Black Belt running through 214 counties in 5 states, where rural blacks constituted a majority that suffered under sharecropping and peonage. Haywood added that in the ghettoes, a mood of race togetherness had arisen, nourished by the church and press. Artists and intellectuals gave that solidarity a historical grounding and engendered a greater appreciation of Negro art, music, literature: "Before long, elements of a nationalistic ideology are at hand." Yet, Haywood added, the middle class sought to protect its interest built on segregation; the fight for full equality in all spheres and for the right of self-determination "up to separation and the erection of an independent Negro state" had to be waged by a radicalized black working class.[33]

Andre Sik, a Hungarian émigré who taught at KUTV, was close to the black students, and his views paralleled (and probably influenced) Patterson's and Ford's assertions that blacks were a specially oppressed race, and no more. In one of the more probing discussions, Sik maintained that the early American bourgeoisie, bereft of colonies commensurate with its expansive appetite, turned to the super-exploitation of blacks, first as slaves, then as "a special group, placed in the position of non-equal members of the nation and society." Unlike Africans who were bound together by common territory, economic system, language, and culture, African Americans had no such attributes and lacked the foundation, or will, to seek national independence. Communists should demand full political and social equality, not self-determination. A political struggle for self-determination was narrowly separatist; it was the cause of marginal producers to carve out a sphere of backward economic life for themselves. It was no menace to the ruling class, which relished the building of a "Chinese Wall" between the races. Rather, Sik argued, the Party should embrace the black working masses as class brothers and sisters, and express its understanding of the "enormous revolutionary role of the racial movement of toilers."[34]

Sik recognized the Negro question as special without embracing self-determination. But his efforts to differentiate Africa and black America made him neglect the bonds of memory, culture, and spirit in black American life, where the name "African" adorned churches and civic and fraternal organizations. He launched a general attack upon sensitive human barometers of black longing (like Du Bois) as self-serving dilettantes seeking to monopolize the Negro market. A mechanical description of black aspirations undermined his effort to affirm the special character of racial persecution and was symptomatic of a grievous weakness in the great debate of 1928: It took place in isolation from African American life. But one point in Sik's analysis stood out: that the virulent racial oppression of blacks yielded super profits from highly exploited labor and formed the cornerstone of capital accumulation in America. Therefore, the struggle of African Americans for equality struck at that cornerstone and had transforming implications, with or without self-determination.

Nasanov charged that Sik did not understand the character of the national struggle under imperialism, where the national movement was precisely a crusade of "petty producers" locked in battle against imperial domination over whole populations. To assure that a national democratic revolution would not take a reactionary turn was simple: Press for the rise of proletarian leadership. Earl Browder, rising to the top in the Party, drew a line between "the national liberation struggle of an oppressed nation" and its "nationalist" bourgeoisie, which "invariably subordinates itself to the interests of the oppressing imperialist power." Haywood complained that it was calumnious to say that self-determination was building a "Chinese Wall" between black and white workers. The concept was not separatist, it was a basis for an alliance of equals between the black population and white workers. Nasanov added that a people's sacred right to choose their own political life was a confirmation of their equality. James Ford, a post-Congress convert to self-determination, declared that by infusing the national striving of the black population with revolutionary content, the Communists had swept away the specter of separatist nationalism and had engendered a stirring promise of black-white unity against a common foe.[35]

In the meantime, Haywood's Comintern star was ascending: He was made a "practicant" in the Negro Bureau of the ECCI. Lenin School students were not ordinarily assigned to political work with a small salary while still engaged in their studies. But Haywood's three years at the school and an evaluation that he "is easily the strongest theoretically" of the black students clinched the job. The post gave him a direct hand in the formulation of a revised resolution in 1930 and placed him in a strong position to influence the execution of the new policy in the United States.[36]

In September 1929 Haywood wrote to the CPUSA, announcing that the Comintern's Negro Bureau had been reorganized as a "Negro Section of the Eastern Secretariat" of the ECCI, responsible for work among blacks all over the world. He added that communication between the Negro Bureau and the Negro Department of the American CP had been "practically non-existent." In coming months the Negro Section would be looking closely at the U.S. Party's Negro work, addressing its "unclarity" on the decisions of the Sixth Congress, and stressing the urgency of getting the Party's "fullest cooperation" with the new section. Brandishing his authority over his seniors, Haywood demanded that the Party forward all materials on its Negro work and on the fight against white chauvinism, along with an assessment of "moods among the Negro comrades."[37]

Otto Kuusinen, still chair of the CI's Colonial Commission, agreed that confusion surrounded the Sixth Congress Negro resolutions and something had to be done. In August 1930 the CI Negro Commission reconvened in Moscow, without the defeated Lovestone faction. The vagaries and unanswered questions inherent in the line were treated with dispatch: Race was clearly subordinate to nation. For Haywood, the assertion that the Negro question was a problem of racial hatred, as distinct from national oppression, was "to contend that the Negroes are oppressed because they are black!" To reduce the tyranny suffered by blacks to a matter of white attitudes about race and color obfuscated the super-exploitation of blacks and encouraged silly liberal nostrums like the healing capacity of time, education (a slap at Du Bois), good will, "tolerance," and wider interracial contacts.[38]

The 1930 resolution declared that political and social equality would be pressed in the North and South, but self-determination was to be the principal political slogan in the South. Communists would support the right of Black Belt Negroes to secede, but would urge them to stay if the revolution was won in the larger nation. Whites would not be obliged to leave the Negro republic, but would be asked to submit to the political hegemony of the majority with full minority rights. With that, blacks would rightfully attain real economic and political power, far greater than the scraps afforded by domination over an impoverished, segregated state. The CI said that self-determination would have no meaning if it applied "only in cases which concerned *exclusively* the Negroes and did not affect the whites." Communists had to oppose "reactionary black separatism." In the North, Communists had to join "the progressive process of assimilating the whites and Negroes into one nation." Finally, self-determination was a slogan for action, not just agitation. It presupposed energetic activity, such as strikes and tax boycotts, linked to the daily needs and suffering of the black population.[39]

AN ASSESSMENT

A persuasive theoretical foundation for a "nation within a nation" was never achieved. A nation was a transient community, not an eternal category. All the statistics marshaled by Haywood and Nasanov did not cast light on the dynamics of social change in the Black Belt and in American society as a whole. Lenin, the ultimate authority in the debate, said that all characteristics of a nation were subordinate to its economic life: National consciousness could be derived from the repressed embryonic "economic property" of colonial and dependent peoples. He did say in his *Statistics and Sociology* that the frozen "prison-house" status of blacks in the rural South could give rise to a desire for a nation. But he also said that with the speed of capitalist development in the United States, "nowhere do the vast national differences shrink so fast and so radically as here into a single 'American nation.' "[40]

Even the Comintern in 1930 said that the Black Belt was "not in itself economically or politically, such a united whole as to warrant being called a special colony of the United States." If not a colony, how then a nation? According to the CI, the Black Belt lacked the "separateness" of a colony; its economic life was uncomfortably "common" to the American nation as a whole. In fact, the larger ruling class was increasingly taking in hand the industrialization of the Black Belt, and "petty producers" were being pushed aside. Segregation fostered a fairly robust class differentiation in cities like Atlanta and Durham (largely through black-owned insurance companies), but it did not bring into being a dynamic bourgeois national consciousness. Structural and technological change in agriculture drove waves of sharecroppers and tenants from the countryside and scattered the potential "stable community on a common territory." Prospects for what Minor called "the deep-going impulse" toward national liberation in the Black Belt were weak, if they existed at all.[41]

A former student at the University of Pennsylvania, James S. Allen (Sol Auerbach) manifested a strong interest in African American life, which drew him into the South in 1930 as editor of the Party's *Southern Worker*. Allen admitted that migration had had an impact on the most extensive areas of the plantation economy. But more than a half-century after the abolition of slavery, the Black Belt retained close to half (49.3 percent) of all Negroes in America. From the start of the Great Depression, he said, northern industries had become incapable of absorbing black migration. Permanent capitalist stagnation was the rule; the task of wiping out the last vestiges of slavery and realizing self-determination in the Black Belt fell to the revolutionary alliance of the emerging black nation and the urban proletariat.[42]

Allen's analysis reflected another basic flaw in the theory of the "nation within a nation": the expectation that capitalism had reached its apex and that the Black Belt would continue to trap the black peasant majority and would continue to deteriorate, provoking a rebellious outcry for national liberation. In the meantime, the proletarian revolution would accelerate in the rest of the United States. The Communists correctly anticipated capitalism's greatest economic crisis. But their expectation of the rapid disintegration of the system was monumentally mistaken.

The "national rebellion" vaguely foretold in the 1930 document, of course, never took place — but a powerful movement for democratic civil rights did begin in the South. Indeed, the rapid development of capitalism, north and south, was stimulating black demands for democratic rights in the larger society; that struggle was an all-class phenomenon that ultimately battered the foundations of the "prison house."

After 1935 black nationhood clearly faded from Communist rhetoric. The concept was formally interred by Earl Browder in 1943, when he declared that African Americans had exercised self-determination by rejecting it. The concept was revived following Browder's expulsion in 1946, but was again laid to rest in 1958.[43]

Should self-determination be dismissed as a "wasted effort,"[44] a musty relic handed down from Moscow? Not entirely. The enterprise might have seemed like fantasy. But the Communists had touched a fundamental issue: democracy as independence, and independence as the right of choice. African Americans, to be free and equal, had to liberate themselves from supplicant status; they had to be free to control the political and social lives of their communities and to redefine the conception of black-white cooperation on the basis of new power relationships among equals. In that respect, the Communists were "advanced" in their approach to the political content of racial equality. They would transform the history of distrust for white promises — promises that regularly deteriorated into betrayal. They would say directly: We recognize and defend your right to choose your own future. We reject the traditional white ruling-class practice of manipulating, controlling, and subjugating blacks. Further, we understand the crucial role of racial hatred and prejudice in undermining joint struggle against the common foe. Killing the "virus" of white chauvinism is not a matter of charity, sentiment, or general benevolence. White workers will never see the socialist millennium while blacks remain in thrall. Therefore, we will cleanse "white chauvinism" from our ranks, root and branch, and without qualification defend your right of political choice.

Driven by the concept of Black Belt nationality, the Communists, at a time of rampant racism and segregation, probed neglected areas of African American history, especially militant and nationalist currents, the sordid legacy of white racism, and connections between black Americans and blacks around the world. Having largely ignored the Harlem Renaissance in the 1920s, they now began to explore African American art and literature.[45]

Ironically, the power of self-determination lay not in its theoretical validity, but in its pragmatic implications. It undercut those who subordinated the struggle for Negro rights to the class question, or who equated the two — thus devaluing the centrality of Negro liberation for revolutionary change. Haywood and others pounded away at "reformist" and "social-democratic" notions of the Negro question as either a class or a race problem, which minimized the transforming potential of the black population. For white workers, black liberation was elevated to first rank in the revolutionary process — making blacks, whose national aspirations were revolutionary in their own right, the indispensable, primary allies of the working class. That was a qualitative break with traditional radical practices concerning the race issue in the United States. No Communist was allowed to forget his or her obligation to forge and defend a revolutionary alliance with nationally oppressed blacks. Communists had to "jump at the throats" of white chauvinists and incorporate the needs and demands of black Americans into every aspect of political life.

The vision of black national oppression as constituting both the vital strength and fatal weakness of imperialism galvanized the Party into unprecedented activities for Negro rights in the 1930s. The theoretical and programmatic elements of self-determination may have been painfully hard to define, but the concept nevertheless drove Communists into a frenzy of struggle for equality and black liberation. Ford and Patterson won their demands, and deeds began to follow resolutions. These two men, along with the other black men and women who threaded their way through those tortuous debates, spoke and acted with growing assurance and confidence in themselves and in the egalitarian aspirations of their cause. That was an exceedingly rare thing in the 1920s.

This does suggest that national self-determination was entirely pragmatic and shorn of a material basis beyond perceived consequences. The sense of a "nation within a nation," born in slavery and nurtured in segregation, is rooted in African American thought. It emerged from the lash, from political subjugation, from the trampling of the cultural heritage of an entire people, from assaults on their psychological makeup and identity. The Negro question was indeed more than a class or racial problem. The forced rupture of community between blacks and whites, and the onslaught on the blacks' historic continuity, culture, and identity had produced a longing for political unity and psychic autonomy—for the realization of black national yearning. The Communists were onto something. National oppression constituted a proper description of what had happened to black Americans. Richard Wright in *Native Son* sought to capture the depth of national oppression in the words of the Communist lawyer, Max, pleading for Bigger Thomas's life:

> Let us banish from our minds the thought that this is an unfortunate victim of injustice. The concept of injustice rests upon the premise of equal claims.... What is happening... is not injustice, but *oppression,* an attempt to throttle or stamp out a new form of life.... Once you see [Negroes] as a whole, once your eyes leave the individual and encompass the mass, a new quality comes into the picture. Taken collectively, they are not simply twelve million people, in reality they constitute a separate nation, stunted, stripped, held captive *within* this nation, devoid of political, social, economic, and property rights.[46]

The problem in the United States, however, was how to fulfill national aspirations when a prospect for the exercise of self-determination within a prescribed geographical area did not exist. In 1918 Cyril Briggs had abandoned the notion of the separate state as unattainable. In fact, Briggs, Moore, and Huiswoud had invested so much in the struggle against Garvey's separatist panaceas that they were at first reluctant to embrace the change of policy. Unfortunately, the American Communists lacked the political imagination and the independence from Moscow to immediately separate the promising kernel of self-determination from the chimera of a "free Negro Republic." In time, they made an unconscious separation by simply not talking about the Negro state. What remained was a belief that racial equality and a "fusion of nations" would come though the empowerment of blacks in deciding the conduct of their relations with whites. As Allen put it in 1932, the objective of uniting black and white workers could not be reached until "Negroes have the freedom . . . to enter of their own free will and without coercion into such a union." Black autonomy was a foundation for "progressive assimilation and a pluralist federation" into a single, democratic nation. The Communists came closer than any other political movement in the nation's history to resolving the contradiction between assimilation and separation.[47]

It has been argued that self-determination was "made in Moscow." The transcripts of the debates certainly show the Russians swarming around the issue and bringing it to fruition. Stalin has also been targeted as the source of the theory. That is possible, but it is of little importance except as a relic of Cold War hagiography. To label the prime symbol of genocidal totalitarianism and the failure of the Soviet model as the author of self-determination may, for some, discredit the theory beyond the point of consideration. But that still does not erase serious theoretical and political issues inherent in the concept. Despite all the confusion, paradoxes, and contradictions, the Negro question as a national question drove the Communists into the vortex of black life, creating an instructive record of black-white interaction and bringing a new influence into a venerable black liberation movement.[48]

A Postscript on KUTV

The African American students at KUTV demanded to be drawn into the CI's discussions of the Negro question. They insisted that a Negro section be set up at KUTV to allow them to explore the global dimensions of the black struggle by collecting and analyzing information on conditions and prospects for change in the black colonies of Africa as well as in the United States. The request was granted, and a Negro Section, with the addition of colonial students, was formed at KUTV under the aegis of the Eastern Secretariat.[49]

From afar, the group began to play a widening role in monitoring the Party's Negro work. From a Comintern platform, it took a hand in shaping the Communist movement's theoretical approach to the Negro question and its work in other parts of the world. Goaded by the renowned dogmatism of the Russian schools, the students became rigid proponents of the new line. When John Ballam, U.S. representative to the Comintern, condemned self-determination as a careless concept, the section members flexed their muscles, calling his speech "chauvinistic" and "liquidatory . . . in regard to the revolutionary strug-gles of the Negroes." They demanded a written statement from Ballam and suggested possible disciplinary action.[50]

The black students' ideological toughness got them through extraordinar-ily hard conditions at KUTV. At any given time, half of them were ill in the school's hospital, and this seriously impaired the wishes of the group "to better prepare ourselves to take an active part on the revolutionary field in the coun-try from which we came." Repeated complaints about extremely cold rooms went unanswered. Sanitary conditions were "deplorable in the extreme," with a perpetual stench from the toilets. The food was bad and poorly prepared; it was more usual than not to find worms in the dining room's compote. The Americans had trouble coping with the "habits and conditions" of "Eastern students," and pleaded for separate rooms.[51]

The African American students spent long hours in class, slogging through courses on political economy, Leninism, dialectical and historical materialism, and the like. But most instructors spoke English poorly, and there was an egre-gious lack of reading materials in English. Yet most of the black students man-aged to get through the KUTV curriculum, which ran an average of eighteen months.[52]

After protests over bad conditions, in early 1930 the students won some changes. The curriculum placed more stress on concrete problems in the United States. Out of a desire for greater access to national minorities in the Soviet Union, summer travel was broadened to include visits to Georgia, Azerbaijan, Uzbekistan, and other regions. The students also became emboldened to chal-lenge racial insults from white students and from unreconstructed Soviets. White students at the "more advanced" Lenin School were charged with racial arrogance and paternalism, and with fostering segregation. In January 1933 the black students summoned Dmitri Manuilsky to KUTV. Walter Lewis of Birmingham and Roddy Lister and Monroe Vallade of Harlem presented a litany of degrading characterizations of blacks in Soviet adult and children's the-ater. Manuilsky promised swift and decisive action. Cleansing racism from So-viet culture was an arduous job, but by 1934 the students reported progress.[53]

For the sixty to ninety African Americans who were schooled in Moscow, the experience was a compound of bewilderment, culture shock, pain, and exhilarating empowerment. They rubbed shoulders with Jomo Kenyatta, Ho Chi Minh, Deng Xiaoping, the Turkist poet Nazim Hikmet, and many other Communists and leftists who were destined to play major roles in anti-imperial efforts of the twentieth century. They were caught in a swirl of international-ism that often tugged at their sense of American reality, but gave them a global frame of reference, built their self-confidence, and encouraged them to create and control their own agendas. All this had a measurable impact on the next phase of the Communists' efforts to forge an alliance with African Americans.

PART II

The Third Period, 1929–33

CHAPTER SIX

The Turn

INTO THE STREETS

In May 1928 Gordon B. Hancock of Hampton Institute noticed something ominous stirring in the South. There appeared to be a changing "work psychosis" among working-class whites, who were now taking formerly shunned "nigger jobs." Urban League investigator and analyst Jesse O. Thomas detected growing "machinization" in southern agriculture; the displacement of unskilled labor was affecting both bottom-rung blacks and poor whites. The special vulnerability of blacks put them under the most direct attack. In Thomas's words, "as soon as a job changes from unskilled to semi-skilled, it becomes a white man's job." Since 1923 crop production had been declining steadily, forcing migration of agricultural workers to cities and industrial areas. The bituminous coal-mining industry, which had absorbed thousands of migrating blacks, was suffering a crisis of overproduction and an excess of miners. The iron and steel industries, which had provided decent wages for blacks, had shrunk consistently. Common hand labor, which blacks had traditionally provided for industry, was being displaced by machines. Pressure from excess white labor had halted the influx of rural blacks into heavy industry. The editors of *Opportunity* were impelled to add ruefully that blacks "ordinarily are taken on as individuals after white workers . . . are cared for.[1]

Before the stock market crash, black observers began to sense the coming nightmare. In the winter of 1929 the *Pittsburgh Courier* noted thousands of business failures, 2 million unemployed workers, and many millions more on the edge of poverty. By spring the *Courier* was warning that "winter and un-employment [will] arrive simultaneously," and those who still held jobs "should hoard their precious dollars."[2]

After years of bruising factional struggle, membership in the American Com-munist Party in the late 1920s and early 1930s was barely over seven thousand. The membership was still largely foreign-born, with Jews and Finns as the major ethnic components. It was concentrated in New York, where one-third of members resided. Chicago had about one-fourth of the membership, fol-lowed by Cleveland and Detroit with less than one-tenth each. New York also provided most of the young organizers who fanned out over the country dur-ing the frenetic early days of the Depression. With its narrow ethnic and geo-graphical base, the Party was usually in a New York frame of mind.[3]

The same ratio held for the Party's black membership. Harlem, with its sprawling mix of social service workers, domestics, clerks, transport workers, professionals, West Indians, artists, businessmen, and paupers, was the focal point of black ideology and culture. It was the dying bastion of Garveyism and other nationalisms, and in the late 1920s it was the concentration point of black Communists. Harlem was the focus of the Party's electoral campaign in 1928, which marked a modest advance in putting the Communists' "Negro face" before the public. "Communism knows no color line," shouted George Padmore from red-draped stepladders in Harlem and Brooklyn, calling on his listeners to consider the uncompromising Party platform: equal pay for equal work, equal access to unions, an end to all discrimination. Richard B. Moore, who was running for Congress in the Twenty-first District, exhorted crowds to reject the belly-crawling bigotry of the old parties. In the midst of the campaign the Party declared its first Negro Week. All units had to study the Communists' "Negro program," with black speakers to lead discussions wherever possible. Open-air meetings in cities across the country were to fo-cus on lynching and also pass the hat for the Party's Negro work. At any time during a Harlem evening the Party would have as many as eight street meet-ings going on simultaneously. With all that, Moore's first foray into electoral politics in a multiracial district netted a scant 296 votes, while Fort-Whiteman, running statewide for comptroller, netted 10,000 votes.[4]

But something else was happening. Hard times had come, with soaring job-lessness, inadequate relief, hunger, and evictions, and the troubles were hitting black communities with exceptional force. In the face of deteriorating housing conditions and unaffordable rents, the Party undertook its most effective work yet in the black community. Richard B. Moore, Grace Campbell, Hermina Huiswoud, and others with long experience in the community wrested the Harlem Tenants League from the Socialists in January 1928. The fight to save the Rent Law struck a responsive chord. The Tenants League had even been noted approvingly by the Comintern, and under pressure from seasoned local organizers, the Party extended full support. The community at last witnessed local Communists giving needed leadership on a pressing issue. The league, with the Party's help, rallied 200 tenants for a Harlem rent strike on January 1, 1929.[5]

At the Party's national convention in March 1929, Otto Huiswoud noted that its Negro work had improved since the Sixth Congress. The Negro Department now functioned under the Central Executive Committee and was charged with directing and implementing the Party's Negro policies. Otto Hall's national tour of industrial areas and centers of black life had brought the Party nearly 300 membership applications from black workers. District Negro conferences were being held to tackle theoretical and practical problems inherent in Negro work. Huiswoud reported that by the opening of the convention, ten districts had organized Negro departments. But shortcomings persisted. There was an insufficient number of trained Negro cadres, Party-influenced unions had done nothing to organize black workers, and virtually no work had been done among sharecroppers and tenant farmers. It was time for an organizing drive in the South.[6]

The 1929 convention was the apex of Lovestone's control of the Party; 90 percent of the delegates were in his corner. Yet he had accumulated debits in Moscow — among them his lack of enthusiasm for self-determination. His forces had no will to resist the demands of black Communists (all from his own group or neutral) for a serious approach to the Party's Negro work. Whatever their factional alignments, Huiswould, Briggs, and Hall felt that both the Foster and Lovestone groups shared blame for the neglect of Negro work during the Party's formative years. In a major step to advance blacks to the highest echelons, Huiswoud, Briggs, Hall, John Henry, and Edward Welsh were elected to the Central Executive Committee. (Apparently, no women were considered.) Welsh was a dedicated Lovestone supporter. Along with Huiswoud, he was a member of the "proletarian delegation" that journeyed to Moscow in May 1929 to plead against Lovestone's removal. He remained loyal to Lovestone and followed him though the byzantine corridors of radical factionalism to the most conservative sectors of the labor movement. Harold Williams, recently returned from KUTV, was appointed as section organizer in Harlem and director of Negro work in New York. After six years in the shadows, Briggs was poised to again play a major role. He assumed the directorship of the Central Committee's Negro Department from Huiswoud, who went on to international work. By December Briggs's dream of a weekly *Liberator* would come to fruition. In the meantime, he pressed for a second "National Negro Week," which was to last ten days. Bucking the indifference of the membership, Briggs insisted that the Party honor the revolutionary tradition in black history exemplified by Toussaint L'Ouverture, Nat Turner, and Denmark Vesey. Party units were called upon to discuss the Negro question, to turn to "the Negro peasantry in the South," to campaign against lynching, and to picket Jim Crow theaters and restaurants. Districts were directed to elect "Negro committees," to raise funds for "energetic prosecution" of Negro work, to hold street meetings, and to run interracial dances to demonstrate defiance of "the capitalist dictum of racial separation."[7]

With all that, the Sixth Congress resolution had not yet penetrated into Party consciousness. The Negro question was still seen as an aspect of the class question, though poisoned by the special, proscriptive nature of racial prejudice. Summing up the results of Negro Week, Briggs noted that the demonstrations against Jim Crow facilities were spotty. White Communists still manifested "a sort of condescending interest in Negro work." But he reminded the comrades that the "age-long oppression of colonial and weak nationalities" had created bitterness toward and distrust of oppressing nations "and the [white] proletariat in particular." Although National Negro Week was over, he concluded, "our Negro work has just begun."[8]

In the spring of 1929 the *Daily Worker* published a series of articles on "the evils of housing in Harlem." The author was Sol Auerbach (soon to become James S. Allen), an emerging Party specialist on the Negro question. Ignoring the thriving cultural life and stable core of homeowners that existed as a counterpoint to the ghetto's misery, Auerbach in these articles made a characteristic Third Period attempt to drive a wedge between the black community's bourgeois and working-class components. He sounded the alarm over the impending expiration on May 31 of the weak Rent Law, which was a last, thin line of defense against landlords. He took his readers on a disquieting walking tour of Harlem housing, through rotting staircases and broken, garbage-filled dumb-waiter shafts. "Higher class" housing at $10 or more a room exacted a toll in harder work, sublets, and rent parties to satiate the landlords' greed. His most searing attack was reserved for the prestigious St. Philip's Protestant Episco-pal Church, which owned a row of tenements called, in mocking tribute to nonpaying tenants, "Rats and Cats Row." He portrayed a middle-class min-istry pouring out Christian piety to the victims of its overpriced, rat-infested flats. Lest he leave an impression of submissiveness, Auerbach ended with news of resistance led by the Tenants League, including the outbreak of partial rent strikes to preempt rent increases and the expiration of the Rent Law.[9]

With an end to rent control approaching, the Tenants League called for an alliance of community groups to save the statutes. But only Party-organized women's groups and the ANLC were willing to support demands formulated with leftist zeal. In a grab-bag of dedication, realism, and sectarian fantasy, signs at demonstrations proclaimed, "Down with segregation and discrimi-nation against Negro tenants!" "Down with rent slavery!" "Defend the Soviet Union!" However, with the crisis building, more than two hundred people answered the call on June 1 to a parade and rally demanding rents commen-surate with income and a ban on racial discrimination.[10]

As rent control expired, increases were imposed on formerly rent-controlled flats. Moore, Campbell, and the others worked to expand rent strikes, orga-nize house and block committees, lambaste the politicians' "honeyed promises," and pressure Mayor James J. Walker to act. In the meantime, the league be-came an unofficial social agency swamped by frightened tenants clutching dis-possess notices. But it had a hard time in the face of the landlords' power, the lack of viable options, and the problems created by its own determination to expose the community's middle-class leaders. Despite that, the league's orga-nizing efforts intimidated some landlords into compromising or even with-drawing rent increases. In the fall of 1929 the New York City Board of Alder-men enacted a rent-control law that offered modest relief. However, the New York state supreme court struck it down, and the housing issue continued to nag the community throughout the Depression years.[11]

By December 1929 the Harlem Tenants League had gained enough notori-ety to have been kicked out of its regular meeting place, the New York Public

Library. The Party's factional quarrel also crippled the league. Moore attempted to remove Lovestone supporter Welsh from the league executive. Both Party and Lovestone supporters packed league meetings. Grace Campbell became so disgusted by the spillover of the Party's battles into the league that she left the Party. In the meantime, many of the league's members were bemused and lapsed into inactivity.[12]

The Harlem Tenants League was the embodiment of the contradictory character of the "class against class" Third Period. Its commitment to the most vulnerable and impoverished sectors of the community was a new departure in the political life of Harlem in the 1920s, where the real estate agents, preachers, and professionals had been looked upon as apt symbols of the black metropolis. But the Party's attacks on conditions in the community often seemed to besmirch the proud notion of a "black Mecca"; its simplistic and ultra-leftist division of the political landscape into friends or enemies wrecked any chance that it might have had to become a widely recognized leader. By virtue of characterizing reform as the front line in defense of besieged capitalism, every partial victory became little more than a confirmation of the system's deceit and treachery; every traditional black leader was an enemy to be isolated and discredited. It must have seemed to many that the Party offered only the choice of revolutionary acts — or nothing. Fortunately for the survival of such work in communities and unions, practical appeals to self-interest often outweighed dogma.

The New York City municipal election campaign of 1929 seemed a suitable vehicle for intensified Communist activity in Harlem. The Party had begun to attract recruits based on its presence on street corners, in legislative hearings, and on picket lines. Harold Williams orchestrated a citywide conference to mobilize support for a new group of Negro candidates: Otto Hall, fresh from the textile strike in Gastonia, North Carolina, for comptroller; Fanny Austin, a domestic worker, for alderman (with the distinction of being the first black woman nominated for municipal office), and Moore for Congress in a special election in the Twenty-first District. In keeping with the new revolutionary line of the Sixth Congress, street-corner speakers fulminated against repression in black communities. When Albert Jackson, an independent ice-wagon driver, was beaten and fired upon, the Party protested against "the guerilla rule of the ice barons" and their flunky Tammany Hall cops. For the police and local politicians, that rhetoric was becoming downright flammable — threatening their perception of a tranquil ghetto. A CP election rally on August 9 was forcibly dispersed by police, and several speakers were arrested. This was becoming a standard procedure. On September 4, the tension reached the breaking point. While Moore spoke on a street corner, police sailed into the crowd and arrested him; the crowd retreated up Lenox Avenue, when bullets were fired in its direction. Two members of the Young Communist League, Sid Resnick and Edith Mann, were dragged into a police car and severely beaten. Solomon Harper followed them to the local precinct and was promptly arrested. The Communists swore they had heard a "Jim Crow" black cop say, "Smash the meeting, smash the damn meeting, and murder the Reds." In mid-September, the Party was back at Seventh Avenue and 138th Street for an election rally under a banner that pointedly proclaimed the "[American] Section of the Communist International." The police blocked the street to prevent the rally; Moore was dragged from a ladder while the now familiar Reds, according to the *Daily Worker,* were singled out for "clubbing . . . so hard that the sound of blows could be heard for half-a-block." Moore and seven whites were arrested when the police plunged into the crowd, which had grown to two thousand.[13]

Such scenes were not limited to Harlem. In June 1929 the Party launched a series of protests against the lynching in Alamo, Tennessee, of Joe Boxley, an eighteen-year-old black farm laborer. A Boxley protest meeting in Detroit's East Side ghetto was broken up by police, despite a permit. On the night when Moore was again being arrested in Harlem, Harold Williams was in Brooklyn to condemn the Zionists in Palestine as "Jewish Fascisti," tools of British imperialism. He was beaten by Zionist youth when someone shouted that he was "an Arab." Three hundred police and two companies of firemen had to quell the ensuing riot. Williams later claimed that it was not the Zionists who broke up the meeting, but the police who were allegedly enraged at the sight of a black addressing white workers.[14]

Death came to a young black Harlem Communist in 1930 and set off a sequence of violence that left yet another Communist dead on the sidewalks of New York. On June 28 Alfred Luro (also identified as Alfred or Albert Levy in some reports) was hauled off a ladder in Harlem and beaten by a group identified in the Negro press as Garveyites. According to witnesses, the police, in the process of "restoring order," joined in the beating of Luro, who died shortly thereafter. On June 30 the Communists led a funeral protest through Harlem. Officer Edmund O'Brien intercepted the marchers and demanded that they show a permit. Thereupon, the marchers allegedly "swarmed over" the patrolman. In the melee O'Brien shot and killed a Mexican national, Gonzalo Gonzalez, who was leading the march. On July 1 there was a second funeral procession. Shortly before its start "100 Negro members of the Communist Party arrived in front of the [funeral] parlor" to escort the coffin to the nearby Spanish Workers' Center, where twenty-five hundred funeral marchers heard the unity of the working class extolled yet again.[15]

The Communist Party in Harlem had grown rapidly enough to mobilize dozens of black members to carry the remains of Gonzalo Gonzalez to a Hispanic workers' center. In the wake of the September 4, 1929, riot, fifteen Harlem residents reportedly joined the Party. William Weinstone claimed that on that evening blacks, voicing anger at the brutality visited upon the comrades, came to their defense. "That proves conclusively," Weinstone said, "that the Negro masses can be drawn into the revolutionary struggle." It really proved that the wellsprings of empathy in the black community came to the surface in the light of unjustified violence. Harlem was the home of veterans of the resistance to the Red Summer, West Indian radicals, people who had experienced labor strife on the docks of New Orleans and in the Arkansas cotton fields. They undoubtedly understood the political meaning of the thud of a police nightstick on the skull of a radical and transferred that understanding to some of the younger generation. Given the dramatic narrowing of options as hunger and desperation filled the life of the ghetto, a turn to communism made sense to some. But faith that a revolutionary awakening came from the blow of a nightstick was more consonant with the old Wobbly tradition of spontaneous politicization than with Marxism. A stable, coherent base among blacks was not going to be built through confrontation with the police. The defense of tenants' rights led by the Harlem Tenants League probably yielded more results than all the violent confrontation with cops.

Within the black community, violence associated with Communist-led demonstrations aroused conflicting responses. For some, the willingness of Communists to risk assault and even death in defending Negro rights obviated doubts about the Reds' sincerity and inspired respect and admiration. But injury and death, especially in the case of black demonstrators, also underscored the pitfalls of a black-Red fusion. For some, the swiftness of the repression must have suggested nothing less than race suicide if vulnerable Negroes were to pursue a relationship with despised, pariah Reds. The Party had to struggle for measurable changes in the material conditions of black life before it could claim to be "the champion of the Negro people." That was the major challenge in days to come.[16]

UNION ORGANIZING — NORTH

On August 31, 1929, 690 delegates gathered in Cleveland to dissolve the largely agitational Trade Union Educational League and form the Trade Union Unity League. This was the Communists' response to the Sixth Congress's injunction to launch "revolutionary unions" to challenge the foundering AFL and to meet the demands of an envisioned revolutionary crisis. Among the delegates were 64 African Americans, chiefly from basic industries.[17]

The 1920s had not proved a propitious decade to launch a new federation of revolutionary unions. Despite the AFL's embrace of bedrock anticommunism and conservative business unionism, the corporate elite in the mid-1920s had consolidated the open shop, had unleashed vigilante attacks on militant unionists, and following Henry Ford's example, had used new assembly-line technology to gain control of productive processes. Company welfare schemes, stock options for workers, and company unions added up to a "new capitalism" built upon suppression, concession, bribery, boss-friendly courts that struck down protective legislation, and high profitability institutionalized by Frederick W. Taylor's "scientific management." Working-class culture had doubtless been affected by a trade-off of intensified, regimented labor for surging consumerism — to the benefit of the two hundred corporations that now owned one-fifth of the country's wealth. Added to the mix of Fordism, consumerism, and the "new" highly rationalized and concentrated capitalism was a coercive Americanism that browbeat immigrants into an Americanization that only deepened nationalistic and self-isolating currents.[18]

Against that tide, desperate miners in rebellious locals defied the national United Mine Workers, striking the Pennsylvania and Ohio fields under Communist leadership. Thousands of mine families were evicted from company houses, picketing was curbed by injunctions, and coal company cops and state police repeatedly raided the strikers' tents and barracks. Imported white and black strikebreakers added to the general woe, while the black scabs themselves were victimized by the bosses' crooked bookkeeping to the point where many received no wages at all.[19]

On September 8, 1928, six hundred miners from rebel locals and the Save-the-Union committees met in East Pittsburgh to form the National Miners Union. Violence in the coalfields spilled into the convention as mobs armed with clubs, knives, and blackjacks descended on the Labor Lyceum. Fighting flowed into the streets and around the delegates' hotels. When the convention finally got down to business, William Boyce, a leading black union miner from Indiana, was elected national vice president. He immediately launched a campaign to oppose strikebreaking and to win blacks to the NMU. He reminded black miners that although the United Mine Workers' constitution banned discrimination, "the words were not worth the paper they were printed on." The truth, Boyce said, was that the UMW did not want Negroes. John L. Lewis, in fact, had been presiding over the elimination of a large component of Negro miners for years. In contrast, the NMU was a "bulwark of defense" of black miners; in this union they were not bulldozed and silenced, but instead were leaders of the organization, which was dedicated to a vigorous fight for full economic, political, and social equality.[20]

In late 1929 a strike, under NMU leadership, broke out in the southern Illinois coal region. The Communists continued to press for black-white solidarity with a steady barrage of resolutions, addresses, and broadsides. James Ford had returned from Moscow and become an organizer for the TUUL's Negro Department. He begged black and white workers to hold onto their fragile, hard-won unity, but the strike was already dying. Interracial cooperation would have to be cultivated on new battlegrounds. Early in 1930 Isaiah Hawkins, a veteran of the Negro Miners' Relief Committee, became the full-time head of the union's Negro Department. He was at his post in 1931 when a major strike, under NMU leadership, erupted in the Pittsburgh area and West Virginia. Six thousand black miners were among the thirty-five thousand who walked out. Black workers at the Pricedale mines in the Pennsylvania bituminous region refused to join the walkout, so the NMU arranged a picnic for the miners. On a hot Sunday afternoon Richard B. Moore addressed the recalcitrant miners and their families. He was at his oratorical best, hailing the union's stand against discrimination, praising black-white unity, and linking the economic crisis, unemployment, the Scottsboro case (see chapter 11), and the miners' strike with the long-time cry for freedom. The following day, the Negro miners at Pricedale joined the strike.[21]

While the Pennsylvania strike dragged on, the NMU began an organizing drive in the Kentucky counties of Harlan and Bell, notorious mine-operator strongholds. Blacks were not as numerous in the Kentucky mines, but they were involved in the bloody Harlan strike called in February 1931. Two militant black miners, Essley Philips and Gaines Eubanks, were indicted on a murder charge — framed, according to the union. When some strikers argued that the strike kitchen should be segregated to prevent a raid by the operators on the pretext that local Jim Crow ordinances were being violated, the Communists argued back for six or seven hours; they finally convinced the workers to eat in the same kitchen.[22]

Black observers were impressed. Charles S. Johnson, writing in the National Urban League publication *Opportunity,* said that the NMU had proved that no permanent obstacle existed to the unity of black and white labor, especially in a time of crisis when the races confronted similar economic circumstances. Rather, the battle was to realize the potential for such cooperation along a broad economic front and to defeat the lingering racial orthodoxies that continued to impede unity. Arthur G. McDowell, writing in the same publication, was moved by "a vivid portrayal of black miners as they emerged from the coal pits arm in arm with white miners and began to march." The NMU's success in uniting workers of both races justified the struggle to unionize black labor, and the Negro miner had "proved his right to be regarded with full respect . . . worthy of the most experienced fighters in the mine union ranks." W.E.B. Du Bois pondered the "odd tendency" of black commentators to reserve sympathy for unionism, even when black workers were involved. In Pennsylvania and Kentucky, he said, black miners "have suffered with their white fellows. They have been starved, beaten, and killed; yet they have stood up staunchly for a living wage, for freedom. . . . They deserve the sympathy of all men."[23]

The Party hailed NMU's projection of "special Negro demands." But it criticized the union's failure to move beyond advocacy of unity as economic necessity to "politicization" of "the struggle against Negro oppression." That would have entailed a holistic appplication of the line to attack the many-sided nature of national oppression: segregated mining towns and other forms of Jim Crow, as well as the death sentences in the Scottsboro case.[24]

In 1928 the Party launched the Needle Trades Workers' Industrial Union, challenging the AFL's despised social-democratic International Ladies' Garment Workers Union. Henry Rosemond, a black furrier, was vice president and executive board member of the union, in an industry that was marked by ethnic insularity, labor-intensive production, close proximity between the boss and workers (the boss often a former worker), and a nasty system of "subcontracting."[25]

Maude White, who returned from Russia in 1930, became an organizer for the union, which by then was a TUUL affiliate. She had been born in McKeesport, Pennsylvania, into a family of fourteen children. Her father was a hard-drinking coalminer and construction worker; her mother worked as a domestic. Through her early teenage years, White did domestic work, cared for the younger children, and was drawn to religion. While in high school she was "saved" by a local preacher, but that experience failed to give her solace or to heal her resentment of life's hardships and the scarring pain of racism. A teacher at the high school, Eleanor Goldsmith, recognized White's intellectual restlessness and latent militancy. She took her to Pittsburgh to hear Scott Nearing lecture on "dollar diplomacy." The meeting was chaired by a black man. Swept into an interracial environment, the excited teenager did not realize that the "club" she joined that night was the Communist Party. Later, a sister of White's was refused a place in the high school glee club, and Goldsmith was fired for fighting for the sister's right to participate. The teacher urged White's parents to allow Maude to live with an older sister in Chicago where, under Goldsmith's tutelage, she would escape McKeesport's stifling environment and enter a larger world of political activism. White finished high school in Chicago and eighteen months later was a student at KUTV. When she returned to the United States in 1930, she threw herself into organizing in the needle trades industry.[26]

White quickly took on problems facing black workers in a trade that had been largely closed to them. The exploitive subcontracting of the labor of black women by white pressers was a priority. The union's policy was to strictly forbid such a practice, but White complained that Communists in the shops dodged the issue for fear of antagonizing the white pressers. Instead of fighting for an equal place for black women in the dress trade, they retreated to "general" slogans about racial oppression. Rose Wortis, a Party leader in the dress trade, told White that the union handled the complaints of black workers "in the same manner" as those of white workers. White had hard questions ready: Did blacks not suffer from special oppression? Did they have no special needs? Was the bosses' treatment of black women really "in the same manner" as the treatment of whites? Such a lack of differentiation obscured the racial discrimination inherent in the situation and was little more than "the union capitulating before the white chauvinism of the boss." But White admitted that a special approach to black grievances was a tough sell to white workers. They resented the entry of blacks into the trade on any basis other than subcontracting, seeing it as an encroachment on their turf. Even militant workers would vacillate and hesitate. But here, she pointed out, was a classic case of how discriminatory wage differentials created by subcontracting hurt everybody. Class-conscious Negro workers had to break down the justifiable distrust of whites among fellow blacks; white Communists had a sacred obligation to lead the struggle to abolish subcontracting and "color caste" in the industry. Hesitation or retreat were out of the question. White pressed the issue in the NTWIU over the next two crucial years, whittling away at some of the worst abuses of subcontracting.[27]

TUUL also agitated for black-white unity and special attention to the needs of black workers in its small, vulnerable unions in the auto, steel, and textile industries. The constitution of the Auto Workers Union said that "we bitterly fight against all forms of discrimination against Negroes." The Metal Workers Industrial League pledged a "special" defense of "especially oppressed" black workers. But such statements were declamatory and not sufficient for the Profintern, which zealously monitored TUUL. Taking a strikingly advanced view, the Profintern said that TUUL had not promoted blacks "to GENERAL leadership and direction of all workers' struggles — black and white." No TUUL union, no matter its vulnerability or the pain of difficult strikes, was exempt from pressure for action on the needs and demands of black workers. And that pressure was shaping the institutional character of the revolutionary unions.[28]

UNION ORGANIZING — SOUTH

How could a small political party with a largely foreign-born membership organize in a vast section of the United States where it had never been visible until William Z. Foster's campaign swing in 1928? One way was to find organizers willing to venture into dangerous territory and pass out literature, make speeches from soapboxes, and live from hand to mouth. Usually their only contacts were foreign-born merchants, skilled workers, and professionals whose origins were in Europe or in the old Socialist or Wobbly traditions. From them, organizers would obtain additional contacts, funds, and access to meeting halls.[29]

Party organizer Tom Johnson gave a backhanded testimonial to the importance of the ethnic enclaves in building the Party in the South. The CP-influenced International Workers Order had some Jewish affiliates in Dixie, whose members Johnson characterized as petty-bourgeois "dead wood," fretting endlessly about the impact upon their businesses of interracial gatherings in their meeting halls. But he admitted that they were always ready with funds and facilities.[30]

Norfolk, Virginia, had a "Jewish-speaking" *(sic)* Party unit with "not a single proletarian element" and a bad case of political paralysis regarding blacks. The unit guided a young organizer, Stephen Graham, to a job at the Southern Spring Manufacturing Company, where 85 percent of the workers were young black women making as little as one dollar a day at sewing. The plant was part of the smokestack skyline of mills and factories in an industrializing city. Graham began to talk to some workers about the TUUL and sometimes visited their homes. On October 15, 1929, he called a meeting to talk union; one hundred fifty workers, most of them black, mostly from Southern Spring, showed up. Local detectives arrested Graham, telling him that he had "no right calling niggers to meetings." His room was ransacked and his literature confiscated. He was charged under an old Virginia statute that outlawed "conspiracy to incite the colored population to insurrection against the white population." Graham was acquitted. However, at the conclusion of the trial he was arrested and held for deportation to his native Yugoslavia. He wasn't a native-born American, and his name wasn't Graham. Nevertheless, this young man was able to cross a cultural chasm to plant the seeds of militant interracial unionism in Norfolk.[31]

Like other mill towns, Gastonia, North Carolina, had absorbed dirt-poor white sharecropping and tenant families who were part of the rural exodus. In early 1929 organizers for the TUUL's new National Textile Workers Union began some muted probing among the millworkers at the Loray Mills in Gastonia. At Loray machines were replacing human labor; surviving workers were beset by speed-up, long hours, and pitiful wages for adults (even worse wages for children). The ubiquitous fibers lodged in the lungs and made the workers ill. Company housing was miserable, sanitation was primitive, and education was nearly nonexistent. The mill's work force of white hill people gradually responded to the appeals of the NTWU's young, grimy, and largely inexperienced organizers. Twenty-two hundred workers struck in early April 1929.[32]

The powers-that-be in Gaston County reacted to the strike with murderous hysteria. Strikers, including women and children, were terrorized, beaten, and evicted from company housing; a mob of vigilantes destroyed strike headquarters. The police chief and four deputies invaded the union grounds without a warrant, and in the ensuing melee the chief was fatally wounded. Amid cries of Bolshevism, "nigger love," and "free love," a trial of fifteen strikers and TUUL organizers ended in a mistrial when a juror snapped mentally at the sight of a bloody effigy of the police chief, introduced as evidence by the prosecution. A second trial in the fall, with the defendants reduced to seven men, including five Communists, ended with convictions and long sentences. On the same day another jury refused to indict anybody for the murder of Ella May Wiggins, a twenty-nine-year-old mother of five who had been killed by company thugs on the way to a union meeting.[33]

In the midst of these events, the Party insisted on making Gastonia a testing ground for the solidarity of black and white labor. The NTWU would use Gastonia to facilitate a long-range goal of wiping out Jim Crow in southern industry. Poor whites who lived on a consoling fiction of racial superiority would learn that the bosses' wrath made no distinction between the races; blacks would shed their historic disdain for "white trash" and see poor whites as allies. In October 1929 the new Southern District of the TUUL and the NTWU held conferences at Charlotte, about twenty miles from Gastonia, in an atmosphere of incipient terror. Black delegates were prominent in both meetings: Charles Alexander, Solomon Harper, and a half-dozen other blacks sat among the white delegates in open defiance of Jim Crow. Foster claimed that white workers in attendance were not the least upset by the blacks' presence.[34]

Interracial solidarity was already a watchword in New Orleans, where the TUUL's nascent Marine Workers' Industrial Union fought to organize that city's thousands of longshoremen, especially black dockworkers who earned as little as thirty cents an hour. But in the southern textile mills only about 5 percent of the workers were black — mainly sweepers, feeders, handlers, and porters. The NTWU had organized some black workers around Gastonia and nearby Bessemer City. In Gastonia itself, there were no black millworkers, but blacks labored in a miserable waste mill that was attached to Loray. The NTWU initially had trouble recruiting them, but as a result of pressure from the Party, the Gastonia local launched an organizing drive among blacks that netted seventeen members.[35]

The ILD claimed that blacks were among the strikers and that the police invasion of the strikers' tent colony was based on the pretext that they "had heard that there was a fight between a white and Negro worker." Scores of Negroes milled about the Gaston County courthouse at the first trial in an attempt to greet the strike leaders charged with murder and conspiracy. When the second trial in the police chief's slaying began in September at Charlotte, the ILD organized a biracial "workers' jury" to observe the proceedings. The "jury" created a sensation when its members refused to be segregated and observed the entire trial from the Jim Crow gallery.[36]

Not a word was spoken about self-determination or the state unity of the Black Belt. Nevertheless, CI injunctions placed organizers under relentless pressure to challenge the region's racial practices. The NTWU ran into trouble persuading white workers to join nonsegregated locals. Jack Johnstone, a leader of the struggle to defend black packinghouse workers in the Red Summer of 1919, was the Party's Central Committee representative at Gastonia. He reportedly sympathized with the view that black-white locals undermined the unionization of white workers. Albert Weisbord, one of the chief organizers, conceded that white workers need not fraternize with blacks or intermarry. That was an unpardonable retreat in the eyes of the Party and its Comintern-Profintern mentors.[37]

Cyril Briggs worried about the comrades "soft-pedaling" the Negro question in the South. No Communist would be allowed to claim that he was unfamiliar with CI and RILU resolutions demanding that Negroes be organized on the basis of full equality. Could Communists get away with a couple of speeches advocating equality "and let it go at that"? Could such declarations be qualified by showing that they did not extend to personal biracial friendships? Or by Communists "throw[ing] up their hands at the specter of intermarriage? . . . emphatically no!"[38]

Otto Hall had been dispatched to Gastonia. Briggs pressed his criticism: Most of the organizers were eager to shift the burden of fighting chauvinism to Comrade Hall. But something happened on June 7, the night of the shootout at the strikers' tent colony. At the moment of the raid that killed the police chief, Hall, a principal target of the union busters, was meeting with black workers at Bessemer City. Though deprived of direction because their leaders had been jailed, rank-and-file white strikers slipped through a police cordon around Gastonia, intercepted Hall's car, spirited him to a railroad station forty miles from Gastonia, and got him on a train to New York City. Briggs marveled at the change in attitude among the first white workers "to come under our leadership." Hall added that although racism was far from ended in Gastonia, a major step had been taken toward its elimination.[39]

The Baltimore *Afro-American's* reporter on the scene was not so sure. But he conceded that for the first time among the poor white southern millworkers, "the necessity of open cooperation with colored workers" had been brought home. In the short run, the Party's "premature integrationism" could not affect a strike that was reeling under repeated blows from a "Committee of 100" organized by the mill operators to spread intimidation and terror. By the winter of 1930 the mills were again working their usual twelve-hour shifts, and the workers were as hungry and miserable as they had been before the strike. Someone who had been there said that "Ella May Wiggins was the only one at peace."[40]

According to James W. Ford, every white southern delegate at the NTWU convention in December 1929 rose to testify to his liberation from the shackles of racism. There were no declarations of allegiance to a black nation, but there were expressions that unity was the only basis for overcoming the rotten conditions in the South. However, the chasm between aspiration and attainment remained: no black delegates from the South were in attendance.[41]

From 1929 through the early 1930s the TUUL remained a mongrel force on the labor front—isolated from the AFL, taking on the most dangerous and intractable strikes, hobbled by its sectarian outlook and dogmatic tactics, harassed by the Party and the Profintern for its inadequacies and failures. Its inner workings were undoubtedly motivated by diktat, but the courage of its organizers and its vision of racial equality, no matter the source, were inspired by concepts of revolutionary necessity and sacred proletarian duty. It experienced a mild resurgence after the election of Franklin D. Roosevelt in 1933. And when it was phased out in 1934, its antiracist consciousness flowed into the founding of the Congress of Industrial Organizations. But in the late 1920s and early 1930s, it won no major strikes. Masses of blacks (and whites) were outside labor's ranks; the Depression squeezed the labor market and made union organization an onerous and frustrating task. The struggle for unity would have to be conducted on many more fronts, and would have to be led by the Communist Party in its own name.

CHAPTER SEVEN

The Communist Party in the Deep South

The decade of the 1920s had been strewn with resolutions calling for building the Party in the South. Nothing had been done save "journalistic protest" against lynching and other outrages. But by the winter of 1930 the Party was free of Lovestone and the theory of the rural South as a reserve of reaction. The Depression was deepening, and suffering in the South was incalculable. There could be no delay in reaching the black population of the South. The Party's 1930 convention called for the Political Bureau to establish three new southern districts, anchored in Birmingham, Winston-Salem, and New Orleans. Negro and white organizers were to be stationed in those cities immediately, and funds were to be provided for "one or two agitators" to assist the organizers.[1]

The Communist Party proceeded to build an organization in the South. At its heart was Alabama. The combination of a black industrial work force in Birmingham with a rural sharecropping and tenant economy nearby was nearly ideal for a synergy of immensely able urban and rural organizers and activists. The local base was augmented by the assignment to Birmingham of the Party's most talented organizers.[2]

Tom Johnson was dispatched to Birmingham. He had been an IWW organizer in northern Ohio. His belief in the revolutionary potential of the black population could not have been tested in a more fitting place—an iron-ore city of mines and mills, filled with a relatively new and young proletariat drawn largely from the countryside, as well as a small, vibrant middle class with plentiful religious and social organizations. Birmingham had faint traces of past labor struggles in the mines and steel mills, of a once potent Knights of Labor, and of a Socialist Party in its heyday. There was also a recent legacy of KKK intimidation and racist violence, which left no hope for a radical fusion of black and white labor. Birmingham was also reeling from the Depression, and predictably, the black working-class women and men were bearing the worst. That winter of 1930, things were so bad in the black neighborhoods that even the largest churches lacked pastors — there was no money among their memberships to pay for a spiritual leader. Deep wage cuts for whites and blacks were common, as were robbery and theft. A report by the NUL noted that "many poor children of unemployed parents can be seen daily on the city dump hunting for cast-away foods or bread that has been sent out by grocers as not being fit for food."[3]

Johnson was soon joined by another white Communist assigned to the TUUL, Harry Jackson. Jackson was a veteran longshore organizer in San Francisco, endowed with Wobbly courage, a taste for combat with the class enemy, and a gritty, profane personality.[4] Neither he nor Johnson feared getting into risky situations. A thin thread of contacts enabled the organizers to get started. An Italian metalworker, James Giglio, had set up a branch of the TUUL's Metal Workers Industrial League. Through Giglio, Johnson was soon meeting with black steelworkers at Tennessee Coal and Iron in Ensley, an industrial suburb. He also walked into the black community, got up on a soapbox, and talked to people about lynching, discrimination, hunger, and the denial of elementary rights, such as education and self-expression. He talked about self-determination in the Black Belt, but according to James S. Allen, "we weren't stupid." Self-determination was defined as democracy at its essence: self-government, self-organization, social and economic equality, the right of blacks to run their own lives without the relentless terror and racism that dogged their steps and made every waking day a living hell. Little was left of a bare-bones class appeal that had been standard just five years earlier; now there was a discernible attempt to touch a brutally oppressed national existence, worsened by the economic crisis. That meeting yielded the first black recruits in Birmingham. Weeks later, a crowd of about two hundred people, mostly blacks, attended an integrated indoor meeting where Walter Lewis, a young black steelworker and new member from Montgomery, joined Johnson and Giglio in addressing the audience. The response was swift and vicious: Giglio's home was firebombed.[5]

Another mass meeting was held in late May with no diminution in the audience's size or change in its racial composition. Eighteen-year-old Angelo Herndon attended that meeting and was mesmerized by the sight of a white man denouncing segregation and calling on black and white workers to stand together to defend their common interests. He had never encountered anything like that before, and the Communist litany of capitalist racism and class struggle seemed to explain the troubles that beset him and his family. Herndon had been born in the small mining town of Wyoming, Ohio, in 1913. His father, who died when Angelo was just nine years old, was a black coalminer, his mother a domestic worker of black, white, and Native American ancestry. A sickly, religious youth, Herndon at the age of thirteen went to Kentucky with an older brother to seek work in the mines. The brothers eventually moved on to Birmingham to look for work in that area's mines, where they encountered miserable working conditions, long hours, and low wages. Herndon also found communism.[6]

With the arrival of spring in 1930 the Communists moved into Birmingham's Capitol Park. From there, they led an improvised march to the local charity headquarters to demand immediate relief. The city passed an ordinance to rein in the Communists' "criminal anarchy." The public clashes in Birmingham, unlike Harlem's street battles, did not take place amid a cacophony of groups competing for the allegiance of an ethnically complex, heterogeneous community. The Party was the only organization that came to town offering resistance to the hunger that was spreading through largely homogeneous and native black Birmingham. Blacks responded to the Party, and did so in far greater numbers than whites. By the fall of 1930 perhaps five hundred people were involved in Party-sponsored activities. In the 1930 election the Communists shook up the state's political status quo, nominating Walter Lewis for governor on a platform of equality, self-determination, relief, and an end to lynching.[7]

It did not take long for Hamilton Fish, one of the most devout anticommunists in the Congress, to bring his investigating apparatus to Birmingham. Witnesses conjured up fantastic stories of maniacal foreigners leading up to eight thousand gullible followers, most of them black. But for the now hardened organizers, attention from a congressional committee only confirmed the impact of their efforts. As the situation grew worse, the Party established new units in metal shops and mines, and among workers on a cotton plantation north of Birmingham. It even began to gain a few white members among the farmers and miners of northern Alabama.[8]

As the winter of 1931 approached, economic conditions were worsening. The Party's ambitious plans to extend the TUUL among those who held jobs in the mines and factories had to give way to the urgent issue of relief for the jobless. Throughout the fall of 1930 the Party organized rallies to address evictions and homelessness. It added a new concept, one that played a major role in the social struggles of the decade: social insurance with minimum cash assistance of $25 a week for jobless workers. The rallies now attracted thousands of people, despite the arrests of Herndon and Johnson at a September meeting and the arrest of Jackson on the way to a rally of unemployed steelworkers in Ensley. In December Joe Burton, an eighteen-year-old black YCL recruit, led a crowd of five thousand from a construction site where they had sought a handful of jobs to the Hotel Morris from where, according to the *Daily Worker*, "the capitalists had fled."[9]

The Growth of Local Leadership

Out of the Party's growing base in the black community came a local leadership, new to communism, but steeped in a rich social and cultural consciousness. Robin D.G. Kelley, in his incomparable study of Alabama Communists, points to the emergence of women who came to the Party through neighborhood relief committees and battles for adequate assistance from the city's welfare board. Addie Adkins, Alice Mosley, and Cornelia Foreman all were drawn to activism through struggles for sufficient relief. Helen Longs joined the Party because of its opposition to the Red Cross's draconian relief programs, which subjected black workers to prisonlike works projects for the lowest relief payments in the country. Estelle Milner, a young Birmingham schoolteacher, organized sharecroppers in Tallapoosa County. A small group of white working-class women led by Mary Leonard was drawn to the local Unemployed Council and from there to confrontations with the city welfare board—demanding food, clothing, decent medical care for desperately poor whites, and respect for women by the authorities.[10]

The cohesion and deep southern roots of Birmingham's black working class produced an exceptional group of leaders, many of whom went on to play important roles in larger arenas. One of these was Al Murphy, born in 1908 in McRae, Georgia, into a family of poor sharecroppers. His was a religious and race-conscious lineage: One grandfather had been a minister of the African Methodist Episcopal Church and a presiding elder under Bishop Henry McNeil Turner, a clarion voice of black emigration in the late nineteenth century. As a marginally educated teenager, Murphy moved in with an aunt and uncle in Tuscaloosa, where he dug ditches, picked cotton, and handled corrosive chemicals in a pipe foundry. At the age of fifteen Murphy came to Birmingham, where he continued his low-paid, onerous labors. But Murphy also enrolled in night school with a vague ambition to find a place in the limited sphere of black politics. When the Depression hit, Murphy's education shifted from night school to the bread line. One morning in the fall of 1930 he read a leaflet calling for an end to lynching, "full rights for the Negro people," and opposition to "imperialist war." That leaflet haunted him; he talked about it with Frank Williams, a friend who had recently joined the Party. Williams brought Murphy to a meeting of the Unemployed Council, and the young man joined the Party almost immediately.[11]

Murphy combined an introspective, analytical approach with a knowing familiarity with the brutal essence of Jim Crow. Feelings seethed inside him, but he rarely, if ever, raised his voice in anger. A rather small man with a body hardened by onerous labor, he found in Marxism an explanation for the racism and exploitation that had shaped his young life. His low-key persona served him well as an ironworker in the Stockham steel plant in Birmingham where he sought to recruit black workers for the TUUL. Among his recruits was Hosea Hudson.[12]

Hudson was born in rural Georgia in 1898 into a sharecropper family. At fifteen he took up sharecropping to help support his family after his mother remarried and left their home. Hudson himself married in 1917 and continued sharecropping until his crop was wiped out by the boll weevil in 1921. In 1923 he moved to Birmingham and found a job as an iron molder at Stockham. Like Murphy, Hudson inherited a long memory, especially from his grandmother, of slavery and of Reconstruction's promise and betrayal. Hudson had grown up protecting his own humanity, refusing to bow before injustice; dwelling in his consciousness was a sense of earthly liberation that was as compelling as the gospel singing that formed part of his religious life.[13]

Hudson joined the Party on September 8, 1931. The date is enshrined in his remarkable writing with a solemnity that one gives to a marriage date or the birth of a child. The oppressive working conditions and the low pay at the foundry were not the immediate inducements to sign up. He was angered by the Scottsboro case (see chapter 11) and the murderous assault on black sharecroppers at Camp Hill. Both of those incidents symbolized in Hudson's mind a cumulative attack on all Negroes. His response was to "national" suffering, and in that sense his feelings typified what the Party meant by the "national question." The Party became a substitute church, extending in Hudson's mind a system of values and a code of moral behavior: "We all thought, 'well, now, this is the real religion,' 'cause they said that Party members shouldn't mess around with another Party member's wife or his daughter... and live a clean life, get out and meet the public, people look upon you as a leader."[14]

Hudson joined the CP with eight other black workers, six from the Stockham foundry. He was elected "unit organizer" of the Stockham group and in that capacity met with other Birmingham unit leaders. He encountered a seriousness and discipline among his black comrades that was transforming for a man who claimed his interests had previously been mostly gospel music and women. The unit organizers talked about new political developments, immediate tasks, the Scottsboro campaign, cases of police brutality, ways to activate all members, checking on fulfillment of assignments, and "criticism and self-criticism." They tussled with the intricacies of self-determination and were comforted that Communists were obliged to support it "to the point of separation," but not necessarily to the act itself. Those meetings were all black; the fashioning of agendas and tasks was an exclusively black enterprise. This reflected in part the difficulty of communication between white organizers from the North and the overwhelmingly black membership of the Birmingham CP organization. The first white comrade Hudson met was Harry Simms (Harry Hirsch), a nineteen-year-old from Springfield, Massachusetts, who became a liaison with the Share Croppers' Union. He was killed in the Kentucky coal strike of 1932.[15]

In late January 1932 Hudson was fired by Stockham along with two fellow workers. By that time Hudson was leading an underground fraction at the plant that had grown to six units with six members each. The sacking of Hudson and his comrades frightened other recruits, and attendance at unit meetings dropped sharply. It was in the dead of winter, Stockham was laying off many workers, and contact with the Party was broken: "We could not see anybody to tell us what to do." On a frosty night, standing at a footbridge, Hudson told his fired comrade John Beidel that he was thinking about going to Atlanta to seek work. Beidel begged not to be left alone; Hudson realized that he could not walk away from Birmingham, and he agreed to help rebuild the units. Within weeks another Party unit had been formed, composed of both working and jobless women and men. The unit moved out to the larger community, building a core of supporters, spreading news of Scottsboro, distributing the *Sunday Worker* and the *Southern Worker,* often surreptitiously drop-ping literature on porches in the dead of night, putting leaflets and newspapers on church steps, and then following up with conversations among those exposed to the literature — always making sure that they were not talking to "police pimps."[16]

In the spring of 1932 Harry Jackson brought a new district organizer to the unit meeting. Nat Ross was a Jewish New Yorker and Columbia University graduate who had briefly attended Harvard Law School before joining the Party. A thoroughgoing Leninist, he insisted on stern discipline and tight orga-nization. Hudson's unit had found a private home that became a headquarters for its members, a place to "chure [chew] the rag," to discuss issues, play check-ers, and cultivate closeness and mutual support. After Ross's arrival, the Party took a major step: It organized an all-day conference on a Sunday in April. Otto Hall came from Atlanta, and so did Angelo Herndon, returning to Birm-ingham after leading a successful demonstration of white and black unemployed to Atlanta's City Hall. Sharecroppers from Camp Hill and Reeltown came, mak-ing this the first full-scale meeting between urban and rural radicals. A Dis-trict 17 bureau was established, composed of Hudson, Ross, Henry Mayfield from the coal mines, Cornelia Foreman, Otto Hall, and a white farmer from Walker County. Since biracial meetings in Birmingham were permitted only between "the better class of Negroes" and a few white ministers, bureau gath-erings had to be secret all-day affairs in the homes of sympathetic non-Party Negroes. Each bureau member was responsible to bring one other to the meet-ing, whose location was secret. Arrangements were generally made to meet on a street corner in early morning during police shift changes. If someone was more than five minutes late, his contact was instructed not to wait; the tardy member, said Hudson, had to "have a veary good reasin for no shoring [show-ing] up on time . . . if they did not . . . we would all give him or her hell."[17]

By early 1932 the Birmingham Party had a coherent southern program: free-dom for the Scottsboro boys; interracial unions; the right of blacks to vote, hold office, and serve on juries; the right of sharecroppers to sell their own crops; public jobs at union wages; unemployment and social insurance; direct cash relief; and full social and political equality. For Hudson and his comrades, such a program arose in large measure from their own experiences. In answer to the relentless charge that the Party was using blacks for its own (read "So-viet") ends, Hudson replied that the poor blacks drawn to the Party "knowed that they didn't have nothing but they chains of slavery to lose." As Hudson saw it, the Party was a working-class political organization, and blacks were members of the working class, an inseparable part of a movement dedicated to breaking "they chains of slavery." How then could a people be "used" by themselves? After all, their identities had become embedded in the Party. The organization became Hudson's spiritual home, a repository of values and a source of education both practical and theoretical. Don West, a Georgia minister, Party member, and co-founder of the legendary Highlander Folk School, attended "Party school" with Hudson in New York and helped him become literate. For all the leading black Communists of Birmingham, a wider world opened. Mac Coad, Archie Mosley, Cornelia Foreman, Henry Mayfield, and Al Murphy all traveled to Moscow in the 1930s. Murphy was a delegate to the Seventh CI Congress in 1935; Coad fought for the International Brigades in the Spanish Civil War. But what they built in Alabama was their most significant legacy—especially the Share Croppers' Union.[18]

The Share Croppers' Union

The movement to build a union of croppers got off to a slow and largely unplanned start. The first few issues of the *Southern Worker* (which began publication in August 1930) had very little on the rural South. In spring 1930 the Party's "Draft Program for Negro Farmers in the Southern States" stressed the role of industrial workers in leading the agrarian movement. James S. Allen expressed similar views in the pages of the Party's theoretical journal.[19]

In 1930 Party member Horace B. Davis was teaching at Southwestern College in Memphis. In January he and his wife Marion drove south from Memphis to the Mississippi delta region and then to northern Alabama. They talked with a white sharecropper "who had his grievances." Davis dropped a hint to the receptive cropper that an organization might help. He then wrote an article that appeared on the front page of the *Daily Worker,* saying that the croppers were "ripe for organization . . . rotten ripe." Something was stirring. Shortly afterward, white tenant farmers in northern Alabama approached the TUUL asking for help in getting government relief. This was the first actual contact between Alabama Communists and rural workers.[20]

Tallapoosa, Lowndes, Lee, and other rural Alabama counties were full of black and white sharecroppers. Black farm laborers were especially tied to cotton, and they lived in landlord-furnished shacks that lacked running water and adequate sanitation. By early 1931 the cotton economy was near collapse. Food and cash advances before harvesting were threatened, debts were mounting, and the crisis in the city deprived rural labor of an economic safety valve. A January 1931 protest march of five hundred sharecroppers in England, Arkansas, inspired the Party to call upon Alabama farmers to organize relief councils, begin hunger marches, demand food and clothing from merchants, and join with urban workers in the fight for bread.[21]

A black Communist from Birmingham dropped leaflets and spread the *Southern Worker* around while visiting relatives and friends in the countryside. The paper soon received letters from sharecroppers and tenants wanting to learn about the Party, asking for instructions on how to fight back, and describing their plight in desperate and poignant terms. The Party embraced more tightly its claims of a revolutionary national consciousness in the Black Belt. Cries of peonage, semi-slavery, and brutal exploitation punctuated the *Daily Worker, Labor Unity, Working Woman, Labor Defender, The Liberator, New Masses, Southern Worker,* and the ethnic press. Descriptions and photos of rural black families barely staying alive in one-room hovels, "old slave cabins," appeared with regularity. The predicaments of white tenants and croppers evoked sympathy, but they had options not available to blacks. Landlords were refusing to turn over to black tenants their rightful share of proceeds from the crop sales. If black tenants and sharecroppers dared protest the "theft" of their crops, they were called "bad niggers" and exposed to violence that was sanctioned and abetted by local sheriffs. Croppers and tenants were increasingly forbidden to raise their own garden and poultry stock, thus being forced to rely on credit and food allowances that were increasingly withheld. Throughout 1931 there loomed the threat of cutoff of food credits. Laborers were receiving as little as three to four cents per pound of cotton after paying out of their own pockets for ginning. Landlords were allegedly stealing Federal Farm Board loans intended for croppers and tenants. Whole crops belonging to tenants were being seized. Wives and daughters of croppers were being pressed into service to white women for as little as a dime a week in some cases, and there was a reported increase of rape of black women by landlords. Black children were not attending school. Landlords were telling tenants and croppers that receiving mail from New York or even Tennessee (where the Party had its regional headquarters) was "against the law."[22]

In February 1931 Angelo Herndon ventured into Wilcox County. He witnessed the sharecroppers' distress and sought to organize them into the Party's United Farmers League. But he was forced to run for his life when local authorities learned of his whereabouts. An attempt to link black contacts with white farmers in northern Alabama foundered when most whites resisted the Party slogans of social equality, which the Party refused to trim or abandon.[23]

The Croppers' and Farm Workers' Union took hold in the flat farmlands of southeastern Tallapoosa County. Estelle Milner, daughter of a Tallapoosa share-cropper, secretly distributed leaflets and copies of the *Southern Worker* in strategic places throughout the area. A former sharecropper and now strug-gling owner of a small farm, Ralph Gray, had had a violent confrontation with a merchant who had bilked him out of federal loan money, after which Gray contacted the Party and asked for an organizer to help him and his brother Tommy build a union. Ralph also joined the Communist Party. The long mem-ory of resistance was part of the Gray family heritage; a grandfather, Alfred Gray, had been a state legislator during Reconstruction and an outspoken de-fender of the egalitarian principles associated with radical Reconstruction.[24]

Mac Coad was sent to Tallapoosa in response to Gray's request. Originally from Charleston, South Carolina, he was a Birmingham steelworker who be-came a Communist in 1930. In the spring of 1931 Coad went to the rural area as "Jim Wright," secretary of the Croppers' and Farm Workers' Union. He ar-rived when several landlords had withdrawn cash and food advances in an at-tempt to force croppers into a newly built sawmill that needed labor for ardu-ous work at miserable wages — work seen as "fit" only for blacks. Coad quietly urged local tenants and croppers to resist the sawmill and to press for contin-uance of food allowances until crop settlement time, for the right to sell their goods where they saw fit, for a two-dollar-a-day minimum wage for agricul-tural workers, and for free school transportation for the children. After two months of organizing, the Party reported that eight hundred farmers had paid a five-cent initiation fee to the "Society for the Advancement of Colored People," a title used to conceal the existence of a croppers' and tenant's union. The CFWU won a temporary restoration of food advances.[25]

On July 1 the landlords of Lee and Tallapoosa Counties decreed that food allowances to croppers and tenants were to be cut off. Scottsboro also became a major concern. The convergence of a case of racist "lynch justice" with the economic demands of the tenants and croppers gave a union a deeper, more political, more racial, and more nationally conscious orientation. The landlords and their police reacted with heightened fury.[26]

On the night of July 15 about eighty black women and men crowded into a makeshift church at Dadeville to hear Coad talk about Scottsboro. Tipped off by an informer, Tallapoosa County sheriff Kyle Young and deputized vigilantes raided the meeting, indiscriminately beating men and women. The gang then went to Tommy Gray's home looking for information on the union — and in the process attacked his wife, who suffered a fractured skull. The following night a hundred fifty croppers again met with Coad in a vacant house southwest of Camp Hill. The sheriff mobilized a posse for attack, but encountered Ralph Gray standing guard about a quarter-mile from the from the meeting. After heated argument, shots were exchanged; Sheriff Young was shot in the stomach, and Gray's legs were riddled with bullets. The meeting house was burned to the ground. As the sheriff was rushed to a hospital, union members took Gray to his home and barricaded themselves inside. They were able to hold off a posse until most croppers had escaped. Gray refused to leave; police reinforcements returned and murdered him while his family watched in horror. His house was burned and his body dumped at the Dadeville courthouse.[27]

The Camp Hill events set off a flurry of rumor, hysteria, and more violence. "Deputies" roamed the countryside, freely terrorizing blacks. Thirty-seven black men, at least nine of them under eighteen years of age, were arrested near Camp Hill. Five union members were charged with carrying concealed weapons or conspiring to commit murder. Frightened tenants and croppers fled to the woods; four black croppers were "sent to cut stove wood," a euphemism for lynching. Coad was forced to flee to Atlanta. Estelle Milner was attacked by police after a local black minister accused her of hoarding ammunition; she suffered a fractured vertebra. Howard Kester of the Fellowship of Reconciliation reported after a ten-day investigation that "several" people had died from wounds suffered in the attacks and had been quietly buried.[28]

The brutal response of Tallapoosa authorities to the union was not lost upon the NAACP. A telegram from Secretary Walter White to branches blamed "the trouble at Camp Hill . . . [on] white men from Chattanooga [who] stirred Negroes to action and then left Negroes holding the bag." The entire episode spelled race suicide for the rural poor, attributable directly to the recklessness of Communists in a region that was dangerous enough without the added radical provocation. The union's use of the name "Society for the Advancement of Colored People" as a cover spurred White to issue a firm denial that the NAACP had had anything to do with the Camp Hill events. The Party press, in vintage Third Period fashion, said the NAACP had "sealed a bond with the KKK" for calling the croppers "innocent dupes" while failing to condemn the peonage and semi-slavery under which Black Belt Negroes lived. Du Bois responded that the NAACP was not dishonest or cowardly: If the "half-starved and desperate" sharecroppers had indeed been induced by the Communists to protest Scottsboro, "it is too despicable for words," because an ill-timed confrontation between "radicals and rednecks" would undermine the fight to save the lives of "eight innocent children." Du Bois was not aware that the sharecroppers had initiated the meeting without regard for the Party's discouragement of "mass" gatherings where a threat of terror existed.[29]

Unlike the Scottsboro defendants, the Camp Hill croppers caught in the police net were already in the CP orbit. There would be no struggle over legal representation; the ILD would do the job. Alabama authorities were leery of another Scottsboro with the possibility of global "mass actions." ILD attorney Irving Schwab got all but seven of the jailed croppers released on grounds of insufficient evidence; the remaining group was freed later after hearings were postponed indefinitely.[30]

Less than a month after Camp Hill, fifty-five members of the CFWU re-grouped five locals into a reconstituted Share Croppers' Union in Tallapoosa County. By September landlords were again threatening to cut off food and cash allowances after the cotton crop was picked. The SCU geared up for a new round of struggle. However, it lacked a leader, and its only tie to the Party between August 1931 and early 1932 was Harry Simms, who provided a tenuous link between district leaders and the SCU. Tommy Gray tried to continue organizing, but his life was under constant threat. His nineteen-year-old daughter Eula, a YCL member, held the union together when Simms left for Kentucky in late 1931. She was an unofficial secretary until May 1932, during which time the union grew to more than five hundred members in twenty-eight locals, ten youth affiliates, and twelve women's auxiliaries. The SCU had also spread to Lee and Macon Counties. The Party noted that "substantial organizational work [among the sharecroppers] has proceeded without interruption for several months although our organizations have . . . failed to give guidance for many weeks." The Party apparently never fully recognized the magnitude of Eula Gray's contribution.[31]

When Al Murphy took over as SCU secretary in mid-1932, he found a resilient, fairly well-organized body in the eastern Piedmont. In a drive to expand beyond that area, Murphy set up headquarters in Montgomery with the help of Charles Tasker, the head of that city's Unemployed Council, and his wife Capitola, who headed the SCU women's auxiliaries. Murphy instituted a rigorous, security-conscious regime, in which meetings were held in small groups often masquerading as Bible discussion clubs. There was a ban on gatherings in empty houses that were vulnerable to detection; the use of firearms was banned except under the most threatening circumstances, and a surface calm, even humility, was imposed to conceal the underlying resolve — and the guns that were always within reach. He set up a system of "captains" for each local, thereby decentralizing the organization and providing new grassroots leadership. He warned the captains against becoming arbitrary and self-centered. Murphy favored an all-black union, but he also welcomed the often clandestine support of poor white farmers. Some whites, especially women, would occasionally venture into SCU meetings to tell tales of suffering and woe that brought tears to many listeners. But open white participation was virtually impossible; J. W. Davis, a white supporter of the SCU, was lynched in 1934. Whites helped by contributing food and supplies to the union and sometimes hiding activists during severe repression. One year after Camp Hill, the SCU had exceeded its strength before the murder of Ralph Gray. Harry Haywood, when head of the Party's Negro Department in 1933, was eager for a firsthand look at the Deep South, the object of his theoretical ruminations. After spending some weeks in Alabama, including attendance at clandestine union meetings that often bristled with guns, Haywood concluded that the union, with its economic and political concerns and its culture of resistance, had become the realization of the revolutionary potential of the rural black population.[32]

Beyond Alabama

Chattanooga, Tennessee, a center of commerce and light industry, had been an active area of TUEL activity. The remnants of the old education league provided contacts, funds, and a modicum of security for Party operations in this relatively "liberal" city. Chattanooga was the second largest sector of Communist activity in the South, the CP's District 17 headquarters, and the home of the *Southern Worker*. Black membership in the Party and its affiliate groups was significant, but not as dominant as in Birmingham. Altogether Chattanooga offered a better climate for biracial activity. The Chattanooga Party ran forums, conferences (including an antilynch conference in November 1930 and the first All-Southern Conference on Scottsboro in June 1931), conventions, demonstrations, election campaigns, and anti-eviction protests. The situation in Memphis, Tennessee, was tougher. When Marion Davis and Tom Johnson attempted to hold an open-air meeting there to protest the arrest of the "Atlanta Six," they were jailed immediately. Lacking a liberal tradition and a stable working class, Memphis posed problems for organizers.[33]

By late 1930 District 17 also had contacts or units in New Orleans, Atlanta, Elizabethton, Tennessee, and Whitney, Alabama.[34] The Party's New Orleans organization grew largely out of the activities of the TUUL's Marine Workers' Industrial Union and the Unemployed Councils. In February 1931 a strike against wage and job cutbacks broke out on the New Orleans docks. In early March injunctions against mass picketing were issued, and 115 workers were jailed, most of them Negroes, according to the *Southern Worker*. Organized protest involving large numbers of Negroes spread to Shreveport, where over five hundred blacks joined with fifteen hundred white unemployed to demand "work or food." But those movements did not receive the same amount of effort that was bestowed upon Birmingham. The New Orleans movement literally hugged the docks and did not directly affect the countryside.

In late 1933 the Party and affiliate groups still lacked the resources for sustained organizing in Louisiana and Mississippi, and thus were unable to tap into sharecropper and tenant discontent. A black organizer, "C. Clark," roved through the Black Belt, spreading news of the Unemployed Councils. Invariably, the croppers and agricultural workers wanted information on how to organize. At Wismer, Louisiana, Clark was able to get fifty workers on the plantation where he labored to strike for a higher wage. However, he was undone by "stool pigeons" who tipped off the riding bosses. He was immediately fired and warned to leave Wismer before dawn. He made his way to Mississippi, where nearly every farmer with whom he spoke described near starvation with no relief in sight. At a field "thick with sharecroppers" he talked about organizing. That evening dozens of women and men crowded into a cabin to hear about the Scottsboro case and testify to their back-breaking labors and endless poverty. But Clark could only give the address of the Unemployed Councils and move on to Sibley, Mississippi, to speak at clandestine gatherings in churches and cotton fields. He estimated that he gave the Unemployed Councils' address to more than two thousand farm workers across Louisiana and Mississippi. But there is no strong evidence that the Party and affiliate groups were able to follow up.[35]

When Harry Simms took a side trip from Birmingham to Atlanta in 1931 to spend time with Angelo Herndon, he was amazed at the difference in the atmosphere. "Gee, you have a hell of a sight better place to work here. In fact it is a paradise in comparison with Birmingham," Herndon quoted Simms. A commercial, transportation, and administrative center of the New South, Atlanta had been the scene of effective unemployed demonstrations that had drawn blacks and whites into common outcry against hunger and joblessness. But to call it a comparative "paradise" says more about the repressiveness of Birmingham than about the liberality of Atlanta.[36]

On March 9 of that year the Party and the YCL attempted to hold a meeting in Atlanta's black business district. Two young white organizers, Joe Carr and M. H. Powers, were charged with detonating a tear gas bomb, although the police later admitted having set off the device themselves out of anger at a leaflet showing a young black and a young white in a heroic handshake. The incident didn't end there. Assistant Solicitor General John H. Hudson dug out an old slavery-era law that had been updated after the Civil War to harass carpetbaggers. Carr and Powers were charged with "attempting to incite insurrection" against the state of Georgia—a capital offense—and circulating "insurrectionary literature" (the leaflet with the black-white handshake). On May 21 Atlanta police raided another CP-sponsored meeting. Mary Dalton, age twenty, from New York and nineteen-year-old Anne Burlak, who had come to Atlanta from NTWU organizing in Greenville, South Carolina, were arrested along with two blacks: Herbert Newton from New York, who was an ANLC organizer, and Henry Story, an Atlanta printer. They too were charged with inciting insurrection and spreading seditious literature. On top of fears of Communist-inspired labor troubles, the arrest of two young white women with two black men aroused the sexual demons that lurked in the mind of the South.[37]

But there was a counter force of sorts in Atlanta. The Commission on Interracial Cooperation had no love or respect for the Reds, but it recognized the madness of resurrecting a statute aimed at slaves and carpetbaggers to trample constitutional rights. The CIC maintained contact with the NAACP and went about quietly organizing public opinion to oppose the prosecution. The ACLU sent its field agent Walter Wilson to cultivate opposition to the indictments among Atlanta's small but active liberal community. The case dragged through nine years of the Great Depression without being brought to trial. And the ILD was bled annually for bonding money to keep the six defendants out of jail. Finally, on August 30, 1939, the indictments were dropped against the Atlanta Six and eleven others, mainly blacks, who had been been charged under the same statute during the bad days of the early 1930s.[38]

Among the Atlanta jobless were white women and men who were desperate enough to join with blacks in demonstrations for relief—even under black leadership. But they were not usually willing to digest the Party's insistence on social equality or to join with blacks in an organized, disciplined setting.

The neighborhood units of the Party in the 1929–31 period appear to have been predominantly black.[39]

District 16 embraced Charlotte, Winston-Salem, Bessemer City, and Gastonia, North Carolina; Greenville and Charleston, South Carolina; and Richmond and Norfolk, Virginia. A small unit had survived the 1929 strike in Gastonia. The all-black Bessemer City group also managed to hang on. The National Textile Workers Union was able to sink some roots in Charlotte; in December 1930 the NTWU attracted four hundred jobless to a biracial meeting. An active chapter of the Unemployed Councils was on the scene in early 1931, running demonstrations against evictions. That year, the Party ran a black candidate, Timothy Williams, for City Council. A chapter of the Young Communist League was also formed in Charlotte, with activity focused on Scottsboro and the defense of a young black, James Wilson, whom the YCL referred to as a victim of a "local" Scottsboro. In July 1931 a Scottsboro meeting in Charlotte attracted five hundred people. However, the dream of interracial solidarity did not take root.[40]

Clara Holden, an organizer sent to North Carolina in 1931, reported that the Charlotte Unemployed Council was composed entirely of black workers. The level of activity in Winston-Salem in the early 1930s was lower than in Charlotte. Sporadic attempts were made to organize the jobless in that city, which lacked Charlotte's working-class base. A minuscule CP organization existed in Charleston, South Carolina. Greenville, however, was the scene of an active Unemployed Council, which had managed to build a biracial organization in the face of intimidation from the local KKK. The desperate situation among white millworkers had even provoked some vague talk that "there will be a revolution" as the heat of suffering melted surface manifestations of racism. An Unemployed Council of five hundred members, "half Negro and half-white," sprang up, with a thirty-member executive board that included four black women and eight black men. But throughout the region, the Party's organizer complained of self-segregation by both races. Small Party units managed to hang on in Norfolk and Richmond, Virginia.[41]

In the spring of 1931 a CP worker complained in *Party Organizer* that "one of the hardest jobs in the South is to overcome the bitter antagonism that the white workers have for the Negro workers. Capitalist propaganda sure has worked." There can be no question that the TUUL's insistence on integrated unions harmed its efforts to build a base in New South industries. Similarly, the Party's absolute commitment to black-white units (or all-black units where necessary) was an obstacle to attracting white workers. Nat Ross believed that the CP in the South should have been flexible in applying its fierce biracialism. He criticized purges of racially prejudiced whites, arguing that to accept only whites who were free of prejudice was a prescription for acute isolation.[42]

To insist that southern whites must enter the CP cleansed of chauvinism was indeed unrealistic in the extreme. But that issue was separable from the question of tolerating all-white TUUL unions or Party units — which the CP would never allow. To understand the sources of the Party's unbending insistence on an unsegregated black-white movement in the South, one has to go back to its failure in Negro work in the 1920s. At the end of the decade the Party had finally admitted the need to win the trust of blacks and to strongly resist any backsliding on social equality. The Communists had come to believe that racial segregation and the savaging of black identity represented both an institutional foundation for American capitalism and its weak point. To compromise with racism in any way strengthened capitalism and wounded its most potent foes. If the Party had temporized with equality, it would have been essentially no different from any other radical or liberal movement that extended a hand to blacks while allowing in its own structures the very circumstances that engendered inequality. Further, concessions to segregation and inequality would validate racism and sacrifice blacks' trust in white radicals. How effective could all-white unions be in a region where a black labor force could be used against them? White workers would be left with the same racial illusions and diversions that had perpetuated white upper-class rule in the Deep South and had made white labor economically vulnerable. Given the deep conservatism and repression in the South, all-white leftist labor and political organizations would have difficulty in any case. Organizational and political compromise on race would have robbed the Party of the potential for becoming part of a culture of opposition and resistance that would eventually influence a larger liberal community and help set the stage for the civil rights movement a quarter-century later. The Communist movement in the South may have been small and unreasonably inflexible, but its contributions to the struggle for equality were significant and enduring.

Chapter Eight

Wipe Out the Stench of the Slave Market

In May 1929 John H. Owens, one of the pioneer black Communists, wrote a letter from New York City to A. L. Isbell, the head of the Party's Negro Department in the Midwest. Owens had just returned from Gastonia and cities along the eastern seaboard where he had been speaking and raising funds for the Party. He urged Isbell to send a special-delivery letter of protest to Robert Minor saying that Owens had received no salary, not even funds for transportation home, and that his family had not received any money either. "The Party is the bunk," Owens concluded.[1] In response, Isbell and three other prominent black Communists in Chicago wrote immediately to the CEC, protesting the "uncommunist and non-bolshevik fashion in which Negro comrades are treated by our Party" and complaining that the CP's Negro work was nothing but pointless "whoopee."[2]

A Negro Department report, probably written by Briggs, acknowledged that the failure of district organizers to share funds with black functionaries reflected a larger underestimation of Negro work throughout the Party. That was impermissible, since the Comintern had placed the Negro question in the United States at the heart of the struggle against capitalism. It had also warned repeatedly about the dangers inherent in "white chauvinism," which had nourished slavery and fortified sharecropping and tenantry, and in the present imperialist epoch sanctioned "super profits" from colonial exploitation. Chauvinism's deep-seated social and cultural savagery "was polluting the ranks of the white workers in America" with "Negrophobia," threatening a fatal split in the working class.[3]

Party leaders claimed that the Owens's situation was symptomatic of the chauvinist disease that had seeped into the very marrow of the Party and its associated labor and ethnic groups. "A real Bolshevik Leninist understanding" of racism, Harry Haywood intoned, held that liberation from the bonds of such oppression was inextricably "part of the question of the proletarian revolution"—a precondition for achieving Lenin's historic alliance of the workers and subject peoples in common struggle against capitalism and imperialism. In freeing itself from the smothering influence of white chauvinism, white labor would assist the Negro struggle for national liberation and thus act decisively in its own interest.[4]

The battle against race hatred was to be considered not a paternal "liberal humanitarian" crusade for purification of the heart, but rather a precondition for engagement of white revolutionaries in the struggle for Negro national liberation and hence for an eventual socialist transformation. Race prejudice was *not* the cause of oppression, as "feeble bourgeois liberalism" and its equally feeble program of "education" would have it.[5]

As long as chauvinism was rampant among white workers, unity was unattainable; without unity, there could be no social transformation. White chauvinism, therefore, was evil, and any class-conscious worker could only cringe when charged with it. Chauvinists were not merely misled by prejudice, they were guilty of the most egregious sin in the Leninist decalogue: wittingly or unwittingly supporting the class enemy and its wage-cutting, strikebreaking, "lynch law" policies.[6]

By locating the source of white chauvinism in the ideology and interests of the ruling class, the Party held an ominous sword over its members. What was more serious than the accusation that a Communist was doing the work of the class enemy? Within the Communist value system, that accusation was far more effective than appeals to humane principles or pleas for "understanding." Although the "stench of the slave market" clung to white workers, racism was alien to their deepest self-interest; they were allowed no respite from self-examination and ameliorative action. Chauvinism could not be expunged by cries of mea culpa and self-indulgent "cleansing" of mind and heart. It had to be purged by demonstrative and energetic "struggles against Negro oppression," to surmount blacks' distrust of white workers.[7]

PRESSURE FOR BLACK LEADERSHIP

The Party's dawning antichauvinism purgatory in 1929 also marked the return of Cyril Briggs to the CP's highest councils. The figure who had shepherded the first group of blacks into the Party, who held to his race-based socialism through a decade of neglect and festering prejudices, whose own career had slipped with creation of the ANLC: This man was now the clarion voice calling the Party to cleanse itself of chauvinism. Pressure to expunge chauvinism and promote blacks to leadership did not come only from within. On this issue the black nationalism and revolutionary socialism of the African Blood Brotherhood reemerged and converged with the Comintern line. The Party was under pressure from both the Comintern and the black revolutionaries to root out the racist malingerers. Briggs, not the Comintern, took on a major role in analyzing and directing CP action against chauvinism. In two pivotal articles in the Party's theoretical magazine, he surveyed the sordid record of the 1920s, acknowledged the slight but measurable improvement in Negro work and black recruitment in 1929, and used the Sixth Congress Negro resolution to whip the Party's membership to greater efforts.[8]

Briggs maintained that chauvinism was still a pervasive influence within the Party. It was manifested in open or concealed opposition to work among blacks, in failure to come out unreservedly as the champion of blacks in their struggles, in hesitancy to fight the union color bar, in unwillingness to draw capable Negroes into leadership of the Party and left-wing unions — using the "rotten slander" that the Negro cadre was incapable and undeveloped. Briggs's indictment suggested that Party members often gave in to trade-union and societal racism. They rankled at directives to fight for Negro rights, which they feared would reduce their influence. This boiled into resentment toward blacks.

Unwillingness to accept Negro leadership within the Party was a major problem. Here was an anomaly: whites ignoring blacks while often projecting themselves as the arbiters and interpreters of the black experience. Briggs said that the tendency of whites to arrogate ideological leadership over black affairs produced "leftist blunders" that had crippled the ANLC and isolated the Party from the black population. Conceptions were pressed upon the black community from the outside, detached from indigenous experience and temperament. This raised a question that Briggs was reluctant to pose: Were Marxism and communism relevant to the needs and interests of blacks?

Although he did not articulate the question, he dealt with it implicitly: The Marxist-Leninist conception of capitalism and imperialism as the root causes of black oppression was valid. In the struggle against the prevailing system, revolutionary nationalism was woven into Marxism-Leninism by Lenin himself. In Briggs's view, Marxist theory was universal and necessarily embraced specific features of the black experience. And who was more qualified to interpret and act on that experience than black Communists? Marxism-Leninism for Briggs was not a "white ideology." But when white Communists pursued policies and attitudes at odds with black comrades and black experience, Marxist "science" was violated, and chauvinism surfaced. The universal principles of Marxist theory could be applied only within a pluralistic embrace of the special characteristics of black life and responsiveness to black Communist leadership. Anything less, Briggs insisted, would distort the multiracial character of the working class and "whiten" Marxism to the point of implosion. He added the devastating charge that white Party leaders, in "utilizing the least militant of the oppressed race," had cultivated toadies and Uncle Toms. With rising anger, he declared that never again would the Party be able to destroy the good work of its militant black cadre as it had done when it "went out of its way to repudiate social equality" at its 1922 convention. He now had, compliments of the Sixth Congress, a weapon that no previous American leftist movement had possessed: the charge that chauvinism was a betrayal of revolutionary theory and practice.[9]

Overcoming Internal Resistance

The stage was set for severe punishment for acts of white chauvinism: expulsion from the revolutionary movement. The Party would now consciously run counter to the racial fabric of American life, casting into a political wilderness those who acted as many other Americans did. A vote against expulsion of those accused of chauvinism revealed the absence of revolutionary mettle and the presence of chauvinism in the judges themselves. This would be a forced march to purification with no doubters or nay-sayers. In Seattle, Washington, "several comrades who objected to the presence of Negro workers at Party dances were expelled." The Central Committee then stepped in and expelled twelve more who had voted against the expulsion of those originally charged. In Norfolk, Virginia, "most of the white members of a Party unit were expelled for refusal to admit the Negro comrades to their meetings." The racial climate of that southern city was not admitted as a mitigating factor. The Party "showed its Negro face" to friends and foes by sending Otto Hall to confirm the expulsions. The approach to chauvinism in the South would be no different than elsewhere; the Party would sooner dismantle whole units than retreat from its stand on social equality.[10]

Nevertheless, a Communist organizer in Greenville, South Carolina, admitted that white workers "absolutely" refused to attend meetings with Negroes. The Party and Unemployed Council in Greenville were virtually all black because of white hostility to the Party's stand on the "'nigger' question." But black workers had begun to challenge the Party's sincerity when they came to all-black meetings — suspecting that they had been "Jim Crowed." The Greenville correspondent complained that the elusive but essential goal of black-white unity could not be accomplished through a dogmatic repetition of slogans about racial equality and self-determination. To engage in endless denunciations or to simply expel a Party member for white chauvinism only accelerated white flight. The answer had to be education showing "the economic necessity for the unity of all workers on an equal basis." A case in point: A 700-member NTWU local in Greenville was thrown into crisis when two of only five black workers in the mill sought to join the union. Nearly half the members of the local objected, with just two Party members supporting admission. The NTWU organizer opted for flexibility. He got a postponement of a vote on accepting the black workers. He then visited members individually, stressing the necessity of interracial organization in the interest of all workers. At the next meeting, he had won a "solid block" of whites for admission. White chauvinism, in this case at least, was overcome by "perseverance and education" and not by "the more crude and dogmatic method," which could have led to the collapse of the local. At the grassroots level, away from the Party center, innovation occasionally won over rigidity.[11]

In the North the District 8 (Illinois) leadership had failed repeatedly to pay Isbell for his full-time Party work. The district's blundering with Isbell had produced "a distinctly anti-Party attitude among the Negro comrades" in Chicago, who had threatened to stop Negro work. That proposed protest action reflected their "politically undeveloped" state. But the decisive issue was white "petty bourgeois elements who are . . . most responsible" for chauvinism and are "sabotaging the Party's Negro work." The bourgeois nationalist heresy, though serious, was subordinated to the fight against white chauvinism. A New York

Communist insisted that having separate ideological standards for blacks and whites was not a negation of racial equality: "Negroes have been for ages oppressed by various groups of whites who have used and abused them. Therefore, the attitude of the Negro workers towards the whites generally is one of mistrust, and rightly so." In answer to the belief of some Communists that "black chauvinism" also existed in the Party, the ideological apparatus responded that such charges often camouflaged white chauvinism. In any case, chauvinism meant oppression of one nation over another: "Can we seriously for one moment entertain the contention that the Negroes are aggressively exercising their national rights over the whites? No! What these comrades mean in making the charge of 'black chauvinism' is that the Negroes in the Party are race conscious as well as class conscious — and this we certainly must commend, and not reject."[12]

White Communists nevertheless were confused when called upon to countenance a seeming double standard in intra-Party race relations by extending to blacks a welcome that went beyond simple equality. An incident in Harlem in 1931, in which whites were cleared from the hall, brought this admonition from the Party leadership:

> But some of the comrades still cannot understand why it was alright to push white workers out of the hall . . . and why it was wrong "to act the same" towards the Negroes who were there. . . . Precisely because we are white workers who realize that the Negroes mistrust the whites . . . we must put ourselves out particularly to win the confidence of the Negro workers. . . . Some tactics of approach which might be permissible towards white workers cannot be tolerated towards Negro workers.[13]

A major pronouncement by the New York District Bureau in February 1931 finally demanded that the membership, already suffering the privations imposed by the Great Depression, accept the primacy of the needs of Negroes. Despite the severity of the crisis, so the line went, whites were still privileged compared to blacks. Any attempt to "blur over" the special demands of blacks (camouflaged by talk of "workers are workers regardless of race") was tantamount to calling for interracial unity while forgetting about lynching, mob violence, and segregation. The special demands of blacks had to be carried beyond the Party into wider struggles, such as unemployment demonstrations and strikes, where whites predominated.[14]

With such internal pounding on white chauvinism, some Communists complained that they could not recruit blacks to a movement that advertised its own prejudices with such vigor. The Central Committee responded that such a complaint was a shabby excuse for not building among blacks. At the same time, the leadership conceded that the struggle for Negro rights could not wait until the Party had purged itself of every vestige of chauvinism. That was a "leftist" fancy that, under the guise of intensive inner purification, actually evaded action as much as did "rightist tendencies."[15]

For the dedicated Communist there was no escape from excruciating self-examination. Although racism was pervasive in the larger society, Communists were forced daily to oppose it, regardless of personal and political cost. Rose Chernin, a veteran Party activist who specialized in defense of the foreign-born, recalled a visit in 1932 to her section committee by Party leader Israel Amter. He told the group that Negroes had been betrayed perennially by whites seeking their support: "what every Communist must do is to be willing to die in defense of any Negro's rights, and it doesn't have to be anything flamboyant or very important — any insult, and there are plenty, directed by a white person against a Negro, is reason enough for a Communist to react, to slap his or her face, hit hard and if you be killed, that's alright too, because . . . without the Negro people we are only treading water as far as making the revolution in the U.S."[16]

The Party's social life often appeared to confound the Communist faith that white workers would ultimately purge themselves of chauvinism. The interracial dance, institutionalized by the Party and the YCL as an exemplar of social equality, often aroused ill feeling in the larger community and sorely tried the comrades' commitment, as well as their physical safety. Blacks had been excluded from a left-wing dance in Detroit, while Party leaders who attended did nothing about it. At the same dance, "a Hindu" was refused admission because he was mistaken for a Negro; a leading comrade fought for his admission, not in the name of equality, but because he was not a Negro! The Linden, New Jersey, branch of the Party expelled one Andrew Matlaga after he refused to allow his daughter to dance with a Negro at an ILD social. Members of the YCL in Washington, D.C., were threatened with expulsion unless they reversed a decision not to invite blacks to a branch dance on grounds that the presence of Negroes "might cause trouble." In Chicago "gangsters" invaded a Party-sponsored social at the Polish Club, enraged at the mixed dancing that was going on. Some white comrades eased themselves out of the hall through a fusillade of threats and insults directed against the Negroes. The police arrived and harassed the blacks while ignoring the intruders. The evening finally ended with a mob attack upon YCL members who had chosen to remain throughout the ordeal. Two days later, at a meeting of the local Unemployed Council, blacks charged that white Communists had been unwilling to defend them and declared that they could rely only on self-defense "by any means necessary." The Party's investigation concluded that its members had yet to grasp their tasks in relation to the Negro question. In a city where one-quarter of the Party's membership was black, the cowardice of white Communists who refused to throw themselves into the path of racist violence was intolerable and potentially fatal for the hope of organizing additional "tens of thousands."[17]

The antichauvinism campaigns sometimes became rooted in beliefs and expectations about what blacks wanted that came perilously close to undermining the Party's own theoretical notions of self-determination. One assumption was that northern blacks, under all circumstances, wanted full assimilation into the Party (and into the society), while chauvinism stood in the way. For example, in Gary, Indiana, blacks and whites routinely sat in different sections at a rally to support the National Hunger March. But Party officials did not permit this "wall" between the races, and they pressured the assemblage to integrate the seating. This incident revealed how a rigid antichauvinism could at times intrude into the social, political, and cultural mechanisms that blacks had built for their own comfort and political development.[18]

Another question concerned the degree to which the struggle against white chauvinism could be pursued without creating serious instability in the Party. Again, the city of Gary was a case in point. The Party and its associated groups in Gary traded charges and counter-charges over the issue of chauvinism until the Central Committee dispatched a "control commission" to investigate the multitude of accusations. After a public inquiry, the commission found that three foreign-born Communists were guilty of refusing to carry out a Party decision to hire black workers at the local cooperative restaurant. But the commission also rejected charges by two black Communists against district leaders, admonishing them not to become unwitting accomplices to attacks "by the right-wing against the Party leadership." The antichauvinism campaigns convulsed the Party, but at times they had their limits. There was an underlying fear of uncontrolled heresy hunting and exploitation of a serious issue for purposes of disruption or factional warfare. There was a trace of a double standard when the Party attempted to keep the campaign at fever pitch among the rank and file, while sealing its leadership from accusations and internecine strife. The weight of the assault continued to fall most heavily on the lower and middle levels, only occasionally reaching the leaders.[19]

Nevertheless, a dread of being caught in a contradiction between egalitarian rhetoric and chauvinist reality drove the Party to act against racial slights in nearly every social situation. Two members of the YCL were expelled in Youngstown, Ohio, when they refused to admit blacks to a local workers' sports club. In Baltimore fifty Communists took over a dance given by the Friends of the Soviet Union after it was reported that blacks had been barred from the hall. Scandalized by the thought that a group purporting to support Soviet Russia, the bastion of racial equality, could commit such an act, the protesters broke through a police guard to capture the dance floor and sing the "Internationale." At a Party-led war veterans' conference, a delegate rose to protest wearying, "unbalanced" emphasis on the Negro question. He was hit with a volley of criticism that pleased Party leaders.[20]

The Party's determination to prove to the black community that it was committed to the eradication of racism led it into public "mass trials" of alleged miscreants. The trials were deliberately structured to make a political point where the outcome was predetermined by the nature of the charge itself. They were not intended to establish guilt or innocence; no one was "cleared" of charges based on the evidence. The trials were a mixture of political theater, public education, self-advertisement, and admonition. They were designed not only to impress blacks, but also to subject the accused to public condemnation and humiliation, coupled with signposts to salvation. Trials broke out all over the country. In Buffalo, New York, an official of the local workers' center was accused of excluding blacks from the facility, even though it was located in the black community. When the trial was postponed after the alleged offender refused to attend what he called "a frameup," the national leadership criticized the local Party for reducing the campaign against chauvinism "to a struggle against the individual." The trial should have gone forward, with or without the "defendant."[21]

ETHNICS AND WHITE CHAUVINISM

The recruitment of one thousand blacks into the Party during 1931 had bared some festering, even worsening racial tensions and prejudices. This problem was especially noticeable among the ethnic groups that constituted the CP's largest constituency. Although avowing Marxist internationalism, these groups often turned inward, using the protective barriers of language and ethnic affinity against the pressures of an unfamiliar and often hostile external environment. Very much like the broader ethnic communities of which they were a part, the Communist ethnics sought material and psychic refuge in their own cooperative businesses, clubs, and fraternal societies.

Many of these groups displayed complex and ambivalent attitudes toward blacks. While foreign-born workers yearned to stay within the secure confines of their own reconstructed communities, they also desired to be accepted into the larger American community. Hence they were receptive to the values and attitudes that carried the stamp of "Americanism" — including "Negrophobia." Beneath the surface of frenzied reactions to blacks who showed up at ethnic social events, one may glimpse not only a desire to protect group exclusiveness, but also the wish to express, however inarticulately, the adoption of "American" ways. By ordering blacks off dance floors, by barring them from their clubs, foreign-born radicals demonstrated that they knew how things were done in America.

While ethnics mimicked what they saw as "American" habits, they were, paradoxically, unfamiliar with the quintessentially American mores and culture of blacks. Also, the distinct contours of white racism, at least, had no analogue in their European experience. The Negro question and the struggle against chauvinism was of little interest; it did not jar their collective consciousness or conscience. For a Party with a predominantly foreign-born membership, this was a major problem.[22]

One Mrs. Estrin was a non-Party "petty bourgeois" tailor's wife who happened to be present in the Detroit Jewish Workers Club in January 1930 when newly recruited black Communists arrived looking for their first Party meeting. They had come to the right place, but Mrs. Estrin "intentionally" told them there was no meeting. The Detroit Party organization said that "little shopkeepers," such as Mrs. Estrin, were like "their big brothers, the big capitalists," and ordered her expulsion from the Jewish Workers Club. The resolution, prepared by Communist members of the club, portrayed the unfortunate Mrs. Estrin as an "instrument" of capitalist treachery.[23]

In the summer of 1930 the manager of a Chicago left-wing Lithuanian restaurant became uneasy about serving some black delegates to a meeting of unemployed workers. Fearing a loss of business, the manager offered the blacks money to eat elsewhere. The Lithuanians called the transaction a "donation"; the Party called it a "bribe" to get the blacks to go away. The incident opened a full-bore attack on the Lithuanian Communists. Party leader William Dunne suggested that *Vilnis,* the left-wing Lithuanian newspaper, dodged the issue of "real estate sharks" who blocked rentals to blacks on the South Side, for fear of losing real estate advertising. Under Party pressure, the editor was removed and the paper was censured.[24]

The Party had an important following among left-wing, ethnically based cooperative businesses and cultural organizations. Increasingly, the Party viewed the ethnic cooperatives, despite their stability, as an ineffective way to raise the oppressed or to bring about a revolutionary change. Festering chauvinism seemed to reinforce in the Party a growing hostility to the narrowness, exclusivity, and small-business outlook of many foreign-language cooperatives. The need for black-white unity in the imminent revolutionary situation overrode any desire to accommodate the insular and splintering ethnic cooperatives.[25]

In early 1931 Maude White complained to Party leader Clarence Hathaway about white chauvinism in the largely ethnic needle trades union. At the same time, Hathaway was dealing with indignation that extended from the Harlem Party to the national Negro Commission over an incident that had taken place in December 1930.[26] August Yokinen, a Finnish immigrant and custodian of the Finnish Workers Club in Harlem, was on duty when a small group of blacks arrived at the club for a social event. Yokinen, who spoke little English, muttered something inhospitable like "your dance is in colored Harlem." A Party member, he later claimed that if he allowed blacks into the club, they would soon be using the sauna, "and he did not want to bathe with negroes." Hathaway, under pressure to respond to Maude White's inventory of racism in the needle trades union, proposed to the Political Bureau that the expulsion process come out of the shadows of internal Party life and into the light as a "mass public trial." As a kind of "shock treatment," the Finnish immigrant's misdeed was to be publicly condemned. The decision set the stage for the largest and most widely publicized trial for chauvinism in the Party's history.[27]

Nearly two thousand spectators, about five hundred of whom were black, crowded into the Harlem Casino on the first Sunday in March, 1931, for Yokinen's trial. According to the Party, 211 members of the audience were official "delegates," representing 133 "mass organizations." Somehow, every delegate was invited to "participate in rendering the verdict." But the actual "jury" of seven blacks and seven whites, chosen to achieve a perfect interracial symmetry, had to render the preordained judgment and outline Yokinen's rehabilitation. Hathaway served as "prosecutor," articulating the Party's line on the centrality of Negro national liberation, the primacy of black and white working-class unity, and the evil of white chauvinism. Richard B. Moore, as "defense counsel," rose once again to impressive oratorical heights. He adopted the only possible defense: Yokinen was guilty of chauvinism, but the "real criminal is the vicious capitalist system." He pleaded for the salvation of the confused Finn who faced the severest of punishments: excommunication from the revolutionary movement. "As for myself," Moore pleaded, "I would rather have my head severed from my body by the capitalist lynchers than to be expelled from the Communist International."[28]

The jury nonetheless found Yokinen guilty of unconscionable chauvinism and expelled him from the Party. However, it decreed that he could be readmitted if he fought racism in the Finnish Workers' Club, joined the League of Struggle for Negro Rights, sold the *Liberator* on Harlem street corners, and led a demonstration against a local Jim Crow restaurant. Yokinen admitted that he had been "poisoned by chauvinism" and pledged to struggle for Negro rights as a condition for readmission to the Party. The trial ended with a lusty singing of "The Internationale."[29]

In the wake of the trial, the *Daily Worker* warned that no Communist would be permitted to mouth abstract words of equality while engaging in concrete racist acts. Harry Haywood declared that the trial and "verdict" were landmarks in the CP's Negro work and proved "to the Negro masses that the Party means what it says." Earl Browder said the trial had won approval and sympathy for the Party, especially among blacks. Both Haywood and Browder credited "the firm Bolshevik line" embodied in Yokinen's expulsion with preparing the Party for its fervent response to the Scottsboro case, which broke shortly after the trial (see chapter 11). Nearly two years later, the Party continued to congratulate itself that the Yokinen trial had dramatized its commitment to drive chauvinism from its own ranks while fighting "tooth and nail to root it out of the working class as a whole."[30]

Some latent problems remained. For those within the black community who were committed to a "race first" agenda, the impact of the trial was mitigated by its underlying objective—achieving "class first" black and white unity. The contention that African American workers wanted proof of the Party's determination to wipe out racism within its own ranks, as a prerequisite to unity, did not impress those committed to various strands of separatist nationalism. Some blacks saw it as an arrogation—contrary to the spirit of self-determination—of their right to define their own political and social interests.

For a broader segment of the black community, no matter how impressive the Party's antichauvinism campaign, its underlying aim of unity based on Third Period "revolutionary" expectations was hopelessly sectarian and not in keeping with the political and ideological climate in either the black community or the nation as a whole. Not surprisingly, the trial and the publicity that attended it did not bring a flood of blacks into the Party.

But the antichauvinism crusade did impress many people, black and white, at a time when segregation, racism, and the remorseless debasement of black identity and culture were societal norms. Thus, the *Chicago Defender* explained editorially "Why We Can't Hate Reds." The Milwaukee CP had dropped a man who had made some "uncomplimentary remarks about workers of the Race. He didn't call us criminals, thugs, or rapists. . . . He said merely that we are 'dumb, cowardly and can't be organized.' " But according to the *Defender,* those words, which been uttered often by blacks themselves, got a white man expelled from a movement to which he was strongly committed. What other group would go so far to prove itself not unfriendly to the Race?[31]

The Yokinen trial was a watershed for Communist-influenced ethnic groups and trade unions. More than Bolshevization in 1925, the forced engagement with white chauvinism, and hence with the Negro question, dragged the ethnic groups out of their insularity and into hard "American" realities. Yokinen in his confessional was obliged to attack the ethnic "clannishness . . . forced upon workers by the imperialists." In turn, the Party would at least defend the ethnics against the black nationalists. Moore, in his "defense" of Yokinen, assailed the "opportunist Negro bourgeois-nationalist misleaders . . . who are attempting to stir up the Negro masses against the white workers, and are attacking the foreign-born workers, Negro as well as white." In the process of cleansing the foreign-language groups of chauvinism, the Party made its black cadre aware of the need to combat black hostility against the foreign-born — especially the belief, promoted most notably by *Defender* publisher Robert S. Abbott, that they constituted a serious source of job competition for blacks. The movement to protect black economic interests against foreigners had to be considered an unprincipled division of the working class, turning the attention of the black population from the real enemy — capitalism.[32]

Two days after the trial Yokinen was seized for deportation to "fascist" Finland. The Party called the action a panicked response to its assault on ethnic racism. Yokinen was now portrayed as a simple "Harlem janitor" who in honestly admitting his mistakes "had become a symbol of unity of Negro and white workers." He was deported in January 1933. The U.S. Circuit Court of Appeals did note his work for readmission to the Party as grounds for deportation. A reward of sorts for the Yokinen episode was the declaration of National Solidarity Day, March 28, 1931, when black and white workers would demonstrate their unity against both lynching and deportation.[33]

A case can be made that the insularity of the foreign-language groups did fragment working-class culture and introduce a regressive and narrow perspective into the left-wing movement. Although the Party was characteristically rigid and heavyhanded in its attempts to cleanse the ethnic groups of chauvinism, ethnic solidarity, buttressed by racism, diluted class consciousness and was incompatible with progress. The question the Party tended to neglect was how to preserve the richness and coherence of ethnic culture, while bringing the foreign-language groups into pluralistic campaigns for equality and democracy.

Labor and White Chauvinism

Labor, the most vital sphere of Party activity, was also where job competition between the races made the struggle against white chauvinism particularly difficult. As we have seen, the TUUL unions were under relentless pressure to advance racial equality. They were repeatedly criticized for underestimating the importance of Negro work and for seeking to shift such work exclusively to black comrades and to the League of Struggle for Negro Rights. In 1931 the Party got the mining, metal, marine, and needle unions to set up Negro departments, which worked against discrimination within the unions and in their respective industries.[34]

Nonetheless Maude White was still confronted with "Negrophobia" in the needle trades union. For example, a dance had been sponsored by skilled custom tailors in Philadelphia on the eve of their strike against local clothing manufacturers. Rank-and-file tailors refused to admit blacks to the event. The Communists in the union were faced with the choice of protesting and possibly losing the tailors at the brink of a strike, or remaining silent and thus becoming accomplices in racism. For Maude White there was no choice. If they even considered the idea of not challenging the action of a small group of tailors, the Communists would sacrifice interracial labor unity and its benefits for "the entire revolutionary movement." Where was the Party's educational work among the tailors? How could the tailors commit such an act when the TUUL was trying so hard to contrast its racial policies with those of the AFL? For White, these questions were vital to the moral grounding and the future hopes of the revolutionary unions. The union had hesitated to "jump at the throats of the one hundred percent bandits who strike the Negro in the face." She invoked those words of Profintern leader Solomon Lozovsky, who warned that no quarter could be given in the fight against chauvinism. Every Communist among the offending workers must wear the brand of a carrier of "bourgeois mentality in the heart of the working class" and "should be thrown out [of the TUUL] neck and crop."[35]

Inevitably, the Yokinen formula was applied to drive white racism out of the unions. Joe Birns was a white furrier charged with using abusive language to Maude White and stating publicly that "it would be better if we had no Negroes in the trade at all." For that he was subjected to a trial. Trouble was brewing in the New York needle trades: Fifteen thousand black workers, nearly one-third of the needle trades work force in the city, were paid from one-third to one-half the wages paid to whites for the same work. Birns's views symbolized the obstacles to overcoming such a situation. His trial would signal a "bitter struggle" in the needle trades union against racism in its ranks. But the trial was not to be considered a fulfillment of the union's obligations. To reduce Birns to a "sacrificial goat," while the union absolved itself of responsibility for a continuing struggle, was unacceptable.[36]

With that in mind, on February 7, 1932, over one thousand people gathered at the New Harlem Casino to witness another carefully orchestrated display of biracial and interethnic solidarity. An oversized jury of nine blacks, eight Jews, two Hispanics, two Italians, one Irish, one Armenian, and one Greek sat in judgment before an audience that was one-fourth black. The legendary Jewish leader of the furriers, Ben Gold, served as "prosecutor," while the black Communist Charles Alexander was Birns's "defense counsel." Gold demanded that Birns be expelled from the union. Alexander claimed that Birns had fallen victim to the "racialist atmosphere" created by capitalism; like Yokinen, he was guilty, but he was contrite, and his crime reflected the chauvinism of the larger society. Not surprisingly, Birns was found "guilty" and "sentenced" to a six-month probation from the union while he carried out instructions to "militantly fight for Negro rights" (and peddle the *Liberator* among his shopmates). The jury also took the opportunity to address the underlying discriminatory conditions in the trade, charging the needle trades union with failure to fight energetically against racism. It instructed the union to increase education on the Negro question and to move against members who exploited blacks under the subcontracting system. The audience had witnessed yet another display of the Party's determination to forge a place for blacks in the unions under its control.[37]

Ultimately, the overuse of trials diluted their dramatic effect, in spite of their groundbreaking characteristics. Writing in 1933, when the fever of the campaign had subsided, Harry Haywood noted, without a hint of self-criticism, that there had been a "widespread tendency to replace consistent and daily struggle . . . for the specific demands of the Negro masses by occasional spectacular . . . mass trials." As the attack on white chauvinism became abstracted from concrete problems and conditions, focusing instead on personal prejudices of individual Communists, the whole exercise skirted self-caricature. It became, ironically, a variation on "liberal" self-flagellation, which the Party condemned at other times. The repetition of trials and heresy hunts began to contribute to the idea that racism was endemic and virtually ineradicable. Earl Browder finally felt compelled to challenge the assumption, which had grown out of the campaign, that the entire working class was hopelessly chauvinist and that racism was "rampant" within the Party.[38]

THE SOUTH

Nowhere, of course, was the challenge of racism in unions more daunting than in the South. Racial issues there went far beyond matters of dance floors, invidious remarks, or the exploitation of contract labor. Racism was manifested in the most fundamental social norm — segregation, which was sustained by state-supported violence and institutionalized by the denial of basic political rights to blacks. In the early 1930s biracial unionism in the South was unthinkable. But that was precisely the Party's goal. The National Textile Workers Union, as we have seen, was instructed to bring blacks into the organization even if every white member deserted. Segregation gave whites a tenuous position on the "mountainside" above blacks. That fortified their illusions in capitalism and thus sustained the system itself. The first injunction to the NTWU was to overcome racial antagonism. That could only be done with a "wide and determined ideological campaign against white chauvinism." The TUUL most likely could have made greater short-term headway among whites in the South by tactical accommodations with racism and segregation. But in the Party's view that would have broken the essential alliance of the working class and the black liberation movement.

One of the first tests of the NTWU's antiracist commitment came in Bessemer City, North Carolina, where in 1929 the union managed to establish a small, predominantly black local. At the first meeting an NTWU organizer, bowing to local custom, stretched a wire across the room, separating the races. When officials of the Party and the TUUL learned of this, Otto Hall was rushed to Bessemer City to condemn the act and to threaten the offending organizer with expulsion from the union. Shortly thereafter, the Party launched its drive to stamp out any suggestion of compromise with segregation in the Gastonia strike. In the early 1930s the TUUL could not transcend racist practices in the South to become more than a marginal force. But its incessant carping and probing on the issue of white chauvinism had a cumulative impact, particularly upon emerging industrial unionism in the mid-1930s.[39]

The Communist Party's antichauvinism campaign of the early 1930s, like most of its ideological crusades, was a mix of idealism and manipulation, realism and fantasy. The "mass trials," expulsions, and heresy hunts often served (as the Greenville organizer noted) as fevered substitutes for the harder educational work in the face of deeply rooted prejudices. Sometimes antichauvinist campaigns degenerated into fantastic accusations, such as expulsions for cooking Aunt Jemima brand pancakes. Still, the campaign was an unprecedented, fervent effort to purge the most tenacious prejudices from the Party's ranks as well as to overcome the historic legacy of black distrust for predominantly white movements. The campaign had its bizarre turns, but given the extent of white racism, who could effectively challenge the notion that extraordinary steps were necessary to exorcise such a tenacious "disease"?[40]

The CP was well in advance of the times in protesting racism in popular culture and sports. Cultural critic Harry Alan Potamkin perceptively exposed racial stereotypes in films when such stereotypes were standard theatrical fare. Although he often wrote in sectarian jargon, he probed the racist subtexts of contemporary cartoons, newsreels, short subjects, and feature films. He noted that the portrayal of Negroes as "indolent idiots" and singing, dancing, crapshooting clowns was a product of the anxieties and rationalizations of the antebellum South that had been transmitted to the entire nation. The Party organized a national protest against D. W. Griffith's antiblack film *Birth of A Nation*. An outraged William L. Patterson organized a protest when he read in the *New York Times* that two Ugandan boys were being housed at the Central Park Zoo, accompanying animals that had been captured in Africa. The white racism inherent in the segregation of athletes in dining, sleeping, and travel arrangements for the Olympic games of 1932 at Los Angeles was chronicled and attacked by the Party's press and by its activists.[41]

The Communists made an important contribution to the search for effective opposition to racism in the way they argued the case. They questioned appeals to morality, abstract justice, and "healing" through "understanding." They stressed instead the need to change power relationships in the interests of all the dispossessed. Missionary endeavors and verbal appeals based upon sentimentality and guilt tended to become exhausted in vapid self-recrimination. Chauvinism had to be fought where it existed—among the white workers. And those workers had to be won over on the basis of their own needs. The Communists stressed self-interest rooted in the requirements of social struggle: Chauvinism was evil because working-class whites could never achieve what they wanted as long as racial division persisted. Blacks were not to be pitied or patronized, they were to be welcomed as indispensable allies in the battle to change the world. They were to be respected for their own history and culture—and for the revolutionary potential inherent in their own struggles for liberation.

CHAPTER NINE

Fighting Hunger and Eviction

In Chicago, in the winter of 1932, the writer and critic Edmund Wilson came upon the Angelus Building, where homeless blacks had taken refuge. He found shattering desolation in a place where even hardened social workers had felt "overwhelmed with horror." There was darkness in the hundred cells dug out of the building's decay; there was cold; there was danger. "It is a firetrap which has burned several times — the last time several people were burned to death. And now, since it is not good for anything else, its owner turned it over to the Negroes."[1]

Beyond Chicago, the country as a whole was in crisis: housing, sanitation, public services, health care, and employment were all affected. The troubles fell hardest upon African Americans. In Pennsylvania only 43 percent of Negro homes had toilet facilities and only 25 percent had bathtubs. Dallas reported 31 percent of black housing "barely habitable" and 19 percent "unfit for habitation." Seven out of ten houses in the African American ghetto in Richmond, Virginia, were on unpaved streets and had major violations of building codes. Similar situations existed in nearly every major city covered by available statistical studies in 1932. In spite of inadequate housing, under the pressures of segregation, blacks continued to pay disproportionately high rentals. In a time of high unemployment, tens of thousands of jobless blacks in urban centers were forced to rely upon the meager resources of private charity and municipal relief. But city mayors complained of heavy relief loads among blacks and warned of the imminent exhaustion of funds. Black groups charged discrimination in the dispensing of relief to black communities. The waiting rooms of employment offices in Harlem were continually filled to overflowing with people hopelessly seeking work. By 1930 the black middle class was feeling the full impact of the Depression, as men and women with college degrees were forced to look for jobs as "red caps," elevator operators, or domestics. But even such marginal work was in short supply.[2]

In late 1929, under Comintern injunction, the Trade Union Unity League had begun to set up councils to deal with unemployment. Still struggling to consolidate its own fragile unions, the TUUL was not equal to the task of simultaneously organizing the unemployed. On July 5, 1930, 1,320 delegates from the Party, TUUL, YCL, and other groups in the Party's orbit (including a scattering from the ANLC) gathered in Chicago to form the national Unemployed Councils. The program for the councils called for unemployed insurance, immediate cash and work relief, public work at union wages, free food for the children of the jobless, and moratoria on evictions. Pervading the program was strong opposition to racial discrimination, recognition that blacks bore the brunt of the crisis, and entreaties to the jobless to unite across the color line. Party-led organizations for dealing with unemployment now stressed the need for an inclusive biracial movement and the priority demand for nondiscrimination in relief. The Comintern had divided the Negro question into a question of self-determination in the South and issue of full economic and social equality in the North. That bifurcation at times seemed to cloud the special dimensions of the Negro question in the northern industrial and urban areas. However, by placing the issue of discrimination as well as the need for unity at the heart of the jobless movement, the cloud began to lift.[3]

In 1929 and 1930 tens of thousands of people drifted through the cities searching for work. With a membership of fewer than ten thousand, the Communist Party set March 6, 1930, as the target date for ambitious demonstrations across the country to demand unemployment insurance. With energy that tested the zeal of its small following, the Communists distributed a million leaflets through the cities and organized innumerable street-corner meetings. Since the Communists appeared to be one of the few groups, if not the only one, seeking to free the nation from its economic paralysis, first dozens, then hundreds, then thousands of people began to flock to the banner of unemployment insurance.[4]

Following the Party's injunctions, members of local Unemployed Councils swept into black neighborhoods, leafleting poolrooms and haranguing on street corners, urging ghetto residents to participate in warm-up demonstrations on February 19, 1930, and then in the March 6 rallies. Like many black communities across the country, Baltimore's ghetto was the scene of noisy street meetings where speakers lamented the injustices of a system that gave $165 million in tax remittances to corporations while the unemployed, black and white, were left to rot. Between February 19 and March 6, the Baltimore Council signed up four hundred blacks, many of whom had recently migrated from the Deep South.[5]

Street demonstrations soon spread across the country—from Philadelphia to Cleveland, Chicago, and Los Angeles. Protests led to bloodshed when police, inflamed by the sight of interracial groups of women and men, initiated violence. At a particularly bloody demonstration in New York City, a black man was one of two seriously injured participants. The *New York Times* noted the tendency of police to single out blacks: "A Negro taken for a communist by the police was chased along Park Row and knocked to the pavement unconscious with blackjacks wielded by several detectives who overtook him." Despite that risk, the Party-controlled press claimed that the growing Unemployed Council in Harlem was playing "a prominent part" in the City Hall demonstrations.[6]

March 6, 1930, turned out to be the most successful day in the short history of the American Communist Party and its affiliated groups. While there was the expected dispute over numbers, photographs and eyewitness accounts attest to the huge size of some of the demonstrations. Black participation captured the attention of both friendly and hostile observers who greeted this either as a sign of powerful new elements joining a heretofore racially narrow movement or as an indication of troubling radicalization of a once docile population. A good deal of attention was focused upon the relatively small demonstration before the White House in Washington, which was dispersed by the use of tear gas, clubs, and blackjacks. The *New York Times* seemed mesmerized by the fact that "those in the Communist demonstration for the most part were Negro men.... Spectators were treated to the unusual spectacle of several white girls walking with colored men during the 'picketing.'... Several of the band of radicals were small Negro boys, nine- or ten-years-old, who carried placards opposing child labor."[7]

The Party and its supporters were gratified by the strong black presence in New York, both on the platform and in the ranks. March 6 was a crushing refutation to the claim that blacks were submissive and conservative. The Party's postmortem on the events stated that black workers delivered a "smashing refutation" to "reformists" who contended that blacks were "too stupid to organize and too cowardly to resist oppression." Briggs's *Liberator*, with an unintentionally patronizing tone, announced that white workers were "pleased by Negro heroism" in the face of harsh intimidation and brutality. Black demonstrators, especially in Washington, D.C., had to fight their way through police lines to join the marches. In the nation's capital, blacks and whites "stood their ground and gave blow for blow until they were brutally driven from the streets with gas bombs and fire hose." The Party press declared with hyperbole that "thousands of Negro workers" were singled out for attack. A policeman in New York allegedly told a group of black women to "go home like good girls and I will call you when I get off." In the heat of street skirmishes, blacks were told to "get the hell out of here and back to Harlem where you belong."[8]

In the South, March 6 represented a coming out of sorts for the Party. The trek to City Hall in Winston-Salem, North Carolina, "marked the first time Negro and white workers openly demonstrated under the Communist Party banner in the South." In Chattanooga, Baltimore, and other southern and near southern cities, placards were raised demanding "full political, economic, and social equality for Negro workers." When blacks were attacked by police in Washington, Winston-Salem, and Chattanooga, an "inspiring spectacle was enacted of white workers springing to the defense of their Negro fellow workers."[9]

The demonstrators, it seemed, were expected to respond to "partial demands," such as unemployment insurance, while also embracing the "revolutionary way out of the crisis." That mixture of a minimum program with a call for socialist revolution did not contribute toward a stable and politically broad unemployed movement. Yet the sheer devastation caused by the Depression mitigated the Communists' sectarianism, which would have been fatal in "normal" times. The movement of the unemployed continued, though it never again achieved the vast numbers assembled on March 6. Still, it spurred hundreds of smaller actions on a local and national scale. Delegations to local relief agencies, city halls, and state capitals — culminating at the end of 1931 and 1932 in national hunger marches to Washington—became a common, recurring scene during the early Depression years.[10]

Blacks were repeatedly pressed into the leadership of countless street marches and delegations. At times this meant that black Communists found themselves suddenly on the front lines. When the reds pushed into a hearing of the New York City Board of Estimate on October 16, 1930, to protest a $7 million increase in the police budget at a time of severe crisis in social services, they were unceremoniously ejected from the hearing room. Maude White, cospokesperson for the delegation, was pushed down a flight of stairs by zealous police. On February 10, 1931, the inventor and indefatigable grassroots activist Solomon Harper, along with Sam Nessin and Alfred Wagenknecht, both leaders of the unemployed movement, noisily interrupted debate in the U.S. House of Representatives on a naval supply bill. Before being dragged away, Harper shouted at southern congressmen that while their white constituents starved, they fed them with racism, intimidated blacks, and condoned lynching. On the first anniversary of the March 6 demonstrations, a delegation of jobless, including a substantial Harlem contingent, marched on the state capitol at Albany, New York. Three delegates, one of them black, were thrown out after shouting their demands on the floor of the legislature. A pitched battle with state troopers ensued, and again the Party lauded the blacks' prominence and courage in the fight. On April 1 more than fifty hunger marchers, of whom about forty were blacks, entered the Maryland House of Delegates and demanded a hearing on assistance to the jobless. Three delegates were permitted to address the House: Legislators were unhinged by the sight of "colored men [who] took papers from brief cases and recited their demands." While the delegates conferred with the governor, a fracas broke out with irate legislators who milled about. The sight of aggressive, self-assured blacks was apparently too much for some politicians, who showed themselves willing to engage in a "lively fist fight." After the state police intervened, two delegates wound up in the hospital and nine in jail.[11]

At a rally at the Philadelphia City Hall, about 40 percent of the demonstrators were blacks. When the mayor saw the crowd, he announced that he was "a friend of the Negroes." That inspired the Communists to follow up with a leaflet castigating him as "an enemy" who had done nothing to stop discrimination in distribution of relief and nothing to stop high rents and evictions of black families. By the fall of 1931 blacks were routinely appearing at the head of unemployed marches to state capitols. In September William L. Patterson led a delegation to Albany to oppose four pending jobless bills and to demand substitution of the Communist program. Speaking as both an African American and a Communist, he attacked the legislators for their inability to deal with growing technological unemployment, a shrinking work force, declining markets, and a catastrophic fall in working-class incomes. The Negro people, he added, were the worst sufferers. Only a major redistribution of wealth would allow workers, blacks in particular, to benefit materially. Patterson demanded that every worker "irrespective of nationality, race, color, or sex . . . get unemployment insurance to the full amount of wages." Vacant buildings had to be opened to the homeless unemployed; blacks had to be granted the right to live anywhere, the right to equal employment, and the right to self-determination for the Black Belt. Within the Depression context, Patterson projected a two-layered "affirmative action" for the working class in general and for the black masses in particular. Thus, the needs of blacks were now on the table as the most compelling aspect of the needs of all working people. By 1932, the unemployed movement in general was pressing special consideration for doubly burdened blacks. An Unemployed Council group burst into the San Diego City Hall to demand a special quota for Negroes in hiring for work on a proposed dam project. Although the demands were rejected, the way in which the Party reconciled the special needs of blacks on a foundation of inclusiveness and interracial unity met with considerable acceptance.[12]

THE COUNCILS IN THE SOUTH

The Unemployed Councils established bridgeheads in the South on the basis of previous TUUL and Party activity. Birmingham, as usual, was in the forefront. Shortly before the national founding convention of the Unemployed Councils in July 1930, an unusually large crowd of blacks and whites gathered in Union Park to demand, among other things, equal cash relief. Police moved in to break up the crowd, including a group of children who were singing, "We are the hunger children who fight for milk and bread / We are the workers' children, who must, who must be fed." The cops struck black and white women without restraint. When the assault ended, eighteen were jailed, while an undetermined number were "taken to the hospital . . . and to the city morgue." In May 1932 Hosea Hudson and two comrades led a three-mile march to protest abuse in work-relief programs. About fifty marchers made it to the steps of City Hall, where a committee led by YCL member Joe Burton sought to meet with city commissioner Jimmy Jones. Burton was set upon by police, who drew guns on the crowd; the youth leader promised to return with larger numbers. The local Unemployed Council, handicapped by arrests of organizers and members, was unable to respond until November 1932, when a demonstration at the Jefferson County Courthouse attracted a crowd of five to seven thousand people, most of them black, the largest biracial gathering in Birmingham's history. On that day Jimmy Jones felt obliged to receive a delegation of fifteen blacks and whites. Mary Leonard, a white Communist who was a native of Alabama, refused to retreat before Jones's baiting questions about social equality. "Yes, why not," she responded, "the Negro people are just as much people as you and I." At that point Jones ordered police to clear the courthouse steps, but many of the protesters managed to hold their ground.[13]

In Greenville, South Carolina, the Unemployed Council faced relentless pressure from the Ku Klux Klan. On April 7, 1931, a "mob organized by mill owners" packed a meeting of the Greenville City Council and monitored council and TUUL members who were presenting a list of demands. Two days later, Mayor E. C. Mann and Chief of Detectives L. W. Hammond led one hundred hooded men on a raid of the small Unemployed Council headquarters. The two city officials watched as the illegally masked vigilantes singled out blacks for physical assault. In early September two blacks were taken from a meeting of the council in the Negro section of Greenville. Eighteen carloads of Klansmen descended upon the gathering, seized the black council members at gunpoint and beat them severely.[14]

Similar demonstrations, with similar groundbreaking cries for equality, occurred from Chattanooga to Atlanta. Clusters of blacks and whites had discovered enough mutual interest to shout together, "Cash for groceries . . . stop evictions."

THE NATIONAL HUNGER MARCHES OF 1931 AND 1932

The national hunger marches at the end of 1931 and 1932 were staples of Communist-led protests during the Depression. They were the culmination of a stream of local demonstrations and marches through the worst years of the crisis. Three marches in mid-1931 in Pennsylvania, Indiana, and Ohio were praised by the Party as models of interracial solidarity. Small detachments of demonstrators broke away to launch street meetings in off-the-path communities where the Scottsboro story would not normally be known (see chapter 11). Scottsboro and hunger became inseparable issues. Communists generalized the specter of the electric chair for the nine youths into a threat against the growing unity of blacks and whites in the fight for food and work. It was the ultimate expression of "the capitalist offensive" against all the dispossessed. If the nine boys died, the entire movement against the depredations of the Depression would suffer immeasurably.[15]

The fusion of Scottsboro and hunger expanded the numbers and augmented the role of blacks in local marches that flowed into the national demonstration. Isaiah Hawkins of the NMU led a delegation to Pennsylvania governor Gifford Pinchot in Harrisburg. Nearly half the Ohio marchers were African Americans, and Herbert Newton, back from Atlanta, was the chief spokesperson. Loala Griffin, a black woman from Indianapolis, was a leader of the Indiana marchers. In Jim Crow sections of Ohio and Indiana, the marchers occasionally veered from their primary routes to challenge local segregation. In Marion, Indiana, white march leaders staged an impromptu demonstration when blacks were refused service at a local restaurant. At Youngstown, marchers pitched signs for segregated seating out of a local cafe. In Mansfield, Ohio, marchers refused "whites only" hotel beds. Such confrontations occurred repeatedly along the march routes.[16]

When the hunger marchers encountered violence, as they usually did, the casualty lists inevitably reflected the interracial nature of the protest. At the St. Louis City Hall, a march and demonstration to demand immediate relief and an end to discrimination at relief stations attracted five thousand people, at least a quarter of them black. An Unemployed Council delegation of twelve found the doors of City Hall locked. When about fifty women, most of them black, who had stood under a scorching sun for hours pushed toward the doors, police fired at the crowd from the third floor of City Hall. Four people were shot, including a Negro, Ben Powell, who was wounded in the abdomen.[17]

Like some local actions, the call to the national march went beyond pleas for racial equality and began to stress the special needs of the doubly burdened black unemployed. The twelve columns moving upon the nation's capital were instructed to emphasize the extremely high rate of Negro unemployment, the existence of racial discrimination in charity and relief programs, and police terror, which was harsher for blacks than for the white unemployed.[18]

By the end of 1931 these activities had captured the attention of black commentators as well as the white press, which assiduously reported the numbers of blacks participating in and leading the protests. The *Pittsburgh Courier* estimated that nearly half of the sixteen hundred people in the national march were Negroes. A "casual count" by the *New York Times* put the number of blacks at over four hundred. On this rare occasion the *Liberator* agreed with the *Times*. The National Urban League noted that most of the Negroes in the line of march "had been picked up on the road and in the cities," suggesting something less than a premeditated commitment. Urban League leaders, however, saw some positive elements in the pull of blacks into radical ranks: The bargaining power of moderates could only be enhanced by the threat of revolutionary influence among the race. But those in power must recognize that time was growing short; persons with leadership qualities, such as Isaiah Hawkins, who was chosen to lead a delegation of jobless to Congress, would embrace the revolutionary cause ever more fervently in the absence of concessions to moderation.[19]

The weary marchers arrived in Washington after the usual confrontation with local police along the way. But all twelve columns could boast that they had firmly opposed segregation wherever it appeared. They had challenged Jim Crow eating and sleeping facilities in Wilmington, Baltimore, and cities below the Mason-Dixon line. Of the twenty leaders who occupied the stage of a rally at the Washington Auditorium, six were black, including the grandiloquent D. R. Poindexter of Chicago. Poindexter subsequently led a delegation to the White House to demand from President Hoover an immediate grant of $150 to each unemployed family and a permanent unemployment insurance fund to be administered by the jobless. At the gates of the White House, Poindexter was "held up by companions while he exhorted his associates to carry on the fight for unemployment insurance until all opposition has been swept aside."[20]

FIGHTING EVICTIONS

The sociologist Horace Cayton was eating in a small restaurant in the heart of Chicago's Black Belt in the summer of 1931 when through the window he saw a long line of "serious and determined" bedraggled black men. He was drawn to their side, intrigued by the quiet dignity of those men who betrayed no trace of the laughter and horseplay that Cayton associated with the unkempt and impoverished. He learned that they were the "black bugs," or "black reds," of Chicago. He asked where they were headed and was told that they were marching to "put in a family" that had been evicted for nonpayment of rent. Cayton was also told that because most Negroes did not know their rights, landlords, without legal sanction, could simply pitch their meager belongings out of windows. But "they, the Communists, were going to see that the people were not treated in this fashion." They came to a dirty street, where the first part of the line had already returned to the house the few possessions of the evicted tenants. A woman stood inside a circle of "black reds," crying and thanking God. The emotional reaction of the Communists reminded Cayton "more of a camp fire meeting than a mob of angry 'reds.' Evidently not all Communists, at least not the black Communists are atheists." With the inevitable arrival of riot police, the marchers stood their ground around a haggard, elderly black woman who had climbed on a soapbox. She talked not about "empty theories" or "some abstract Utopia," but about "bread and jobs, and places to sleep in." The woman was pulled from the soapbox; clubs came down on heads with sickening precision; shots were fired. It was over in a minute. Cayton was sure that he would read about another "red riot" in the next day's papers, that red agitation among blacks was growing, and that America really was in danger.[21]

The fight against evictions was led by the Unemployed Councils with occasional assistance from the League of Struggle for Negro Rights. By 1930 the councils had become accustomed to returning the belongings of evicted families to vacated flats. If the council's "flying squadrons" found the doors locked, they broke them down; if physical force was not enough, they used tools to gain entry. Brown Squire, a Negro Communist on Chicago's South Side, became something of a legend for his ability to quickly round up "some of the boys" to return the often pitiful belongings of the evicted.[22]

The sight of blacks and whites enduring police violence together apparently had a profound effect on some ghetto residents. Claude Lightfoot was a twenty-one-year-old graduate of Virginia Union University who had been drawn to the Garvey movement in 1930. Like thousands of other South Side blacks, he hung around Washington Park during hot summer nights, listening to Garveyite, Communist, and various religious speakers. When all-white crews laid trolley tracks on the fringe of Washington Park, in full view of the black jobless, Lightfoot led demonstrations that resulted in seventy-five jobs for Negroes. He became a Communist when he joined an "eviction riot" and witnessed how whites "shed real blood in defense of Negro workers."[23]

Brown Squire recalled an incident when police arrived at an eviction site before the UC flying squadron and forced the group to run a gauntlet of blackjacks and nightsticks as they returned furniture piece by piece, "covered with workers' blood." On another occasion, the burly Squire wound up scuffling with a Negro politician who had attacked a white UC member. With a black comrade, he pondered the change in attitude from 1919, when they had defended their community with guns against whites, to 1931, when they "beat up a Negro capitalist in defense of a white worker."[24]

From Detroit to Brooklyn to Norfolk, Virginia, city life was punctuated by sullen ceremonies of returning possessions to the homes of the evicted, as well as occasional rent strikes.[25] Ultimately, the violent reactions to these acts culminated in death and in outpourings of anger and grief. Not surprisingly, the big explosion came in Chicago's Black Belt.

On February 10, 1931, the Unemployed Councils first entered the South Side in an organized body with a march through the community. The Party admitted that only one in twenty in the ranks was black and that "the Negro masses looked [upon the march] with skepticism and some with hesitation and indifference." The comrades chose not to retire from the Black Belt. They organized a hunger march to Springfield, the state capital; they sent delegations to City Hall to demand adequate relief; they established six branches of the LSNR on the South Side. On August 1, two days before the fatal events that shook the community, hundreds of blacks participated in a Party-led antiwar demonstration.[26]

In late July the "colored Communists" restored four families to their homes in a single day. For three weeks before August 3, Unemployed Council Branch No. 4 was intervening in three to five evictions a day. On July 24 the Mid-South Side Property Owners Association met with representatives of the state's attorney to complain of inaction by the police in curbing Communist meetings in Washington Park and the reds' practice of moving ousted tenants back into vacated flats. The association demanded vigorous prosecution of "housebreakers." But the authorities were not anxious to rile the large crowds that gathered at eviction sites. In one incident the police collected $25 from their own ranks to "prevail upon" a landlady to allow an evicted tenant to return to her apartment. But that spirit soon gave way, perhaps under pressure from real estate agents and landlords to get tough with the reds. Ominous reports were brewing that "Chicago is going to face a situation more grave than that of 1919."[27]

On August 3 UC Branch No. 4, had already moved against three evictions when it received word that Diana Gross, a seventy-two-year-old Negro woman, had been evicted. Her furniture was being restored to her apartment when police arrived to arrest the "ringleaders" at the request of an anxious landlord. As an angry crowd of neighbors and UC members surrounded a police wagon that already held three demonstrators who had been seized, a second wagon arrived. At that point, the picture dissolves into chaos and confusion. The police accused the crowd of attacking the driver and crew of the second vehicle, seriously injuring three officers and forcing police to fire their weapons in self-defense. The Communists and bystanders accused the police of firing pointblank into a knot of demonstrators. Three black men fell dead: Abe Grey, a Communist and member of the Unemployed Councils; John O'Neal, a member of the UC; and Frank Armstrong, who may also have been a member of the UC. Twenty-one people were arrested. At the coroner's inquest, witnesses testified that the black victims were neither armed nor resisting arrest.[28]

The presence of Henry W. Hammond, an attorney for the landlord group and the Chicago NAACP, at the July 24 landlords' meeting had thrown the Party into a paroxysm of accusation: The black bourgeoisie had joined the city government in a battle of "the dirty dollars of the landlords against the lives of the working class." Mayor Anton Cermak was thrown on the defensive — as were black clergymen, editors, and educators who met on August 6 with city officials to discuss ways of preventing "further communistic activities" in the Black Belt. They admittedly faced an unaccustomed challenge to their own leadership. Thus, while bowing before the raw power of city authorities in blaming "red agitation" for the bloodshed, they warned that the community could not for long resist the reds' appeal unless the misery of the ghetto was alleviated. Reverend J. C. Austin complained that he had addressed several Washington Park meetings, but that he could not talk religion to men with empty stomachs. Reverend Harold L. Kingsley said that he had predicted the events of August 3. The Communists were manipulating drifting, declassed, desperate men and women; he could not address the angry drifters after the riot because "I can't tell a hungry man to be patient." The community leaders' statement, adopted with the approval of city officials, noted that the "only cure" for events like August 3 was unemployment relief.[29]

Mayor Cermak said he had information that the Communists were well-fed fellows "with an aversion for honest toil." The city elite applauded the police for their "firmness" and "moderation." But the conservative black newspaper *Chicago Bee* said that it was useless to bait the Communists; given the ghetto's misery, it was a wonder the whole race hadn't turned red. The black *Chicago Whip* said that something was very wrong with a system so rich in resources, brains, and money as to allow so many to starve. The breakdown of law and order should be blamed not on the Communists, but on the system's failures. Why not exert the energies expended pointlessly on the red menace to correct the evils that gripped the Black Belt?[30]

Despite Cermak's flippant remarks, he had to admit that jobless people could not pay rent. Under the impact of August 3, he announced a temporary suspension of evictions. The nightly Washington Park forum on August 4 drew a huge crowd to hear Party speakers declare a partial victory, but also castigate the city for not acting until Negro blood had been spilled. The Party reported that in the days following the killings, five thousand blacks had joined the Unemployed Councils, five hundred had applied for Party membership, and "hundreds of others" had joined the ILD.[31]

The coroner's inquest became a battle between the Chicago district attorney and the ILD. Hundreds of South Side unemployed packed the courtroom where the ILD presented to the coroner's jury its claim that the killings had been provoked by the police. The jury eventually absolved the police and city authorities of responsibility in the deaths of Grey, O'Neal, and Armstrong.[32]

On August 8 the Party and its affiliates staged a "mass funeral" for Grey and O'Neal.[33] Party members flooded the South Side with tens of thousands of leaflets headlined "They Died for Us!" claiming over half a million unemployed in Chicago, including "over fifty thousand . . . Negro workers who are doubly exploited and persecuted."[34] Thousands of Black Belt residents waited in long lines to view the bodies of the victims. After a sung service, the mourners poured into the street to march to a point where the bodies of the slain men were to be shipped to Mississippi for burial. The procession was a combination of genuine grief and political huckstering. Along the sidewalks "scores of boys and girls hawked copies of the *Daily Worker*. 'Come on and join us,' the marchers continued to yell at those who looked on." The reporter for the *Chicago Bee* captured the sweep and emotion of the funeral: "All ages were represented. White and black children wearing red sashes joined hands and marched while singing. Black mothers and white mothers marched with infants in their arms. Old men and old women, too old for work, paraded, sang, and clapped their hands. At the playing of the 'Internationale' by a band which led the parade, men and women sang lustily and held up the fist of the right hand."[35]

The August 3 bloodletting did not bring an end to evictions or to the efforts of the Unemployed Councils to stop them. When the tension abated, the bailiff's office began serving writs again. The police were more cautious in handling crowds, but more ruthless in harassing the Unemployed Councils. However, in the spring of 1933, the Communists were still moving furniture back into the homes of evicted tenants in Chicago's Black Belt.[36]

What of the hundreds on the South Side who joined the Party in heat of anti-eviction protests? Michael Gold, writing in the *Daily Worker,* admitted that "some of them have been driven away. The Party in America has not yet worked out some simple consistent plan that would hold such masses." Often the problem was simply the internal tedium of Party life, which was at least as much a part of being a Communist as the excitement of confrontation at eviction sites. To be a revolutionary required paying dues and special assessments (for the South, for example), distributing the Party's press, working in "mass organizations," "checkup" on various financial and press circulation quotas, building audiences for public events, mobilizing people for demonstrations, participating in "educationals," enduring "criticism and self-criticism." This huge commitment of time and energy became too much for many blacks and whites after the heat and passion of a given struggle faded. Many left — not with anger or recrimination, but because the normal rhythms of life did not allow for the abnormal rhythms of a revolutionary existence. Sometimes a change in lifestyle — getting a job, leaving the city, getting married, having a child, becoming ill, or losing interest — was cause for an exit.[37]

What of those blacks who remained? Many who were recruited in the early and mid-1930s stayed for months and years. Sylvia Wood, Claude Lightfoot, Nate Sharpe, and others remained Communists for their lifetimes. Despite a high turnover, the South Side section of the Party in the early 1930s began to take on the cultural expression, texture, and even the cadences of black life that had been largely transported from the Mississippi Delta to Chicago. As it had for the blacks recruited in Birmingham, Marxist theory offered a compelling explanation for the exploitation and discrimination felt throughout Chicago's Black Belt. Some members, like Lightfoot and Ishmael Flory (along with Haywood and Hall, of course), contributed to the theoretical development of the Party's evolving policies. Richard Wright, for more than a decade, was the Party's most prominent literary figure and articulator of the emotional content of national oppression.[38]

Lightfoot tells of Harry Haywood coming to the South Side in 1932 as a representative of the national organization's Negro Department. He appeared at a large section meeting, with all the "authority" and inflexibility of his years at the Lenin School. Haywood had come to expel Poindexter for some sort of "deviation." In his Party-style monotone, Haywood laid out the particulars: Comrade Poindexter did this, Comrade Poindexter acted without the Party's approval, Comrade Poindexter did that, and on and on. There was a stir in the hall; a woman cried out: "Oh, Lord, the Party's gonna expel Poindexter!" There were sighs and discordant sounds from Poindexter's admirers, especially women. Poindexter responded: "If my Party sees fit to sever me from the revolutionary movement which I have served faithfully, so be it. If I soiled Communist principles while leading the unemployed, while fighting for relief, while standing at the citadels of power and demanding justice for the working class— while [voice rising] comrade Haywood was studying at the Lenin School, so be it, so be it." At this point, shouts of indignation and support for Poindexter filled the hall. Haywood turned to the section leaders and signaled a retreat "for consultation." Later, Haywood reappeared to announce that in view of Comrade Poindexter's "self-criticism," the Party would withdraw its charges. Poindexter's celebrated rhetoric and the audience's responses, punctuated with "yes," "tell it!" and "amen," were not, to say the least, typical of Party meetings. But they had become typical on the South Side where, according to Lightfoot, section meetings often took on the sounds and spiritual tension of a Delta revival.[39]

Three weeks after the "mass funeral," the Chicago Communists were back at it, this time at United Charities, where they demanded relief for four destitute families that had been denied assistance. Demonstrations at relief agencies, public and private, had become commonplace occurrences during the Great Depression. Especially in black communities, where many lived on the margin of starvation, the local charity or relief station virtually held the power of life and death over the people. From that standpoint the battle for relief had a directness and urgency second to none. Typical of the street politics of relief was an incident in Harlem in 1931, when a crowd stormed a relief station after being exhorted at a street meeting of the local Unemployed Council. The demonstrators complained about the plight of Negro women who were forced to wait for hours to apply for nonexistent menial jobs. The fury of relief agency protests sometimes spilled into courtrooms. On September 2, 1932, thirty Communists and supporters shouted their outrage at sentences handed out to two people who had been in the middle of a disturbance at the Harlem Relief Bureau. A white woman, Eleanor Henderson, wife of a Columbia University economics instructor, was given ten days in jail; Sam Brown, a Negro, received six months for the same charge. Mrs. Henderson reportedly was among the first to condemn this unequal punishment as a racist caricature of justice.⁴⁰

In November 1932 a twenty-seven-year-old mother of four children was buried on Long Island after a mass funeral at the Harlem Workers' Center, sponsored by the Harlem Unemployed Council and the LSNR. The Party claimed that Mrs. Estelle Smith, her husband, and four small children, one of them an infant, had been denied relief by charity agencies and were forced to live on eleven cents a day given them by the Home Relief Bureau. A diet of cabbage and beans, along with the burden of caring for her family during pregnancy, had seriously weakened Mrs. Smith by the time she bore her fourth child. Communists in Harlem charged that she was mistreated and neglected while in the hospital. She died shortly after the birth of her child. At her coffin, blacks and whites pledged to avenge her death by organizing to destroy hunger and starvation. Her husband was then elected a delegate to the Second National Hunger March on Washington, on December 5, 1932.⁴¹

On December 22, 1932, the Communists found the body of a Negro man in an abandoned building on West Fortieth Street in Manhattan. The building for some time had been "home" to assorted vagrants, some of whom had joined the New York Unemployed Council. The unidentified man was given the name "Skippy Baritone," and a combined protest march and funeral procession was organized. Behind the hearse, carriers bore a placard that read, "He Died of Starvation," flanked by a huge red flag. Other signs charged the city commissioner of welfare with complicity in "Skippy's" death. As the cortège, led by the Red Front Band, made its way through the garment district to Union Square, the now anticipated confrontation with police erupted. "Skippy Baritone" was laid to rest at a burial ground owned by a Party affiliate in Mount Olivet cemetery in Queens. For the Party, "Skippy Baritone" had been rescued from the dust and ashes of his own decay. In death, the humanity, identity, and dignity of all black men and women who lived and died as anonymous outcasts were reaffirmed.⁴²

But critics were not about to ignore the element of manipulation and opportunism in the "Skippy Baritone" funeral. The *Pittsburgh Courier* commented wryly that "past masters in the business of 'demonstrations,' New York Communists will grasp any opportunity to stage one." With a Third Period belief in "them or us," nearly any self-serving device could be, and usually was, rationalized by the Party. Not only were the sensitivities of the larger society often ignored, but often those of workers and blacks themselves — with results that skirted burlesque and invited scorn. With all that, the "Skippy Baritone" incident, and scores of others like it, pounded into the consciousness of the broader public what the nation and the system were doing to its black members.[43]

In the early Depression years, very few had taken on that task.

CHAPTER TEN

Nationalists and Reformists

Always, for the Party, there was bourgeois nationalism and the "national revolutionary movement of the Negro people." Both were shaped and driven by social class, but the internal nature and relationship of class forces within those distinct modes were strikingly dissimilar. The two were also contradictory.

Bourgeois nationalism hadn't changed; it was still personified by the remnants of the Garvey movement and by the merchants, strivers, and assorted professionals who sought to maintain their own ghetto through subordination to the dominant capitalism.[1]

On the other side of that bourgeois coin was "reformism," personified by Du Bois and the NAACP. The Negro reformists sought assimilation into the larger society though class collaboration and piddling concessions. Their goal, according to the Party, was to prolong a dying system by luring the masses into their murky, compromising channels. Thus, they were "social fascists" — part of capitalism's last social democratic line of defense against revolution.

In the Party's view, both the bourgeois nationalists and reformists were from the same class and had a common denominator: to undermine revolutionary working-class unity and save capitalism.[2] Against them stood the national revolutionary movement, led by black workers.

The Party's relentless attack on bourgeois nationalism and reformism exemplified a "vulgar" determinism that departed from traditional Marxist theory on the national question. In the fevered Third Period, there wasn't much discussion about how, under national oppression, the subjugated bourgeois class calls upon its "native folk" to rally to national self-determination. The working class had to join that fight and support bourgeois demands like freedom of movement and free education, which "affect the workers no less, if not more, than the bourgeoisie."[3] All that was lost in demands for proletarian hegemony in the black community.

Black Communists were counseled to "*clearly dissociate* themselves from all bourgeois currents in the Negro movement." White Communists were warned not to balance nationalism among black comrades with their own more serious white chauvinism. White racism was always the primary danger, yet chauvinism and nationalism were "two roads to the same camp" of racial division within the working class. Cyril Briggs was obliged to couple his call for struggle against white chauvinism with counsel to black Communists that they must combat "the segregation tendencies of the Negro workers themselves." The New York District routinely admonished its black members to "conduct tireless activity among the Negro comrades against all remnants of distrust, suspicion and super-sensitiveness in regard to white revolutionary workers."[4]

But Briggs's own simmering nationalism occasionally bubbled to the surface. An editorial in the *Liberator* entitled "The Need to Hate" hailed a black college student who attributed his academic successes "to the fact that I hate white people." Briggs commented that "the ordinary and necessary attitude of hating one's enemies will not be to the liking of either the white imperialist oppressors or their servile middle class tools.... It would be a good thing for the Negro race if all Negroes did hate all white people."[5]

A week later Briggs wrote an editorial entitled "A Correction and Self-Criticism." He had been censured by Earl Browder as an example of the proclivity of some Negro comrades to capitulate "to the propaganda of the Negro bourgeoisie and petty bourgeoisie intellectuals of race hatred directed against all whites without distinction of class." Briggs now reminded his readers that the white ruling class and its agents — white and black — were the scourges of the black masses, while the "revolutionary workers" were their staunch allies. Hatred there must be, Briggs stated, "but that hatred must be directed solely against the oppressing class."[6]

Richard Moore also periodically got into trouble for "nationalist" deviations. At a meeting of the Party's Negro Commission in January 1929, Moore was reminded that he had not yet left the church as the Political Committee had instructed. He now gave in, announcing that he was resigning from his denomination "not because he agree[d] with the perverted statement," given out by the Party, that he had "an anti-Communist attitude" in regard to religion, but because his "Communist work in the church [was] not yet fully understood even by Communists," and he did not wish to perpetuate "illusions" about the nature of his church membership.[7]

In his report to the Party's Eighth Convention in 1934, Harry Haywood complained that petty bourgeois nationalism had seeped into the CP's black membership. Some black Party leaders were being called Uncle Toms. Doubts persisted among black CP members about the commitment of white workers to the struggle for Negro rights; some argued that Negro work could not develop until the Party had cleansed itself of all white chauvinism. Some black comrades used the charge of white chauvinism to "cover up their shortcomings and weaknesses as well as their petty bourgeois nationalist tendencies."[8]

"RACE LOYALTY" AND CAPITALISM

In the larger black community, the notion of "race loyalty" struck a chord despite the national crisis. The Harlem Business Men's Club in 1931 launched the first of several "Don't Buy Where You Can't Work" campaigns, claiming that the community was letting "millions of race dollars" slip through its fingers by patronizing white businesses. The *Pittsburgh Courier* claimed that its "Build As You Buy Campaign" would produce profitable black enterprises to provide financial support for community churches, schools, and housing. The socialist-minded Du Bois in 1932 argued that blacks had the ability to furnish the capital "to establish a black industrial world" (presumably along cooperative lines). The dream of economic survival within a segregated market appeared to be gaining fresh support.[9]

William Patterson countered that "race loyalty" was fealty to a black bourgeoisie that sought only to get black workers "to spend their wages in the stores or deposit in the banks of these petty business men." Theirs was "a cash register loyalty" that gave them "the first whack at the pocketbook of the Negro consumer." They were "treacherous fellows" who salivated over "herd[ing] us into a segregated blacktown so as to force us to be supporters of blacktown grocery stores, shops, etc." The subordinate state of the black bourgeoisie caused it to work even harder to curry the favor of the white ruling class. White big business tossed some crumbs to black entrepreneurs, but none that would threaten its own interests, even in the ghetto. White big business and black small business had forged an alliance—sealed by "bribes" in the form of concessions, loans, and mortgages—that created some slight common interest between them.[10]

The Party occasionally admitted that the interests of the black middle class were not always identical with those of white capitalists. The petty bourgeoisie did not escape racism. The *Liberator* admitted that black businessmen were hurting from the penetration of white-owned chain stores into the ghetto. Patterson conceded "great points of difference between the white ruling class and the Negro capitalist group." Subservient black business needed concessions from white capitalists to extend the ghetto—the only territory available to it. But such concessions were rarely, if ever, granted.[11]

The Party could have concluded that such factors quickened prospects for an alliance between black working people and the Negro bourgeoisie. That would have been consistent with the theoretical concept of the all-class character of the national question. A segment of the African American petty bourgeoisie clearly had "progressive" attributes; the discriminatory practices of the larger society set up a potential conflict between black-owned business and white corporate power. At best, the black bourgeoisie was a vulnerable stratum that vacillated between capitalists and workers. The Party's caricature of thieving landlords, gouging shopkeepers, and "prostitute intellectuals" clouded middle-class battles for reform in education, housing, economic life, and the judicial system—reform that advanced the black working class as well.[12]

Despite all that, the Communists raised probing questions about ghetto capitalism as a survival strategy. They were not alone in this endeavor. T. Arnold Hill of the National Urban League claimed that the "economic structure of the race is yet too weak to support big business run exclusively for Negroes and competition too severe for inexperienced entrepreneurs and for shoestring investments to succeed." For Hill, the struggle for jobs in the larger society held greater promise.[13]

Loren Miller, the left-leaning city editor of the *California Eagle,* noted that no group, save the workers themselves, had been hit harder by the crisis than the black bourgeoisie. Race consciousness was being pushed by that besieged group to entice black workers to expend their meager resources on black business. But "trying to blackjack patronage out of the worker with racial arguments and race glorification will only go so far." The worker's slim hope for gain from race-based spending was the "far fetched possibility" that his purchasing power might contribute to a developed black capitalist class that would build factories to employ black workers. But a middle stratum with capitalist aspirations was obliged to place its limited surplus funds in "established white investments," which did not employ blacks. The black worker was left to pursue his interests in the cauldron of industrialism. The middle stratum, in its own interest, should support the struggles of black workers for justice.[14]

Eugene Gordon, another young radical intellectual, wouldn't concede that the bourgeoisie was sincere about race loyalty. That fidelity was less a matter of racial exclusiveness than "a propellant of individual achievement within the race." Such climbing did not assure that others would be drawn upward, nor did it assure immunity from white racism. The experience of one of the leading black capitalists, Charles C. Spaulding, a banking and insurance magnate in Durham, North Carolina, was instructive. Spaulding had once been cursed and tossed out of a smoke shop in neighboring Raleigh by a lowly white sales clerk. The incident was emblematic of "the state of black capitalists in free America."[15]

As the Depression deepened, business news appeared to confirm pessimistic assessments of black capitalism. The heralded Binga State Bank of Chicago had collapsed in 1930; the Douglass National Bank went under in 1932; black-owned Victory Life Insurance and National Benefit Life became insolvent in the same year. In 1928 the Colored Merchants Association had begun to promote cooperative wholesale buying and efficient retail businesses. By the end of 1932 three CMA stores in Harlem had declared bankruptcy. By the summer of 1933 CMA itself was in ruins. John Nail, who in 1931 was the leading black real estate agent, tore into the belief that "race patronage" could succeed. Black bankers and businessmen, Nail said, could never compete with white capital. The only long-term solution was to somehow merge into the white business world "and quit thinking of ourselves as Negro businessmen, but as businessmen." Black commentator William Occomy, writing in the *Business Review* in 1931, questioned the ability of capitalism to make room for black entrepreneurship without a significant redistribution of wealth to ease the burden on the black population. The power of government had to be exercised to redistribute wealth at least to a moderate extent. Without that, blacks would have no chance to create an independent ghetto economic base, and the Communists, already on the move in the ghetto, would make major inroads among blacks.[16]

For the Communists, the cold reality remained: Black workers, now more than ever, were forced to seek jobs in the factories, farms, and stores controlled by white capital. The illusion of salvation through black enterprise built on race loyalty was being fostered deliberately to divert blacks from the struggle for unemployment relief, social insurance, and the opening up of all fields of work to their labor.[17]

The belief in a plot was typical Third Period excess. Yet the limitations of black capitalism were a serious concern. Its historic weaknesses suggested a poor alternative to the struggle for economic and social survival in the larger economy, public and private. Race-conscious buying and selling could offer only limited help in the absence of a struggle against the racist underpinning of the economy and against discrimination in employment and relief.

As the Party emerged from its severe sectarianism, its position on black business became softer and more nuanced. Internal discussions noted that white capital dwarfed black capital, even the small portion of the latter that penetrated the ghetto. But the *Harlem Liberator* in 1933 finally conceded that it was "not opposed to Negro business as such." That would be giving "objective support" to white business over black enterprise — something Communists would never do.[18]

The Communists in the early 1930s gave little thought to the possibility that "race loyalty" could transcend black capitalism. Their narrow view was a consequence of sectarianism and a sometimes simplistic approach to the complex interactions of class and race. The theory of the national question should have led to recognition of a strain of race loyalty grounded in a culture of struggle against oppression. Also, by reducing the ghetto to little more than a field for exploitation by petty black capital, the Party's line could be misunderstood as a simplistic contempt for the ghetto and for the community's racially grounded allegiances.

"Lickspittles" and Betrayers

The Communists' churlish attitude toward the black middle class was numbing. When two black physicians decided to sell their homes in a New York suburb after protests by white neighbors, the *Liberator* called their action "true to the treacherous code of their class." When a black assistant pastor in Chicago complained to police about distribution of a Communist antilynch leaflet in front of his church, he was accused by the *Daily Worker* of "helping lynching." When the minister advised his congregation to reject the assistance of whites and "fight their own battles," the Party's paper accused him of "open support for the bosses' plans of isolating the Negro" to intensify his oppression. When the 1930 convention of the Negro Ministers' Evangelistic Alliance of America passed a resolution denouncing communism in the black community, the *Daily Worker* countered that the convention had failed to say anything about lynching and unemployment, and ran its story under the headline "Negro Sky Pilots Help Lynching."[19]

Leading intellectuals and academics, such as Robert R. Moton, W.E.B. Du Bois, Kelly Miller, William Pickens, and Mordecai Johnson, were described in Party polemics as "intellectual prostitutes" who have "fattened and grown [upon] . . . segregation." Old nemesis Miller was called "one of the most astute bunk spreaders," one who used his Howard University platform to play the Republicans' "clever procurer." John D. Rockefeller III's visit to Fisk University in 1931 triggered a Communist attack upon the "Jim Crow Negro College." Why was Rockefeller, this representative of "peonage and debt slavery," welcomed by the Fisk faculty? The answer: "they too profit by this system which brings starvation and death to the masses but petty jobs for them." The Party dismissed Tuskegee as a "Jim Crow technical school" whose president, Robert Moton, allegedly prevailed upon students "to slavishly accept the degradation heaped upon them by American imperialism." Horace Mann Bond was virulently attacked by Patterson for publishing an article that pleaded for both races to place their faith and trust in the "more genuine Southern white gentlemen." Patterson replied, "For cringing base cowardice, for pure belly crakling [*sic*], award this the first prize."[20]

The CP identified the Urban League as among the black community's "most deadly enemies," fawning before the capitalists and doing "nothing for the Negro masses." Generalizations often escalated into specific charges, such as an allegation made in 1931 that the Urban League had recruited black strikebreakers in a Boston longshore strike.[21]

The NAACP was a special target. Its claim to leadership in the battle against racial injustice collided with the Party's aspirations. The NAACP's solid middle-class credentials, its anticommunism, its faith in the legal system, and its status as a pillar of the community all earned it special enmity on the part of the Communists, which dissolved only gradually with the coming of the popular front in later years.[22]

Although the Party could not accept reform as an end in itself, it held to the Marxist view of an organic connection between reform and revolution. Without a struggle for reform, a revolutionary movement failed to win the confidence of the masses, who could not survive on abstractions, but needed realizable victories. Yet the Party still continually accused the NAACP of wast-

ing its time on "petty reforms" and on legal challenges to segregation ordinances, while Jim Crow became ever stronger without the force of law. A clash
of basic values and assumptions about how to achieve black liberation (and
about the nature of "liberation" itself) reached its climax during the celebrated Scottsboro case (see chapter 11). The Party had a simple explanation
for the NAACP's circumspection and dread of mass action. The "reformist
traitors" were doing the job of social fascists — diverting blacks and whites
from forming "fighting alliances" in the streets. Communists did their own
variation of race-first rhetoric by claiming that the "white capitalist masters"
who controlled the NAACP assigned to it the task of fostering illusions about
the "boss courts."[23]

The Party's mindless quarrel with Du Bois was an offshoot of its campaign
against the NAACP. Whenever Du Bois offered a seemingly radical idea, the
Communists treated it as an affront to their own claims to militant leadership
of the black masses. The 1932 conference of the NAACP was shaken by criticism of the association's handling of the Scottsboro case and its tepid response to the effects of the Depression on blacks. Du Bois seized the moment
to try to move the organization to deeper involvement in economic and social
issues. He suggested electoral ticket splitting, selective voting, and the formation of an independent labor party rooted in a black-labor alliance. Harry
Haywood dismissed the suggestions as "demagogic prattle," merely signifying that "old methods are no longer fit to serve the cause of [his] imperialist
masters." Du Bois's call for political independence, Haywood claimed, was a
repackaging of "old reformist" illusions in radical-looking wrappers because it
was no longer possible to line up Negro masses behind the "old reactionary
parties."[24]

Summarizing the differences between the ANLC and the NAACP, Du Bois
had charitably put the two on the same plane, claiming that their programs
were in "essential agreement." The comparison was a handy vehicle to convince
his readers (and probably himself) that the NAACP was ready for change. Du
Bois reiterated that he had for many years "warned against an attempt to solve
the American Negro problem simply by the capitalistic program of accumu-
lating wealth." Yet, he admitted, the NAACP was in a difficult position in face
of the power of capital. The answer was to seek to preserve the "possibilities
for good" in the system, while correcting its excesses and abuses. Instead of
revolution Du Bois chose reform through "sacrifice, patience, clear thinking,
determined agitation and intelligent voting."[25]

Cyril Briggs might have greeted Du Bois's favorable assessment of the ANLC program as a validation, but he did not. For Briggs, the act of comparing the ANLC and the NAACP sullied the revolutionary integrity of the moribund group. Du Bois's gentle search for common ground was a "deliberate and politically crooked" attempt to cover up fundamental differences. His effort to tug the ANLC into a social-democratic framework did not sit well, to put it mildly. Briggs dismissed Du Bois's claim that both organizations shared a belief in "increased democratic control of industry," which reeked of spineless class collaboration through such palliatives as profit sharing. He also scoffed at Du Bois's claim that both groups shared an advocacy of "interracial cooperation," which had the odor of a middle-class tea party. The NAACP's interracial conferences on unionism were only gab fests between white bosses and their "tools" in the black community. So that no one could misconstrue the differences between the two organizations, Briggs said the issue boiled down to a "program of struggle" versus "bourgeois petitionism" anchored on pathetic appeals to the (nonexistent) conscience of the ruling class.[26]

The Garvey movement in the early 1930s was a shell of what it had been a decade earlier. But the Party was not about to be less confrontational with separatist nationalism than it was with reformism. The Garveyites still played "the bosses' games" in advocating "race first" and advising blacks to shrug off the rest of the (white) working class. With the Garveyites, the battle sometimes became violent. The CP charged that St. William Wellington Wellwood Grant, head of the UNIA's Tiger Division, made it a regular practice, in league with the New York cops and Tammany Hall, to "gang" and bully CP street-corner meetings.[27] (Under pressure from the Party in late 1933, Briggs acknowledged that despite the corruption and ideological malfeasance of UNIA leaders, the Garveyite rank and file were "good fighters, willing and ready to wage a relentless struggle to free Africa, the West Indies, and the 'Black Belt' of the Southern states." Communists were obligated to win over that honest but misled group: "We must overcome the mistakes we have made in the past of antagonizing them — mistakes from which the *Liberator* has not been free.")[28]

INTERNATIONALISM AND NATIONALISM

When discussing communism, the Garveyites focused repeatedly on the Party's tight embrace of the USSR. The Soviet example did not impress the UNIA; it merely demonstrated that under communism blacks would still be a minority. The CP would not retreat; defense of Soviet Russia was part of its standard appeal to African Americans. The USSR was proclaimed to be the living embodiment of racial justice and self-determination. Blacks were urged to march with that global movement, headed by the USSR, on the road to freedom for all oppressed national minorities.[29]

The Soviet Union enjoyed considerable sympathy and some prestige in black circles in the 1930s. The middle class often raised the Soviet specter as a club against government-sanctioned racism. Du Bois was one of the first black intellectuals to contrast the seeming success of the Soviet experiment with capitalism's exhaustion and paralysis. He claimed playfully that when Russian youth heard that America was making work for the idle by using men with snow shovels instead of machines, the young Soviets suggested that the Americans try spoons. The *Pittsburgh Courier,* despite its attachment to the status quo, pointed to the labor shortage in Russia as a stark contrast to the hordes of jobless and the bread lines in the United States. Soviet intolerance for racism, manifested in summary treatment of whites judged guilty of that transgression, received sympathetic coverage in the African American press. The scores of black Americans who went to the Soviet Union in the early 1930s to work as artisans, laborers, and engineers also got considerable attention from the black press, as did George Padmore's election to the Moscow Soviet in 1931. A tremor ran through the black media when Kelly Miller Jr., son of the conservative Howard University dean, left the United States in 1931 for an "indefinite stay" in the USSR. William N. Jones of the Baltimore *Afro-American* routinely praised the Soviets' social and economic safety net. Dean E. P. Davis of Howard University, while in Moscow in 1936, found the new "equality" constitution of the USSR to be a model of educational, social, and economic fairness. A. L. Foster, leader of the Chicago Urban League, who toured the Soviet Union in 1936, stated that "it is the Communists alone, who offer colored people just what they say they are fighting for — political, social, cultural and economic equality."[30]

The black press also followed the heart-tugging saga of a young black Communist and his upper-class white wife who went to Soviet Russia to escape hostility to their marriage. The husband, Herbert Newton, survived his indictment for "insurrection" in Georgia, but he was unable to cope with the antagonism of his white father-in-law, Colonel John C. Emery, a wealthy banker. Jane Emery's marriage to Newton was revealed in 1934, after the couple was involved in a stormy eviction proceeding. The young woman was forced to undergo a psychiatric evaluation of her sanity because of her marriage to a black man. In

1936 the Newtons and their two children moved to Russia where, Jane Newton declared, "my marriage will be approved."[31]

Even so the Party's Soviet-centered internationalism did not always sit well with the various streams of nationalism that ran through black life. The situation worsened when the Party yielded to Soviet state interests (paradoxically, in the name of internationalism), and when those interests seemed to take precedence over black priorities.

THE MAKING OF *BLACK AND WHITE*

The problem was illuminated by the story of twenty-two young blacks who went to Moscow to make a film. In early 1932 James W. Ford returned from Europe with a proposal from the Comintern for black artists and writers to create a movie in the USSR about blacks in the United States. Ford turned to Louise Thompson to set up a committee to recruit the participants and arrange the trip. Thompson, a thirty-one-year-old graduate of the University of California, had arrived in New York in the late 1920s on an Urban League fellowship at the New York School for Social Work. Unhappy with the school's stress on palliatives at a time of crisis, she left to become editorial secretary to Langston Hughes and Zora Neale Hurston under the patronage of Mrs. Osgood Mason. After a spin through the eddying Harlem Renaissance, Thompson parted company with Mason over the patroness's efforts to fashion her into a "primitive Negro." She went to work organizing seminars on race and labor issues for the Congregational Educational Society. But Thompson became resentful of the elitist attitudes of the employer participants in the seminars. She was moving leftward—attending Marxist classes at the downtown Workers' School and organizing a "Vanguard Club" with artist Augusta Savage to promote political discussion among the Harlem intelligentsia. She was also becoming fascinated with the Soviet experiment, and in 1931 she established a Harlem chapter of the Friends of the Soviet Union. It was in that role that she was approached by Ford.[32]

The film was to be called *Black and White*. W. A. Domingo hailed the project as an unprecedented departure from racist stereotypes in film. *Black and White* "will trace the development of the Negro people in America, their work, their play, their progress, their difficulties—devoid of sentimentality as well as of buffoonery." Thompson set up an interracial committee to recruit the actors and finance the trip. On June 14, 1932, twenty-two young black Americans sailed for Moscow. In a group drawn from lower middle-class and white-collar working-class backgrounds, only the singer Sylvia Garner and the actor Wayland Rudd, who had appeared in *Porgy,* had acting experience. The others — among them Langston Hughes, Dorothy West, Ted Poston, Henry Lee Moon, and Loren Miller — were writers, lawyers, postal clerks, insurance agents, students, manual workers, and a farm laborer. There was only one self-acknowledged Communist in the group — Alan McKenzie, a young salesman. (Thompson joined the Communist Party in 1933 after her return from Soviet Russia.) On the transatlantic voyage, political tugs and potential splits appeared when a majority voted down a proposal to cable a plea for the freedom of the Scottsboro defendants.[33]

Greeted in Moscow as *Negrochanski tovarishi* (Negro comrades), the group was housed in the stylish Grand Hotel and received VIP treatment. But the proposed film was turning into an embarrassment bordering on disaster. The screenplay opened with a tale of black Alabama steelworkers struggling to organize a union and unite with fellow white workers. Given the times, that was not totally unreasonable. But the story line did not avoid stereotype and was replete with wild improbabilities. At the end, embattled black workers used a radio to call for white unionists in the North to rescue them from a brutal race riot. The unionists rushed to Alabama, where somehow soldiers of the Red Army linked up with them.[34]

Langston Hughes nearly wept over the inanity of the script. But he declined an invitation to salvage it. Karl Junghans, a German director, who spoke little English and knew even less about the United States, attempted a rewrite, but it was rejected by the production company, Mezrabpom, the CI-connected German film group. With the film in limbo, most of the cast left for a tour of Black Sea ports. The film's future became the subject of intense speculation by American correspondents in Moscow. Rumors abounded that the Soviets were cooling on the project, fearing that its release would hurt their chances to win diplomatic recognition from the United States. Colonel Hugh Cooper, the American chief engineer on the Dnieperostroi dam project, had allegedly used his access to Stalin to stop the "un-American" film. Comintern leader Dmitri Manuilsky acknowledged to black students at KUTV that Cooper had threatened to delay completion of the dam if *Black and White* went into production. When the group returned from the Black Sea, Moon, who had not gone on the tour, was waiting with an issue of the *International Herald-Tribune* that featured the headline "Soviet Calls Off Film on U.S. Negroes; Fear of American Reaction Cause." Within the group, two contending factions formed.

Moon and Poston ironically mimicked the polemical jargon of the Communists, accusing Mezrabpom of "right opportunism" and "base betrayal of the Negro workers of America and the International Proletariat." Thompson, the outspoken defender of the project, was dubbed "Madame Moscow," while Moon's growing antagonism toward Hughes exploded into a stream of vituperation.[35]

By late summer 1932 American correspondents in Moscow were churning out lurid stories of abandoned, starving, and uncompensated American Negro youth "adrift in Uncle Tom's Russian Cabin." The majority of the group asked for the Comintern's intervention to get the film back on track. Hughes and Miller pleaded with the ECCI that abandonment of the project would seriously damage the prestige of the world Communist movement. Moon and Poston accused Mezrabpom of colluding with the Kremlin to kill the film in the interests of Soviet foreign policy. The CI agreed that the film should be made despite Mezrabpom's ineptness. But no date was set for production to begin; the project was dead.[36]

Returning to the United States, Poston and Moon piled on more accusations: The Russians had ditched the film, caving in to "the forces of race prejudice" in the United States, because they feared Japanese advances in Manchuria and were courting Washington to gain diplomatic recognition as a counterweight to the Japanese. Their allegations struck a chord with Floyd Calvin of the *Pittsburgh Courier*. He concluded that the Soviets had bowed to racism, which proved "that the Communists are, after all, on the whole, white people and will sacrifice Negroes to monetary advantage just as the white people who control the capitalist system in this country will sacrifice them."[37]

Responding to Moon and Poston, fifteen cast members issued a statement calling their claims "fake" and "ridiculous." Louise Thompson reiterated that there had been no political intrigues — just script problems and technical difficulties. Without an approved script by mid-August 1932, the film had had to be postponed due to weather problems. She informed readers of the *Crisis* that members of the cast would be invited to return to the USSR in 1933 to complete the project. But Manuilsky, facing questions from black students at KUTV, seemed to confirm that the Soviets were seeking a deal with the United States: "Comrades, I put this question to you: if the Soviet Union were to be confronted by the danger of a major war, and . . . in the interests of preserving the dictatorship of the proletariat, were to be interested in at least the benevolent neutrality of America, would it have the right to maneuver occasionally on this or that issue?"[38]

The film was ultimately the victim of an oxymoronic "conscious inadvertence." A realization dawned upon its sponsors that Mezrabpom had neither the artistic nor the technical capacity to complete the project. And somewhere in the process, the Soviets' enthusiasm probably waned as prospects rose for gaining diplomatic recognition from Washington. Floyd Calvin decided that Russia was a growing world power and increasingly pursued national interests that could conflict with its commitment to achieve racial justice across national borders. For better or worse, the resolution of the racial crisis would have to come on native ground. Blacks would always be "forced back to the old truth, that this country, with all its faults, is the home of their history in modern civilization, and of their hopes for the future." In the view of black nationalists, the interests of a "white" polity would always take precedence over black interests. As reformers saw it, linkage with Soviet Russia threatened political ostracism and isolation. Ultimately, the episode showed that the black-red fusion was not without problems. When internationalism descended to dogma, it became virtually impossible to admit that state interests do collide with internationalist principles. Failing to confront that fact with candor, the Communists lost credibility among some sectors of the African American community.[39]

Padmore's Apostasy

The trajectory of George Padmore's life from ardent Communist to leading pan-African black nationalist presents another dimension of the problem. When Malcolm Nurse metamorphosed into George Padmore, his talent and his capacity for hard, selfless labor captured the attention of William Z. Foster and other Party leaders. In his early days in the Party, Padmore saw the organization as an instrument for winning an equal place for blacks within American society. At the same time, his vision was narrowing to Africa—hinting that he would follow the footsteps of Edward Blyden, the nineteenth-century nationalist, to a home in Liberia. Foster saw enough promise in Padmore to take him to Moscow in late 1929 to report to the RILU on the founding convention of the TUUL. Padmore's journey to Soviet Russia as a foreign quota resident of the United States earned him a refusal of reentry to America. But that may not have been important to him, for Padmore was becoming a significant figure in international Communist circles and his return to the United States was not on the horizon.[40]

Padmore soon became head of the Profintern's Negro Bureau. In that capacity he produced pamphlets and contributed articles to the *Moscow Daily*

News. His ascent in world Communist circles was nearly dizzying: arbitration of internal factional conflicts in the Chinese Communist Party, election to the Moscow City Soviet, occasional carrying of funds to overseas parties — all this while still in his twenties.[41]

Padmore was also involved heavily in the Hamburg conference held in July 1930, which formalized the ITUCNW as a federation of workers' organizations. There, he excoriated Garveyism, warned against pan-Africanism, and pilloried the reformists. He strongly advocated spreading propaganda for national freedom among colonial soldiers. The principal vehicle for such work would be the monthly *Negro Worker,* to be published within the friendly confines of Hamburg's old waterfront district. James Ford would be installed as the monthly's first editor.[42]

During 1930 Padmore was living in Vienna, unable to get into Germany to assist in consolidating the ITUCNW. Life was trying for him; he knew little German and had few contacts and little money. Perhaps the isolation stirred in him an Afrocentric longing that narrowed his political vision to what he knew best and to what reflected his own roots — the suffering of blacks under British imperialism. After a few months under Ford's editorship, the *Negro Worker* was turned over to Padmore. He managed to get to Hamburg in 1931 and began a very productive period, editing the monthly and writing twenty-five pamphlets in a single year. The best known of them was *Life and Struggles of Negro Toilers,* which was saturated with data on the conditions of black labor on three continents, the status of black organization, and a precise calculation of the surplus value created by colonial labor. His writing was generally free of jargon and was built upon an accumulation of solid information on economic and social conditions in the colonialized world. But the most impassioned aspect of his work concerned notions of racial oppression, with solidarity along class lines playing a rather subsidiary role.[43]

In May 1931 the executive committee of the LAI met in Berlin. Padmore was elected to its General Council as a West Indian delegate. From that point, his identity as an American was obliterated; he never again represented a U.S. organization. He was also beginning to advocate a two-phase variant of Leninist revolutionary theory in the colonial world: The first phase would be a racially grounded bourgeois revolution to overthrow white imperialists, in which Communists would cooperate with the nascent black bourgeoisie. The second phase would be a socialist revolution led by the emerging native working class.[44]

By June 1933 the Nazi takeover of Germany was in full swing. By mid-year, the Hamburg office of the *Negro Worker* had been ransacked and Padmore, among others, had been jailed. The journal had been kicked out of Germany and was using a post office box in Copenhagen. Before the end of the year Padmore was deported to England, where the authorities reluctantly permitted him to enter on his British passport. In London he was drawn deeply into the African and West Indian community, while he also labored to produce the *Negro Worker* under increasingly difficult circumstances.[45]

On August 13, 1933, the Comintern decided to suspend the *Negro Worker* and what was left of the ITUCNW. Padmore later claimed that this awakened his latent suspicions that such actions reflected a desire by Soviet Russia to reach an accommodation with the Western powers, especially the British Foreign Office, in the face of the growing fascist threat in Germany. He followed the logic of his deepening tendency to define imperialism in racial terms — and to cast doubt on an international movement led largely by whites. The August–September 1933 edition of the *Negro Worker* featured an "Au Revoir" from Padmore announcing the end of his editorship of the journal. Acknowledging that the monthly was virtually bankrupt, he urged that the struggle for colonial freedom should continue, no matter the cost, in solidarity with "our white class brothers." In the late summer of 1933 Padmore resigned his posts as secretary of the nearly moribund ITUCNW and as editor of the *Negro Worker*. He subsequently rejected an invitation from the Comintern to explain his action. On February 23, 1934, the CI's International Control Commission expelled Padmore from the Communist movement.[46]

Neither the *Negro Worker* nor the ITUCNW actually folded. In May 1934 publication of the monthly resumed in Copenhagen under the editorship of Otto Huiswoud, who used the nom de plume "Charles Woodson." A "working committee" of the ITUCNW itself was resurrected in the summer of 1934, but was forced out of Copenhagen and relocated for a time in Brussels. In November 1935 the *Negro Worker* was being published out of the offices of the renamed *Negro Liberator* in New York. With the emergence of the popular front in 1935, the RILU decreed that the working committee of the ITUCNW be reorganized and enlarged — with unions, peasants' groups, unemployed movements, tenants' leagues, fraternal societies, and educational groups to affiliate with the ITUCNW. The RILU also directed the *Negro Worker* to comply with French laws in order to secure a permanent home in Paris and to prepare a broadly based global conference of Negro workers in the French capital.[47]

The ITUCNW continued its anti-imperialist rhetoric with a new united-front line. The united front was to "struggle against exploitation, imperialist war... [and] for liberation and self-determination for Negroes." Granted, the campaign against colonialist violence was for the moment narrowed to protest against Italy's war upon Abyssinia. But internal RILU directives still spoke of semi-underground work to contact black seamen and colonial workers with ITUCNW's program.[48]

As a courier, Padmore had occasionally delivered funds to Senegal and other colonies. His break with the Comintern in 1933 was probably triggered by cutbacks in clandestine funding and perhaps also cuts in the arming of colonial unions and leftist organizations. But that could be justified on political grounds: They were unproductive interventions that undermined the security of native activists and vitiated their influence. Further, the need to compromise with the West in the face of the fascist threat could also be justified. The long-term viability of the movement against colonialism faced the greatest threat from fascism. Drawing the Western capitalist states into antifascist collaboration would strengthen the democratic, anticolonial forces in those societies; the hold of those states over their colonies would be weakened and riven by contradictions as the struggle against fascism went forward. There should have been room for Padmore and the CI to seek an understanding of each other's position. But that is not how changes of policy were implemented. Padmore's incipient racial nationalism and evolving social-democratic views shredded his loyalty to the Comintern and marked him as an enemy.[49]

The revived *Negro Worker* released a torrent of invective against Padmore. In an allusion to his continuing association with Garan Kouyaté, a former CI operative in Nyasaland who was now branded as an enemy agent and embezzler, Padmore was called "a petty-bourgeois nationalist with connections with agent-provocateurs and enemies of the Negro liberation struggle." There were vague charges that he had compromised former comrades by consorting with alleged police agents. He was attacked for saying that whites did not understand Negro psychology. (When black Communists had routinely leveled the same broadside in the 1920s, it had rarely provoked a reaction.) For the CI, that implied an unbreachable barrier to working-class unity. Padmore had placed racial solidarity above class; he had preached the divisive doctrine that blacks must fight for their own, primarily racial interests against all whites.[50]

In the end the *Negro Worker* lamented Padmore's "rise and fall... as a revolutionary fighter," adding that many non–working-class elements that had cast their lot with the workers were not steeled for hard struggle. Padmore allegedly tired of the difficult fight to win white workers in metropolitan areas to the battle against imperialism. From that frustration came the chimerical scheme to free Liberia from the clutches of its colonialist creditors by raising millions to pay its debts. He had condemned Garvey as a financial charlatan, but he now favored a utopian scheme to hurl dollars at the feet of the imperialists. According the the Communists, two warring souls — the anti-imperialist and the "Negro nationalist" — raged within Padmore. The nationalist soul won.[51]

Liberia loomed large in the CI's attack on Padmore's alleged betrayals. (He characterized the accusation that he dickered with the Liberian bourgeoisie as "chief" among the "monstrous lies" leveled against him.) The first broadside announcing Padmore's expulsion from the Communist movement stressed his truckling to "national reformists" to collect funds for a Liberian bailout. *Inprecorr*'s opening salvo ridiculed the notion that Liberia could be salvaged without global anti-imperialist struggle. To believe that "bribes" could free Liberia from vast profits taken out of the hides of native workers was worse than naive — it was doing the enemy's work.[52]

The CI did not confuse Padmore with another pro-Liberian "George Padmore," as his biographer claimed. In the RILU records is a plaintive letter written by Arnold Ward, a West Indian black who ran the Negro Welfare Association in London. That small, independent social welfare agency raised funds to provide summer excursions for the black children of London's slums. Ward floated on the periphery of the ITUCNW, and in turn the Committee published occasional fund appeals for his group. In November 1933 Ward wrote William Patterson asking what had become of George Padmore. He knew him well; shortly after the suspension of the *Negro Worker*, Padmore had uncharacteristically pressed upon Ward "a scheme . . . for buying out Firestone in Liberia" by raising $5 million. Ward wrote that Padmore had cursed "everything that is white — capitalist, socialist, communist; everyone is no good only Negroes is *[sic]* good." Padmore was also quoted as saying that the CI had let Negroes down; America and Britain were both going fascist. All that remained for blacks was to "develop Liberia and migrate us all back there."[53]

Padmore went on to become a major influence in the African liberation movement that erupted after World War II. He had a powerful impact on the thinking of a new generation of expatriate colonial radicals. For him, communism had become polluted by the exigencies of state power embodied in Stalin's rule of Russia. In Padmore's evolving thought, communism's engagement in state relations with colonialist powers had corrupted its mission to liberate the oppressed. Pan-Africanism would fulfill that failed mission and advance libertarian political systems for new African states by rejecting the polarities symbolized by the United States and the Soviet Union. His doctrine evolved into an "Africa for the Africans" precept, espousing a variant of social democracy, with state control of basic production and distribution. Scorning the obsessive anticommunism of the "god that failed" school, Padmore sought to maintain both his anti-imperialist focus and his resistance to communism. That was the basis for the "nonalignment" that characterized the emerging Third World after World War II.[54]

But Padmore's pan-Africanism was not able to plot a comfortable path between anti-imperialism and anticommunism. Ironically, a "pollution" similar to what he ascribed to communism due to its dealings with the West also seeped into pan-Africanism. Padmore began to promise that if Great Britain would only work toward self-determination for its colonies through gradual constitutional reform, bulwarks would be built against communism. The colonialists obliged. It turned out that they were amenable to concessions to the colonies — including political independence — as long as economic, cultural, and military dependence was maintained as a Cold War requirement. By accepting nominal independence as an alternative to communism, the former colonies were obliged to forego the more thorough and transforming changes in the economic and social spheres that deeper and more complete revolutions might have accomplished. Pan-Africanism represented reform, bargaining, and promises to contain latent militancy in the populace. In the words of political scientist Azinna Nwafor, "the storm centers of popular uprising for African emancipation were in fact headed off with the aid of Pan-Africanists, who represented themselves to the colonial authorities as the only force capable of curbing the violence of the masses." In country after country, the flag of independence flew as dependence upon the economic and social structures of the colonialist powers actually deepened.[55]

Padmore became the embodiment of converging reformism and racial nationalism — two things that the Communists always believed to be organically connected. For the CP both currents rejected the centrality of class in the formation of racist structures, refused to confront the capitalist essence of racial oppression, and ultimately sought accommodations with the dominant order. Padmore had stepped over a line into the heretical world of class collaboration. As a result, he was consigned to the scrap heap with the likes of

Garvey, the Sanhedrinites, the petty capitalists, and an array of apostates and "misleaders."[56]

REFORMISM, NATIONALISM, AND THE INNER LIFE OF BLACK COMMUNISTS

In the early years of the Depression the reds were all over ghetto street corners and meeting halls — still relative strangers to black life who preached in strange words. Nevertheless, they claimed the sole franchise and uncontestable truth in the battle for liberation. The CP seemed to be saying to blacks: it's us or the hell of betrayal by misleaders. Blacks who would march under the Party's banner would have to cut themselves off from traditional approaches and would have to trust that white workers would cast off their encrusted racism in the name of revolutionary unity.

In view of such demands, how did scores of racially conscious black women and men come to join the Party, accept its fundamental policies, rise in its ranks, and, in many cases, commit an entire adult life to a movement with which they came to identify? First, they understood communism as a global, multiracial movement whose theory, Marxism, knew no racial bounds. For William Patterson, the thought that Marxism, a universal "science of society," could not apply to the African American experience "denied the equality of blacks."[57]

Race and class converged in an ideological comfort zone where expressions of fierce racial opposition to the dominant society meshed with passionate class partisanship. Simple facts did not have to be articulated: The bosses were white, the lynchers were white, the landlords and merchants were white. Smoldering racial feeling could be vented through contempt for a *white* ruling class. That fully satisfied the class-against-class posture of the Party in the early 1930s. Some black Communists, like Cyril Briggs, would slip on the high wire of finely balanced class and racial antagonism — losing the class reference and turning his anger against all whites. But he would quickly recover that balance by refocusing on "the need to hate" bosses.

Even ideological struggle against other sectors of black life could induce in black Communists an affirmation of their racial consciousness. They attacked the black bourgeoisie's obeisance to the white ruling class, so that the middle class became a cabal of Uncle Toms bowing to powerful whites. Garvey and his followers, when under attack, became cowering supplicants before a white government; Du Bois and other intellectuals became fawning apologists for the white economic and legal establishments. In the words of black playwright Julian Mayfield, "You scratch a black man in the Communist Party and you're going to find a black man." There was little sign that black Communists were haunted by the specter of racial inauthenticity.[58]

The CP logically included in its demand for self-determination a solemnization of national consciousness communicated in black culture. "Negro Weeks" launched by Cyril Briggs in 1928 and 1929 were the start of a long tradition of celebrating fearless revolutionary heroes: Toussaint L'Ouverture, Gabriel Prosser, Denmark Vesey, Nat Turner, Frederick Douglass — racial idols who were sumbols of the national revolutionary impulse. "Militant Negro manhood" was for the Communists a dialectical response to national oppression and a legitimate manifestation of the struggle for national identity. In this regard, the Communists absorbed a sliver of Garveyism's male-centered heroic black Spartacus.[59]

In the heavily segregated society of the 1930s, fraternization with whites in a largely white movement was a mark of equality. The Party's practice of sending white organizers into black communities and placing whites on black-oriented publications like the *Liberator* troubled only a few black Communists. The whites generally were in subordinate positions, working under the direction of blacks who guided the Party's activities in predominantly black areas or institutions. They generally accepted black leadership and provided useful experience. Patterson believed that the essential issue in that relationship was the political and emotional capacity of those whites to fight racism and to respect the qualities and capabilities of black leaders. Theoretically at least, powerless white workers did not have the capacity or will to manipulate and control blacks. Like their black comrades, they looked at society from the bottom up.

In response to the allegation that the Party wished to use blacks to aggrandize its own (and Soviet) interests, Hosea Hudson said: "So any guy that say that the Party was using Negro people is just lying, that's all. Because the Party is a working class political party, and it takes in all workers, and the Negroes happen to be part of that working class. How they going to use them? I mean, when these people raise the question of they 'using' us, how they going use us when we're part of the working class?"[60] But in case white workers failed in their "proletarian duty," black Communists would continue to defend their commitment as the embodiment of their national consciousness and of their racial and class interests.

CHAPTER ELEVEN

Death to the Lynchers

In February 1931 a writer for the New York *World* noted that the incidence of lynching had increased sharply in 1930 — as a direct result, he stated, of the stock market crash of 1929. The Depression had caused social unrest and fanned mob hysteria among the unemployed. Arthur Raper, an expert on lynching for the Commission on Interracial Cooperation, conducted an extensive study of the phenomenon in the early 1930s. The commission was an organization whose caution often rankled even the cautious NAACP. Its conservatism made Raper's conclusions seem even more startling: "Lynching and the threat of it are now primarily a technique of enforcing racial exploitation — economic, political, and cultural." Lynching was a way to perpetuate "peonage, low wages, restricted work opportunities, and inferior education." Consequently, blacks suffered from inferior schools, fewer parks, poor public health, greater morbidity, poor police service, and "a small pauper allowance or relief order."[1]

The motive behind lynching was a constant: "the Negro must be kept in his place." While the rural mob of "low cultural and economic rank" engaged in lynching most frequently and most crudely, the wealthy exercised more subtle forms of the practice "to maintain their control over Negro labor." For the poor, the racial dogma was vital to prove their superiority; as lynchers, they became society's protectors and were able to flourish weapons, hunt down the accused, render judgment, and destroy their prey through torture, dismemberment, and burning. Thus they would for a time be able to forget their own miseries. So Negroes are lynched, Raper concluded, "and native-born white lynchers, some with property and more with none, are seldom indicted and never convicted."[2]

After the Sixth CI Congress, Communists began to comprehend lynching as an instrument of national oppression — an undiluted assault on the essence of culture and identity. Harry Haywood and Milton Howard counted, from 1882 to 1928, four thousand Negroes, including seventy-five women and girls, who had been hanged, burned, or mutilated by lynching. "Ruling class savagery," marked by such atrocities as a baby torn from the womb of its pregnant mother, had a purpose: "to strike terror in the hearts of the oppressed Negro people so that they dare not strike out for liberation." Thus, blacks were not lynched because they were a despised caste; rather, they were despised because they were an intensively exploited national minority. Seventy years after the end of slavery, the capitalists and landlords had sacrificed black humanity on the altar of super-profits erected by national subjugation.[3]

As the first rocky decade of CP history ended, lynching and "legal lynching" were finally being stressed by the Party. In mid-December 1929 Charlotte, North Carolina, was the scene of a modest antilynching conference held by the International Labor Defense, where local blacks and a handful of whites gathered to hear Simon Gerson, a young New Yorker, condemn the recent lynching of a Charlotte-area farm worker. In early 1930 Charles Alexander, an African American, was elected to the ILD board as an organizer with special responsibilities among Negroes. At the same time, instructions went out to all ILD regional groups to add black organizers. The ILD called a "mass protest conference" on lynching on May 18, 1930 — pledging to distribute a half-million antilynch leaflets and recruit five thousand blacks. The tempo of antilynch protests was stepped up with a series of rallies in North and South, including events in Charlotte and Winston-Salem, North Carolina; Greenville, South Carolina; Atlanta; and Chattanooga. "Sacco-Vanzetti Anti-Lynch Day," August 22, 1930, involved one hundred fifty thousand people across the country, according to the ILD (whose fervor may have led to suspiciously inflated figures). The Elks Hall in Sioux City, Iowa, was denied to a group seeking to stage an antilynch meeting; that at least showed that the protest was spreading into the nation's heartland.[4]

The Fourth ILD Convention, held in Pittsburgh in December 1929, marked a major effort by Communists and their allies to deal concretely with lynching and the treatment of blacks by the judicial system. The defense organization criticized itself for previous failures. Events surrounding the convention signified change. The Monongahela House Hotel, the convention site, refused to house the thirty blacks among the three hundred delegates. A protest demonstration was hastily staged in the hotel lobby, where the delegates declared a boycott and moved on to another location. That exhilarating act raised the spirit of the gathering and lent passion to resolutions calling for blacks and white allies to arm themselves against lynching.[5]

Mob violence was increasing in 1930, but William Patterson asserted that the ruling elite could no longer rely on "mobs slyly provoked into murderous action." White workers were allegedly less willing to be manipulated into committing racist outrages, so that the bosses were forced into their own courts to do the job, making the courtroom as deadly for Negroes as the deserted back roads of rural America. In North Carolina alone, the *Southern Worker* charged, five Negroes had been legally executed in a single week of 1930. By mid-1930 the ILD was moving into defense of blacks under legal attack. In Crescent Springs, Kentucky, the ILD defended a nineteen-year-old youth accused of assaulting a white woman. In Chester, Pennsylvania, a black laborer, Andrew Turner, was accused of manslaughter in an auto accident. The ILD came to his defense, charging that he was the victim of a "speed maniac."[6]

So great had ruling-class fear of growing Negro assertiveness become, the CP argued, that Scottsboro notwithstanding (see below), the perennial rape pretext was being abandoned. Instead, blacks were being dragged before the bar and "legally lynched" for nothing more than refusing to accept their conditions with docility.

The case of Euel Lee ("Orphan Jones"), an elderly agricultural worker from the eastern shore of Maryland, illustrates the practice of legal lynching not involving rape. Lee's prosecution resulted from his insistence upon receiving his "rightful pay" from a wealthy white farmer in Snow Hill, Maryland. He was charged with killing the farmer and his two daughters in the fall of 1931, and was nearly lynched on the way to jail. The ILD alleged that Lee was being framed for a murder that resulted from a "bootleg feud," and that he had been abandoned by the NAACP. At the first trial, in January 1932, ILD lawyers Bernard Ades and David Levinson attacked the systematic exclusion of blacks from the petit jury. The judge rejected that significant challenge, though he was unable to recall a single black juror in his twenty-six years on the bench. After Lee was sentenced to death, the ILD appealed to the Maryland Court of Appeals and won an unexpected favorable ruling: The procedures used to select juries violated the Fourteenth Amendment. A second trial was ordered with three token blacks on a jury panel of two hundred. After their quick disqualification, Lee was again found guilty and sentenced to death. This time the appeals court upheld the verdict. After the second conviction, the ILD battled all the way to the U.S. Supreme Court, which refused to review the case.[7]

Though overshadowed by Scottsboro, Lee's case received strong support from the Party and its affiliates, which organized scores of demonstrations, rallies, and petition drives in a futile campaign to save Lee from the hangman's noose. At the same time, the Party pressed its struggle for Lee through the justice system; his principal attorney, Bernard Ades, fought with such vigor that Maryland authorities got him suspended from practicing law in that state. While Ades litigated, the Party typically derided the legal system and warned "the workers [to be] on guard against legalistic illusions in the 'fairness' and 'justice' of the lynch courts."[8]

Acts of brutality against scores of organizers sent into the South represented another kind of repression. For the Party, it was not the same as what blacks faced, but still a confirmation of the antiradical intent of the violence committed against blacks as well as a vindication of the white organizers' work. In the eyes of southern authorities, northern white organizers and southern black activists constituted a single focus of red rebellion. Thus, violence against the black community was often accompanied by red-baiting forays in search of "outside agitators" and hysterical claims that traditionally submissive Negroes were being corrupted by northern Communists.[9]

Repression of Communists in the South was severe, becoming entwined in some cases with growing antiblack violence and with attempts to prevent antilynch protest. TUUL and ILD organizer Paul R. Beverhouldt was pulled from a platform in Salisbury, North Carolina, where he was leading a protest against the lynching of a sixty-five-year-old black woman, Laura Wood. The Party counted Tom Johnson and Horace and Marion Davis among the secondary radical victims of lynch terror when they were threatened and arrested in Memphis in 1930 for protesting the indictments of the Atlanta Six. The arrest of ILD organizer Lowell Wakefield and the repeated jailing of Harry Jackson in Birmingham in 1931 were counted as part of "a most ferocious ruling class drive of terror." In Dallas, a local reporter created a minor sensation when he charged that two Communist organizers in the area had been kidnapped and flogged by the local Ku Klux Klan. The murder of Ralph Gray and the other

Two generations: Cyril Briggs and Charlene Mitchell,
Los Angeles, 1960. Courtesy of Charlene Mitchell.

Claude McKay. Schomburg Center for Research in
Black Culture.

Richard B. Moore. *People's Weekly World.*

Harry Haywood, 23 August 1948. *People's Weekly World.*

A banner raised for black-white unity by unionists at a May Day parade in the 1930s. Schomburg Center for Research in Black Culture.

Richard B. Moore and August Yokinen (both seated) at Yokinen's trial for white chauvinism, Harlem, 1931. *The Liberator.*

James W. Ford addressing a legislative hearing, 1932. Corbis-Bettman Archive.

An interracial salute at a banquet for Robert Minor, 30 August 1934. *People's Weekly World.*

Unemployed marchers in Harrisburg, Pennsylvania, demand relief and a moratorium on evictions, 2 March 1933. Corbis-Bettmann Archive.

Women demand an end to lynching. Schomburg Center for Research in Black Culture.

A young demonstrator carries a jeremiad for the Scottsboro
Boys. Schomburg Center for Research in Black Culture.

Angelo Herndon flanked by brother Milton (on left) and James Ford and Robert Minor (on right). *People's Weekly World.*

Louise Thompson addressing a meeting to protest the rise of Nazism, 22 November 1938. *People's Weekly World.*

The battle goes on. A street corner speaker for the postwar Civil Rights Congress protests police brutality in the early postwar years. Schomburg Center for Research in Black Culture.

sharecroppers at Camp Hill and the arrest of Willie Peterson in 1931 on the charge of murder of two white women were all tabulated as part of lynch terror. And, of course, the arrests of the Atlanta Six themselves were characterized as part of the pattern of "lynch justice." News stories in the radical press dealing with the Atlanta case tied it to a wave of vicious killings of blacks in 1930 — in Sherman and Honeygrove, Texas, Oakdale, Tennessee, and other places. Herbert Newton declared that even though the state of Georgia had executed "John Willie Clark, Willie Kirkland, John Bryant, George Grant, and several others . . . no number of lynchings will keep the 'Atlanta Six' from carrying on our work."[10]

Another link between reds and antiblack terror was forged in Atlanta. On June 10, 1930, four hundred disgruntled whites formed the "American Fascisti and Order of Black Shirts. . . . to combat the Communist Party and to discourage the teachings of communism and foster white supremacy." The immediate impetus for the secret order, supposedly inspired by Benito Mussolini, was the impending trial of a white gas station attendant who had killed a fifteen-year-old black youth. Calling upon the people of Atlanta to protest the possible conviction of a white for killing a Negro, the Black Shirts also asserted their intent to fight communism and "put white men to work."[11]

"Lynch terror," in the Communist view, was not limited to the South. The northern variant brought death to Lee Mason, a black Communist congressional candidate who died on September 7, 1930, after being severely beaten by police in the midst of anti-eviction activity. Louis Alexander, a black ILD worker, disappeared from Barberton, Ohio, in 1931; three white police officers were charged with kidnapping. In Cleveland two black members of the local Unemployed Council, John Grayford and Edward Jackson, were killed by police bullets at a protest against the eviction of an unemployed Negro. The Harlem killings of Alfred Luro and Gonzalo Gonzalez, and the fatal shooting by police of three black anti-eviction workers in Chicago, demonstrated that the deadliest brutality was aimed at people of color to "to split the skull and body of the American working class."[12]

Increased recruitment of the "best proletarian Negroes" did not deter internal criticism of the antilynch campaign: Too much contact with the black community was being channeled through misleaders and preachers; the antilynch campaign was not linked sufficiently to self-determination; the campaign was not spurring southern organizing (except in Alabama). Such pressure was symptomatic of the ideological rigidity of the Third Period. But that pressure served a purpose, for antiracist campaigns were highly susceptible to re-treat — even among the hardiest. The Party's constant pounding on the meaning of lynch terror meant that unions and unemployed groups could hardly ignore the issue.[13]

The League of Struggle for Negro Rights

In October 1930, in a last gasp, the ANLC had launched National Anti-Lynching Week, and its "Southern provisional organizing committee" managed to put together an antilynch conference in Chattanooga in November. The southern meeting was noted for issuing invitations to churches, fraternal organizations, and labor groups, including representatives from AFL unions. But the ANLC kept insisting that anticapitalism be the basis of a movement against lynching, which virtually killed off any cooperation from other groups.[14]

In any case, the ANLC's days were numbered. In December 1929 the Comintern's Anglo-American Secretariat (spurred by Harry Haywood's Negro Section) had pointed to the Party's continuing "grave shortcomings" — among them the weakness of the ANLC and the lack of meaningful work in the rural South. That stinging communication led the way for a new organization, calibrated to the Sixth Congress, to replace the ANLC.[15]

The League of Struggle for Negro Rights, founded at St. Louis in late 1930, demanded "confiscation without compensation" of southern plantations, the land to be distributed among black and white small-scale farmers and share-croppers. It advocated self-determination (including "complete independence" from the U.S. government) "with full rights for the toiling white minority." The new organization fashioned a large agenda for Negro rights; at its heart was a promised aggressive campaign against lynching as the major manifestation of national oppression.[16]

The LSNR had problems from the beginning. The ILD was becoming more active and more effective in exposing lynching and in defending blacks caught in the snares of the system. The Unemployed Councils acted against evictions and hunger. What role was left to the LSNR? The issue was complicated by the Party's mantra that the struggle for black equality must not be "dumped" on the LSNR. But the question was not so much the compartmentalization of Negro work in LSNR as the need to find a role that would allow it to sustain itself, grow, and make a contribution. If the ANLC was narrow, the LSNR in the climate of the Third Period was even more cramped, all the more so because of its origins in Haywood's Comintern roost and its out-of-touch program.[17]

CI's PolCom insisted that the LSNR be an undisguised Party auxiliary to "openly advocate the Communist programme." Despite its unambiguous call for Black Belt self-determination, the LSNR was given virtually no role in the South, where the Party itself was instructed to expand its work. The league would later manage to establish a national leadership with Langston Hughes as honorary president and a national council composed of representatives of TUUL unions and Party-affiliated organizations. As the popular front dawned in the mid-1930s, the LSNR showed some vigor in fighting for jobs and relief. It eventually grew beyond the ANLC, claiming a membership of ten thousand at its peak. The LSNR demonstrated, picketed, circulated the *Liberator,* held rallies, and called antilynch conferences. But it never developed a broad following independent of the Party.[18]

SCOTTSBORO

The trial at Scottsboro, Alabama, of nine black youths accused of rape erupted in early April 1931 in the midst of the Communist Party's campaign against white chauvinism. Scottsboro broke barely three weeks after the Yokinen trial (see chapter 8), at the height of a drive to pound into the comrades both a renewed sensitivity and a compulsion to respond to the perceived growing national oppression of the black population. Already that spring the International Red Aid had warned that anti-Negro lynchings "were more than ever the methods used by the dollar bourgeoisie to break the counter-offensive of the workers" against the Depression. With such intense ideological preparation, the Party was primed to respond to Scottsboro. The cry "they shall not die!" began to echo across a nation haunted by the Depression. Activists marched, leafleted, begged for money, and organized. They wore themselves out in the fury of their commitment, in spite of their own economic suffering, acting in the belief that the fate of the defendants was linked inextricably to their own lives. Scottsboro became a legal and political struggle that reverberated throughout the decade, reenergizing the movement for equality, highlighting the issue of African Americans and communism, and focusing attention on racial oppression to an extent not seen since the Dred Scott case in the mid-nineteenth century.[19]

On March 25, 1931, nine ragged and frightened black youths — Charlie Weems, Ozie Powell, Clarence Norris, Olen Montgomery, Willie Roberson, Haywood Patterson, thirteen-year-old Eugene Williams, Andrew Wright, and Andrew's thirteen-year-old younger brother Leroy (Roy) Wright — were hauled from a train at Paint Rock, Alabama, and accused of raping two white women hoboing on the same train. Also on that day, James S. Allen had returned to Chattanooga, where he and his wife, Helen Marcy (Isabel Auerbach), had established the *Southern Worker*. He had been visiting a family of black sharecroppers on a plantation near Sumter, South Carolina. On the way home, he pondered the "slave-like" conditions on that plantation and the chain gang that he had observed on the old Savannah Highway. He was beginning to understand "modern plantation slavery." Back in Chattanooga he discovered another chilling "social accompaniment of the plantation." The afternoon papers shrieked about the arrests, raising fear of a wholesale lynching.

Lowell Wakefield, who had just arrived in Chattanooga as southern ILD organizer, and Marcy departed hastily for Scottsboro. It took less than a day for them to become convinced that the defendants were being railroaded to the electric chair, if not to an unscheduled "necktie party." Without hesitation, they concluded that the frame-up was rooted in a drive to subjugate Negroes even more thoroughly. The sight of nine frightened, confused black youths, two of whom were barely more than children, underscored their impression of a murderous contempt and racial vindictiveness bordering on madness. Their interpretation, derived from their politics, turned out to be right. A frame-up was in the making.[20]

On April 2 the first Scottsboro article appeared in the *Daily Worker*. The nine boys who had taken the freight train bound for Memphis to search for work had already become "nine workers" ensnared by a "campaign of terror" orchestrated by local bosses and courts to instill fear in black workers and "to smash growing unity of white and black." Scottsboro in the Party's eyes meant class struggle and more. The carnival-like atmosphere filled with blood lust, the demonstrable animus toward the nine youths, the revived slave-era stereotypes of sexual predators defiling white women, the relentless march to the electric chair all exposed a vile and cavalier contempt for the lives and property of blacks, which constituted national oppression. Scottsboro was "part of a campaign of terror against the Negro workers and impoverished farmers and sharecroppers of the South, to 'teach the nigger his place,' lest he join with his natural comrades, the white workers and poor farmers of America in their struggle against starvation and boss rule." By April 9, all the young men had been convicted and sentenced to death, except thirteen-year-old Roy Wright, whose case was declared a mistrial.[21]

Already there had been a long, deadly procession of lynchings, as well as convictions and executions, of blacks with only the faintest stir of public attention. Scottsboro would be different. The number of the defendants, their youth, the threatening environment around the courtroom, the circumstance of "bumming"—all too common during the Depression—the stunning rapidity of the trials, and the savage sentences would not be soon forgotten. The ILD dispatched attorney Allen Taub and organizer Douglas McKenzie to Chattanooga. As the trials continued, the Communists in Chattanooga located the families of the youths living in the city. They found "hopeless, defeated, bewildered" kin who from their own experience understood what blacks could expect from southern "justice." But they did not grasp the underlying causes, which seemed inexplicable—and without explanation, they could not grasp a solution. The Communists addressed the relatives respectfully, without patronizing them or adopting an attitude of false familiarity. They told them that the struggle for the freedom of their children was the obligation of the entire working class; they offered devoted and expert legal support. But they said that "boss" courts would never dispense justice without the relentless pressure of a mass movement. They promised to summon that movement and to persist until the boys were freed. "For the first time" in the lives of those parents, "white men were not telling them what to do, but asking their support on the basis of complete equality." One of the mothers repeated through tears: "You are angels from heaven!"[22]

Before the trials began, the Interdenominational Ministers' Alliance of Chattanooga retained attorney Stephen Roddy "for the purpose of seeing that the boys get justice." When Roddy arrived at Scottsboro, he denied that he had been hired to defend the youths; the ministers had sent him down only to "look things over." The judge appointed a local lawyer who bordered on senility and allowed Roddy, an alcoholic, to participate despite his own vague and half-hearted delineation of his role.

Roddy offered no defense. He did not request an adjournment to familiarize himself with the case, called no defense witnesses, overlooked pertinent questions, and failed to seize upon blatantly contradictory statements by prosecution witnesses. He later confirmed that the arresting officers could not ascertain that the nine boys were rapists. The two doctors who examined the women found them in good physical and mental condition with no lacerations or bruises around the sexual organs. Semen found was "non-motile," showing that the two women, Victoria Price and Ruby Bates, who were known to be prostitutes, had last had sexual intercourse at least twenty-four hours before the time of the alleged rapes. Roddy never attempted to explore the implications of the devastating medical evidence.[23]

Dr. P. A. Stephens, secretary of the alliance, wrote to the NAACP asking for assistance. Walter White, the NAACP secretary, had his legal assistant respond on April 2, asking the alliance's lawyer to draw up a "statement of facts" on the case. The venerable NAACP would exercise caution before taking on a possible gaggle of rapists. Stephens's letter turned out to be the start of a tumultuous legal and ideological battle between the NAACP and the Communists for control of the case and for the support of African Americans and the larger population.[24]

On April 10 Taub and McKenzie announced that the ILD had been retained by the defendants and their families, and would file an appeal for a new trial. On the same day the ILD secured the services of a southern lawyer, George W. Chamlee of Chattanooga, a former county attorney general and grandson of a decorated Confederate veteran. The ILD's chief lawyer, Joseph Brodsky, contacted Clarence Darrow to inquire whether the famed attorney would handle the anticipated appeal to the Supreme Court. A meeting was proposed for April 11. Darrow relayed the information to Walter White, who claimed that the NAACP had things under control; the ILD's only intention was to make "Communist propaganda." The meeting never took place. On April 24 the *Daily Worker* published a letter from William Pickens, now a field secretary for the NAACP, congratulating the Communists on their fight "to prevent the judicial massacre" and enclosing a contribution for the ILD. That was jarring for the nearly paralyzed NAACP, whose only resolute act had been to stop Darrow's meeting with the Party's defense arm.[25]

Soon after the verdicts were handed down, the NAACP was swamped with inquiries from its own branches, individuals, media, and other organizations. Many were puzzled by the association's silence in the face of the growing notoriety of the case and the torrent of ILD press releases. Negro papers were running Communist materials favorably comparing the ILD's vigor with the NAACP's sluggishness. This, as some noted, was contributing to growing sympathy for the Communists.[26]

Under growing pressure, the NAACP became ensnared in a tangle of prevarication and deception. White told the Pittsburgh branch secretary on April

20 that "through our local branches and through a group of ministers at Chattanooga an attorney was retained to represent the boys." Thus, he falsely connected the NAACP to the incompetent Roddy—and ignored the fact that the Chattanooga branch was moribund. On the same day, he was asking Stephens in Chattanooga how the ministers felt about Roddy. "How far," he asked, "will [the ministers] be willing to cooperate with the NAACP *should we decide to enter the case?*" (emphasis added). On April 24 the association finally issued a press release claiming that Roddy "had been retained by the NAACP." However, not until May 2, in a memorandum written by White to the Ministers' Alliance, was mention made of a potential written contract with Roddy and Moody, pending White's ability to win the defendants to the NAACP. By June 1 White's falsifications had hardened: "the NAACP has been in these cases from the beginning"; Roddy had been hired at the start by the NAACP and the ministers; he had been vilified unfairly by Communists, although he had displayed courage and "made an honest defense of the boys."[27]

Something more troubling than the debate over who was first in the field was emerging. On April 25 Mrs. Janie Patterson, mother of defendant Haywood Patterson, appeared on a Harlem street corner to address a "mass rally" sponsored by the ILD and the LSNR. That was the start of the Scottsboro mothers' involvement in an ever expanding global arena. The Communists had offered hitherto anonymous southern black women the opportunity to become active players in the battle for their sons' freedom. The mothers found their voices; they became partners, friends, and "comrades" of the Party and its allies. They soon traveled to every corner of the country to speak for their sons' lives; in 1932 Ada Wright, mother of Andrew and Roy Wright, went on an extended and often tumultuous tour of Europe. Mary Craik Speed, an Alabama socialite who turned to communism, found that her patronizing "affectionate regard" for the black women cooks, washerwomen, and field hands of her youth had fallen "like scales from [her] eyes" when she joined the mothers of Olin Montgomery and Clarence Norris on one of the innumerable lobbies to the White House. Their hard lives and surviving aspirations made Speed appreciate their character and fortitude. The mothers (Claude Patterson, who was also active, was the only living father) turned out to be crucial to Communist control of the case. Their involvement also brought the Party to a rather belated recognition of the potential "organized power" of women workers.[28]

The Party and the ILD offered a united front to all who would join in the struggle for the boys' freedom. Public meetings were being held in halls and churches all over the country. Another round of "united front conferences" in more than forty cities began on May 15. On June 1, two hundred delegates, most of them black, overcame police harassment and gathered in Chattanooga to demand freedom for the boys, to plot strategy, and to cheer a message from Roy Wright that read: "Fakers can't fool me. I am for the ILD."[29]

A New York conference was convened, with scores of notable American writers and artists attending, under the auspices of the National Committee for Defense of Political Prisoners. Rienzi Lemus of the Baltimore *Afro-American* complained that the New York gathering was "hogged" by the Communists. He had a point. The potential for a genuinely broad response to Scottsboro was mitigated by the Party's ideological posturing and the trouble that was brewing with the NAACP.[30]

But the urgency of the situation obliged many nonleftists to overlook the Party's disdain for "misleaders and betrayers." A Chicago conference, sponsored by the most firmly rooted Party organization in the black community, drew representatives from 118 Negro churches and 16 black social clubs. Such gatherings set fund-raising goals, organized "tag days" to raise money, planned block and neighborhood committees, and projected new demonstrations and parades. Each Party unit was directed to assign two to four members to the ILD and the LSNR, which were given the task of spearheading the "mass defense." Unions and ethnic organizations under Communist influence were enjoined to denounce the verdicts. The TUUL was bombarded with messages from George Padmore, demanding that it "come forward" for the Scottsboro boys. An ethnic Communist from Philadelphia reported that his comrades declined to organize Scottsboro block committees, citing their inability to communicate in English. He rebutted that a few words in broken English would suffice. There was to be no let-up, no excuses.[31]

William Pickens, now thoroughly chastened by his hasty contribution to the ILD, could still not restrain his admiration for white men in Oklahoma City who went to jail "on behalf of Negroes in another Southern state" — and who had been charged with raping white women, no less. Everywhere throughout a southern tour he found Communists "protesting consistently against the Alabama horror.... As long as I have a fighting corpuscle in my blood, I will feel a kinship with the courage of people like that." Herbert Benjamin, head of the Unemployed Councils, recalled the legendary confrontation between a tenants' group and a balky landlord in the Bronx. "All right, all right," the landlord exclaimed. "I'll fix the plumbing and paint the halls—but I can't free the Scottsboro boys!"[32]

A barrage of international Scottsboro protests began with Berlin streetcar workers. Demonstrations spanned the globe from Havana to Europe, to Moscow, to Australia and New Zealand, to Japan, South Africa, and Latin America. Demonstrators hurled bottles and smashed windows at the U.S. Consulate in Dresden when consul officials refused to accept a petition. A spring demonstration in Chemnitz, Germany, was broken up with twelve wounded and one killed. In Havana a crowd of demonstrators attacked a branch of the National City Bank of New York. Albert Einstein and Thomas Mann joined other well-known Germans to form a Committee for the Deliverance of the Scottsboro Boys. Thirty-three members of the British Parliament protested the trials and convictions. Alabama governor Benjamin Miller received cables from women workers of Soviet Keralia and from representatives of three hundred thousand German trade unionists acting in the midst of Hitler's ascendancy. The attorney general of Alabama, Thomas E. Knight, informed Montgomery telegraph company managers that they would be liable for contempt citations if any more messages "of an illegal, libelous, scandalous or obscene nature are delivered." The *Afro-American* declared that the most powerful and attractive feature of the Communists' interest in the American Negro was the vast, international scope of protest.[33]

Still, there were problems. The Party's proffer of a united front, though fulsome, was undercut by its Third Period dogma that unity be forged "from below" and was anchored on support for the ILD and CP's handling of the defense. Once the NAACP declared that it had entered the case, the Party prepared to do battle against the "social fascists." Soon the conflict with the NAACP took center stage, burying the united font in an avalanche of mutual accusation.

On April 23 two Chattanooga ministers got the defendants to give the Ministers' Alliance (and consequently the NAACP) "priority" in the case. The following day, the parents who could be reached by the ILD repudiated that authorization—with the nine defendants backing their parents. Thus began a bruising tug-of-war between the NAACP and the ILD for the defendants' support. White made a hurried trip south to offer the boys the NAACP's standard litany: The association works under the Constitution and the nation's laws; the ILD and the Communists are working to overthrow the government; their objective is to "make Communist propaganda," even at the price of sacrificing your lives; the Communists' threats to judges and the governor will "damage your appeals"; and finally, do not add communism to the vile hatred already heaped upon you "because you are black and . . . are accused of raping white women."[34]

White had a fallback position: Should the NAACP be forced to withdraw, he would blame the reds and the "ignorance and stupidity of the boys' parents." The parents had "been flattered and filled up with a lot of flamboyant stuff. Unhappily, they are of the type of Negro who would believe anything said by a white man, no matter how absurd." In White's mind the parents' ignorance had become inseparable from their class status and their poverty: They were "pathetically ignorant and poor . . . bewildered by the catastrophe that has swooped down upon their sons." Pickens said that the families were "the densest and dumbest animals it has yet been my privilege to meet . . . cattle . . . hopelessly entrapped" by the Communists. He taunted the boys by telling them that the reds were "trotting out your bewildered mommas all over the country." Dr. Charles McPherson fretted that bloody events at Camp Hill had shown that "there are too many poor colored people [who are] absolutely *defenseless* living in small towns and communities, living peacefully perhaps to have a radical organization bringing its propaganda which they can not and may not absorb. Something must be done."[35]

On the terrain where race and class converged, there were unexpected consequences. The Communists had made no secret of their belief that underlying the controversy over "mass action" versus reliance on the legal system was something deeper — a confrontation of opposing class forces and social temperaments. They regarded the defendants and families as "class brothers and sisters." The parents and the sons were not simply passive victims; they were both symbols and catalysts, setting "the masses in motion not only for the freedom of the boys, but also for their constitutional rights." They commanded respect for their symbolic and political importance, as well as for their class, their race, their suppressed nationality, their humanity, and their capacity to resist.[36]

The NAACP was hampered by the class chasm between it and the defendants. White never managed to achieve trusting and respectful relations with the boys and their families. For him, Scottsboro was a symbolic injustice — one to be challenged, but one to be combated mainly to salvage the reputation of a venerable defense organization. White could only interpret the families' allegiance to the ILD as the result of ignorance and stupidity. He could not imagine that they were responding to an offer of solidarity, concrete expressions of social equality, and diligent labors for their sons' freedom. White complained that the families were deferring to whites "in preference to what might be said by the finest and most trustworthy Negro alive." His statement ignored the pivotal role of black Communists. Also, White's "finest" often could not suppress their antagonism, haughtiness, condescension, and outright contempt for the families and the boys. All this only solidified the bonds between mothers and sons, and the Communists. White asked Andy Wright why he wanted to stay with the ILD. He replied that it was his mother's wish. White responded that "superior age did not mean superior wisdom." Andy looked at the urbane secretary with pleading eyes: "Mr. White, if you can't trust your mother who can you trust?"[37]

Both sides of the controversy measured Scottsboro in terms of their respective political ideologies and ambitions. But the Communists were better able to translate political abstractions into human commitments. The reds had cultivated a sensitivity to impoverished, vulnerable families that was beyond the reach of the middle-class NAACP. In this situation at least, the perceived bonds of class led to a strong biracial respect, while a shared racial identity, riven by class differences, could not prevent one group within the race from despising another. Thus in response to White's claim that the parents were too ignorant to know what they wanted, Mrs. Mamie Williams Wilcox (mother of defendant Eugene Williams) said, "We are not too ignorant to know a bunch of liars and fakers when we meet up with them."[38]

The battle over the boys' allegiance raged through the summer and into late 1931. The carnage at Camp Hill in July (see chapter 7) drove the NAACP and the Ministers' Alliance into shriller denunciations of the Communists for supposedly goading poor, uneducated blacks into suicidal acts. The NAACP became increasingly driven by its own ideological demons. Pickens, in a speech on June 7, accused the Communists of being willing to see the boys lynched if that would "give them material for still more sensational propaganda among the more ignorant of the colored population." The defendants themselves were being torn apart by the succession of visitations, arguments, promises, warnings, and pleading from the NAACP — countered by repeated ILD mobilizations of the families to undo the association's efforts. The NAACP found itself in the public arena, contesting the ILD for control of the case, for money, sympathy, ideological justification, and bureaucratic survival. Inevitably, each side accused the other of reckless expenditures of the nickels and dimes collected from the hard-pressed public of Depression times. Few things could have been more inflammatory.[39]

The most compelling tactical disagreement was between mass defense and exclusive reliance on the courts (what James Allen called "drawing-room dickering and submissive favor-seeking"). The NAACP, even as it came under black leadership, reflected its roots in white progressivism and a belief that racial oppression would be ameliorated through rational discourse, gradualism, good will, and conciliation — which included, of course, faith in the prevailing social system and its legal institutions. Only Du Bois questioned the system. But Du Bois also rejected the underlying assumptions of mass defense, which placed confidence in the willingness of the white workers to struggle for black liberation. The promise of mass action by an alliance of black and white labor brought a heated reply from Du Bois: "That kind of talk is like a red rag to a bull. . . . White labor had been the black man's enemy, his oppressor, his red murderer. . . . Whatever ideals [it] strives for in America, it would surrender nearly everyone before it would recognize a Negro as a man."[40]

Anticommunist writer George S. Schuyler argued that the South would never tolerate mass action replete with wild threats and an absence of mandatory restraint and intelligence. The rantings of the "turbulent and radical elements of both races" would only unlock the racist beast within southerners of all classes. "Anyone who is familiar with the southern psychology," Schuyler said, "knows that no class issues are involved." The only hope was to maintain an unprejudiced and nonthreatening demeanor before those "good whites" of better breeding.[41]

Such talk was "petty bourgeois defeatism," said leftist Eugene Gordon. It implied that Negroes should wait submissively until the "good whites" handed them justice. But patience was not justified in light of the pivotal role of those "good whites" in suppressing blacks. The ILD's militant approach promised liberation rather than the illusions peddled by the NAACP that blacks could find equity in "capitalist courts." Negroes were coming over in increasing numbers to mass defense. They would claw at the contradictions within bourgeois democracy, ceaselessly pressure the legal system, and engage in irresistible battle until the will of a racist structure should be broken and "this fetish of 'white supremacy'. . . pickled in the brine of the past."[42]

The Party and its supporters would not budge from belief in the insepara-
bility of strong legal defense and pressure from the streets. William Patterson,
who became ILD secretary in November 1932 upon the death of J. Louis Engdahl, actually figured out a way to make expert legal defense an endgame of
radicalization: "The ILD believes that only mass pressure can bring about the
release of a class war prisoner; that pressure must be supplemented by legal
defense... [which] must be of the most expert character. Every legal technicality must be used. The more far-reaching the knowledge of the lawyer retained by the ILD, the more easily and effectively can the worker be shown
that the guarantees of justice... are meaningless." Legal expertise was welded to
sectarianism. What remained however, was committed, seasoned legal support.[43]

The argument went beyond strategy and tactics, to the deeper level of ideological goals. James S. Allen contended that "if the NAACP had been the vic-
tor... not only in the purely legal question of defense but on the more important point of ideological leadership over the Negro masses — the struggle would
have been stifled and its revolutionary potential left undeveloped." On the
other side, Pickens was almost gleeful that the red card could be played more
effectively than the quest for justice. He wrote White that "Roddy told me
confidentially that Judge [Alfred E.] Hawkins told him that the CHIEF ISSUE
now is the REDS — that if they were out of it, it might be simpler; that he (the
trial judge) did not really think the boys should be put to death, but that the
Communists are more of an issue than are the FACTS of the case." White
wrote to a wavering Roderick Beddow (an Alabama attorney whom he desperately sought to hire), appealing not to Beddow's faint sense of racial justice,
but to a higher patriotism: "Whatever the difficulties, we must continue in these
cases, as they have developed into being infinitely more important than originally was the case, due to the Communist activity." In another message to Beddow, he wrote: "Checkmated... in their attempts to utilize this case for propaganda, [the Communists] will be effectively set back in their sinister designs
and you will have rendered a great service of lasting benefit to our country."[44]

Through the fall months of 1931 some defendants who had been pulled to
the NAACP fell away. Defendant Ozie Powell wrote to White in September that
his mother had selected the ILD, and "she nows *[sic]* the best for me." Clarence
Norris's mother finally persuaded her son, the last holdout, to sign with the
ILD. By December George Chamlee wrote exuberantly to George Maurer at the
ILD national office that all the boys were now firmly in its camp. On January

4, 1932, White wrote a scolding letter to defendants Willie Roberson and Charlie Weems: "You and the other boys have vacillated, changing your minds so frequently that it is impossible for any organization or individual to know just what you want. . . . You have chosen your counsel and that settles the matter so far as the NAACP is concerned." On that same day the NAACP announced that it was formally withdrawing from the Scottsboro case.[45]

Also on that same day, the Negro Bureau of the Party's Negro Department convened, with Wakefield, Maurer, and Brodsky joining LSNR head B. D. Amis, Harry Haywood, and Party custodian Max Bedacht in discussion. The mood was buoyant. Scottsboro was becoming the "spark" of which Lenin had spoken — the instance that propelled the masses into motion. The bureau instructed Brodsky to draft a letter to Clarence Darrow and civil liberties lawyer Arthur Garfield Hays. The two famed lawyers had been brought back into the case by White, but had withdrawn when the ILD gained control. The letter would not ask the attorneys to submit to ILD's direct oversight — which they had already rejected — but only to work with the ILD's lawyers. However, a cynical and manipulative note was struck. With such mutual distrust, there was no expectation that Darrow and Hays would accept. But the offer would squeeze them between the desire to serve justice and loyalty to the NAACP. That would strain the ties between the lawyers and the association, "driving a wedge" between them. Finally, the anticipated "refusal of [Darrow and Hays] to cooperate would give us a valuable opportunity to expose the entire policy of these attorneys and the NAACP." Nastiness still abounded.[46]

An appeal to the Alabama Supreme Court of all the Scottsboro convictions was argued by Chamlee, Brodsky, and Irving Schwab on January 21, 1932. On March 24 the Court affirmed seven convictions. On October 10 the noted constitutional lawyer Walter H. Pollak, who had been retained by the ILD, argued the appeal before the U.S. Supreme Court. A month later, the Court overturned all convictions. The startling decision was based on the "denial of effective and substantial" counsel. Because the defendants "stood in deadly peril of their lives . . . the failure of the trial court to give them reasonable time and opportunity to secure counsel was a clear denial of due process."[47]

Justice George Sutherland noted that among the three grounds for reversal offered by the defense (no fair trial, blacks excluded from the jury, denial of counsel), only the issue of counsel was considered. With the NAACP's disingenuous story about being on the scene from the beginning, about the phantom Chattanooga branch and the ministers hiring Roddy, about Roddy's correct and courageous behavior—it is not likely that the association would have appealed on the grounds of denial of counsel—the only grounds acceptable to the high court.[48]

The case was returned to Alabama for retrial. The first round was over.

Summing Up the First Stage

Scottsboro's prominence yielded some important insights into the ways in which race went to the core of American social and institutional life. It also revealed a lot about the Party's engagement with African Americans. The allegation that the Communists were willing to see the boys die to demonstrate capitalism's brutality was a grievous misreading of their ideology and emotional involvement. Execution of the defendants would be a victory for the despised "dollar bourgeoisie," which allegedly sought to drown the unity of black and white workers in an ocean of hatred and recrimination. It would be a "lynching, an institution which is rooted deeply in the damnable economic system which gives it birth and nourishes it"; it would undermine rising class struggle against wage cuts, evictions, rural peonage, and all manifestations of exploitation. The boys' execution would be a major blow against the resistance to "capitalist reaction." Had the executions occurred, there is little doubt that the subsequent mourning and sense of defeat would have eclipsed what was felt for Sacco and Vanzetti. On the other hand, the Communists believed that victory would constitute a real advance for biracial unity and revolutionary consciousness. The cry of "they shall not die!" had a resonance and sincerity that stemmed from such unyielding conviction.[49]

Charges that the Communists engaged in dangerous, inflammatory conduct toward the courts were overstated and deflected attention from a racist judicial system in Alabama. Those controversial telegrams, of which the Alabama attorney general had complained, ridiculed the icons of judicial detachment and betrayed a blissful ignorance of judicial decorum. But they were more like religious allegories, envisioning retribution for sinners, than actual threats. The most "threatening" telegram was sent to Governor Miller on April 9, 1931, by B. D. Amis for the LSNR, stating that "this organization ... demands that you stop this legal lynching and holds you responsible to stay the hand of the lynch mob." Judges and politicians could hardly fear a metaphorical working class holding them "responsible" for due process.[50]

One of the peculiarities of the Third Period was the extent to which the Communists implied in their actions that the bourgeois order, for all its alleged bankruptcy, was susceptible to the pressure of an aroused public. Scottsboro, with all the talk of a revolutionary awakening, was about democracy and justice for African Americans and the rest of the powerless. On the surface, the Party railed against bourgeois democracy, derided its own victories as "perpetuating illusions," stupidly attacked the chief justice of the Alabama Supreme Court *because* he dissented from the majority (he was allegedly offering a "gesture ... to stop, if possible, the development of the mass movement"), and derided "petitionist nonsense" even as it petitioned zealously. But at a deeper level, mass defense probed bourgeois democracy's armor, bared the contradictions between its rhetoric and reality, marshaled global attention, and created lingering embarrassment. The state of Alabama stiffened under the onslaught of protest, but in the end the spotlight cast by mass defense upon its legal processes made the state fear for the sanctity of its practices and contributed to its dropping charges against four of the defendants in July 1937.[51]

On the day the Supreme Court rendered its Scottsboro decision, Communists were poking wildly at cherished beliefs in blind justice; they demonstrated on the Court's steps and fought with District of Columbia police. But the justices had to be mindful of the national and global protest. The Court was the ultimate custodian of the nation's purported values and social stability. In that role, it was sensitive to the political climate. The Scottsboro decision reflected awareness of the conflicting tides of racism, legal conservatism, and growing protest; it evaded the denial of a fair trial in the face of racist mobs and pointedly ignored the systematic exclusion of blacks from Alabama juries. But the decision *did* throw out the convictions. William Patterson warned predictably that the partial victory held the danger of deepening "illusions in the justice of the courts." He might well have added that victory also elevated the idea of mass defense and gave renewed strength and confidence to the disinherited.[52]

Jay Lovestone's fading faction hailed the Party for rescuing the case from the obscurity that was the usual fate of such brutal attacks upon Negroes. But the quarrel with the NAACP and the insanity of "social fascism" prohibited unity with other forces. The Lovestoneites contended that the CP had a poor grasp of what a united front was supposed to be: an alliance of equals in agreement on a minimum program, and not an appeal to follow the Party. The quarrel with the NAACP diverted attention from the Scottsboro boys' would-be executioners.[53]

Much of that criticism was persuasive. In later years, without acknowledging the despised Lovestone group, the Party would adopt those very precepts for a united front. However, in fairness, the Party's conflict with the NAACP came after the association had attempted to wrest the case from the Communists. Both sides shared blame for the resulting controversy. But the Party's problems ran deeper than the Lovestone group's criticism. They stemmed from the CP's belief that its revolutionary outlook mandated sole leadership of African Americans. As long as the Party spoke of establishing "hegemony over the Negro liberation struggle itself," it would often antagonize those who questioned or opposed it and would negate its own claims to be fighting for self-determination.

Ideology, with its metallic toughness, can lead to manipulation and self-serving political warfare. But the impact of the Party's stubborn sectarianism was far more complex and contradictory than appears on the surface. The CP's often asinine political temper was exhibited in the shadow of the worst economic crisis in the nation's history. Under that circumstance, revulsion toward the Party's policies was often blunted — especially among blacks. Tough, sacrificing, Communist tactics seemed to many to be not unreasonable under the circumstances.

Yet the sensitive, sophisticated, and cooperative tactics of the popular front in the mid-1930s often had a high political price. Although more effective than Third Period bombast, the popular front unity often required a difficult balancing of principle and compromise. In 1937 and 1938 the ILD subordinated its own role within the broadly based Scottsboro Defense Committee to the liberal Alan Knight Chalmers. While Chalmers engaged in time-consuming and ultimately futile negotiations with Governor Bibb Graves to pardon the remaining Scottsboro defendants, the ILD was pressured to maintain a painful silence. That experience demonstrates that the sectarian years and the popular front years cannot be reduced to separate and simplistic categories of evil and good.[54]

Mass defense contributed to a resurgence of a militant mood within the black community. By 1933 Scottsboro "had made some dent" on Negro students. A black southern educator was quoted by Roger Baldwin as saying, "This Scottsboro case has taken a lot of rabbit out and made us fight." Black schoolchildren in Philadelphia struck for the release of the boys; black fraternities and sororities passed resolutions, petitioned, raised money, and demonstrated. Beyond the campuses, Negro editors reported that working-class blacks had become favorably disposed to the Communists and to their militant efforts to free the Scottsboro boys. One editor observed that Scottsboro, in addition to the Party's integrated social life and its urban battles against evictions and for relief, "would advertise Communism, recommend it highly, and make a strong appeal to a certain number of a much abused race." Asbury Smith, Baltimore minister and member of the board of the Urban League, said that "the Communists go out and fight for Negro rights. The International Labor Defense is communism in action for Negro rights and Scottsboro is the supreme example."[55]

The unity of southern black and white workers in battle to free the boys was more hope than reality. A deeply rooted element of delusion and irrationality persisted on the plane where southern white men of all classes contemplated the conjunction of race and sex. Schuyler had a point; so did Du Bois who worried about illusory expectations of support for embattled blacks from the white southern masses. Yet the Communists hit on a generalized, symbolic truth about the persecution of the Scottsboro boys. The Depression had been marked by raging economic anxiety and growing social and racial tensions. The nine black youths on that train, even before the accusations of Victoria Price and Ruby Bates, had been wounded by hard times. With other young folk, black and white, they were bumming freights in a search for work—microcosms of the country's economic and social breakdown. The freight ride and the racial brawl underscored the need for the dispossessed of both races to join in battle for mutual survival. The Communists brought to the fight to save the boys a refusal to descend to patronizing charity and fleeting moralism. The whole country, blacks and whites, they said, could no longer ignore the scarring, miserable racial oppression that continued more than a half-century after the end of chattel slavery. Scottsboro was a cornerstone of justice for all.

CHAPTER TWELVE

The Search for Unity and Breadth

As a melancholy holiday season approached in the fall of 1930, the *Chicago Defender* published a wry editorial cartoon entitled, "Unemployment Solves One Problem." Two jobless workers, one black, one white, are seated on a park bench. The black says: "I was just thinking — when times were good my old buddy here wouldn't work with me. He said I wasn't white like he is and kept me out of a job. Now, times have changed and hard times have hit him, and he's willing to chum with me."[1]

Would the leveling tendencies inherent in the Great Depression dissolve the centuries-old "Negrophobia" of much of the white working class? Du Bois's views still hung over the Party, especially his insight that Marx's profound revelation about the centrality of the class struggle in human history did not apply to the United States. Here, black labor suffered from capitalism, but "the lowest and most fatal degree of its suffering comes not from the capitalists but from fellow white laborers" who heap upon the Negro all manner of discrimination. Those white workers are not manipulated by capital; they know what they are doing as they scramble to climb over Negroes still immobilized by slavery, disenfranchisement, and the color bar. For that reason, American Communists cannot get a respectful hearing unless they turn against black labor; their "shrill cry" is ignored "because and solely because [the CP] seeks to break down the barriers between black and white."[2]

The difficulties of getting white workers to join with blacks were often disheartening. The problem was underscored by poignant letters to the national secretariat, especially from the fragile beachheads established in the South. By 1932 the Party had not yet sunk any meaningful roots among black workers through TUUL unions. But the Unemployed Councils and various ad hoc campaigns reached directly into black neighborhoods and connected with those communities. Such bodies attracted blacks, often in greater numbers than whites. Such was the case in Norfolk, Virginia, in November 1932, when Party organizers launched a rent strike of about a thousand families who held firm against abuse and provocation by city authorities (while their organizers were repeatedly jailed, heavily fined, and generally harassed). The strike was confined to black tenants, though some white workers were showing increased sympathy and were "beginning to come to us for aid against evictions."[3] After a month the strike had started to wane, and one UC branch of over two hundred members had already begun to break up under the pressure of arrests and fines. The black workers were willing to fight to the end. But, they asked, where were their white comrades?

In Richmond, the unemployed movement had organized 250 black workers "and a few whites." It turned out that one of those few whites was Palmer Weber, who became the leader of a small band of Communist students at the University of Virginia. He later left the Party, to become a New Deal and CIO activist, founder of the movement to abolish the poll tax, and the first white southerner on NAACP's national board. His friend in the Richmond UC, James Jackson, was among the first African American Eagle Scouts in the South and later became a leader of the Southern Negro Youth Congress and the Communist Party.[4]

Charlotte, North Carolina, was a promising location, where "a very large section of the Negro population is with us." They were "actually starving" and were willing to fight. At a demonstration at the local Salvation Army, the police refrained from attacking black speakers, out of fear of "Negro defense squads" (the correspondent noted that "again we have no white workers"). Despite enormous obstacles, the demonstrators had forced the Salvation Army to return blacks to charity lists after they had been eliminated due to alleged UC or CP membership. But without support from the white unemployed, there was danger of a deep racial divide, resulting perhaps in race riots. The black comrades understood the difficulties, were willing to go "into open battle," but were pessimistic. Two weeks later, another letter described increasing cold weather, comrades weak from hunger, and a dropping off of activity due to widespread illness. Two white Communists, Kenneth and Lydia Rottger, had been convicted of fomenting a riot at the Salvation Army and had been sentenced respectively to eight months on the chain gang and eight months in the workhouse. At the trial, the defendants forced their lawyer to agree to refer to black witnesses just as he would to whites — if he refused to use "Mr." or "Mrs." for blacks, he would address whites the same way. In the cold and muddy winter of Charlotte in the worst year of the Depression, that was a victory.[5]

Separate black and white units in Charlotte were criticized by the Central Committee. Dave Doran, a young YCL organizer who later died in Spain, countered that they were unavoidable in the South, with its all-black neighborhoods and all-white mill villages. Despite the difficulty, efforts were being made to coordinate racially separate units and to engage in "constant struggle" for black-white unity. White organizers were concentrating in white areas in response to complaints from blacks about the paucity of whites in the movement. Doran in turn chided the center for demanding "the mechanical placing of a Negro comrade into activity in a white mill village, without . . . political clarification of the white workers." That was mercilessly dogmatic and endangered the black comrade's life. But Doran admitted that the Comintern was right to criticize the CP for shying away from white areas. Such were the difficulties of interracial organizing in much of the South in 1932.[6]

The only functioning Party units in District 17 were in Alabama and Tennessee. Chattanooga, Tennessee, had a "fairly good base of Negro party members," but suffered from "the complete absence of white workers." In Georgia, there were nearly a dozen loosely organized CP members in Atlanta, and a group of just three in Rome. A new organizer in Atlanta, Joan Barbour, complained about failure to receive funds from the center and was obliged to apologize for such transgressions as failure to include self-determination in leaflets for rural counties and use of a lower-case *n* for Negro. In Louisiana, Party and YCL organizations in New Orleans were small and riven by conflict between black members and a white organizer over his allegedly haughty and bureaucratic behavior.[7]

Alabama's devoted core of black industrial workers and sharecroppers remained largely intact under increasing assault by the authorities. But the relatively generous resources bestowed upon Alabama did not win over many whites. An All-Southern Conference for Civil and Political Rights, held in October 1932 in Birmingham, drew three hundred blacks and fifty whites. Nearly one thousand blacks were turned away for lack of space. Otto Hall, arriving from New York, was arrested, beaten, and dumped on the outskirts of the city. The local ILD office was raided and trashed. Shortly before the conference, Klansmen in full regalia marauded through black communities and around the meeting hall, threatening to break up the meeting, "even if we have to kill some." The Party's District Bureau noted that most of the white members of the ILD turned away from the hall at the sight of Klansmen, as well as cops with machine guns.[8]

Before August 1932 the Share Croppers' Union had had a low profile, with no systematic organization or planned activities. Meetings would be led by a speaker wearing "a revolver openly in his scavage," making "sharp and fiery" speeches that encouraged others to arm themselves. After the meetings all would leave, uplifted emotionally, but without "any particular tasks." When Al Murphy became the organizer in the spring of 1932, he changed all that, creating small locals of about ten members, including women's and youth auxiliaries. Murphy made a strict accounting of SCU's membership, county by county; in 1932 there were 778 members.[9]

But the problem of establishing ties with whites remained. The unit in Collegeville, Alabama, was criticized for canceling a march on the local Red Cross because of the absence of white workers. That inspired Murphy to seek ways of winning whites to the union. He had seen white tenants sitting among Negro croppers in their homes, "cracking jokes," dipping snuff, and borrowing food. He had met a white cropper who worked halves with a black cropper — eating in his home, dividing the crop, depending on him for information and advice. Although none of the black SCU members had approached the whites about joining the union, hard times had provoked white tenants and croppers into saying that "us white folks and you colored fellows [should] get together and raise hell."[10]

Such experiences, Murphy warned, should not "drive us off into a pool of overestimation" about unity. Desperation and misery made whites willing to seek some degree of association between the races. But their core belief was still that blacks were willing to do what white men say and accept merciless exploitation without grumbling. Such "valuing" of the Negro reflected the white landowners' culture; their condescension and false confidence had filtered down to poor rural whites. Nevertheless, Murphy agreed that white tenants were falling into debt slavery, forcing them into penury and powerlessness (they too were denied the vote) similar to those of the black farmers. In Camp Hill's wake (see chapter 7), whites now realized that the SCU was fighting for all tenants and croppers, and some now wished to join. But the black croppers were reluctant and distrustful. Some whites who were friendly now had ridden with the sheriffs to Camp Hill and had been in the courthouse mob that ached for a lynching. There was the haunting presence of Pat Heard, a white tenant who sought to join the union and even declared that he would go to Camp Hill to kill the landowners who had taken everything from his family. He might be "a pretty good fellow now," one who had finally located the source of his suffering, Murphy conceded. But the black croppers remembered that it was Heard who knocked down Ralph Gray's door "and helped drag him to the car after the sheriff shot him through the mouth and killed him." Murphy noted wryly that perhaps the SCU should wait awhile to recruit Pat Heard.[11]

That left a gnawing question about how to organize white farmers. Against the grain of the Party's national leadership, and a major part of the District as well, Murphy advocated the formation of an all-white Tenants' League featuring an interchange of delegates with the SCU. Eventually, the league could become a source of recruitment for the union. After all, the SCU's attractiveness was growing. On one plantation it had won croppers the right to sell their own crops. On another the union had won an allotment of clothes and shoes for a desperate cropper and his family. A program was in place based on the right to own and sell cotton at ten cents per pound. SCU was seeking to organize large plantations. Conditions for an all-white tenants' organization were improving, as SCU activities accelerated. But without support from the Central Committee and from the district, that proposal was fading from view.[12]

The Unions

In southern industrial centers, the corporations exercised their powers of social manipulation to divide white and black workers. They would drag out the specter of "social equality," terrorize black workers, and harass organizers. For its part, the TUUL remained hobbled by a failure to attract blacks. Despite their opposition to the AFL's racist policies, the revolutionary unions were suspect in the eyes of many black workers. A mine strike began on January 1, 1932, in largely white rural Kentucky, where employer resistance was ferocious and often deadly. The strike was fatally wounded by the NMU's poor preparation, empty pockets, and bullish sectarianism, as well as the UMW's hostility. But the handful of striking black miners were prominent among those willing to carry on. Anne Reeve, reporting for the *Daily Worker* from Bell and Harlan Counties, was thrown into jail under a sweeping injunction as soon as she crossed the Cumberland Gap into mine country. Help came from black families who pressed against Reeve's ground-floor cell window, plying her with food and old magazines. Black miners sang and prayed with white miners. But the strength of the mine operators, the weaknesses of the union, and the hostility of the government crushed the strike and prevented any real progress in biracial unity.[13]

The TUUL's needle trades union survived into 1932, buoyed by modest growth following a successful strike against New York dress manufacturers in 1931, in which six thousand dressmakers had won increased wages and improved working conditions. But the Party did not consider the participation of three hundred black workers out of thousands in the industry to be adequate. Earl Browder, however, insisted that winning even a small number of blacks was more important than winning any other group — so long as the Negro question "registers with ten-fold effectiveness in creating difficulties for the capitalist class and improves our chances of advancement." According to TUUL leader Jack Stachel, the union failed to take special steps to win black workers; battles against discrimination were fought only rarely; "outrageous actions" by some white workers were not handled with "sufficient political firmness." The New York dressmakers' strike mirrored the contradictory and transitional situation in the small radical unions in 1932: A growing awareness of the need to respond to the special conditions of black workers — and an occasional effort to do so — was counterbalanced by tenacious chauvinism and inattention.[14]

The Unemployed Movement

Astronomical rates of joblessness and economic privation among blacks drew them in increasing numbers to the UCs and into fervent demonstrations against hunger. Detroit was one city that had not been known for black-white cooperation among the working class. The influx of black workers, mainly from Alabama, into Ford's auto plants in the 1920s had been spurred by good pay and paternalism. However, by 1932 wages at Ford had dropped 50 percent below the 1929 level. Speed-up had doubled and tripled; drillers, grinders, lathe and punch-press operators, and foundry workers (virtually all of whom were black) were laboring at a feverish pace and contributing involuntarily to growing unemployment. At the Briggs auto body plant, blacks were earning ten cents an hour less than white workers; a sign in the women's lavatory said that any female worker "caught talking to Negroes" would be fired immediately. Such were the indications that employers were cultivating racial tensions at a time of deepening crisis.[15]

On March 7, 1932, unemployed Ford workers, some of whom had been laid off that very morning, gathered for a hunger march to the Ford plant at River Rouge, Michigan. The marchers, called together by the Auto Workers Union and the Detroit UC, demanded among other things an end to discrimination against blacks in jobs, relief, and medical services. More than three thousand were on hand, among them nearly four hundred blacks, mainly from Ford's rolling mill, foundry, and steel mill. Skirmishes broke out at the Dearborn city limits, where police firing tear gas sought to block the road to the Rouge plant. Some marchers managed to reach Ford's employment office to present their demands. They were met by reinforcements; shots rang out from police revolvers, leaving four dead and twenty-three seriously injured. (One of the wounded, Curtis Williams, a black former Ford worker, died from his wounds months later.) "Unity" had come to the dead.[16]

In the largely segregated city of St. Louis in midsummer 1932, the UCs won a battle that set a standard of black-white cooperation among the jobless. After the city eliminated fifteen thousand families from relief rolls, the local UC called a hunger march on City Hall on July 8. Five thousand people responded and waited under a scorching sun while a committee met with city officials to demand an immediate reversal of the cutbacks. The mayor was forced to relent; money suddenly materialized, and instructions were issued to provide relief for all the unemployed coming to relief stations. On July 11 ten thousand blacks and whites turned out to support a group that was to meet with the mayor to discuss additional demands. When the group failed to reappear, word spread that the mayor had refused to meet with them and that they would not, or could not, leave City Hall. One hundred women, most of them black, supported by two hundred ex-servicemen, marched on the mayor's office, only to be fired upon by police using shotguns and gas grenades. Throngs of blacks were among the last to be driven away by the attack, in which four people sustained gunshot wounds, scores were beaten by police, and forty-eight were arrested.

A wave of sympathy for the demonstrators swept through the city; religious leaders condemned the "un-Christian" shootings, and the local press voiced fear of worse upheavals ahead. Under mounting pressure, the city restored all those who had been cut from relief rolls. However, the forty-eight jailed demonstrators were held incommunicado for two days and subjected to beatings and psychological pressure. Thomas Beezley, an unemployed laborer, committed suicide after he was released on bond. News of Beezley's suicide spurred the Party to organize new delegations of a broader character, achieved through the vaunted "united front from below." The CP, which by its own admission had been a weak and narrow group of ninety members in a city of a million, doubled its membership. That still constituted a very small number, but the new recruits brought a surge of energy to the Party's work among the jobless. The Unemployed Council organized seventeen block committees in a single day — largely, but not exclusively, in black neighborhoods.[17]

Throughout 1932 the work of the Unemployed Councils to win nondiscriminatory relief resulted in some effective, sustained interracial cooperation. In Chicago, where the pressure on city and county relief agencies was unswerving, a new plateau of comfort between blacks and whites emerged. Indigent whites shed their inhibitions about appealing to the black leadership of the councils for help. The Cook County Bureau of Public Welfare was also forced into negotiations with Brown Squire, the relentless black organizer for the South Side Unemployed Council. In November 1932 the relief agency declined to accede to Squire's demand that every family on assistance be given six dollars for Thanksgiving. But the director agreed to seek funds for partial payment of rents for those facing eviction, despite a state-mandated policy of refusing such payments.[18]

Hit-and-run demonstrations at relief stations helped in gaining concessions from relief officials. During the summer of 1932 the Illinois Emergency Relief Commission had appointed a "special committee to treat with" the Chicago UC and the Socialist-led Workers Committee on Unemployment, to consider cases that the Cook County bureau had not settled to the satisfaction of the unemployed groups. By the end of 1932 the Urban League in New York City and other places had become accustomed to referring many in desperate straits to the UCs. When all else failed, the Urban League indirectly acknowledged the efficacy of "mass action."[19]

THE BONUS MARCH

The Bonus March on Washington by twenty-five thousand war veterans in the late spring and summer of 1932 drew blacks and whites from all regions of the country. For Communists, it became a battleground within a battleground to confront the race issue. The Workers Ex-Servicemen's League had been set up by the Party following demonstrations on March 6, 1930, in part as an improvised workers' "defense corps." By late 1931 the WESL was calling for payment of a deferred pay increase — called a "bonus" — for veterans of the Great War. At the December 1931 hunger march a caucus of more than four hundred veterans agreed to make the bonus their primary issue. In April 1932 James Ford and Samuel Stember appeared for the WESL before the House Ways and Means Committee. Before they were thrown out, they condemned the bourgeois "illusion" of dependence upon the legislative process and said that they would be back with twenty thousand more to secure the bonus and unemployment insurance. The WESL followed up by creating a National Bonus March Provisional Committee, headed by ex-marine Emmanuel Levin, the business manager of the *Daily Worker*. But unrest among veterans across the country erupted in a trek that did not wait for the reds. In Portland, Oregon, W. W. Waters led three hundred veterans across the country to the nation's capital. The tattered march picked up thousands more along the way, including scores of blacks. The WESL found in Washington a spontaneous assemblage including some "advanced revolutionary workers" and a body of "declassed workers, ruined farmers and representatives of small propertied elements ruined by the crisis." The Party would have no easy time getting control of the crowd and imposing its standards of black-white unity.[20]

WESL veterans in the Chicago, Detroit, and Cleveland contingents made forays through the camps to contest Jim Crow. Joe Gardner, a militant veteran from Chicago, had been elected leader of the Illinois contingent, which was three-fourths white. When the Illinois militants found the Negro veterans of the Camden, New Jersey, encampment segregated, they stormed and blustered until the group desegregated. At the much publicized "Pennsylvania Avenue barracks," two hundred black veterans had been confined to the top floors. Sol Harper led a charge against Jim Crow in a stronghold of the "Waters clique." After the protest, the "barracks" was integrated without complaint from veterans from the Deep South.[21]

Roy Wilkins was impressed by the climate of biracial amity that radiated in part from the left. Asked by the *Crisis* to explore the racial angle in the Bonus March, Wilkins was struck by how there appeared to be no visible color line when "Southerners, Northerners, blacks and whites, met in the Army of Despair." Whites welcomed the irony, music, and humor that blacks injected into the grimy camps, and they drew sustenance from the clarity and moral authority of the black ex-servicemen. There was no time for division; cooperation and understanding came from the pressures of a common cause. Black toes and white toes protruded from the same tent flaps and oversized corrugated boxes. Captain A. B. Simmons, a Negro from Houston, Texas, reported that even on the march through the South, homes had been opened to blacks and whites, who took meals, hiked, and rode together. If the bonuseers could unite across racial lines, Wilkins asked, why couldn't the entire fabric of American life be desegregated?[22]

Anacostia Flats and the other camps were destroyed by military action ordered by the Hoover administration. During the mopping up, the police invaded a WESL meeting in an abandoned church. The gathering was billed as a conference of rank-and-file veterans. James W. Ford, among a group of black and white Communists and leftists, was arrested.[23]

Hunger, not ideology, was the driving force behind the bonus army, said J. Max Barber of the *Pittsburgh Courier*. And in the face of that hunger he, for one, was ready to join with any party that offered a program of relief, a "recasting" of an unjust political economic system, and a refusal to "insult me by Jim Crowing me." How dare the "Communist bogey" crowd bully and badger him, since "there is something rotten in a political system which does not guarantee a right to a job and a place in the nation's economic life. And bogeys won't cure the situation."[24]

A Presidential Election

In 1932 James Ford was rapidly becoming the Party's symbol of its internal egalitarian life and its commitment to advance blacks to its leadership. In May he was nominated for the U.S. vice presidency on the Party's ticket. Ford embodied an emerging temperament. There was something regal about him; he was unfailingly courteous, natty, imposing, efficient, and often aloof. Ironically, that lordly detachment marked him as a potential mass leader, capable of commanding the respect of followers and other leaders alike. The locus of black Communist leadership was shifting, if ever so subtly. Harry Haywood turned inward to become an ideological enforcer. B. D. Amis was diffident and had not been able to spark the LSNR; William Patterson was burrowing into the ILD. Otto Huiswoud and George Padmore were in Europe. The other pioneer Communists, such as Cyril Briggs and Richard Moore, were drifting into the background as a result of "nationalistic" flare-ups that at times ran counter to the Party line. A new generation of activists was emerging. While they made their bows to dogma, the old battles against Garveyites, Lovestoneites, and the others seemed irrelevant compared to the urgent requirements of the crisis. Ford never lost his impatience with ideological hairsplitting (though he yielded to no one when called upon to attack enemies). Above all, he was a practitioner, a Party man, and a bridge between past and future.[25]

The CP's nominating convention at the Chicago Coliseum turned into a celebration of its modest but meaningful growth among blacks. By mid-1932, with the impact of Scottsboro, battles against unemployment and evictions, and the growth of the Alabama Share Croppers' Union, blacks constituted nearly 10 percent of the Party's membership—around thirteen to fifteen hundred. At the nominating convention four thousand blacks were among a crowd of more than twelve thousand that overflowed the Coliseum. Clarence Hathaway nominated Ford, declaring that "for the first time in American history, a political party names a Negro for Vice President... not as an eye-catching device, but because it is our fundamental policy. For this Negro freedom we will fight until death." There was an outburst of joy for what many freshly recruited Negro Communists affectionately called "the comrade party." Ford and presidential candidate William Z. Foster were seized by a cheering, chanting crowd and carried around the hall. Roger Didier of the *Pittsburgh Courier* exclaimed: "shades of Danton and Robespierre... when 12,000 Reds, wildly, fanatically chose James W. Ford as their party's standard bearer for vice president... even a callous reporter was dazed."[26]

The convention reflected a change from the overwhelmingly foreign-born, faction-ridden Party of 1929. Among the black delegates, many of whom took the rostrum to declare their devotion to the Party, were sharecroppers, dock workers, teachers, unemployed auto workers, domestics, garment workers, miners, and students. Blacks delivered half the speeches, and one of the most riveting speakers was a Florida sharecropper who urged blacks and whites to organize jointly, "if not in city streets and buildings, [then] take to the woods, but organize." Among the quarter of the delegates who were black, women finally emerged as fully engaged participants. Laura Osby, a new recruit from the Chicago stockyards and candidate for state representative, was moved to guileless emotion in saying that "we Negroes love the Communist Party." The *Afro-American* observed that "the whole attitude of Negro workers was one of intense belief in the movement. There was a sense of belonging, of being an integral part of the assemblage. They were at home."[27]

The campaign put together an unprecedented "Ford-Foster Committee for Equal Negro Rights" (Ford's name, in nearly all matters, preceded Foster's). Chaired by William N. Jones of the *Afro-American,* the committee was en-

dorsed by middle-class black leaders, such as Mrs. Vivian Allen, industrial secretary of the YWCA; William Porter, former Republican leader in South Carolina; Kelly Miller Jr.; Countee Cullen; and others. The economic crisis and
its crushing weight on blacks had squeezed endorsements from people who
would ordinarily have disapproved of the Party. In the depths of the Third
Period, the Party, without a signal from the Comintern, sought to achieve a
true united front. Even Haywood's standard bourgeois bashing was pushed
into the shadows.[28]

These developments reflected the disquiet over doctrinaire narrowness that
was beginning to stir within the Party at large. An internal document circulated in the Negro Department in mid-1932 maintained that Party-sponsored
groups should not be held to an Olympian political standard. The International Workers' Order was not an "avowed" revolutionary organization. It was
a fraternal society that sold cheap insurance. Its worth should be gauged not
by the numbers expelled for various deviations, but by the sum of "ideologically backward" workers won to its banners. The IWO should also be allowed
to organize all-Negro branches where necessary, to address "the stubborn fact
of the backwardness of masses of American workers." In a similar vein, the ILD
national convention in October 1932 lashed out at the "old, stupid sectarianism" that prevented winning people from all strata, especially the middle class
and professions. Frank Spector, an ILD assistant secretary, criticized its "stubborn refusal to connect . . . with organizations upon a concrete defense issue"
and its reluctance to admit into its ranks those who did not accept its full
program. He granted that the ILD's remorseless attacks upon "reformist leaders" had been used to reject relations with their organizations.[29]

In 1932 the CP ran dozens of black candidates in every region for everything from alderman and mayor to lieutenant governor and governor to members of Congress. All the Party candidates stressed the issues of unemployment
insurance and racial equality. Getting elected was not a serious goal. Campaigns
were "mass actions," political sounding-boards; in Ford's words, they were a
means "to mobilize workers in the struggle for their immediate needs." When
asked about chances for the Party's black candidates, Ford replied, "The Communist Party is not stupid; we know that better than 4 million Negroes in this
country cannot vote . . . and besides this, there is a great anti-Negro sentiment
which the Party goes up against when it puts forth Negroes as their candidates."
The black-white Communist ticket won 102,991 votes — a minuscule number,
but one that was still impressive compared to past performances. It showed

that there were whites across the country who were not dissuaded by Ford's place on the ticket. That in itself was progress.[30]

The Herndon Case and the Search for Breadth

In the summer of 1931 Angelo Herndon was severely beaten by police in Birmingham, Alabama, who tried to link him to the killing of two white women. He was charged with vagrancy, jumped bail, and was sent to Atlanta by the Party to organize the unemployed. Only nineteen years old, the slightly built, bookish young Communist arrived in Atlanta as bankrupt city and county relief centers shut down, affecting thousands of people. On June 29, 1932, Herndon and a handful of comrades labored through the night to distribute leaflets over the city calling for a march the next day of "whites and Negroes together, with our women folk and children." They would march on the Fulton County Courthouse to demand relief for the jobless. Nearly one thousand careworn blacks and whites answered the call, crowding around the county commissioners' offices, where they extracted promises of immediate relief without racial discrimination. Eleven days later Herndon was arrested. After two weeks without bond, he was charged with attempting to incite insurrection and to induce others to resist the lawful authority of the state of Georgia. The indictment, including the charge of circulating political literature, came under the same pre–Civil War act that had been used against the Atlanta Six in 1930.[31]

Attorney Benjamin J. Davis Jr. immediately went to Fulton County Towers, where he offered to defend the young Communist who was facing a possible death sentence. Davis was the scion of an Atlanta family that had risen from slavery to prominence in the black community. His father was the publisher and editor of the *Independent,* a banker, and a leading figure in the Republican Party in Georgia. Davis Jr. had earned his bachelor's degree at Amherst College where he also played football; in 1932 he graduated from the Harvard Law School. With those credentials, he appeared to be on the way to a relatively comfortable life. But he was a restless nonconformist with a hatred for Jim Crow. His parents worshipped capitalism, but they never forgot where they had come from or pushed from memory the murderous violence that nurtured King Cotton. With that heritage, Ben Davis Jr., who had been practicing law for barely six months with his partner John Geer, was drawn to Angelo Herndon's case.[32]

Herndon was likewise drawn to Davis—who with his partner agreed with the ILD that the defense should be based on Herndon's innocence, the unconstitutionality of the Georgia insurrection statute, the exclusion of blacks from grand and petit juries, and the constitutional rights of speech and assembly. Davis became the pro bono lead attorney and began diligent study of the books, pamphlets, leaflets, and old copies of the *Daily Worker* that had been seized from Herndon. He also immersed himself in the local CP branch, which consisted of three whites and seven blacks, headed by a sixty-year-old black ironworker. He was on his way to becoming a Communist.[33]

At the trial, Davis launched a vigorous, though unsuccessful, challenge to the jury system. He objected so strongly to the use of the word *nigger* in the courtroom that the judge reluctantly barred its utterance. He demanded to know how Herndon could be punished for upholding rights enshrined in the nation's most revered traditions. On the stand, Herndon gave a dramatic recitation of the horrors of the Atlanta jail, the suffering of the city's jobless, and the bankruptcy of capitalism.[34]

Prosecutor John H. Hudson, in his summary, cried out: "Must the State of Georgia sit idly by while [the Communists] organize and mobilize your Red Army? . . . Send this damnable anarchistic Bolsheviki to his death by electrocution and God will be satisfied that justice has been done." With emotion that was unprecedented in a southern courtroom, Davis read from one of Herndon's seized pamphlets, describing the lynching and burning of a pregnant black woman. Such acts were the real insurrectionary deeds, he declared— adding that Hudson's piety was a cloak for evil, that he knew as much about communism "as a pig knows about a full-dress suit." Any verdict other than innocent would turn the Constitution into a meaningless scrap of paper, destroying the democratic rights of every Georgian, white and black.[35]

The trial ended on January 18, 1933. The all-white jury found Angelo Herndon guilty and sentenced him to eighteen to twenty years of imprisonment.[36]

One might have thought that Scottsboro would have drained the energies of the CP and the broader left. But somehow Communists and leftists found new reserves to fight for reversal of Herndon's conviction. Scottsboro's symbolic power was unquestioned, but the Herndon case had elements that compelled a broad appeal without precedent. The attack on Herndon was an attack on ideas and beliefs—sacred to a large public. His own scholarly and self-abnegating demeanor contributed to wide support for his case.

The *New Republic* said that the sentence virtually proved Communist allegations about "capitalist-ruled courts in the Deep South and elsewhere." The *Nation* charged that Herndon's only crime was being a black militant who spoke out and organized the unemployed on a nonsegregated basis. The Negro press was almost unanimous in its condemnation of the conviction. The *Daily Worker,* without its usual "social fascist" prattle, noted approvingly that "many Negroes, liberals and intellectuals already have come forward with promises of support."[37]

The Atlanta ILD, despite continued carping by the national office, pursued local liberals and helped form the uncommonly broad Provisional Committee for the Defense of Angelo Herndon. Its membership embraced black and white Atlantans, and included local religious leaders, academics, workers, merchants, and trade unionists. Among the participants were the city's best known black Baptist minister, Reverend J. Raymond Henderson; the outspoken Socialist Mary Raoul Millis; and the young historian C. Vann Woodward. The *Daily Worker* advised ILD members within the committee to push for Herndon's immediate release on bail (especially in light of the abominable conditions in which he was held), free speech, and the right of the CP to a legal existence. Communists in the larger group should show "any honest worker or intellectual that the ILD is sincerely interested in forming a real front, and not in dominating the whole action." Although the bitterness between the national NAACP and the ILD over Scottsboro still festered, the local branch of the NAACP quickly offered support in the appeals process. The winds of change were blowing while the battle to free Angelo Herndon went on.[38]

SCOTTSBORO IN 1932

In 1932 the Scottsboro campaign's impulse for breadth and black-white unity made faltering progress. Learning that the ILD was having trouble paying the highly respected attorney, Walter H. Pollak, whom it had retained, Walter White and Arthur Spingarn offered financial assistance on condition that the funds go directly to the attorney. That warming led to a proposal by the NAACP to engage in general fund raising for the Scottsboro defense. William Patterson surveyed the financial burdens on the ILD and, prevailing over Party hardliners, accepted in an exchange of letters with White brimming with uncharacteristic civility. The NAACP's efforts yielded nearly $12,000. But bickering over finances never wholly ceased. In mid-1933 Patterson dragged out a disputed $7,000 payment in 1931 to attorneys Darrow, Roddy, Moody, and Beddow, from funds raised by the association. "Not one cent of the money... found its way to the defense of the Scottsboro boys," Patterson complained. The NAACP's standard reply was to accuse the ILD of careless bookkeeping and sloppy handling of money.[39]

A compelling image of a united black-white struggle to free the Scottsboro boys came from an unexpected source. Ruby Bates had written a letter to a boyfriend on January 5, 1932, in which she stated that "those negros did not touch me." Of the two accusers, Bates was never the enthusiast. Victoria Price was older, and wiser in the convoluted sexual mores of the South. She had a profane tongue and a robust sexual imagination, and she painted a salacious picture of demented black teenaged rapists. Price understood that failure to accuse the boys of rape would tar the two women as vagrant whores. By charging rape, they became upright southern women whose virtue had to be avenged against black sexual predators. But Bates had grown uneasy under Price's manipulative and dominating personality. A spark of conscience was never extinguished. Further, neither her jobless state nor her hunger was eased by the notoriety of the case. Bates's letter slithered through Chattanooga's back streets, inevitably catching George Chamlee's attention. By the end of 1932 Ruby Bates had decided to "go over" to the defense.[40]

On the left, Bates became a symbol of the inseparable destinies of the black and white southern poor. She came from a sharecropping family, afflicted by mean-spirited, boozy men. The family's hardscrabble life took them back and forth between cropping and mill work. With a miserable mill job in Huntsville, Bates and her family were the only whites in the black section of town. Despite the myth of total segregation, the racial divide vanished at the lowest layers of southern society. There, among black people, Ruby Bates and Victoria Price played, drank, slept, loved—giving the lie to the shibboleth that no white woman, however degraded, would give herself to a black man.[41]

An unsteady, evasive Ruby Bates appeared as a surprise witness at the second Scottsboro trial in April 1933. Her testimony brought the stinging rebuke that virtuous white women did not lie about the most heinous of crimes; she had defiled the good name, honesty, and purity of white womanhood for "Moscow Gold." But again, on the left, Bates became a symbol of the latent integrity of the South's white poor—proof that their suffering could bring a yearning for justice for white and black alike. She marched with the Scottsboro mothers, shared their grief and pain, won their gratitude, appeared in May Day parades with clenched fist aloft, spoke at innumerable rallies, petitioned and led delegations, met with politicians, learned to say "comrade." She spoke in her unschooled voice about the mills, about her hard life, about sensing that "if people would all work together instead of against each other it would help everbody." Bates's recantation of the rape charge was dismissed by Alabama prosecutors and judges with ill-controlled anger. But for the Communists she embodied potential: From ignorance and degradation, a democratic, egalitarian, even revolutionary consciousness could emerge.[42]

J. Louis Engdahl accompanied Scottsboro mother Ada Wright on a long European tour in 1932. At times they were enveloped in the deepening shadow of fascism. Mrs. Wright was arrested in Czechoslovakia, expelled twice from Belgium, and barred from speaking in several German cities. While the European trek went on, the Party's Negro Department anticipated Engdahl's reassignment after the tour. It proposed to the CP leadership that Patterson become national secretary of the ILD; a motion to that effect added that the Negro Department was opposed to placing Patterson in a lower position, such as head of Negro work in the defense organization. Black Communists would fight for the establishment of African American leadership at the highest levels. On November 21, 1932, J. Louis Engdahl died in Moscow. Patterson's appointment was then confirmed.[43]

REELTOWN

In early 1932 CP farm specialists Harold Ware and Lem Harris described to the Negro Department the acute crisis in cotton: soil erosion, the boll weevil, falling prices, displacement of human labor by mechanical cotton pickers, competition from expanding cotton production around the world. The Depression had dried up production credits, which were the croppers' life blood. Landowners were getting a handful of black youth to wear uniforms with "Tractor Driver" in red letters and to run the machines to displace the sharecroppers.[44]

The crisis required new strategies. Croppers and tenants needed decent free land to raise food; an effective relief system without discrimination had to be instituted in ravaged rural communities; all debts owed to landlords and banks had to be abolished. The decline of sharecropping and the rise of wage labor in agriculture would require, in the long term, more of a standard labor union agenda for the Share Croppers' Union.[45]

A bloody outcome of the debt crisis came in Reeltown in Tallapoosa County, Alabama, at the end of 1932. The SCU had regained momentum in the county after Camp Hill, when it forced a Tallapoosa plantation to allow croppers to sell their own cotton and to continue to receive winter food allowances. But an SCU organizer, Luther Hughley, was arrested for vagrancy and later charged with kidnapping a Camp Hill white woman. The charges were dropped after black croppers and tenants crowded the arraignment and the ILD girded for another mass defense.[46]

While tensions were smoldering in Tallapoosa County, Al Murphy and five SCU organizers attended the National Farmers' Relief Conference in Washington, D.C. Some SCU delegates asked Harris if they "should build a fort" against the murderous hostility of the sheriffs. His advice was the same as that of Murphy and other Communists: Such actions would be premature and would provoke the sheriffs. Harris advised the SCU members never to hold meetings in empty houses, never to face the lights of cars or flashlights, never to walk in large groups, and never to take armed action before notifying the Party or the SCU leaders, "unless it is impossible to get out of a snap without fire."[47]

The "snap" occurred on December 19, 1932, when armed sheriffs sought to enforce a writ of attachment brought against Clifford James by his creditor, Notasulga merchant W. A. Parker. Sheriff J. Kyle Young, who had been wounded at Camp Hill, had been to James's house in early December for an unannounced search that yielded SCU membership blanks and literature. James, like other farmers in the area, was attracted to SCU's program; he became a union leader in the area and a Party member. With the Depression, James could no longer meet payments on a six-year-old loan from Parker, who asked Deputy Sheriff Cliff Elder to serve the writ on James's livestock.[48]

Parker had become convinced that something had happened to hitherto compliant black debtors: The "spirit of cooperation" had been poisoned by Communists. Deputy Sheriff Elder went to James's house to serve the writ, where he encountered several men who were ready to prevent the seizure of James's livestock. When one of them, Ned Cobb, gently advised Elder that he wouldn't "get any mules today," the sheriff raised his gun, threatening to come back with reinforcements and "kill all you niggers in a pile."[49]

Elder returned that afternoon with three other men. Cobb faced the jittery group, who immediately recognized that they were confronting armed union members. As Cobb turned to enter James's house, he was hit with bird shot. An exchange of fire followed. When it subsided an SCU member, John McMullen, was dead and several others were wounded, including Cobb, James, and Milo Bentley. Sheriff Young gathered a posse of over five hundred men from four counties. After the shootings, police discovered a local union membership list in James's home. More than twenty people were rounded up and jailed; some were wounded but accorded only minimal medical care. Among those arrested were persons not involved in the shootout, but whose names were on the confiscated list. Whole families fled in terror to the backwoods as vigilantes broke into homes, pistol-whipped inhabitants, and seized guns and other property. After Cobb was treated for minor wounds at Tuskegee Institute's hospital and told to leave, Dr. Eugene Dibble notified the sheriff's office. Cobb was later captured, but Bentley was wounded after firing at the deputies. Clifford James, wounded in the back and shoulder, hid in a ditch for nearly two days. He managed the seventeen-mile trek to Tuskegee for medical aid. After being questioned by Dr. Dibble, James was turned over to the Macon County sheriff, thrown into a dank cell at the Montgomery County jail, and made to lie on a floor naked and delirious. He died on December 27 of infected wounds and pneumonia. Milo Bentley had been placed in similar circumstances and died on the same day.[50]

James's widow charged that "while Dr. Dibble was pretending to look after Cliff's wounds, he sent a student to the Sheriff's office and a deputy came right over and took him to jail, where he died." The *Pittsburgh Courier* noted that at the height of the Reeltown events, the Memphis *Commercial Appeal* called upon Tuskegee to turn its attention to the threat of communism, warning that the "enemies of law and order" who had appeared at the institute's doorstep had "established a foothold among the race that Tuskegee Institute is endeavoring to make into law abiding, useful citizens."[51]

A segment of the area's black middle class feared Communists in their midst. The SCU, however, enjoyed substantial, if muted, popularity across the countryside. The police were convinced that local blacks were giving guns and ammunition to the union. There were signs of sympathy from some whites. When a posse member lifted an axe to finish off the wounded Judson Simpson, he was stopped by Homer Jackson, a white, who hid Simpson for two days. The ILD claimed that "many [blacks] were hidden and sheltered in the homes of poor white sharecroppers who realized that this was their fight too." Some whites quartered black neighbors on the December 19 night of terror. A white doctor, W. S. Hanson of Reeltown, treated some of the wounded croppers and tenants.[52]

Five of the arrested sharecroppers went on trial for assault with a deadly weapon. Despite the ransacking of the ILD's Birmingham office and the arrest of Party organizers, a successful rally was held on January 2, 1933, to protest the arrests and to denounce Tuskegee. Shortly thereafter, three thousand mourners, most of them black, followed two caskets draped with the hammer and sickle to burial. The trial was postponed when scores of blacks and some white sympathizers clogged the courthouse. When the proceedings got under way on April 24, county officials attempted to block the main roads in order to stop black farmers from attending. Yet croppers and tenants managed to appear and were seated when defense attorneys Irving Schwab and W. A. Morrison protested the barring of blacks from the courtroom. The defense also challenged the exclusion of blacks from jury service and contested every racial slur uttered by prosecution witnesses. The five croppers were convicted of assault with a deadly weapon and received terms of five to fifteen years. Various charges against others dragged through the courts for years. Cobb was given a sentence of twelve to fifteen years, despite testimony that he had remained unarmed throughout the shooting.[53]

The battle at Reeltown and environs did not halt the SCU's growth. From 778 members in November 1932, the union grew to nearly 2,000 organized in 73 locals by June 1933. It spread into counties south of Tallapoosa and over the Georgia border, and added scores of women's auxiliaries and youth groups. The Party established five new rural units as Reeltown became a hymn of resistance throughout the rural South.[54]

THE SECOND NATIONAL HUNGER MARCH

As 1932 drew to an end, the energy of a tumultuous year was channeled into the second preholiday National Hunger March. Colorful, defiant, even profane, the marchers gloried in their interracial presence as they snaked through Jim Crow Maryland into Jim Crow Washington, D.C. The *New York Times* seemed beguiled by "a high-stepping Georgia Negro in a rainbow colored beret with scarf to match, [who] stepped jauntily... to the martial music of the 'Internationale.' Behind him trudged a woman of his own race, a coonskin coat flopping about her ankles and a happy smile on her broad face." But things were grimmer than conveyed by the *Times*'s giddy affection for racial stereotypes. On the dreary slopes of Capitol Hill, the marchers were hemmed in by eight hundred police armed with tear gas, riot clubs, and blackjacks, while Klansmen burned a thirty-foot cross on the other side of the Potomac. Nevertheless, the cry for unity went on. Even the young caught the spirit: Seventy-four children, black and white, pushed against resistant police lines at the gates of the White House, pleading for insurance and for relief without discrimination for "hungry children."[55]

The police estimated that over 15 percent of the nearly three thousand marchers who got to Washington were black women and men. The *New York Times* claimed that "nearly half" of the marchers were black. One reporter commented that "even with [their] drabness . . . these marchers made a colorful picture as the sun played on white and black and red skins." Delegations from Georgia, Louisiana, Virginia, and other parts of the South were led by blacks and whites. One black observer noted the spectacular convergence of cultures in the lusty singing of "Onward Christian Soldiers" and "The Internationale." Garland McKay of the *Washington Tribune* pondered the marchers' example for the Jim Crow capital. Black marchers appeared to be indoctrinated with steely suspicion for the "capitalist press." The previous year, many blacks had jumped in — hoping simply to get food and a place to sleep. But in 1932 black marchers were thoroughly briefed and fully represented in "committees" that confronted Vice-President Curtis and House Speaker John Nance Garner with demands for cash relief and unemployment insurance. McKay concluded that "the Communists really practiced the brotherhood of man."[56]

Summing Up

Robert Minor assessed the state of the Negro question and the Party's Negro work as the nation entered a new epoch with Franklin D. Roosevelt's election. In cities and towns where Negroes constituted 9–18 percent of the population, they made up 66–90 percent of the unemployed. Displacement from jobs by whites and ferocious wage cutting had hit black communities hardest. The black bourgeoisie had suffered devastating setbacks, exemplified by insurance companies that bore as many policy lapses as new business.[57]

Minor noted that the results of a questionnaire on the radicalization of the black community, distributed by the National Urban League to business and professional groups, corresponded with internal Party evaluations of its strengths and weaknesses among blacks around the country. There was a reported drift away from religious institutions and a growing interest in radical ideas among working-class and sharecropping blacks. In Chicago (which Minor extolled for "a most splendid record" in the Party's Negro work), unemployment and evictions drove many Negroes to communism. Despite considerable middle-class opposition, the Chicago Party had recently recruited around 430 black members, "the proudest achievement" to date in Negro work. Indianapolis and South Bend, Boston, Detroit, New York City — all registered growth among blacks. But little activity and growth were reported in Pittsburgh, where blacks numbered 25 percent of the unemployed, though only 8 percent of the population. The report confirmed the Party's influence among sharecroppers and tenants in parts of the South, noting that croppers opened floorboards to strangers they had come to trust, revealing copies of the *Daily Worker* and other Communist literature. A black church leader reported that no literate Negro family in the rural districts around Atlanta was without Communist literature. Minor granted that such a claim "is a bit exaggerated," and wished that the small Atlanta Party group "could thoroughly deserve that compliment."[58]

The Urban League had concluded that a vaguely defined but broad sympathy for the CP in the black community had yielded only spotty organizational commitment and growth. Minor agreed. He added that the revolutionary unions had not consolidated gains made among blacks, like those in the coal strike of 1931. Had the Party given organizational permanence to the advances made among blacks in the unemployment, hunger, and anti-eviction struggles? It had not. The *Liberator* remained a sore point, hobbled by undisclosed "editorial" problems and unable to reach more than a minuscule readership. Chicago had the only regularly functioning Negro Department. In District 2, which included New York City, the Negro Department was "so weak that it is almost negligible." The national leadership's repeated injunctions to the districts to establish functioning Negro departments had been carried out in only three or four districts.[59]

White chauvinism in the Party had often turned out to be more egregious than reported. A problem of enormous magnitude, according to Minor, was the Party's failure to consistently advance the special needs and specific demands of blacks. In the mine strike the Party had set limits for the Negro question — advocating solidarity of black and white, but not dealing forthrightly with the special oppression of the Negro.[60]

Minor might have dug deeper regarding the anomaly of sympathy among blacks and little organizational growth. He did not discuss the growing concern within the CP itself about sectarianism, which ran counter to the religious and cultural values of many blacks. Nor did he consider that it might be unrealistic to ask blacks to throng to a revolutionary movement that as yet existed at society's margins. The Party's paltry size and limited resources made it difficult to reach many sectors of the black community. The problem of winning white workers to the struggle for black liberation continued to be central to the Party's difficulties. Without broad support from the white working class, disquiet among blacks about their own vulnerability in embracing the Party would not dissolve. That was understood within the CP. The tumultuous events of 1932 had yielded just enough evidence of a changing racial consciousness among white workers to offer encouragement. But the attainment of large-scale white commitment to the struggle for black liberation was a long way from fulfillment.

The Communist issue had begun to claim the attention of black editorial opinion. In 1932 Du Bois launched an unprecedented symposium on the Negro and communism in the pages of the *Crisis*. That discussion touched upon socialism, nationalism, Marxism, imperialism, Soviet Russia, and self-development vs. alliances with radical whites. Carl Murphy of the *Afro-American* said that the Communists were latter-day abolitionists, "for which Allah be praised!" The *Norfolk Journal and Guide*'s P. B. Young admired the Party's saving hand to drowning men. Some hailed the Party for welcoming blacks "into high and lowly positions" in its ranks. Quite a few saw a useful lever to force the white elite to make good on its democratic claims. E. Washington Rhodes of the *Washington Tribune* warned that if the flirtation between reds and blacks became more serious, "the white American must blame himself." W. P. Dabney, editor of the *Union* (Ohio), said that the Communists came to blacks with brotherhood, not charity, with deeds, not words. Yet the larger society could still exorcise the red menace by ostracizing racism: "Will Pharaoh heed?" In a country saturated with anticommunism, the majority saw something good in Communist efforts.[61]

But some editors doubted that the Party could penetrate the Negro's faith in "the ultimate justice of American democracy." Another doubt also remained. Du Bois was joined by I. Willis Cole of the *Louisville Leader* and William Kelley of the New York *Amsterdam News*, who asked if communism had any relevance in the United States, where workers often formed the backbone of the lynch mob, while bourgeois institutions often opposed disenfranchisement and segregation. Roscoe Dunjee of the *Black Dispatch* rendered a stereotypical portrait of the reds, but was also poignant and nearly prayerful. For years he had hoped to witness poor whites awakening to their own interest in unity and cooperation with blacks against a ruling class that had deliberately driven the races apart. And now the poor white man, shrouded in red banners, had come to his door. He staged marches and carried banners through the heart of Dixie — saying that the Negro's miserably oppressed life must vanish. Had white wrath against blacks become a spent force? Had the prospect of revolutionary change in the nation's social and racial attitudes become enough to invest hope in the Communists? Dunjeee could not say: "There stands the poor white with a bomb under his arm — yet love in his heart for me. What shall I do about it? Does that unsanitary looking human being hold within his grasp my rainbow of promise, and the power which I so sorely need?" That remained the key question.

PART III

The New Deal and
the Popular Front, 1933–36

CHAPTER THIRTEEN

New Deals and New Directions

REDS, BLACKS, AND THE NEW DEAL

The coming of the New Deal did not initially provoke the Communists into new thinking. Franklin D. Roosevelt's early policies seemed to lend credibility to the CP's "social fascist" mantra. His election to the presidency brought the growth and concentration of state power and a strong bond with corporate capital. Momentum toward state capitalism was accelerating — accompanied by efforts to eviscerate class struggle in the name of the higher good of the nation. The two major building blocks of Roosevelt's crisis program — the National Industrial Recovery Act and the Agricultural Adjustment Act — seemed like corporate fascism swathed in nationalist fervor. The NIRA's "codes of fair competition" were formulated under the preponderant influence of big business. The Agricultural Adjustment Act favored large farms and agribusiness — intensifying the squeeze on sharecroppers and tenants. All this seemed to validate the Third Period claim that reformism and fascism were two sides of the same coin.[1]

The Communists were not alone in charging that the New Deal was doing nothing to relieve the misery of blacks. Much of the Negro press and major black organizations turned against the NIRA and its agency, the National Recovery Administration. In May 1933 the Rosenwald Conference on the Economic Status of the Negro warned that special measures were needed to assure that blacks would not be driven out of their jobs once wages were equalized. Such measures were not forthcoming, despite assurances from the Roosevelt administration that it would "not forget the special problems" of black workers. As the codes emerged, blacks were doubly victimized — by joblessness where wage equality was applied, and by low-paying jobs where wage equality was not applied. Southern capitalists and politicians mobilized to enforce wage differentials through threats, through exemptions in places where blacks were concentrated (the Urban League estimated that 3 million black workers were excluded from the codes), through manipulation of loosely drawn codes, and through the establishment of formal wage disparities for the South. The NAACP charged that under Title 2 of the NIRA (the public works section), local contractors, given control of hiring, were providing little or no work for blacks. For blacks, the acronym *NRA* became "Negroes Roasted Alive," "Negroes Ruined Again," "Negro Robbed Again," "Negro Repressive Act," "Negro Run Around."[2]

The AAA seriously wounded black agricultural labor. While landlords received the lion's share of acreage reduction payments, sharecroppers complained that they often did not get even the paltry payments earmarked for them. Landlords often forged the signatures on cotton parity checks meant for tenants and croppers or pocketed the checks after getting illiterate recipients to endorse them without knowing what they were signing. Landlords began to resist government work programs and cash relief, claiming that their tenants and croppers preferred relief to labor and were being "ruined" for return to the fields. Worse, AAA's cotton reduction program had caused widespread tenant evictions in the Southeast. NAACP secretary Walter White maintained that "more than 100,000 Negro and white sharecroppers and tenant farmers" had been cast off the land as result of AAA policies. Despite pleas from black organizations, the Department of Agriculture steadfastly refused to appoint black advisers.[3]

But there were glimmers of hope in the New Deal, which — joined to anger over the new administration's failures — gave renewed energy to protests. The most persistent and focused attack against New Deal discriminatory practices came from John P. Davis and Robert C. Weaver. Davis was raised in Washington, D.C., graduated from the famous Dunbar High School, got his bachelor's degree from Bates College, and graduated from Harvard Law School. At Harvard he met Weaver, who was working on a Ph.D. in economics. From conversations over poker and coffee with Weaver and the few other blacks at Harvard, Davis became committed to social activism. With his law degree in hand as the New Deal was beginning, he joined Weaver to form the Negro Industrial League, a two-man operation that lasted through the summer of 1933. The two young men trudged from one congressional hearing to another, demanding that an often distracted and uninterested Congress pay attention to the impact of the NRA upon black labor.[4]

Roosevelt deftly kept the southern segregationists under his tent while making overtures to blacks. By the end of summer 1933, Weaver had been coopted into the administration as an assistant to Clark Foreman, the liberal white southerner who served as adviser on Negro affairs in the Department of the Interior. In the fall Roosevelt stated that one of the underlying principles of the NRA was the elimination of "inequalities and class distinction," adding that he had appointed "twelve men of the colored race and twelve of the white" to sift out complaints of discrimination. Harry Hopkins, Roosevelt's relief czar, made a decent effort to prevent the concentration of rural relief aid in the hands of landlords. He also sought to establish a modicum of equality in cash and work relief under the Federal Emergency Relief Administration.[5]

When Mabel Byrd arrived in Washington as the only Negro staff member of the NRA's Division of Research and Planning, no office awaited her. Instead, she was given a desk beside black census tabulators on the segregated tenth floor of the Commerce Department building and was warned not to use white stenographers. Her projected study tour of southern cities was squelched by NRA director Hugh S. Johnson, who characterized such a trip by a northern black woman as "preposterous." Working from Washington, Byrd confirmed through her research that NRA had actually accelerated the displacement of black workers. Sectional wage differentials facilitated racial discrimination; racist practices were tolerated by enforcing agencies in which not a single black served; discrimination ruled the New Deal's Civil Works Administration and its Public Works Administration. She proposed a policy stipulation that discharge or displacement of blacks due to higher wages and hours would be regarded as "an unfair operation of the [given] code."[6]

Byrd's proposal was ignored by the NRA bureaucracy, and in late 1933 she was told that her services were no longer needed. Davis was embittered by her firing, especially in view of the fact that blacks had been pressing for representation in the NRA from its beginning. And now, in its second year, the NRA did not employ a single Negro "with a rank equal to that of a clerk."[7]

Byrd's experience at NRA outraged the Communists and the broader black community. Marguerite Young, of the *Daily Worker*'s newly established Washington bureau, wrote that people like Byrd who joined the administration were not "betrayers" but committed activists who sought to advance democracy and progress from within the government. Byrd commanded respect for her identity as a "Negro Woman, Economic Expert," and principled foe of racial discrimination.[8] Not only did stories like this one reveal a new flexibility in attitude, but also the creation of a Washington bureau was a tacit admission that the New Deal was worthy of reportage.

Weaver's appointment in the Department of Interior put an end to the Negro Industrial League. Davis, however, became increasingly committed to the role of critic outside the system. In September 1933, with some money from the Rosenwald Fund, help from George E. Haynes of the Federal Council of Churches, and the sponsorship of the NAACP and fifteen other organizations, the Joint Committee on National Recovery was born.[9]

From the beginning, the JCNR struggled to make an impact with an annual budget of less than $5,000 and a staff that never exceeded two members. Davis built on Byrd's work — exposing discriminatory NRA codes in the cotton mills of Georgia, the steel mills of Alabama, the sawmills in the pine forests of the South. He challenged AAA marketing agreements that were extended to whites only. He sought to discourage black ministers and lay leaders from sanctioning lower wages for black workers. The JCNR collected letters complaining of unfair treatment and sought to bring those complaints before government officials. Davis, with his technical adviser Rose M. Coe, managed to appear at more than a hundred public NRA hearings. He caused a minor sensation in late 1933 when he released confidential minutes of an NRA meeting, which suggested that the agency was considering lower wages for Negroes. Threatened with a government investigation, Davis demanded instead that government snoops expend their energies to investigate New Deal bias. The government backed off. But with limited resources, the JCNR was increasingly confined to issuing reports and engaging in public education to expose the inequities dogging black workers. Its single victory was to get the NRA to decree that it would not sanction lower wages and hours for black workers. But in the end, that was a pyrrhic victory, as wage equalization accelerated displacement of black labor.[10]

Throughout the JCNR's existence, the NAACP remained its chief sponsor. Although White never fully trusted Davis and his uncompromising assault upon New Deal racial policies, he did understand the value of the JCNR. He resisted pressure to scuttle it and ridiculed the prissy reaction of the "the dear old ladies of the YW" to Davis's expansive and courtly personality. But the JCNR hit financial bottom in mid-1934. Davis struggled on until he joined with Ralph Bunche and the Social Science Division of Howard University to sponsor the Conference on the Economic Status of the Negro, held in May 1935. When that conference laid the foundations for a National Negro Congress, with Davis as chief organizer, the JCNR died.[11]

By this time Davis was beginning to view racial discrimination as systemic to capitalism. Hope for progress lay in the labor movement, which showed signs of awakening, and in prospects for a black-labor coalition. He met James W. Ford and became acquainted with Benjamin J. Davis Jr., who had jettisoned his legal career to become a Communist functionary and editor of the *Harlem Liberator*. By late 1934, John Davis was fully committed to the Party's concept of black-white working-class unity and to its longstanding ambition to forge a pro-labor coalition of black organizations. For all intents and purposes, he became a nonpublic Communist, and he played a major role in linking the Party with key sectors of the black intelligentsia.[12]

A subtle shift in the CP's political culture was taking place. Some Communists were impressed, if not mesmerized, by the New Deal, while CP leaders fretted over their admiration of the enemy's new clothes. In July 1933 the Central Committee called an extraordinary national conference to stiffen the Party's revolutionary backbone. The meeting produced the *Open Letter,* which exhorted the CP membership to reject empty paper resolutions, to end its alleged laxity, to exercise tighter organization and accountability, and to energetically win the working class to a revolutionary outlook. The *Open Letter* also conceded that the New Deal was not fully matured fascism, but was tending in that direction with the aid of reformists. With unacknowledged irony, the document's call for broadening the struggle for labor rights and for black liberation was framed by an intuitive sense of new openings presented by the New Deal.[13]

The *Open Letter*'s exhortation to "end idle chatter" about reaching the masses encouraged some of those in the Party's sphere to seek a wider arena. A handful of Communists and leftists concerned with the farm crisis joined AAA and became convinced that the JCNR's criticisms of the agency were justified. Davis gained a sympathetic audience among the "pro-tenant group" at AAA, which included Rexford G. Tugwell, Alger Hiss, John Abt, Margaret Bennett, and others, who together initiated an unprecedented level of interaction between Marxists and liberals.[14]

Many young black Communists of the Depression decade had already been politicized by mainstream movements before their encounters with the CP. They were not Moscow-trained and were less doctrinaire than an earlier generation. Ralph Turner joined the Party in Peoria, Illinois, in the early 1930s under repressive conditions that forced his unit to function underground. Turner's public political work was as head of the local NAACP, organizing in the area encompassing Rockford and Peoria, even as the Party continued its ideological warfare against the association. Merrill Work, from a prominent academic family, was the director of the Urban League's community center in Brooklyn, New York, in the early 1930s when he moved into the Party orbit. Struggling to feed a hundred thousand people with a fund of $75,000, Work concluded that charity was certainly no answer to the crisis. He became secretary of the Harlem Unemployed Council, but his reputation as an Urban League activist followed him into the jobless movement. Democratic politicians attempted to coax Work into cooperation with them — and Work, sensing possibilities in the New Deal, kept those contacts alive. After Bill Crawford graduated high school in 1934, he did occasional domestic work in Westchester County by picking up jobs at one of the notorious "slave corners" in the Bronx. When he joined the Party, he was involved in the Household Workers Association (an attempt to bring unionism to domestic workers) and the NAACP Youth Council. He continued those contacts as he found in the CP the embodiment of his father's socialist vision and his own working-class outlook. Frank Sykes in Detroit had his own interpretation of the united front from below. He insisted on maintaining his church membership after he joined the CP in the early 1930s.[15]

LYNCHING AND THE NEW DEAL

Lynching worsened in the early years of the New Deal. The administration's stated aim of wage equality brought a surge of mob violence in the South and border states. Walter White reported that the Alabama mob murder of Dennis Cross on September 24, 1933, marked the seventeenth lynching of the year, more than twice the 1932 rate. (The ILD counted forty-seven lynchings in 1933.) The hanging and immolation of George Armwood in Princess Anne County, Maryland, on October 18, 1933, was also blamed by White on "efforts of certain Southern forces to terrorize Negroes into acceptance of wage differentials and lower economic status under the National Recovery Act." In the absence of federal intervention, leading church organizations pleaded with the president at least to speak out. On December 6, 1933, Roosevelt spoke, conceding that "that vile form of collective murder — lynch law . . . has broken out in our midst anew" and sullied the biblical commandment against killing. "We do not excuse those in high places or low who condone lynch law," he said. However, he took no action.[16]

In the last days of 1933, in response to growing black protest against lynching, senators Edward I. Costigan and Robert F. Wagner of New York introduced a bill to make lynching a federal crime. It languished without support from the White House. When it was reintroduced in 1935, the bill had extensive backing. But the Communists opposed it — scorning its underlying illusion of "capitalist justice," deriding its omission of the death penalty for lynching, condemning its silence on legal lynching and frame-ups, and expressing fear that its definition of a mob ("three or more persons acting in concert . . . to kill or injure") could be used against the left.[17]

Those differences over the Costigan-Wagner bill underscored the Party's contradictory relationship to the black mainstream. At no other time was the middle-class movement's analysis of the roots of lynching more in tune with the views of the CP itself. But the Party's ideology-first standard blinded it to the progressive antilynching tradition inaugurated by Ida B. Wells and absorbed into the NAACP. At least William Patterson admitted that the ILD's "narrow, sectarian outlook chokes its growth organizationally and politically." But he was unwilling to apply that self-criticism to the antilynch bill. The ambitious antilynch conference and public hearing in Baltimore in November, 1933, on the Armwood lynching, sponsored by the ILD and the LSNR, won the support of scores of organizations and local branches of the NAACP. But the gatherings also expended energy on attacking "the toothless anti-lynch bill." When a broad spectrum of the black community at last strove to force a federal commitment to stop lynching, the Party adhered to its rigid view of class forces and class struggle, thus nourishing an image of the Communists as political interlopers who sought to impose their own agenda on the community.[18]

Yet the Party and its organizations in 1933 and 1934 pressed with characteristic vigor the battle against lynching and for the constitutional rights of blacks. Across the South, scores of black witnesses were produced to prove the systematic elimination of African Americans from southern juries. Demonstrations were organized in seven major cities to protest the lynching in Tuscaloosa of Dan Pippin and A. T. Harden in the summer of 1933. The ILD in Maryland produced a public affidavit (sent to the president) naming the lynchers of George Armwood (to which it added the state attorney and local commander of the American Legion). The Theodore Jordan Defense Committee, made up of two dozen organizations, was formed by the ILD in the late winter of 1933 to defend a black man accused of murdering a railroad steward. Also, innumerable Scottsboro conferences were held in 1933, and Richard B. Moore and Ada Wright toured seventy-two cities for the defense. As the tempo of antifascist demonstrations quickened in 1934, the ILD and other groups wove the arrest of German Communist leader Ernst Thaelmann, the Scottsboro case, and the jailing of five thousand political prisoners in Cuba into a single fabric of protest against what they viewed as linked variants of fascism.[19]

Inevitably, there were losses, such as the execution of Euel Lee in Maryland in 1933. There were also victories. A black thirteen-year-old charged with rape was acquitted in Virginia after ILD-inspired public protest; in Arkansas, for the first time, blacks were placed on federal jury panels, partly in response to pressure exerted in the Scottsboro case and other instances. Unemployed worker Jesse Griffin was released after being charged with "inciting to riot" on a Pennsylvania relief line. The trial in Minneapolis of James Johnson, who was accused of killing his alleged attacker, was postponed indefinitely when the ILD announced that it would press for blacks to be included on his jury. Norman Thibodeaux, cut down from a lynch rope in Labadieville, Louisiana, by a white bridge tender, was taken by the ILD to New York where he was shielded from danger. In Detroit the ILD forged an alliance of twenty-two organizations to win freedom for aptly named ILD member James Victory, who had been falsely accused of attacking a white woman.[20]

THE SCOTTSBORO AND HERNDON CASES

In January 1933 William L. Patterson persuaded dubious Party and ILD leaders to hire Samuel Leibowitz as defense counsel in the retrial of the Scottsboro boys (see chapter 11). Leibowitz had not previously been particularly concerned with racial justice, and his political horizons did not extend much beyond New York's Democratic ward politics. But he was, with the exception of Darrow, the most prominent trial lawyer of his time. For Leibowitz, fame and moral authority awaited; he would be lifted above the tawdry world of mob defense in a way that could advance his political ambitions. He would publicly disclaim sympathy for the views of the ILD, would try the case solely on its merits, would not receive a fee (and would not even accept reimbursement for expenses), and would stress his belief in the "desire of the people of the South to deal fairly with the colored man." In Patterson's view, Leibowitz's engagement might contradict the canard that the Communists were more interested in martyrdom than acquittal. Though often rigid in his ideology, Patterson also possessed a lawyerly precision and a hardheaded sense of how to achieve increased public backing through solid courtroom defense. A marriage of convenience, based on mutual need, was duly arranged.[21]

After a change of venue to Decatur, Alabama, the second round of trials opened in another vengeful atmosphere before Judge James E. Horton. Leibowitz launched a withering defense. Amid prosecution shouts of "Jew money from New York!" defendant Heywood Patterson was again sentenced to death on April 9, 1933.[22]

Through the first three months of 1933, there had been little in the way of Scottsboro protests, since Leibowitz had extracted an agreement that the Party would go easy on public protests during the Patterson trial. With the trial over, the self-imposed restraint on mass action was ended. Five days after the verdict, thousands gathered in New York's Union Square to rekindle street protest. Black participation reached a new level as hundreds of people marched and rode buses from Harlem. Observers acknowledged that more blacks than ever before flowed into Union Square, including entire church groups and even a contingent of Harlem Girl Scouts. Scores of blacks were injured in tussles with police as organized clusters sought to march back to Harlem after the rally. Thousands had listened to a broad band of speakers, such as Roger Baldwin of the ACLU, religious leader John Haynes Holmes, and J. B. Matthews of the Fellowship of Reconciliation, who joined Patterson, Moore, Ford, and other Communists on the platform. Upon his return from Decatur, Leibowitz was greeted by a crowd of three thousand at Penn Station. His cautious relationship with the Party warmed when he said, "Had it not been for the International Labor Defense, those nine Negro boys would be in their coffins now."[23]

For the moment at least, the contentious relationship between the Party and the black middle class appeared to lessen. But new Scottsboro groups were emerging, some of which appeared to be fund-raising rackets, while others seemed legitimate. In the view of some Party leaders, new challenges to Communist control of the case foretold an effort to undercut mass protest. William Patterson fretted that Leibowitz's loud advertisement of his ties to the Democrats was aimed at "divert[ing] the pressure of mass opinion" into the very party that bore responsibility for Scottsboro.[24]

The Party moved quickly to reassert its leadership. A National Scottsboro Defense Conference was called, which pushed the LSNR's omnibus civil rights bill — a document with twenty-two sections outlawing all forms of discrimination and leveling severe penalties for lynching and other acts of terror. That gathering produced the CP's version of a united front — the National Scottsboro-Herndon Action Committee, under the provisional chairmanship of Ben Davis. Joining the CP, LSNR, and ILD on the new committee were the Fellowship of Reconciliation, various left-wing unions, church organizations, and the Conference on Progressive Labor Action. Heading off the attempt of William Davis of the *Amsterdam News* to launch a Washington demonstration, the Scottsboro Committee and its allies hurriedly called for a mass march in early May. As a result of shortage of time, Depression poverty, heavy rains, and a loss of momentum, only four thousand people turned out. Nevertheless, Ruby Bates, behind the lusty shouting of rain-soaked marchers, led a delegation to the White House, where they presented petitions to Vice President John Nance Garner. By the following spring Scottsboro demonstrations were again a common occurrence in Harlem. In March 1934 police used tear gas and smoke bombs to break up an open-air meeting called to greet Ada Wright on her return to New York after visiting her sons in Alabama.[25]

The brief era of good feeling between the Party and groups outside its own coalition was coming to an end. The CP's effort to find new ways of connecting with the African American mainstream continued on a zig-zag path.

The George Crawford case, which unfolded in January 1932, brought renewed friction between the CP and the NAACP. The case began with the murder of a wealthy white woman, Agnes Boeing Ilsley, and her maid on Boeing's estate at Middleburg, Virginia. Crawford, a black former convict, was arrested in Boston and charged with the crime. After he was extradited to Virginia, the NAACP took the case under the direction of Charles H. Houston, then vice dean of the Howard University Law School. The association billed it as "more important than Scottsboro" and claimed that the defense would challenge the exclusion of Negroes from juries and fight for Crawford's innocence by producing alibi witnesses. The jury challenge was denied when the county jury commissioner testified that he could not find a qualified Negro to serve. Houston, to the Communists' chagrin, assured the court that he held it in "profound respect and high regard," and announced that he would not seek a reversal. Martha Gruening, whom the Communists pointedly identified as a "liberal," wrote a well-researched article with Helen Boardman in the *Nation* (and another in *New Masses*), charging that defense attorneys never sought out alibi witnesses. Ultimately, Houston engineered a deal whereby Crawford, after being convicted by an all-white jury of murdering Mrs. Ilsley, pleaded guilty to killing the maid in exchange for a life sentence. The ILD hectored Houston through the mid-1930s, alleging that he had prostrated himself before a Jim Crow court, acquiesced in an unfair trial, failed to explore exculpatory evidence, and abandoned an innocent client. The Crawford case became for the Communists an example of spineless capitulation compared to the uncompromising defense of the Scottsboro boys. There was an unrecognized price in all this: Houston was not wholly unsympathetic to the Party; he had defended Bernard Ades against disbarment in Maryland. He was embarrassed and anguished by the affair (even as he defended himself against Gruening's charges). The time had not yet arrived when the Party would stop turning friends into enemies.[26]

In late June 1933 Judge Horton turned aside the jury verdict in the Patterson case, setting the stage for a third round of Scottsboro trials. The judge's virtual rejection of a white woman's claim of rape against blacks in the Deep South was unprecedented—and in the context of the times, remarkable. Leibowitz congratulated the entire South for its "courageous and brilliant" son. He heaped praise upon Horton while calling the Decatur jurors "lantern-jawed morons" (which struck Brodsky as "stupid and impolitic, as well as revealing a stubborn loyalty to the Southern elite").[27]

The Party, however, pointed to Horton's peremptory dismissal of the defense claim that blacks were deliberately excluded from Morgan County juries. He had done nothing about the lynch atmosphere surrounding the trial or about the state's attorney's race baiting, red baiting, and anti-Semitism. Two months earlier Judge Horton had brusquely declined to set aside the Patterson verdict. What had happened in two months? Predictably, the Party pointed to its renewal of mass pressure. Although the Party's inner circle may have felt relief over Horton's action, it was publicly irritated by the praise heaped upon the judge, viewing such approval as feeding illusions in the courts and undercutting the role of the ILD in saving the boys' lives.[28]

Some voices in the black community also noted that the judge's reversal of Patterson's conviction prevented a review of the Alabama jury system by higher courts. The *Pittsburgh Courier* even speculated that Horton was an instrument of Alabama's desire to preserve its Jim Crow jury system, even at the cost of delaying Heywood Patterson's execution. William Patterson's concern was more complex and actually kinder to Horton. He worried that if Horton were unable to maintain control of the case, it would be turned over to Judge William W. Callahan, a notorious bigot with KKK connections.[29]

Patterson was right to be concerned: The third trial began in late 1933 before the dyspeptic Judge Callahan, whose crude bias was manifest. Convictions and death sentences for Patterson and Clarence Norris quickly followed. On June 28, 1934, the Alabama State Supreme Court upheld the convictions. The case was again on its way the U.S. Supreme Court.[30]

The collaboration between the ILD and Leibowitz was becoming increasingly strained. As Leibowitz's political ambitions grew, he became restless under the ILD umbrella, and was especially annoyed by the ILD's aggressive use of Bates. In June 1933 he sought out black leaders to explore the prospect of forcing the Communists out of the case. He was disappointed to find a lack of enthusiasm for launching a competing coalition in the face of the impressive global campaign organized by the Communists.[31]

Leibowitz's opportunity for a clean break came in the fall of 1934. A former well-digger from Birmingham, J. T. Pearson, had approached Victoria Price in the summer of 1934, calling himself "Charles Price" and claiming to be "a second or third cousin." According to later testimony given on November 4 by Victoria Price, Pearson told her that he could get her out of the distasteful case and, at the same time, get her $500 for "signing a paper." Price went to the Huntsville police chief, H. C. Blakemore, who told her to "play along." Two weeks later Pearson reappeared with New York lawyer Samuel Schriftman (whose pseudonym was "Daniel Swift") and raised the ante to $1,000. Price testified that the lawyers described the paper as a promissory note of some sort to the effect that she would not appear at the next trial. (She added senselessly that the pair told her that she could go to Decatur and "tell them you sold that little piece of paper for what money there was in it.") She allegedly agreed to accept the $1,000 payment.[32]

Pearson had contacted the ILD in June 1934, saying that Price might be willing to recant. Brodsky, with the Bates disavowal in mind, believed that checking out Pearson was obligatory. Schriftman, who was associated with the ILD, allegedly met Pearson in Birmingham in mid-August and settled on the $1,000 offer. On October 1 Schriftman, joined by Sol Kone, a Brodsky associate, flew in a chartered plane from Cincinnati to Nashville for a rendezvous with Price and Pearson. At the same time, under Huntsville police surveillance, Price and Pearson drove toward Nashville and were intercepted along the way.

Acting on information provided by Pearson, authorities arrested the two ILD men in Nashville and quickly extradited them to Alabama to face charges of bribery.[33]

When the story broke, Leibowitz flew into a rage, threatening to withdraw "unless all Communists are removed from the defense." He quickly met with four Harlem ministers and William Davis of the *Amsterdam News,* who was ready to use his paper to help wrest the case from the ILD. Leibowitz's assistant and an attorney were dispatched to Kilby Prison in Montgomery, while a delegation of clergy went to Chattanooga to seek out the parents. Unlike previous efforts to undercut the ILD, this one partly succeeded. Leibowitz had an advantage that Walter White never had: He had bonded with the boys. Heywood Patterson and Clarence Norris immediately signed on with Leibowitz. Even Ada Wright endorsed a letter instructing the ILD to cease "any actions or steps with reference to these cases."[34]

Leibowitz now recited a litany of charges against the CP and ILD (which he had never before uttered in their two-year association): Scottsboro was a propaganda show for the Party and a cash cow for fund raising; the case "was used to stir up trouble between black and white in the South." The parents were stupidly sent "barnstorming around the country," while judges and officials were bombarded with insulting telegrams; the boys' lives were jeopardized for political purposes. But the meticulous criminal lawyer apparently never looked hard at the circumstances surrounding the alleged bribery before severing his ties with the ILD.[35]

Those circumstance might have cast doubt on the whole affair. At the November 4 hearing Price could not reconstruct a single sentence uttered by "Swift" or Kone offering her a bribe to change her testimony. It was only "Mr. Price [Pearson] . . . [who] told me to sign not to appear at the trial if I didn't want to, and to change my former testimony."[36]

The two men were supposedly "caught red-handed trying to bribe Victoria Price." Some reports said that when arrested, "they were carrying the $1,500" in one-dollar bills in a briefcase. Why they needed 1,500 one-dollar bills to pay a $1,000 bribe was never explained. The mystery does not end there. Claims that the money was taken directly from the two lawyers were contradicted by reports that it was recovered in a police cruiser. A stringer in Huntsville, working for the black *Norfolk Journal and Guide,* reported that the money was found by "Deputy Sheriff Corcoran" in the car in which the men were placed after arrest. When the deputy "reminded them of the money they were leaving behind [they] responded that it wasn't their money." A nearly identical report was filed by Moscow film veteran Ted Poston. Scottsboro's stridently racist *Jackson County Sentinel* avoided saying that the men had carried the money by reporting that "Swift, when arrested *is said* to have had $1,500 on his person. His luggage was not searched, but was held by Nashville authorities" (emphasis added). What happened to the alleged briefcase? If not in a briefcase, where exactly was the cumbersome pile of cash hidden? Why would a deputy "remind them" that they had left the money? Was it an almost comic stab at baiting Kone and Schriftman into a trap? All this should have been enough for further inquiry — suggesting possible entrapment with Price's connivance. Such things were not entirely unknown in those environs. But Leibowitz wasn't interested in pursuing the matter.[37]

The trial of Schriftman, Kone, and Pearson opened in mid-1935. Kone and Schriftman apparently had had enough of Alabama justice (among other things, they had been illegally extradited from Tennessee). They did not appear for trial, and each man forfeited $2,000 in bail. The state of Alabama never pursued them. Pearson, the alleged instigator of the whole affair, did appear; Alabama authorities declined to prosecute. The scandal faded from sight.[38]

The Scottsboro defense had fractured at a critical moment. In the midst of the bribery affair, the Alabama Supreme Court on October 3, 1934, denied the appeals of Patterson and Norris. Anticipating those rulings, the ILD had arranged for the appeal to the U.S. Supreme Court to be handled by Walter Pollak and Osmond K. Fraenkel. From a sanitarium in Russia, where he had gone to recover from exhaustion, William Patterson accused Leibowitz of breaking with the ILD out of jealousy over the choice of Pollak and out of opportunism driven by political ambition. Leibowitz had wished to argue the case before the highest tribunal; at that juncture, the appeal was the only available mechanism for him to remain in the case. He was wounded by the prospect of being cast out of the limelight. The Party granted that Leibowitz was a brilliant trial lawyer, but he was no constitutional expert. His hunger to go before the Supreme Court added up to placing "personal aggrandizement" ahead of the boys' interests. True to the dire predictions of Party hardliners (who had never wanted Leibowitz in the first place), the political shoe dropped in the fall of 1935. Leibowitz sought the Democratic nomination for Kings County district attorney. He lost.[39]

The ILD had to face the prospect that contending lawyers would argue before the Supreme Court. Joseph Brodsky concluded that the boys' lives were the ultimate priority: nothing should undermine an effective appeal, even if that meant an accommodation with Leibowitz—to whom he turned over ILD's Scottsboro records.[40]

Brodsky's action struck hard in favor of the view that the struggle for the boys' freedom outweighed the urgency of "proletarian hegemony" over the case. That decision was perhaps more transforming than was noted in the heat of the moment; it set the stage for more enduring cooperation with broader forces, but not without infighting and backsliding. Ben Davis journeyed to Montgomery on October 18 to win back the boys. Calling the bribery episode a frame-up and castigating Leibowitz as a turncoat, Davis got Patterson and Norris to switch back to the ILD. This started a cycle that echoed the agonies of 1931.[41]

As a new tug-of-war for the defendants began, Leibowitz helped found the American Scottsboro Committee, despite a widespread feeling, among blacks in particular, that the last thing needed now was competing defense groups. Leibowitz had hoped that a new group cleansed of red associations would win support among southern moderates. He was disappointed. "Moderate" anticommunism was not unconnected to racism, and racism remained. As for Leibowitz, he was still a "New York Jew lawyer" who had defamed the South.[42]

The CP decided to cooperate. A letter from the Scottsboro-Herndon Committee to the American Scottsboro Committee struck a self-critical note: The defense movement in the orbit of the ILD had resisted groups that sought to work independently to free the boys. It was time to accept without conditions whatever other groups were willing to give. It was time to renounce, once and for all, any notion that others must walk with the radicals on a revolutionary road in order to cooperate. In capital letters, the communication declared, "WE MUST ACCEPT WHATEVER HELP WE CAN GET FOR SCOTTSBORO. WE MUST ACCEPT HELP EVEN THOUGH IT COMES ON THE BASIS OF SCOTTSBORO AND NOTHING ELSE."[43]

The Scottsboro defendants bounced back and forth no fewer than five times between Leibowitz and the ILD before the pressure of the impending hearings forced both sides to reach an accommodation. In January 1935 the U.S. Supreme Court agreed to review the convictions. During this time the Scottsboro-Herndon Committee had sent a delegation to William Davis to try to dissolve differences and join forces. The Communist-led National Student League had joined with the social-democratic Student League for Industrial Democracy in coordinated Scottsboro actions. The Communists had also sought to cooperate with the Socialist Party. Finally, a deal was made: Leibowitz would argue for Norris; Pollak and Fraenkel would argue for Patterson.[44]

Meanwhile, throughout 1933 Angelo Herndon languished in jail in frail health; the Party worried about a life-threatening situation. In March 1934 a delegation led by playwright John Howard Lawson was dispatched to Georgia. After meeting with assistant prosecutor John H. Hudson, who flew into an anticommunist rage, and Governor Eugene Talmadge, who professed his "love for niggers," the delegation finally saw Herndon, who complained of acute isolation and censorship of his mail. The group went on to Alabama to see the Scottsboro boys, who were being held in even more severe conditions. The delegation's report concluded that the violations of civil and human rights in Georgia and Alabama eclipsed their worst fears; the political landscapes of those states were blighted with bigoted politicians who sought to "Hitlerize" the region, threatening blacks, poor whites, liberals, and intellectuals. This brought another surge of activity, expanding public awareness of Herndon's situation and the constitutional issues involved in his case.[45]

Nonetheless, on May 24, 1934, the Georgia Supreme Court upheld Herndon's conviction. Four days after the court ruling, Hudson launched "red raids" on the Party's Atlanta office and the homes of known black and white radical activists. Don West, a young white minister and poet from northern Georgia, became Hudson's prime target. West had been a founder, with Miles Horton, of the Highlander Folk School in Tennessee. Later, he became Georgia state organizer for the CP and leader of the local Herndon defense committee. He had slipped away from the ostensibly secret Party office shortly before the raid and became the focus of Hudson's search. Benjamin Davis managed to trundle West into the back of a Ford, cover him with sacks, and spirit him out of Georgia. Several weeks later, under mounting repression, Davis too left Georgia for New York.[46]

Georgia authorities succumbed to pressure. In mid-June 1934 the state offered bail. With bondsmen refusing to provide the funds, the ILD was forced to turn to liberals to raise the prohibitive sum of $15,000. After incessant pleading, and the painful accumulation of dimes and dollars, Joseph Brodsky and the Reverend A. J. Martin presented the bail money to dumbfounded Georgia authorities. On August 4 Herndon departed by train for New York. Hundreds of blacks and whites greeted him as a hero at stops in Washington, Philadelphia, Trenton, and Newark. On the evening of August 7, a crowd of more than six thousand gathered at Pennsylvania Station in Manhattan to greet Herndon. Robert Minor was the first to reach him, with a fulsome hug and kiss; his brother Milton embraced him, as did Ruby Bates. James Ford and Ben Davis hoisted Herndon to their shoulders and carried him up the stairs where the crowd, which had strained to see the weary youth, greeted him with upraised clenched fists. The crowd swarmed into the streets, paraded, sang, shouted slogans, and wound up at a mass meeting in Union Square. Ten days later a crowd of four thousand greeted Herndon at Rockland Palace in Harlem, where the "frail light-brown-skinned youth" said, "They can send me to the electric chair, they can wreck my body, but they cannot break the spirit of the working class." More than ever, the Communists had become a very visible part of black political life.[47]

The days of ideological combat based on anticipation of revolutionary crisis were ending. By the end of 1934 it was evident that the system still had a capacity for reform. Labor had awakened to the possibilities of section 7A of the NRA, which was aimed at assuring collective bargaining. The order of the day was to deepen democracy to facilitate working people's progress. This in turn required the cleansing of racism from the nation's institutional life. Freedom for the Scottsboro boys and Angelo Herndon was an inseparable part of that objective, and required the broadest cooperation. Before formal edicts from the Comintern, the seeds of the popular front were being planted.

RED AND BLACK AT FISK AND HOWARD

Black students added their energies to the rising radical temperament. Ishmael Flory arrived at Fisk University in the fall of 1933 to pursue graduate studies in sociology. On December 15 a seventeen-year-old Tennessean named Cordie Cheek was lynched. Flory promptly called a campus meeting, featuring Professor E. Franklin Frazier, to condemn the lynching and press other demands, including a course in black history. After denial of a permit to march through Nashville, the students staged an on-campus demonstration. Flory flooded the Negro press with reports of the action, hoping to spark a national student antilynch movement.[48]

Flory next decided to act upon faculty member Charles S. Johnson's suggestion that he tackle segregation at the University Social and Sports Center. Flory again resorted to press releases to force Fisk (and associated schools that shared the center) to end segregated seating at the arena. He then took on the Jim Crow Loew's Theater in Nashville, where the Fisk University Octet, an offshoot of the disbanded Jubilee Singers, was engaged to perform. Flory called a meeting of the student body in the name of the Denmark Vesey Forum (associated with the Communist-led National Students' League) after the president of the Student Council declined to act. At the meeting a petition was circulated demanding cancellation of the performance. Flory also sent out another fusillade of press releases.[49]

In the meantime the university dean got wind of the protest; he convened the university's Executive Committee, which canceled the engagement. But Flory was accused of damaging the school by linking its Octet to a theater that herded blacks into an upper balcony. He responded that "when a Negro university becomes engaged in Jim Crow performances, it ceases to be the concern of the university, but the concern of twelve million Negroes." The Executive Committee voted to expel Flory "for the good of the university." That vote was upheld by a faculty majority, with Frazier and Horace Mann Bond among only seven dissenters. Flory was sent packing with the claim that he had not been expelled, merely "asked to withdraw." Walter White of the NAACP was troubled by this expulsion of a student "who had the courage and the manhood" to stand up for right.[50]

In the early spring of 1934 Howard University students demonstrated on Capitol Hill against segregation at the restaurant of the House of Representatives. The courageous act grew from an enlivened political environment at the federally funded university, where a small but active unit of the National Students' League had been established. By mid-1935 Howard was besieged by charges that it had become a cesspool of Marxist subversion. Kelly Miller, by then retired from Howard, accused President Mordecai W. Johnson (who had uttered kind words about the USSR) of "allowing the facilities of the university to be used as a forum where communism could be preached." The worst offense had been an economic conference on the condition of the Negro, held in the spring of 1935, at which the JCNR and the Political Science Department had given a platform to James W. Ford and the Socialist Norman Thomas, among others. A congressional committee was dispatched to the campus, but it could find no galloping "red menace." Nevertheless Arthur Mitchell, the Negro congressman from Chicago, "insisted that a house cleaning is most urgently needed." Mitchell was more worried about congressional cutbacks in appropriations than about students being infected with Marxism. To Miller's consternation, Secretary of the Interior Harold Ickes, whose department was responsible for Howard, saw no problem in Dr. Johnson allowing the "doctrines of communism" to be explained to Howard undergraduates. The turmoil at Howard went on for months.[51]

COMMUNISTS, LABOR, AND THE NEW DEAL

In the midst of growing labor activism sparked by the New Deal, a strike in St. Louis in spring 1933 showed that the TUUL was not quite moribund, especially when it came to tapping the potential of black women. The seasonal nut-picking industry in that city encompassed sixteen factories and three thousand women, 90 percent of whom were blacks who received half as much pay as the white women workers. A Communist with family connections in one of the factories got three black women to attend a meeting where pointers on organizing were offered along with standard ideological fare. Further meetings followed, and on May 15, 1933, a hundred women walked out, demanding a pay increase. Three weeks later a thousand black women struck; the next day white women walked out in solidarity. A central strike committee was set up to coordinate the spreading strike and feed twelve hundred strikers with the help of the Party and UCs. The women armed themselves with "brick sandwiches" to confront strikebreakers and resisted efforts to isolate them from the TUUL. By the end of May, at the height of the season, the owners capitulated, offering a substantial pay increase and recognition of the TUUL's Food Workers Industrial Union. After the successful strike shop committees were established, shop stewards trained, and an educational and social program developed—including baseball teams and picnics for the largely youthful work force. That strike became a spark and model for grassroots unionism in other small industries in St. Louis.[52]

In Chicago eight hundred young women, both black and white, won a partial victory in a strike against the B. Sopkins Dress Company in July 1933. Black strikers, singled out for brutal treatment, forced the Chicago Urban League to allow James Ford to speak for them at a league conference on labor conditions in Chicago. They successfully resisted Sopkins's efforts to get the AFL textile union to intervene. The strikers won an accord that included a provision for equal pay for equal work without discrimination against black workers. The St. Louis and Chicago strikes were held up as examples of the powerful capacity of black women to lead both black and white workers, advancing the culture of biracial unionism and underscoring the important role of women in the emerging labor movement.[53]

In 1933 California's San Joaquin Valley was the scene of perhaps the largest agricultural strike in the nation's history when fifteen thousand cotton pickers walked out under the leadership of the TUUL's Cannery and Agricultural Workers Industrial Union. The strikers had to endure the jailing of leaders, the usual vigilante violence orchestrated by the growers, and the hostility of the AFL. The strike also had to overcome deep-seated prejudices along complicated fault lines: southern whites against blacks, whites against Mexican-American workers, blacks and whites against Mexican-Americans. The strike camps, where workers from Oklahoma, Missouri, Arkansas, and Texas mingled, became classrooms in union solidarity and antiracism, as Communist and leftist organizers calculated the cost of division in the shadow of the bosses' guns and thrust the results before the strikers. Soon white Okies were electing blacks as picket captains and camp heads; Deep South families shared utensils with blacks and drank from the same mugs. In addition, both blacks and whites were obliged to gain a new respect for fellow Mexican-American pickers; they were not "greasers," but brothers and sisters with determination and intelligence who would stand up to provocations, jailing, beating, and murder.[54]

In Bridgton, New Jersey, another agricultural strike by a largely black work force broke out at the Seabrook Farms. After a two-week beet harvest strike, punctuated by seventy-five arrests and beatings, the dispute was submitted for arbitration. The cannery betrayed its promise to rehire all striking workers, refusing specifically to take back Negro strikers. Blacks and whites joined in continuing the walkout. The dispute reached a climax when a score of black women pulled the beets picked by strikebreakers from the trucks on which they were loaded. The black leaders of the cannery workers' local became targets for a KKK klavern in rural New Jersey. Barracks fires, drive-by shootings, and burning crosses made Seabrook a highly visible issue in the black community — especially when black strikers armed themselves to defend against Klan attacks.[55]

The AFL, however, was becoming the major battleground as the opportunities presented by the NIRA fused with the miserable conditions of industrial workers to produce an unprecedented strike wave in 1934. The concentration of radical and Communist activists in dual TUUL unions had isolated many of the most experienced and dedicated activists from the mainstream AFL unions and from newly emerging, independent non-Communist unions. Formal pronouncement of the popular front at the Seventh CI Congress and its rejection of dual unions finally pushed the TUUL into its grave.[56]

The struggle for the incorporation of blacks into the labor movement was also shifting to the AFL's terrain. At times the battle went on in the face of the Party's own historic weaknesses. In the auto strikes that erupted in Detroit in 1934, the TUUL's Auto Workers Union had been quickly supplanted by the Mechanics Educational Society and various AFL unions. Communists in the mechanics' union had refused to demand the inclusion of blacks in the tool-and-die section of the industry, resurrecting the old tautology that there were hardly any black tool-and-die makers in the first place. The elementary lesson had to be taught all over again in the AFL's hostile environment: Discrimination had to be fought with unqualified conviction.[57]

San Francisco's labor scene was different. There were only twenty-three blacks among the five thousand members of the AFL's San Francisco local of the International Longshoremen's Association when the longshore workers struck in May 1934. Scores of black dockers defied picket lines to work for inflated wages. The ILA local vowed never to allow more blacks into its ranks. However, as the strike progressed, the left-wing rank-and-file, led by Harry Bridges, shaped the union's agenda. The key demand — a union hiring hall — promised to end the racial discrimination that was part of the notoriously corrupt "shape-up" system. From that point through the general strike in the summer, blacks joined picket lines and in large numbers faced repeated attacks by company goons. The rank-and-file won the hiring hall; from that victory the black longshoremen of San Francisco joined local black leaders to bombard the AFL convention meeting in that city to end powerless Jim Crow federal locals and promote industrial unionism on the basis of racial equality. This set the stage for a showdown on industrial unionism and racism in the AFL.[58]

In Alabama the NIRA had spurred the rapid growth of unionism in the Birmingham-Bessemer area, where thousands joined local AFL trades and labor councils in 1933 and 1934. The Alabama coalfields sprang to life under the UMW. By the end of 1933 dozens of new locals had been organized, and large numbers had struck for union recognition. The Party's efforts to influence these developments were enhanced by Clyde Johnson, a young white Minnesotan and former student leader at New York's City College, who had recently arrived in Alabama to take over the CP's labor organizing. Soft-spoken, earnest, and intrepid, Johnson was able to form rank-and-file committees in unions that now enjoyed a modicum of protection from the federal government — a very different situation from that of the weak, now largely defunct, National Miners Union.[59]

Blacks, who constituted more than 60 percent of coal miners, had to put up with incessant harassment and were confined to unskilled jobs, such as coal loading and pick mining, while whites held exclusive claim to skilled and machine-based jobs. The UMW boasted of nondiscrimination, but generally turned its back on black workers. The Communists, represented by a core of black miners, formed a rank-and-file committee that pressed for advancement of blacks in mine jobs and union posts. When in early 1934 the UMW accepted the NRA code that set lower wages for southern coal miners, the Communist-led rank-and-file movement called an unauthorized strike that won the support of fifteen to twenty thousand miners. In the midst of that walkout, the Communists saturated the mining camps with leaflets calling for elimination of the freeze that kept black workers in the most menial and lowest paid jobs. The strike spread to another fourteen thousand miners when the operators rejected a change in the mine code to allow a small wage increase. Almost immediately violence erupted, and three black miners and a young white miner were killed. On September 16, 1934, deputies opened fire on a rally of twenty-five hundred miners, both black and white, on the edge of a company-owned village in Jefferson County. Two black miners were killed. Throughout the strike wave the Communists continued to press for unhindered job mobility for blacks and advanced other demands that resonated with black workers and their families, such as stopping the operators' deductions of back rent and relief payments from miners' checks. The 1934 strikes dissipated, but in the fall of 1935 seventeen thousand miners struck against regional coal operators. Aside from a small wage increase, the UMW finally won union recognition in the struck mines. That important victory in a bastion of the open shop and company unionism was won in large measure through the spirited participation of black miners.[60]

In June 1933 Nat Ross had bemoaned the Party's failure to realize the potential of building black-white unity in the first strike wave. But he saw something new in the 1934 and 1935 strikes. Black workers proved to be "union men to the core." White workers were beginning to grasp their own interest in ending the lynch terror that enforced wage disparities and meant declining standards for both races. "What stood out during the strikes," Ross wrote, "was the growing solidarity of white and Negro labor, together in the union hall, and side by side on the picket lines facing the machine guns."[61]

The rank-and-file movement among the miners eventually seeped into the community and affected other industries as Communists sought to organize relief workers and the unemployed. During a laundry strike in Birmingham in the spring of 1934, rank-and-file miners, against the will of the local UMW and AFL leadership, marched downtown to join the picket lines — only to be broken up by police. But the same AFL leaders who opposed the solidarity picket line joined a mass meeting called by the Birmingham Labor Council to protest police brutality in the laundry strike.[62]

The Party's strongest link to Alabama workers was the International Union of Mine, Mill, and Smelter Workers, an outgrowth of the old Wobbly-led Western Federation of Miners. The Alabama locals of this union were overwhelmingly populated by black ore miners. When John Davis, a white Communist, was expelled from the Bessemer local by union bureaucrats, the predominantly black membership voted unanimously for his reinstatement along with two expelled black Party activists, Nathan Strong and Ed Sears. In May 1934 eight thousand ore miners struck Tennessee Coal and Iron, Republic Steel, and other mines, demanding higher wages and union recognition. The companies evicted dozens of striking miners; five strikers, all blacks, were murdered by company gunmen, including a black secretary of a local. Clyde Johnson organized a campaign to prevent evictions and to secure cash assistance for the strikers from Bessemer relief agencies. Social consciousness and a social agenda were hallmarks of the Mine, Mill, and Smelter Workers, which defined its role in far broader terms than wages and hours. The union became a civil rights movement, embracing the struggle for black and (in the Southwest) Mexican-American equality. It developed a social life marked by interracial solidarity expressed in song and skits, and a multifaceted cultural life built around the union local. The social agenda of left-wing unionism also included a major role for women's auxiliaries, which often grew out of rank-and-file committees and became indispensable factors in reinforcing the mettle of male strikers. The women's auxiliaries, whose membership in Alabama was overwhelmingly black, also provided steady support for picket lines and other strike-related activity.[63]

In Louisiana, on the New Orleans docks, blacks constituted a majority of the seven thousand longshore workers. Over the four years of Depression, their wages had shrunk nearly 85 percent. The TUUL's Marine Workers' Industrial Union organized a series of local strikes from 1931 to 1933 at targeted docks. The stoppages were aimed at combating wage cuts, short hours, and miserable working conditions. They also sought to send a message to the city that black longshoremen would fight efforts to undermine their presence on the docks. Again in 1934 the New Orleans docks pulsated with strikes. ILA head Joe Ryan revoked the charter of a black ILA local because of its refusal to accept an unfavorable arbitration. But the members of the local refused to end the strike and joined with whites who had also rejected arbitration. Longshore strikes at Beaumont and Galveston, Texas, relied heavily on the support of black workers. At Galveston black cotton handlers, though not members of the ILA, struck in sympathy with the union strikers. When shipping companies brought in a hundred white strikebreakers, black dockers joined the strike, putting aside their unorganized status. The ILA won that strike, and according to John P. Davis, its success was due in large measure to the support of unorganized black workers. Blacks also participated in longshore strikes along the Atlantic seacoast. In Portsmouth, Virginia, thirty black dockers were jailed along with scores of white strikers for preventing the loading of a ship. In the historic West Coast longshore strike (which triggered the San Francisco general strike of 1934), black workers played a prominent role, leading Harry Bridges to pledge that his union would never exclude black workers from full participation.[64]

As Communists increased their activities in the AFL, they sought to build rank-and-file committees within the larger mainstream unions. Of fundamental importance, the Communist-led rank-and-file groups fought for the rights of black workers, including inclusion of African Americans at all levels in the expanding unions. During the strike wave of 1934 Communists targeted wage differentials based on race, fought segregation, and insisted that every vestige of union discrimination be addressed and eliminated. As we have seen, the Party was rarely satisfied with the level of commitment to Negro rights in the TUUL unions. But persistent education and political pressure on the TUUL cadre produced a core of unrelenting advocates of black rights who went on to affect the racial consciousness of the Congress of Industrial Organizations.[65]

In mid-1935 John P. Davis took stock of the black workers' relationship to the strike wave. He found that they had been prominent, despite being proportionately less unionized than white workers. They had gained ground from the efforts of the TUUL unions and the rank-and-file committees, and also involved themselves in many strikes, often in the face of unresponsive and hostile AFL leaders. The textile strike of three hundred fifty thousand workers, led by the old-line United Textile Workers, had not been welcoming to blacks. Negro workers had been Jim-Crowed into segregated locals and controlled by corresponding white locals, and there had been almost no black organizers.

Yet the southern textile strike was bolstered by fifty thousand black workers who joined the walkout. The union's head of southern locals had declared that integrated unionism would not emerge for "the next fifty years." Despite that, black workers refused to be excluded. Massive black participation in the strike won the admiration of Francis J. Gorman, chair of the strike committee.[66]

Black labor was involved in union efforts across the country—in the mine strikes in Alabama, in textile strikes in the Carolinas and Georgia, in packinghouse and steel strikes in the Midwest, in the western agricultural strikes, in New York laundry strikes, and in the union struggles among sharecroppers in the Deep South. The shibboleth that blacks were scabs and would not unionize had been decisively disproven. The image of the black strikebreaker was dissolving as the new era of industrial unionism was dawning. Faced with super-exploitation at the hands of industrialists and big planters, and the hostility of much of official unionism, "the record of the Negro union man during the last two years is worthy of the highest praise."[67]

The Party heralded the surge of black unionism. But James Ford warned that union organization in 1934 remained weak among Negro workers. It was the duty of Communists and leftists to extend the fight for full participation and equal rights into the heart of the AFL. His words reflected a growing disquiet among leading Communists in the midst of the invigorating growth of labor struggles. The healthy tension between racial equality and self-determination was fading. National self-determination in the Black Belt was weakening as the demand for equality was becoming part of the economic and social mainstream. The New Deal was creating both a new possibility and a new casualty: the possibility of democratic growth of the struggle for equality and the casualty of self-determination in the Black Belt. Nat Ross noted that Communists in the Alabama strikes often failed to make the connections between wage differentials under the NRA, the struggle for the freedom of the Scottsboro boys, and the right of self-determination. Harlem, the center of African American life and culture, would become the principal arena for determining the outcome of this ideological tension.[68]

Chapter Fourteen

Harlem and the Popular Front

In Harlem, on a single day in the spring of 1933, the Harlem Unemployed Council fought seventeen evictions, returning possessions in three cases; a major Scottsboro meeting was held at the Abyssinian Baptist Church; a Harlem branch of the Food Workers Industrial Union was formed; and three hundred people demonstrated at the Home Relief Bureau, demanding money for rent and nondiscriminatory work at union wages. Hammie Snipes, a truculent ex-Garveyite, suffered one of his many police beatings at the bureau. Such a day defined the life of a Communist for the small number of Harlem residents who joined the Party.[1]

In January 1933 the Party had launched a campaign against discrimination at Harlem Hospital after black doctors and nurses complained of discrimination, poor health care, and corrupt administration. A mass meeting resulted in the formation of the Peoples Committee against Discrimination in Harlem Hospital, composed of workers, unemployed, small-business people, and assorted professionals. Ahead of the Comintern and the national Party, the campaign successfully built a multiclass coalition. It also marked the start of the CP's cooperation with Reverend Adam Clayton Powell Jr., then assistant pastor to his father at the influential Abyssinian Baptist Church. At the same time, thirteen new ILD branches were formed in Harlem, and four thousand residents asked to join the defense group in the wake of the second Scottsboro convictions.[2]

Nonetheless, the national Party was critical of the Harlem Section for allegedly ignoring the "united front from below" and becoming too cozy with misleaders. The section's internal ideological health didn't seem so great either. At a membership meeting of the section's scattered and weakly led clubs, blacks and whites sat on different sides of the room—a dismal occurrence after the antichauvinism campaigns. At a subsequent meeting of the bureau of District 2, a Harlem activist stated that the black members "claimed that all the white comrades are white chauvinists."[3]

Matters came to a head with the hurriedly organized Scottsboro march on Washington in early May 1933. A fairly broad March Committee had been set up that attracted "reformist fakers." Harry Haywood was enraged that the Harlem comrades had welcomed them, had not demanded that the reformists accept "our program," and had not pressed for a demonstration of concrete deeds "in order to expose them." To make matters worse, William H. Davis of the *Amsterdam News* organized his own group to go to Washington. Some members of the National Scottsboro-Herndon Action Committee had the temerity to link up with Davis's clique. "We have grounds to expel these elements" from the action committee, Haywood warned. The odor of petty-bourgeois black nationalism was wafting over Harlem's black leaders.[4]

There were other problems as well. The New York LSNR was in shambles. The *Harlem Liberator* was bedeviled by financial difficulties and had become a nest of non-Party factionalists. The ILD was flooded with literally thousands of applications, but it lacked a stable core and had yielded only about a hundred recruits to the Party. The section leadership—headed by Steve Kingston, like Snipes an ex-Garveyite—was well intentioned but fractious and irresolute. A District 2 leader concluded that "someone who has authority" had to be assigned to Harlem on a full-time basis.[5]

After the July 1933 *Open Letter*, Earl Browder acknowledged that the Party had still "not yet made a decisive change in our work in Harlem." Haywood left no doubt that the nationalist deviation would be the target of an ideological and organizational redirection. The Party's leading black figure, James W. Ford, was coming to Harlem as section organizer.[6]

Ford's arrival brought a tightening of discipline and greater organizational stability. It also diminished the role of the old revolutionaries—principally Cyril Briggs and Richard B. Moore. Under Ford, loyalty to the Party would be primary. Briggs and Moore would not publicly challenge that, but they shared a latent (at times manifest) emphasis on race that would collide with evolving Party policies. For Briggs, at least, the "Socialist Commonwealth" remained a path to something politically deep and emotionally felt—liberation of the race. Ford, with his trade union background and his unbending commitment to interracial working-class unity, arrived in the midst of rising labor militancy. That only sharpened the emerging ideological tensions.[7]

The crucial issue of jobs increased those tensions. In the summer of 1933 there was a burst of the sporadic "Jobs for Negroes" movement. Conditions in Harlem in the first year of the New Deal remained abominable, with 80 percent of heads of families and 64 percent of single men unemployed. Into the picture stepped a Chicago transplant, Sufi Abdul Hamid, sometimes called "the Black Hitler" for his anti-Semitic rhetoric. He was complemented by two fiery street-corner orators, Ira Kemp and Arthur Reid. Sufi began aggressive picketing of the stores along 125th Street, demanding jobs for blacks. Kemp and Reid joined forces to form the African Patriotic League, which advocated a boycott of white-owned businesses as a step toward ultimate black control of Harlem's economic life.[8]

The Harlem Communists responded by inviting church and civic groups to join in forming a Provisional Committee against Discrimination to secure jobs for blacks at chain stores—thus avoiding antiforeign hostility had ethnic "mom and pop" stores been targeted. The W. T. Grant chain was pressed to hire blacks until they constituted half the work force. Whites were not to be fired, but transferred to other stores. Unproductive negotiations dragged on for weeks, and in August 1933 the coalition prepared picket lines.[9]

Ford insisted that the Grant campaign be terminated. The issue was hotly debated in the Harlem organization with the participation of members of the Central Committee and National Negro Commission. An especially contentious issue was the shaky disposition of white workers in the section's demands. Ford charged that the struggle for jobs was not projected on an *inclusive* basis; white workers would be forced out of Harlem, and black-white unity would be ruptured. Absent from the proposal was even a hint of trade union organization. Haywood accused the Harlem comrades of an inexcusable lapse of Marxist logic: They would concentrate their fire "not against the capitalists and the government, but against the white workers!"[10]

Richard Moore asked: Wasn't Ford placing the responsibility for forging black-white unity on the backs of black workers? Why all the hand-wringing about antagonizing white workers who survived off the meager resources of the ghetto? The Party's task, Moore said, was to fight for jobs for black workers and then rally whites to support that fight—not the reverse. He complained that the community would not understand a jobs strategy that protected white workers. Things then got personal. Moore and Briggs viewed Ford's "personality, ruthless style, and reliance upon the Central Committee as a mixture of opportunism and Uncle Tomism." Haywood undoubtedly had Moore in mind when he spoke about leading comrades who conjured "veiled inferences that...those who are seriously carrying out the work of the Party are 'Uncle Toms.'"[11]

Ford and Haywood addressed the longstanding question of the viability of the segregated ghetto economy. Did the Party wish to imitate the self-serving tactics of Reid and Kemp, snatching a handful of jobs for favored supporters while abandoning the fight against Jim Crow in the larger economy? The struggle for jobs would never be won on the fragile, narrow ghetto plane. It had to be carried across the city and across the country — binding the issue of jobs for blacks to black-white unionism. "The unbreakable solidarity between Negro and white workers" now depended on discrediting the black nationalists and reformists.[12]

The dissidents asked: What happened to white chauvinism as the primary obstacle to working-class unity? Haywood agreed that it was the main danger, but accused the Harlem comrades of using the issue to conceal their capitulation to nationalism. He rejected the mechanical categorizing of "major" and "minor" dangers under all conditions. In a particular circumstance, the minor peril can become primary. That was what had happened in Harlem, Haywood insisted, where petty-bourgeois nationalism had become the "main danger" in the controversy over the jobs issue. He even assailed the "logic" of silencing the struggle against nationalism until white chauvinism was completely eliminated.[13]

Despite such heat, the polarization was hardly justified. The Harlem Section's approach and Ford's proposals were not far apart. Both sought to advance black employment while protecting white workers in different ways — one through transfer of whites to other jobs, the other through reduction of their hours (at no decrease in pay). Both agreed that the campaign had to be extended across the city. The conflict has since been blamed on the Party's disquiet over Briggs's and Moore's "independent power base" in the community, as well as their freewheeling agitational style, which collided with the Party's centralist discipline. The argument is persuasive, but such disagreements could not erupt into organizational shake-ups, expulsions, and lingering resentments without the underlying accusation of ideological heresy. The well was poisoned when Harlem leaders were accused of caving in to bourgeois nationalism. As in the early disputes over self-determination, the op-

portunity for a healthy diversity of views within the framework of shared political values was sacrificed to "the line."[14]

CHANGING OF THE GUARD

In the midst of the section's turmoil, Richard Moore accompanied Scottsboro
mother Mrs. Janie Patterson on a punishing national tour. After the third conviction of Haywood Patterson in late 1933, Moore again took to the stump at
rallies and demonstrations across the country. His impassioned speeches continued to mirror his belief that Scottsboro was "one of the historic landmarks
in the struggle of the American people and of progressive forces throughout
the world for justice, civil rights, and democracy." By April 1934 Moore was
feeling the effects of political and physical burnout; he resigned as general
secretary of the LSNR (to be replaced by Harry Haywood). No one apparently
urged him to reconsider. In 1935 and 1936 he was field representative of the
ILD in Boston, where he contributed to the movement against the Italian invasion of Ethiopia and did valuable educational and cultural work. But his Boston
assignment largely severed his Harlem ties.[15]

In early October 1933 Cyril Briggs was relieved of his post as editor of the
Harlem Liberator. Briggs, who had maintained wide community contacts, was
cast as the sectarian who had made the *Liberator* a boring and costly mouth-
piece for his personal views. The paper (a euphemism for Briggs himself) was
accused of harboring non-Party elements who were attempting "to drive every
Party comrade out of the *Liberator*" by incessant bickering with CP members
who were attempting to set things right. Consequently, the staff had become
demoralized over the weekly's financial and circulation problems. Briggs, in
the meantime, was accused of undifferentiated attacks on all Garveyites, regardless of rank.[16]

Briggs admitted a sectarian error: In castigating Garvey's troops for assaulting Party street meetings, he had failed to distinguish between bad leaders and honest members of the rank-and-file. Briggs also conceded that he
should not have published in the paper the names of persons whom he had
accused of mishandling funds for the *Liberator*. One irate couple named by
Briggs "several times violently attacked me, once throwing a loaded bottle at
my head . . . and another time entering the office with a lead pipe . . . with the
declared purpose of braining me." Such were the travails of daily life in the
struggle. Briggs blamed "these mistakes" on his "growing isolation" from the
section leadership since Ford's arrival.[17]

But Briggs bitterly challenged Ford's allegation that the New York District had "squandered" $2,000 on the *Liberator* while "section functionaries were starving," calling it false and inflammatory. Briggs also confronted those who accused him of political narrowness. Under its new editors, the *Liberator* had become an "open organ of the Party"; community news had disappeared, as had the paper's role (under Briggs) in generating cultural activities — especially the Liberator Chorus, the Liberator Orchestra, and the Liberator Kiddies Rhythm Band. Briggs fiercely resented his removal at a moment when the paper's community outreach was beginning to win support.[18]

Like Moore, Briggs was a "disciplined comrade" who accepted the decisions of Ford's Section Committee on the reorganization of the *Liberator* and his reassignment to the staff of the *Daily Worker,* where he continued to write about lynching and racism. He also continued to write articles for the *Liberator* and managed to keep the Crusader News Service afloat. But like Moore, Briggs was no longer a factor in the radical politics of Harlem.[19]

Briggs's departure marked the end of an era for Harlem Communists. The voices of a generation schooled by the Great War and its aftermath were quieted, if not silenced. But that could not be attributed solely to James Ford and his agenda. It had deeper roots in the nation's and the world's rapidly changing social circumstances. The coming of the New Deal, the stirring of industrial unionism, the rise of fascism, and the threat of a new world war all were undermining the Third Period's theoretical assumptions. The New Deal forced the Communist movement to adjust to the new vitality and potential for reform. The Depression had weakened the economic base of black nationalism, despite the occasional outbursts of nationalist-tinged jobs campaigns. The new prominence of industrial unionism would affect blacks of all classes no less than whites; new strategic alliances were in the making that placed less emphasis on ghetto survival and far greater stress on interracial trade unionism. Such vast changes ultimately weakened the influence of the old African Blood Brotherhood group and opened the way for a new generation of Communists with stronger ties to the union movement and the ability to cultivate more cordial relations with the community's mainstream organizations.[20]

The departure of Briggs and Moore in some measure reflected a national drive to "Americanize" the Party. In June 1934 the Party reported 11,298 native-born members (40 percent) and 17,570 foreign-born members (60 percent). In the opening months of the year, more native-born (3,014) than foreign-born (2,242) new members had joined the Party. By mid-1935 black membership stood at 2,227 outside of District 17 (Alabama and its environs), which was 90 percent African American. Adding in District 17, black members totaled about 11 percent of Party membership, with the vast majority native-born. The African Caribbean presence in the Party diminished as a by-product of the events of late 1933, even though there was no conscious attempt to do so.[21]

Ford brought in Merrill Work to manage the financial affairs of the *Liberator* and Maude White to serve as managing editor. Ben Davis would soon follow in the post of *Liberator* editor, while White was reassigned to Cleveland. James Ashford became head of the Harlem YCL. Thoughtful, dedicated, and selfless, Ashford had been something of a legend in Detroit. In Harlem he lifted the Young Liberators (the youth arm of the LSNR) from a moribund state to a vigorous community presence. Manning Johnson was brought in from Buffalo to lead trade union activity in Harlem. Abner Berry came from Kansas City to work for the LSNR. The Texas-born Berry, at this time thirty-two years old, had been a printer's devil in Chicago, a steelworker in Gary, Indiana, a city editor of the *Houston Informer,* a longshoreman on Houston's docks, and a functionary whose radical roots were in the ANLC of the mid-1920s. A brother of the dancing Berry Brothers, he was articulate, humorous, skilled, and sharply attuned to community moods. He was the embodiment of the new generation of confident, nondoctrinaire black Communists. All of these newcomers to Harlem leadership were native-born African Americans.[22]

Ford also sought to advance black women within the Party and its orbit. In addition to appointing Maude White, he encouraged Louise Thompson to collaborate with the artist Augusta Savage to build the social and educational Vanguard, which ran a public forum and Marxist study group, sponsored dance and theater activity, and created a vibrant social life. The artist Aaron Douglas found his political voice in the Vanguard; Langston Hughes and other writers and poets were regular participants. Thompson also became a full-time functionary in the National Committee for the Defense of Political Prisoners and was the first black organizer for the International Workers Order.[23]

Williana Burroughs, a graduate of Hunter College, joined the Party in 1926 through the ANLC and attended the Sixth CI Congress. An elementary-school teacher in the New York school system, she was fired in June 1933 when she led a demonstration at the Board of Education for decent lunches for the children of the unemployed and against discrimination faced by black teachers. In 1933 Burroughs ran for city comptroller and in 1934, for lieutenant governor. She was director of the Harlem Workers School, and during the hearings on the Harlem riot of 1935 she was one of the Party's most effective witnesses. In 1937 she returned to the USSR to work as an announcer and editor of English-language broadcasts for Radio Moscow. This enabled her to reunite with her two sons, whom she had placed in Soviet schools in 1928.[24]

Audley Moore was born in Louisiana into a family whose vision of liberation was sparked by Garvey. She came to New York after the Great War to see Garvey's ships and wound up in Republican politics. While still juggling UNIA membership and Republican activism, Moore witnessed a Scottsboro demonstration. Seeing an outpouring of blacks and whites "doing something for our people," she joined the Party. A large, striking woman with a soaring voice and a penchant for picturesque language, Moore fused the Marxist and nationalist traditions of Party activism. With only a fourth-grade education, she was nevertheless equally at home in Harlem's back-room politics, in intellectual salons, and in the world of hairdressers, domestics, and laundry workers.[25]

Bonita Williams was also an effective presence for the Party in Harlem politics. Widely respected for her dependability and commitment, Williams was the leading woman in the LSNR. She wrote poetry, fought against retail profiteers in Harlem, and was an indefatigable presence in a variety of campaigns.[26]

One of the first steps of the Ford leadership in Harlem was to build and consolidate a Marxist study center, the Harlem Workers School, which registered 125 students in the fall of 1933 and featured "short courses and lectures on the national question." But national self-determination was fading, and a variant was emerging: the idea of the centrality of the Negro question in all of the CP's activities. *Centrality* came to mean that every issue confronting the working class and its allies was significantly affected by the conditions and struggles of the Negro people. In virtually no arena of activity could the Negro question be neglected or ignored; the battle against white chauvinism could never be undercut or trivialized. The quest for unity in every field of work required continuing and expanding struggle, on a priority basis, for racial equality—now more and more defined as the essence of liberation.[27]

By the start of 1934 the Harlem Section had grown to twenty-eight units whose activities included consolidating the ILD (which had stabilized at around five hundred members), organizing unions in local industries, increasing unemployed and relief work, building the LSNR, and disseminating the Party and LSNR press. The LSNR was placed directly under section control, while

Ford sought to shore up the Party's influence in its "bridge" organizations, gambling that the league could grow and develop politically more than the less controllable ILD.[28]

The Harlem Party was signing up new Party members in the area's laundries and in the small shops in both upper and lower Harlem. The local CP was also assisting tobacco workers, house painters, and needle trades workers by offering help to their unions and laying plans for the development of a Harlem trade union center (in part to counter A. Philip Randolph and Frank Crosswaith, who were organizing Harlem workers under Socialist banners). The Communists had also begun to organize women domestic workers, attracting as many as two or three hundred women to regular meetings. Block committees of the UCs were being buttressed, with regular meetings being held and functioning executives put in place.[29]

In early 1934 the CP broadened its Scottsboro fund appeals, enlisting artists ranging from Helen Morgan to Groucho Marx to Bennie Carter, Buck and Bubbles, Bill Robinson, and Fletcher Henderson in hugely successful Scottsboro benefit dances. The Scottsboro dance floor held the swaying figures of liberals, Socialists, Communists, as well as those of the full range of the Harlem mainstream. On March 17, 1934, thousands of Harlemites awaited Ada Wright; when the meeting was dispersed violently by police, local residents hurled a fusillade of "ripe fruit and missiles" from their windows; many fought with police, and throngs repeatedly regrouped after gas wafted over them. To observers, Scottsboro protest had transcended by far the limited circle on the left. Community groups and the anticommunist *Amsterdam News* echoed the protests of Sol Harper, speaking for the LSNR, that the police had been out of control and "wild cops" had instigated a riot.[30]

Large numbers of blacks participated in the mammoth New York May Day parade. One of the most poignant moments was provided by Eulah Gray, the seventeen-year-old niece of Ralph Gray, who sang the sharecroppers' union song: "Lenin is our leader, we shall not be moved!"[31]

After a successful effort to win the right of Harlem residents to register for Civil Works Administration jobs anywhere in the city, the LSNR took on the transportation industry. In response to the Central Committee's decree to make transportation its "concentration," LSNR tried a drive for jobs and union recognition at the Fifth Avenue Coach Company, whose buses were routed through Harlem. Despite spirited interracial picketing, a boycott flopped with little support from white bus drivers and a weak effort to enlist broad community involvement.[32]

In the meantime, Reverend John H. Johnson, pastor of St. Martin's Protestant Episcopal Church, launched the Citizens League for Fair Play after Blumstein's Department Store (the largest in Harlem) rejected his request that it hire black sales clerks. The league constituted itself as a "united front" with a middle-class phalanx of sixty-two religious, business, and social groups joining—as well as Reid and Kemp. The boycott of Blumstein's commenced in June 1934.[33]

The Blumstein's boycott seized Harlem's imagination, while the Communists declared that the middle-class sponsorship of the campaign was courting a fatal schism between black and white workers. But large picket lines were thrown up around the store, and the Communists, concerned about being isolated from a popular campaign, had members and supporters, especially whites, join the lines in a show of solidarity. By August Blumstein's ended its resistance; a buoyant Harlem victory parade underscored the dreaded nationalist undercurrents when whites were told to leave the line of march.[34]

Shortly after the victory over Blumstein's, the Citizens League began to fracture. It was attacked from the outside by Sufi Abdul Hamid, who saw his dreams for a lucrative labor agency punctured by the coalition that "stole" his campaign. Many suspected that Reid and Kemp, on the inside, were trying to get control of the jobs process by charging the coalition with weeding out dark-skinned young women. The Communists admonished that when a job fight ends in a fight for job control, a "labor racket" beckons.[35]

At the same time the Young Liberators began picketing the famous Empire Cafeteria on 125th Street, demanding "counterman" jobs for blacks. That campaign followed large demonstrations led by the ILD at a Cleveland restaurant where Ada Wright had been refused service. There had also been a successful campaign in Detroit, where union members had boycotted a supermarket chain, winning an increase in the hiring of black clerks. In Harlem hundreds of Communists and supporters, both black and white, came from all over the city to join the picket line. James Ashford coordinated what was becoming a crusade that even involved white Empire employees and left-wing workers from the nearby home relief bureau. Local residents were impressed when young whites scuffled with police. Empire quickly capitulated and hired four black countermen without making any cuts in the white work force. This was a boost for the Communist contention that jobs campaigns pitting blacks against whites were counterproductive and ultimately self-defeating.[36]

As disquiet over nationalism in the jobs movement spread among members of the black middle class, the Party's approach to jobs became more persuasive. Communists used their influence in the Home Relief Workers Association to fight discriminatory and discourteous treatment of blacks at relief agencies as well as harassment of white workers who practiced personal and political solidarity with blacks. As a result of union protests, blacks were added to the bureau grievance machinery and black investigators who had been fired were rehired. In December the Party, along with the ILD, LSNR, and UCs, again took on discrimination at city relief bureaus. That campaign won widespread support from Harlem church and civic organizations, even getting endorsements from the New York branch of the NAACP and from William H. Davis of the *Amsterdam News*. Groups supporting the campaign formed the Joint Conference on Discriminatory Practices, whose initial meeting was held at the Abyssinian Baptist Church, with Moore and Ford joining Powell, local politicians, and the head of the New York NAACP on the platform. At the end of 1934 the relief bureaucracy agreed to promote several blacks to supervisory positions and to hire more black investigators, making relief work the largest field of Negro employment by New York City.[37]

Events in Harlem mirrored what was going on in other parts of the country from mid-1934 to 1935. In the East, pickets led by Communists ringed chain stores in Philadelphia. The Pittsburgh LSNR rallied against discrimination in distributing relief; Cleveland students linked to the LSNR and ILD won an ordinance outlawing discrimination in public facilities after Ada Wright was refused service. In the Midwest, the LSNR in Chicago joined with the American Consolidated Trades Council to launch a drive against job discrimination.In the South, the New Orleans UC pressed the mayor of the city for nondiscriminatory relief for the jobless. In five southern states, the Socialist and Communist Parties agreed to a joint campaign against regional wage differentials. In the West, Thomas "Ace" Walton, a black leader of the Los Angeles Unemployed Council, organized demonstrations (which were often violently suppressed) against the discriminatory administration of the county relief program. Nationally, in January 1935 Washington, D.C., was the scene of the National Unemployment and Social Insurance Congress. One hundred and fifty black delegates joined with fifty whites in a special subsession to hammer out an action program for the attainment of national unemployment insurance. Representatives of the Urban League worked with Communists, liberals, and religious activists (including members of Father Divine's cultist Peace Mission).[38]

ACCELERATING THE POPULAR FRONT

Communists could now embrace coalition politics unburdened by the sectarian imperatives of the Third Period. Nudged by signals from the Comintern to extend a hand to Socialists and liberals in antifascist cooperation, the CP began to jettison its crude attacks on bourgeois organizations and individuals. With regard to the black community, the churches, fraternal and professional groups, and Greek-letter societies were no longer simply vessels of bourgeois reformism, but multiclass entities whose social and religious values reflected their often progressive aspirations. If religious organizations sought social justice on the basis of theological belief, was not the shared desire for that justice more vital than ideological differences over religion? This new tolerance extended to Father Divine and his cult, whose members were "toiling people" and whose views coincided with the Party's opposition to war and fascism as well as its advocacy of social insurance. If college fraternities and sororities mixed their bourgeois striving with a hatred for discrimination, wasn't that more important than quibbles over middle-class ambitions? Had there not been a self-inflicted wound in the Party's Third Period notions of class war against the leadership of such groups? It was time to approach social clubs, lodges, church groups, and civil organizations with an outstretched hand. After a very brief stint as head of the LSNR, Harry Haywood was dispatched to Chicago, where he exercised his passion for expulsions and tormented Richard Wright for his fixation on lumpen proletarian characters. The voice of strident opposition to "reformist misleaders" no longer had a national platform.[39]

James Ford, the paragon of Party orthodoxy, led the way to the popular front. He was among the first Party leaders to counsel Communists to participate in black organizations modestly and in a "sensible and human" spirit. In mid-1935 the Harlem CP had fractions in the Elks, in two churches, in the Harlem Caribbean Union (whence came Samuel Patterson, head of the Scottsboro-Herndon Action Committee), in a couple of Greek-letter societies, and in the Puerto Rican United Front against Discrimination. There were similar developments in other cities, especially Chicago, where Communists were very active in churches, civic groups, and unions.[40]

Although the Party and its affiliates continued to struggle with political, organizational, and financial problems, growth characterized the mid-1930s.

At the start of 1935 the Harlem Party's black membership had grown to over three hundred with eighteen shop units; the ILD had over a thousand members in eleven branches; and the Unemployed Council had over three thousand registered members. In the fall of 1933 Langston Hughes had been named president of the LSNR. Nationally, 15 percent of new recruits to the Party in 1935 were black, with notable gains in black membership in Louisiana, North Carolina, Georgia (along with Alabama), and the industrial states of the Midwest. Of course, for both blacks and whites there were persistent problems of turnover as the stress and responsibilities of Depression-era life overwhelmed the demands of the movement. The black membership, and the larger group of non-Party supporters, still constituted a minuscule segment of African American life. There was still societal anticommunism, lingering cultural gaps between the movement and the black community, the Communists' lack of resources, and nagging doubts among blacks about the fidelity of white workers. But with the deemphasis of sectarianism, the political impact of that membership was becoming far greater than its numbers.[41]

INTERNATIONALISM IN THE MID-1930S

When Benito Mussolini attacked Ethiopia in late 1934 and 1935, the CP already had a long record of involvement in anticolonial activity. Throughout the early 1930s the Party and its allies demonstrated often against continuing U.S. occupation of Haiti, protested U.S. colonialism in the Philippines, and excoriated Firestone's influence in semicolonial Liberia. In 1934 the Party strongly supported the Cuban left against the imposition of a reactionary regime. In that same year Ford traveled to Havana to address the convention of the Cuban National Labor Confederation in the face of threats from then Colonel Fulgencio Battista to break up the meeting and arrest its organizers. In 1933 the ILD had established sections in South Africa and Madagascar. When ITUCNW's *Negro Worker* was forced out of Europe in the fascist wave, it settled for a short time in the offices of the *Harlem Liberator*. Scottsboro marches were often coupled with slogans against the "war danger."[42]

The Second U.S. Congress of the League against War and Fascism in Chicago in the fall of 1934 brought Communists and leftists together with mainstream black leaders, such as the prominent lawyer Edith Sampson, Mabel Byrd (who was elected vice president of the league), social worker Thyra Edwards, Arthur G. Falls of the Chicago Urban League, and others. The meeting linked the liberation of people of color around the world (including the United States) with the defeat of fascism and war. The Party's antiwar message stressed competition for colonial booty as the essence of advanced imperialism and a major factor in igniting a new world war.[43]

The CP's anti-imperialist sensibility came into play quickly in the Ethiopian crisis. Allegations that the Soviet Union was shipping strategic goods to Italy were countered with charges that the British were abetting the movement of Italian troops to East Africa, the French were hindering efforts by the League of Nations to stop the invasion, and in the United States Wall Street was rooting for the "plunder of Abyssinia" to protect the house of Morgan's investments in Italy. The Party's resolve stiffened when the Soviets opposed the Ethiopian invasion. By the fall of 1935 the *Daily Worker* proudly displayed the words of William N. Jones of the *Afro-American,* who wrote: "It is my earnest conviction that Soviet Russia today [is] the nation most actively and effectively opposing Italian plundering of Ethiopia." Soviet opposition stamped Mussolini's war as imperialist and against the interests of both the Italian workers and the Ethiopian people. William L. Patterson, writing in *Inprecorr,* hailed "the heroic Italian workers who . . . are calling for the defeat of their 'own' imperialism."[44]

For American Communists, any attempt to define the Ethiopian conflict as a race war was an egregious error that would obscure its imperialist nature and turn white workers against black workers. Yet that is what seemed to be happening in Harlem and other black communities where voices were raised condemning the white man's war against African peoples. With an issue that dramatically uplifted their agenda, the nationalists in Harlem quickly congealed into a coherent force. The UNIA, the African Patriotic League, and other nationalists talked about raising black volunteers for Ethiopia, boycotting Italian goods, and driving Italian merchants out of Harlem.[45]

Abner Berry proposed to the nationalists that a broadly based defense committee be created to raise funds for besieged Ethiopia and organize mass demonstrations against Italian aggression. The UNIA agreed, but with a wounding caveat: It would have nothing to do with whites. In a tactical move that would have been impossible months earlier, the Communists agreed to join with the nationalists to form a Provisional Committee for the Defense of Ethiopia that was dominated by an antiwhite mood. A member of the Party's Italian Bureau then sought to meet with the committee, but was rebuffed. Yet the Communists said not a word about maneuvers to divide the working class. Sol Harper and William Fitzgerald managed to arrange the appearance of a UNIA figure before the Party-led Italian Workers Club, whose members greeted him warmly and reached into their pockets to support the Provisional Committee. The ice was at least partially broken. The Garveyite left the meeting convinced that the struggle against Mussolini had friends in the Italian community. Support for a boycott of Italian merchants weakened. Energies were then focused on a delegation to the Italian consulate and on a mass march against Italian aggression.[46]

Ultimately, the Committee rejected the race-war interpretation of the conflict. Its first public meeting on March 7, 1935, showed surprising breadth given its initially narrow ideological base. Religious and community leaders joined Arthur Reid and James Ford in a rousing call to action. Adam Clayton Powell Jr. eloquently underscored the antifascist nature of the struggle for the survival of the fragile East African kingdom and linked that battle to defeating the "Coughlins and Huey Longs who in America represent the spirit of fascism." Ford wiped out any simplistic notion of racial causation: Japanese sympathy with Ethiopia was merely a fig leaf to cover its aggression in Manchuria; Mayor Fiorello LaGuardia and Ed Corsi, head of the city's relief bureau, were "enemies of Italy." In Chicago, Harry Haywood was dragged off a rooftop by "red squad" cops while attempting to address ten thousand "Hands off Ethiopia" marchers, both black and white, who had defied the city's refusal of a permit for the event.[47]

By the fall of 1935 broad, liberal-led alliances like the New York City Committee for Ethiopian Independence were convening large rallies. Given the stress on Mussolini, skirmishes at Italian consulates broke out all over. In New York Jane Craik Speed, late of Birmingham, was arrested on charges of disorderly conduct on the complaint of Prince Guido Colonna of the consulate. She led a group of women who sought to present a petition and, according to the prince, "spilled ink all over his suit and shirt" when he denied them entry. A full-scale Italo-Ethiopian war broke out in the fall, and angry rallies erupted in response in every major city. In Harlem a black-Italian riot was narrowly averted. But across the country the focus remained on the internationalist, antifascist, and anticolonialist character of the protest.[48]

The Harlem Riot

Harlem erupted on March 19, 1935, when a teenager was grabbed by the manager at the Kress store on 125th Street for stealing a knife. A policeman dragged the young man into the basement and released him through a back entrance. Black customers believed that the boy was being beaten and angrily overturned counters and merchandise. Louise Thompson passed by; she advised the police to provide answers and told them that if they did so, the crowd would disperse. Instead, the store was closed; rumors kept spreading that the young man had been killed. When outraged Harlemites turned to Party headquarters, the first response of those on the scene was to channel spontaneous rage into disciplined protest. The Young Liberators threw up a picket line at Kress and started an impromptu street meeting. Someone hurled a rock through Kress's window. The police promptly broke up the meeting, dragging a speaker from a lamppost. Within an hour, not a window was left intact along 125th Street. When the turmoil ended, one person was dead, several wounded, and over two hundred jailed.[49]

Ashford's Young Liberators threw together a leaflet headlined "CHILD BRU-TALLY BEATEN!... CHILD NEAR DEATH." It urged a boycott of Kress and called for an end to police brutality in Harlem. The YCL issued a similar leaflet with similarly untrue claims. But the thrust of Communist activity was to discourage "Boss... Race Riots in Harlem." Whites circulating through the crowds were generally presumed to be reds who had become part of the landscape of protest against hunger and joblessness. They were not touched. The Harlem riot never became a race riot; large stores owned by blacks were looted, while some white stores that hired blacks were spared.[50]

The riot's aftermath was marked by a frenzy of red baiting as New York's right-wing press and the Manhattan district attorney sought to finger the Communists for fomenting the chaos. Ford issued a press release saying that the CP always discouraged riots in response to hunger and police terror in Harlem. Underlying the events was the indescribable poverty in Harlem, where the "masses live on the brink of starvation." An investigation into conditions in Harlem was needed, and the Party was ready to cooperate, Ford claimed.[51]

A community with no deeply rooted anticommunist feelings viewed the "outside agitator" theme as a red herring to deflect attention from economic and social despair. For Harlem leaders, the riot was principally an "economic revolt"; they did not believe the claims of Communist instigation.[52]

The LaGuardia administration also hesitated to jump on the anticommunist bandwagon. Instead, it established the Mayor's Commission on Conditions in Harlem — accepting the community's demand for emphasis on Harlem's misery. The Party chose Ford, Williana Burroughs, Louise Thompson, and Robert Minor to testify on its behalf, with the advice of two lawyers. Thompson described what she had seen on the evening of March 19 — the anger, the attempts by the Young Liberators to channel the riot into constructive protest, the hostility of the police who "could have prevented the riot if they had acted properly" and who were the immediate cause of the unrest. At a deeper level, she said, "the people were mainly expressing their spleen against their conditions under which they were living."[53]

The two-month-long hearings gave the Communists ample opportunity to offer their views on Harlem's plight. They took full advantage, and what they said resonated with Harlem's labor, religious, political, and social organizations. A pattern of cooperation emerged that spread to the streets and meeting halls over the next few months. In style and content, the polished and professional demeanor of Burroughs, Thompson, Ford, Berry, Work, and others created a comfort zone for Harlem's middle-class leaders. The "bad old days" (in Hosea Hudson's words) when dead bodies were paraded through the streets dissipated in a swirl of coalition building. Making its own interpretation of Comintern edicts, the Party was engaging in broadly progressive and humanist politics. Even the confrontational hangovers from the Third Period had an unmistakably compassionate and multiclass content. "Flying squads" of black working-class housewives led by Bonita Williams swarmed over local butchers demanding 25 percent price cuts and ripping up the old prices when they won their demands. Rent strikes hit the middle-class enclave of Sugar Hill, activating a good part of Harlem's upper strata.[54]

The Party-inspired Joint Conference on Discriminatory Practices found new life when city officials at the riot inquiry boorishly denied racial bias in dispensing relief. The group held a "mass trial" of the bureaucrats at Reverend William Lloyd Imes's St. James Presbyterian Church. Imes, Powell, and Channing Tobias of the YMCA (to whom the Communists had apologized months earlier for lumping him with "misleaders") served as "jurors," while Ben Davis and Loren Miller led the "prosecution." Some city administrators and politicians began to feel the pressure, and in the summer of 1935 relief officials opened two new bureaus under black supervisors. Former skeptics and outright opponents of the Party, such as A. Philip Randolph, became convinced that cooperation with Communists was possible. When the Works Progress Administration was inaugurated in the summer of 1935, a Party-led coalition, recalling the widespread bias manifested in its predecessors, demanded a fair share of jobs for blacks. The usual rallies, marches, and demonstrations, spearheaded by the CP-influenced relief workers' union, led to the adoption by the WPA of a policy of inclusive hiring and promotion on public works projects.[55]

In a rare official departure from anticommunism, the final report of the Mayor's Commission concluded that "while one . . . would hesitate to give Communists full credit for preventing the outbreak from becoming a race riot, they deserve more credit than any other element in Harlem for preventing a physical conflict between whites and Negroes."⁵⁶

THE CULTURAL FRONT

In the ABB days Cyril Briggs had been interested in both the aesthetic and ideological content of black culture. He wrote on black theater and hovered on the edge of the Harlem Renaissance — challenging exotic and pathological stereotypes and exploring manifestations of national consciousness in African American art. In 1933 Briggs wrote that "the art of an oppressed people . . . must reflect and support the struggles of that people for freedom, for national liberation." He claimed that black artists around the *Liberator* were promoting "genuine Negro culture, with its proletarian content (work songs, songs of revolt, etc.) as against the prostitution of Negro culture to suit the commercial aims of the 'Negro Inferiority' dictum of the white ruling class." That formulation connected authentic black culture to proletarian origins, forging an inseparable bond between a national cultural consciousness and class struggle.⁵⁷

But a broad and satisfactory convergence of those themes was often blocked by judgmental, if not arrogant, sectarianism. James W. Ford in the early 1930s said that revolutionary black art was not emerging quickly enough. "Among the Negroes, for instance, who is there besides Langston Hughes?" he asked. However, his notion of revolutionary culture was limited to "building up the intellectual opposition to the traitorous leadership" of the NAACP. Michael Gold also awaited the authentic black proletarian voice. His old comrade Claude McKay seemed to be mired in "animalism" and in an exaggerated "racial patriotism" that ascribed all the joy in the world to Negroes. At least that is what Gold got from McKay's *Banjo* (1929), which contained too much "anti-white prejudices" for his taste. But having observed the racism that McKay faced, Gold could not blame him. McKay wrote with fire and lush humor, capturing the "real talk . . . real poetry" of black workers. But, according to Gold, he had yet to discover "those proletarian Negro themes" that would rise above the primitive "Negro joy" that was so appealing to "white literary bums" like Carl Van Vechten. So many promising Negro artists were wasting their talents on "the gutter-life side of Harlem." "What a crime against their race!" he exclaimed. But in time "Negro Tolstoys, Gorkys, and Walt Whitmans" would arise. The

Negro's true voice "will be a voice of storm, beauty and pain, no saxophone clowning, but Beethoven's majesty and Wagner's might." Gold's own voice combined unprecedented respect for black art, cultural puritanism, a paternalistic Euro-American reference point, and a sad ignorance of the "beauty and pain" in jazz and other aspects of black culture.[58]

In 1930 Phil Schatz, then a very young YCL member, wrote that "Negro culture is perhaps the most genuine workers' culture in America," despite being corrupted by bourgeois patrons who encourage spirituals about "Jim Crow heaven." On the contrary, the Negro worker often found solace in singing about an earthy woman or about the next train to another grimy job — instead of " 'sweet chariot comin' for to carry him home.' " Even when he sang spirituals, he sang of his struggle to fill an empty stomach and be free of the bosses' ire:

> *I tol' my cap'n that my feet was col'*
> *"God damn yo' feet, let the car wheel roll."*

There it was, Schatz exclaimed, a grasp of exploitation and class distinction in the folk tradition. But with all his uncommon awareness of black folklore, Schatz's rigidity blinded him to the revolutionary implication of that "sweet chariot coming for to carry me home."[59]

V. J. Jerome, who became the Party's cultural ideologist, tried to combine the mournful spiritual with the clarion call to revolution. Unfortunately, his effort bordered on parody and compared poorly with the lusty singing of Share Croppers' Union members who transformed "Give Me That Old Time Religion" into "Give Me That Old Communist Spirit" or turned "In Dat Great Gittin'-up Mornin' " into "In Dat Great Revolutionary Mornin'." Jerome wrote:

> *Dad-dy is a Com-mun-ist,*
> *Locked up in de pen;*
> *Di-dn' rob nor di-dn' steal*
> *Led de work-in men.*[60]

However embarrassing, Jerome's effort encouraged more authentic voices to create music and poetry out of the burdens of southern rural and northern urban life. As Robin Kelley has pointed out, the *Southern Worker* in the early 1930s published many "personal expressions of exploitation and resistance" by both men and women. That was also true of the *Harlem Liberator*, while *New Masses* opened its pages especially to the poems of Langston Hughes, which combined the edgy, sardonic language of the ghetto worker with a fulsome "Good Morning Revolution." Richard Wright in one of his early poems, "I Have Seen Black Hands," synthesized black national assertiveness and multiracial internationalism:

> *I am black and I have seen black hands*
> *Raised in fists of revolt, side by side*
> *with the white fists of white workers.*[61]

Eugene Gordon was among the first in the Communist orbit to attempt an extensive Marxist analysis of black literature. His critique was unsparing. He found in the post–Civil War black writers "a peculiar national psychosis caused by a suppressed nationhood." That suppression drove black writers to a yearning for the freedom and bourgeois comfort of their former white masters. Charles W. Chesnutt's sentimental folktales had an Olympian detachment that moved white critics to note that there was nothing in his writing "to indicate that [Chesnutt] was colored." Du Bois had felt the lash of racism like the characters he created in *The Quest for the Silver Fleece* and *Dark Princess.* However, Gordon contended that Du Bois also manifested a "personal psychosis": He resented whites in general for ignominiously denying the black bourgeoisie entry into the white bourgeois world. Gordon claimed that Paul Lawrence Dunbar's earlier poems reflected his origins in the world of the black worker, but that his later works exhibited a desire "to be with the class that he had adopted." Thus, he later only trivially and artificially needled the ways of parasitic whites while reducing black workers to "atmosphere." Claude McKay, the "retired radical," in *Home to Harlem* did not tell a story of workers who worked; he dealt with "'workers' " who "lie concealed in the rat holes of Harlem by day, drinking until sodden ... perpetually on the verge of committing murder to possess the body of some woman."[62]

Wallace Thurman, Countee Cullen, and Rudolph Fisher fared only a little better under Gordon's microscope. Thurman was a dilettante absorbed in the portrayal of "white and colored degenerates"; Fisher's characters were suggestive of "cheap vaudevillians" bereft of class consciousness. All wrote for the white upper class, which demanded stereotypes to fit into its notions of what the Negro should be. Even Langston Hughes was rapped for an alleged shortage of class consciousness in *Not without Laughter.* Granville Hicks found his novel about "situations and events that the revolutionary must regard as of only secondary importance ... something of a shock." Walt Carmon was dis-

appointed that *Not without Laughter* was a "race novel." But he consoled himself that "under its black skin, there is red proletarian blood running through
it." With all its faults, Carmon declared, "It is *our* novel."[63]

Gordon concluded that "if the novelist's workers must have illusions, then
these workers . . . must have also disillusionment evolving into sanity of mind
and clarity of vision. If there be no class-conscious action following this awakening into reality, there should be at least, a forecast of it." Aside from arguable
points about specific writers — and his neglect of women writers, such as Zora
Hurston, Nella Larsen, and Jessie Fauset — was there nothing to be learned
from despair or from the lives of people who mixed joy with suffering, whose
foibles, petty cruelties, and small triumphs constituted a kaleidoscope of means
of survival and gave insight into the ways of the modern capitalist world? Marx's
own scattered writings on literature and art did not suggest a mechanical imposition of class struggle (which was inherent in all things anyway) upon art.
Any artistic expression had value if it focused on humanity and pointed to
what Engels called the dawning of the human epoch. Yet Gordon's plea for
black literature built upon the working-class foundation of African American
black life was an important contribution to the quest for an authentic black
aesthetic free from the demands of white commercial culture.[64]

Lawrence Gellert was the prime collector of Negro music in the CP orbit.
He claimed to have seen a letter from John Lomax, the discoverer of Huddie
Ledbetter (Leadbelly), to a friend, in which Lomax said, "My chauffeur . . . Leadbelly is a nigger to the core of his being. In addition he is a killer. . . . He is as
sensual as a goat." That provoked Gellert into attacking the Lomaxes for racist
pathology and reduction of black folklore to carnal minstrelsy. Before long
Leadbelly himself was ensnared in the controversy. According to Gellert, he
had been promoted by the Lomaxes as the South's supplicating "'good nigger' " who only killed another black man — enough to rate a pardon.[65]

Nonetheless Leadbelly later became an icon of the left, which viewed his
songs and his life as emblematic of the travails and triumphs of the rural black
population. As the popular front expanded, Gellert's formulaic variant on "socialist realism" weakened, and a more holistic "black and white people's culture" emerged, which heralded folk art as the honest articulation of the experiences of working people of all races and ethnic backgrounds. That concept
placed black culture within a vastly pluralistic cultural universe, so that the
artistic and musical contributions of blacks, whether or not they had explicit
political content, ranked as first among the works of artistic equals.[66]

In the spring of 1934 the left-wing Theater Union presented *Stevedore*, a work by two white Communist playwrights, Paul Peters and George Sklar. Drawn from Scottsboro, Rosewood, Camp Hill, and recent longshore strikes, *Stevedore* electrified its biracial audiences. The plot involved false rape charges, a black dockers' strike, a white mob attack on heroic black strikers, and black and white workers beating off a common enemy—to the tears and cheers of the audience.[67]

Perhaps at any other moment *Stevedore* might have been dismissed as didactic, manipulative theater. But in the context of the times, the play's heroic and dignified portrayal of black workers was a revelation. Nineteen thirty-four was the year of the strike, and the play vibrated with the emotional force derived from that reality. J. A. Rogers hailed *Stevedore* for promoting black self-respect with humor and art. It was measurably better than the minstrel-tinged *Green Pastures* or *Emperor Jones*. The image of white workers rushing to aid Negro comrades was "unreal," but it showed the audience "the only real solution to the 'race' problem"—black and white workers together putting "the henchmen of the capitalists to flight, as they surely will some day." High praise came from Walter White, William H. Davis, and William Pickens, who said that "nothing like this has ever happened on the American stage under the management of white people." Mike Gold, of all people, was uneasy with the play's didacticism. No matter. *Stevedore* exemplified the transforming potential of the interracial working class. That too was an aspect of the changing political and intellectual climate in the nation.[68]

Another ground-breaking theatrical event in 1934 was the Theater Guild production of John Wexley's *They Shall Not Die*. Wexley, according to Brooks Atkinson of the *New York Times*, succeeded in creating "militant social service," which drew audiences into emotional engagement with Scottsboro. But acclaim was by no means universal. Roy Wilkins was so upset over the play's negative portrayal of the NAACP (called the ASPCP, or American Society for the Protection of Colored People) as "yellow" frauds "who would sell out to white folks" that he considered legal action for libel. CP critics were not enthralled by the play's focus on the courtroom and the "struggle between lawyers," to the detriment of mass pressure. Particularly galling was the flattering portrayal of the "romanticized humanitarian lawyer" (Leibowitz), who sought "abstract justice" without concern for the social issues involved. But Communist critics conceded that *They Shall Not Die* was attuned to the capacity of uptown middle-class subscribers of the Theater Guild to digest political drama. The Marxist critics might have noted that the Scottsboro boys themselves were largely voiceless and cowering in contrast to the impassioned, articulate white lawyers. There was no comparison with Langston Hughes's one-act play of 1931, *Scottsboro, Limited,* in which the nine boys were at the core of the drama. With cadences that anticipated the work of Clifford Odets, Hughes had the boys shouting defiance in verse:

> *Who does want to die?*
> *That's why all the free black men*
> *Have got to fight,*
> *Or else we will all die in Poverty's night.*[69]

Stevedore and *They Shall Not Die* underscored the growing determination of the left to advance and treat black themes with heretofore unequaled partisanship and dignity. The plays also revealed the limits of the white imagination in exploring those very themes. Again, the left's impulse to ground artistic renderings of the black experience in the working class offered a variant to white commercial domination of the black image and helped pave the way for a deeper, authentic African American theater.

One of Cyril Briggs's last efforts before his removal from the *Harlem Liberator* had been to form a theater group around the weekly in June 1933. With the upheavals in the Harlem Party in the summer and fall of 1933, the theater project had faded from sight. But it reemerged in the ferment of 1935 on a wider plane. In the wake of the Harlem riot, cultural figures in and around the Party, both black and white, formed the Friends of Harlem to create theater, dance, and music projects. Its first major accomplishment was the Negro People's Theater, whose company was drawn from the casts of *Stevedore* and *Green Pastures,* under the direction of the noted black actors Rose McLendon and Chick McKinney.[70]

The NPT struggled with two sometimes opposing aspirations: to build a theater by and for the black community, and to develop a universal prolabor repertoire. Its first production was Clifford Odets's searing set of morality sketches on the recent New York taxi drivers' strike, *Waiting for Lefty.* But the work about white taxi drivers and distinctly Jewish workers and intellectuals did not translate well into a portrayal of blacks "deep down in the working class." Nevertheless, the community responded warmly. Five thousand people packed the cavernous Rockland Palace to see the play—the largest single Harlem audience ever assembled for a theatrical production. NPT was a pioneering effort by Communist and left-wing artists to create an African American theater primarily to serve the black community while at the same time embracing pluralistic working-class culture.[71]

Across the country theater groups that addressed the black experience sprang up. The Worker's Theater, Theater Union, and New Theater League joined the Negro People's Theater to constitute a radical antiracist theater arts movement — something strongly attractive to black artists despite the Party's often doctrinaire and puritanical dicta on proletarian culture. Blacks were also part of a growing "soapbox theater" created by organized labor. Black students in a workers' education program in Atlanta presented labor plays and skits on campus lawns and building steps; textile workers in Mobile, clothing workers in Louisville, and union members in Nashville developed plays with "no color line among the actors or in the material." A waitress in Texas fashioned a chilling script out of a conversation she had overheard between two men who had participated in a lynching. The soapbox theater was a labor-based precursor of the Federal Theater Project — often dramatizing ideas about race and class that it believed the working class should know of and think about.[72]

In the visual arts, change was also taking place. Dissatisfied with a 1934 exhibition sponsored by the Citizen's Committee of Harlem, six local graphic artists organized the Harlem Artists' Guild. Aaron Douglas, Augusta Savage, Romare Bearden, Charles Alston, Henry W. Bannarn, and Gwendolyn Bennett combined to forge cooperation among black artists and to tell the nation that blacks were "destined to play an important part in the art of America." The guild later pressured the WPA to secure assignments for black artists; it boycotted Jim Crow art exhibits in the South and challenged the discriminatory practices of arts-funding foundations.[73]

The Communist-led John Reed Student Clubs helped create revolutionary literary reviews with fashionable titles of the times — *Left Front, Left Review, Leftward, Cauldron, Blast, Dynamo, Anvil, Partisan Review* (which in 1934 was the organ of the New York John Reed Club). Richard Wright was a rising star in that firmament and in 1934 served as editor of *Left Front.*[74]

SOCIAL LIFE

By 1935 the Communist Party and its supporting organizations had attained the size and breadth to constitute a distinct social and cultural entity. After the years of battles against white chauvinism, the Party had by no means eliminated the scourge. But as Ishmael Flory pointed out, the social life within the

Party was immeasurably more egalitarian and nonracist than the society beyond its meeting rooms and social halls. Flory had returned to Los Angeles in 1931 after graduating from the University of California at Berkeley. He was drawn to the Scottsboro case and soon began attending a discussion group at UCLA sponsored by the CP-led National Students League. Within that context, he became friendly with the working-class students, most of them Jewish, in the UCLA branch of the league. At a social event he won a waltz contest, establishing himself as a contributor to the group's social life. Especially among the growing number of young people to enter the Communist orbit, the dances, parties, picnics, summer camps, ball games, demonstrations, lobbies, concerts, movies, and folksong fests that framed their social and political lives had become distinctly interracial. This was not an embellishment but the cultural and social essence of the Party and its affiliates. It became a marker of the Party's political behavior in unions and community organizations. The point was not lost on the Federal Bureau of Investigation, which routinely instructed its agents and informants that they could spot reds by the presence of Negro friends and Paul Robeson recordings in their home.[75]

Inevitably, interracial camaraderie would settle on the sensitive ground of black-white romances and marriages. Although no statistics are available, there were undoubtedly scores of such unions—far more than in the larger society. A considerable number of marriages took place between blacks and Jews. Jews were the largest ethnic component in the Party's orbit and had a rather strong spiritual and emotional bond with oppression. A majority of the interracial marriages were between black men and white women. Louise Thompson Patterson attributed the larger number of such unions to white women's "freedom" in approaching black men, which she ascribed to the protective stance of "defying racism" adopted by white women. However, there appeared to be more marriages between white men and black women away from the Party's New York center. In Detroit, which had a stronger working-class base, there appeared to be an almost equal number of interracial marriages between white men and black woman as between white women and black men.[76]

This situation caused considerable social tension. From the outside, the Party occasionally had to defend itself from assertions that it used white women to "lure" black men; in 1935 the *New York Amsterdam News* commented editorially about the reds putting "a proletarian blessing on the Lindy Hop and now the Union Square blondes and brunettes are stealing most of the devoted Harlem swains from their one-time dance partners." Audley Moore resented "white women taking the black men." In Harlem there was a mini-revolt by black women who demanded that the party forbid such unions. There is no sign that this occurred in other parts of the country. In any case, the Party, devoted to racial equality from the workplace to the bedroom, would never have considered such an edict. Interracial unions were personal decisions that arose from a collective commitment to equality on all levels. All that was left was to try to alter the social situation in the Party so that black women advanced to full recognition and white men learned the social graces to become comfortable with both white and black women in social settings.[77]

The vast majority of African Americans who became Communists lived parallel lives—in the Party, in the black community. There were many friendships between blacks and whites within the Party. Even in Alabama, where the CP was 90 percent black, the sharply limited contact between the races did not fully prevent respectful relationships between white and black Communists, as Al Murphy recalled nearly forty years later. Yet the bonds of race were powerful in all ways. Black Communists maintained special ties with each other within the Party; most also lived in the larger black community, where a variety of social relationships abounded that were not dependent upon the Party. Louise Patterson, for all her absorption in the Party and the IWO, "never relinquished [her] friendships with people who were not Communists." For the most part, the world of the Party and the world of black community life coexisted in relative harmony. But some blacks, especially among the leadership, found in the Party an insular social, intellectual, and workplace home that tended to cut them off from the larger world. By the mid-1930s the race and national partisanship encapsulated within the Party had nearly silenced those critics in the African American community who considered black Communists to be servants of a white political movement.[78]

The figure of Paul Robeson unified the diverse cultural, racial, national, and political strands that ran through the Communist-influenced left. When he returned from his European stay in 1935, he became highly visible in virtually all arenas of radical activism and culture. His imposing presence, his rich baritone, his superb intellect, his uncompromising internationalism and support for the USSR, his fierce advocacy of Africa and African culture, and his uncanny fusion of anger and humor, militancy and gentleness all combined to represent the character, the talent, and the principles that many Communists wished the world would see in their movement. He exemplified the spirit and content of a movement that sought to give voice and substance to antifascism and anticolonialism, to peace, and to black liberation. Robeson became the living manifestation of a profoundly national consciousness—promoting African languages and culture, pointing to independence and freedom for all peoples of African descent—a consciousness based in a pluralistic world of many cultures and national identities. For Robeson the linkages were unbreakable between African liberation and antifascism, antifascism and internationalism, internationalism and freedom for black Americans, freedom for black Americans and support for labor. Over the next two decades and well into the Cold War, the towering figures of Robeson and Du Bois (who moved into the Party's orbit in the postwar years) would sustain the hopes and morale of a besieged generation of leftists.[79]

CHAPTER FIFTEEN

Toward a National Negro Congress

THE LAST BATTLE WITH THE AFL

In January 1935 thousands of people gathered in Washington, D.C., for the CP-inspired National Congress for Unemployment and Social Insurance. T. Arnold Hill, then acting executive secretary of the National Urban League, was one of many voices calling for action to facilitate the entry of blacks into the emerging industrial union movement.[1]

The need for action was compelling. Around the nation many observers wondered if Negro workers could long resist the pressures to break strikes in the face of the AFL's racism. Before the issue of the union hiring hall attracted the support of black longshoremen in San Francisco (see chapter 13), "several hundred" had crossed the picket lines to accept high-paying jobs. Three black longshoremen had been killed defying a strike on the Houston docks. The Kohler Company in Wisconsin was actively courting black workers to disregard the walkout against its plumbing works. On the other hand, the hiring of black construction workers in St. Louis under NRA regulations had prompted AFL members to walk off the job and physically assault black laborers who were eager to join the union. So severe was the racial discrimination of the AFL Railroad Brotherhoods in the Midwest that blacks and sympathetic whites sought to organize an Independent Organization of Western Lines to push integrated unionism. The numbers of black strikebreakers had so far been small, but could that last in the face of the labor federation's hostility?[2]

In April 1934 William N. Jones of the *Afro-American* noted that the AFL was gaining under the NRA. But its shabby record on racial equality and its lack of black leaders threatened to widen the gap between black and white workers. There was a need, Jones concluded, for black labor to wage a "bitter fight" for its rightful place in the rising labor movement.[3]

The national convention of the AFL was held in San Francisco in the fall of 1934. It was quickly besieged by black longshoremen who had given strong backing to the dockers' strike. They joined with local Negro leaders to picket the convention— paraphrasing Marx's famous Civil War dictum with signs that read: "Labor Cannot Be Free While Black Labor Is Enslaved." After summary rejection of their resolution calling for an end to Jim Crow unionism, A. Philip Randolph demanded the appointment of a committee to investigate the AFL's policy on organizing Negro workers. It was time to put an end to limp excuses, inaction, and empty resolutions, as well as to the spurious claim that separate Jim Crow charters were demonstrations of the federation's inclusiveness. After prolonged shouts and cheers, the convention agreed to at least appoint a Committee of Five under the control of the Executive Council to investigate the conditions of black workers.[4]

The all-white committee was appointed by AFL president William Green eight months later. Nevertheless, black activists chose to present an exhaustive indictment of the federation's cozy accommodation with its affiliates' racist charters and practices. John P. Davis, representing the JCNR, offered a program to abolish Jim Crow unions, elevate blacks to the AFL Executive Council, employ black organizers, and launch a national educational campaign to show that "there can be no American labor movement that's worth a tinker's damn until Negro and white workers are organized together." Randolph endorsed Davis's proposals—stressing that concrete acts, like expulsion of discriminatory unions, should be joined to the educational campaign. The Committee of Five responded with its own plan: Biased affiliates should "take up" the issue of inequality in rules and in the ranks; the AFL should issue no more charters to unions that continued to deny entry to blacks; it should launch an educational campaign to get the white workers "to see the weakness of division and the necessity of unity between black and white workers to the end that all workers may be organized."[5]

Less compelling than Davis's proposals, the committee's recommendations were still a historic advance. A plea for a positive response came to William Green from T. Arnold Hill, who warned that the labor movement could never function as an instrument of security for the nation's workers unless the AFL outlawed Jim Crow. Hill's jeremiad echoed rising voices in the black community: If the Negro was to cast his lot with labor, labor must cast its lot with the Negro.[6]

Blacks backed those words with action. After a decade-long struggle, the Brotherhood of Sleeping Car Porters won an overwhelming vote for the union in mid-1935 in an election conducted by the National Mediation Board. And after scores of attacks on Randolph and his vacillating tactics, the *Negro Liberator* hailed the victory as a milestone in the battle to win union representation for black workers. In the flush of that victory, Randolph's Socialist colleague, Frank Crosswaith, pulled together a Negro Labor Committee of 110 unions claiming to represent 350,000 workers. Hewing to the Socialist Party line, it vowed to work exclusively within the AFL to end the color bar. In a reprise of Crosswaith's old battles with the reds, the founding conference refused to admit Arnold P. Johnson from the left-wing Emergency Home Relief Bureau Employees Association, except as a nonvoting delegate. Johnson withdrew. The Resolutions Committee referred all the "hot" resolutions on Herndon, Scottsboro, Ethiopia, and fascism to the incoming executive. William Green sent a letter to the conference voicing approval for its faith in the American Federation of Labor.[7]

All that fell on the AFL's deaf ears. Green and the AFL Executive Council quashed the report of the Committee of Five, accepting instead an alternate proposal from George Harrison, president of the lily-white railway clerks' union, which called only for "education" on the status and conditions of Negro workers. The fifty-fifth convention of the AFL opened in Atlantic City on October 7, 1935. Green's presidential address did not even give a nod to the Negro question. The struggle over industrial unionism and the unrestricted granting of industrial union charters were the burning issues. To be sure, those questions affected the organization of black workers. But the linkage was buried in the tumult, highlighted by the famous fistfight between John L. Lewis of the United Mine Workers and Bill Hutchinson of the Carpenters' Union.[8]

On the last day of an exhausting convention, the Executive Council put Harrison's "Supplemental Report on Colored Workers" before the delegates.

Randolph castigated the Harrison report as a cynical evasion; the AFL's inaction was particularly galling at a moment when the government was expanding federal projects whose jobs were controlled by Jim Crow unions. In the closing hours, Randolph submitted the Committee of Five recommendations for a vote; they were rejected. The convention then endorsed the "education" proposal submitted by Harrison — who had admitted on the floor that "we do not admit Negroes to our Brotherhood." Black leaders within and without the labor movement became convinced that nothing more could be hoped for or gained from the American Federation of Labor.[9]

The Committee for Industrial Organization was founded by eight international unions on November 9, 1935 — a milestone in a three-year period from 1934 to 1937 in which the American working class accomplished what it took English workers nearly a century to do: the unionization of basic industries. Faced also with a historic choice, the emerging industrial unions would adopt a general policy of racial inclusion and equality in building their organizations. Once again the American workers chose the progressive path — but under some pressure by an increasingly multiclass movement in the black community and by the Communist-led left.[10]

A movement among blacks to secure the position of African American workers in the industrial unions brought the strategic outlook of much of the black community into alignment with the Communists. This trend had been in the making for some time. In 1932 Charles S. Johnson had concluded that the bloody miners' strike confirmed the need for biracial action to destroy the racist orthodoxies in the labor movement. The Rosenwald Conference of 1933 had discussed the possibilities of a Negro-labor alliance more extensively than ever before in such a venue. The Amenia Conference in the same year had declared that only a well-organized interracial labor movement could compel justice from government and business. By the mid-1930s several major developments had converged: The Depression still held millions, especially blacks, in the grip of poverty; the landmark National Labor Relations Act (Wagner Act), preventing employers from interfering with workers seeking to bargain collectively, became law; the industrial union movement broke with the old-line, racist and sexist craft unionism. The fascist threat on a global scale (many blacks saw themselves as the first targets of fascism) hastened the movement to unify disparate antifascist forces. Electorally, African Americans accelerated their movement to the Democratic Party, embracing Roosevelt's neo-Keynesian economic reform. With the exception of Du Bois's advocacy in 1934 of a separate black economy, nationalist currents remained ghetto-bound and increasingly marginal. As Loren Miller declared: "The gaudy dream of a self-sufficient Negro economy vanished overnight. This structure collapsed decisively not because of a lack of Negro ability but because the capitalism on which it depended fell down. No amount of intra-group loyalty could have availed to save it." At the same time, the old antilabor conservatism of the Booker T. Washington school eroded as the Negro-labor alliance gained wider support among blacks. Through mid-1935 the Party influenced and drew sustenance from these trends as it continued to shed its notions of prerevolutionary crisis and social fascism.[11]

THE WORKERS' COUNCILS

In April 1934 the National Urban League formed the Workers' Councils to educate and mobilize black workers to battle Jim Crow unions and thus to usher in a "new deal for labor." T. Arnold Hill said the NUL would not abandon its longstanding efforts to win capital's support, but "we can expect little from these sources if the Negro himself is too listless or too uninformed to win labor to his side."[12]

An unusual event occurred in the fall of 1934. Atlanta police raided the southern regional offices of the NUL in a search for "communist literature" — carting away material on the Workers' Councils. Lester B. Granger, now secretary of the organization founded by rich white philanthropists, said that it was no disgrace to be red-baited; Communist-led movements were to be welcomed for spurring new directions:

> The march of black labor is steadily toward the left, away from the counsel of the old-time race leadership and toward an alignment with radical leadership in politics as well as industry. One cannot belittle the effect which the gallant defense of the Scottsboro boys by the ILD is making on the rank-and-file of Negro workers, or the value of . . . radical speakers to Negro audiences. They now speak from the pulpits of churches, where a few years ago they would not have been permitted inside the doors. . . . radical leadership has discovered an intelligent approach to black workers and is finding a sympathetic audience.[13]

By 1935 the Urban League reported forty-two Workers' Councils in seventeen states, embracing over thirty thousand workers. The councils were engaged in educational programs and were working for passage of the Wagner labor bill. The NUL convention in 1935 articulated the new mood of labor partisanship and militant commitment to unionism. Ella Baker of the Harlem Adult Educational Committee, destined for legendary leadership of the freedom movement of the 1960s, debated the venerable Nannie Burroughs on the need for the Urban League to become even more fiercely prolabor. Granger announced that the league was now in full-scale battle with the AFL over its racist policies.[14]

In the same year the Twenty-sixth Conference of the NAACP in St. Louis accepted a revised program written under the direction of Abram L. Harris. It committed the association to "worker's education, a study of the economic history of the race, unionization of black and white labor," and a pledge to "study plans to bring about a government for the benefit of the workers, as well as organization and cooperation of all workers and intellectuals for the immediate improvement of economic conditions." The conference authorized the formation of Workers' Councils in areas beyond the Urban League's reach.[15]

At the same time, blacks observed the maturing conflict between John L. Lewis's Committee on Industrial Organization and the white AFL craft unions. In December 1935 Lester Granger and John P. Davis met with Lewis and his deputy John Brophy (who had resigned from the Committee of Five to protest the rejection of its proposals). They agreed that the member unions of the CIO (still at that point within the AFL) would become vehicles for one last battle against the AFL's craft bureaucracy. However, there was little doubt that the CIO would soon bolt from the AFL to form a new federation. William N. Jones perceived the outlines of a powerful coalition, including the "Lewis group," the Communist Party, and the reenergized Urban League and NAACP, both now committed to a labor movement in which black labor might reap the benefits of unionization.[16]

The Communist Party was initially wary of the Workers' Councils. James Ford perceived little more than a ploy by the NUL to harness black workers to an antiwhite, anti-union program — a reflexive and ill-informed response to an old nemesis. Manning Johnson, reporting on the CP's Negro trade union work in New York, maintained that through the councils the Urban League sought to establish "a mass base for the Negro reformists in practically every big city throuout [sic] the country."[17]

By December 1934 the Party had altered its position and had begun demanding admission to the Workers' Councils of all organizations and trade unions, whether all black or interracial (a prescription for gaining entry for the TUUL unions). The councils were responsive to such demands, but the Party was plagued by the revolutionary unions' nagging organizational inconsistencies. Representatives of those unions rarely showed up. In New York a Party member actually became president of the local council, but he seldom appeared at meetings. Such behavior was fodder for the reformists, who were accusing the reds of joining the New York Workers' Council in order to wreck it. Yet the Party reiterated its new-found belief that the Workers' Councils were of "tremendous importance" in bringing together black organizations to fight for an end to Jim Crow unionism.[18]

THE CIO

Some of the founders of the Congress of Industrial Organizations were not noted for their dedication to racial justice. But black workers were essential to the CIO's prospects. They averaged 17 percent of all semiskilled and unskilled workers in the packinghouse industry, 69 percent of tobacco workers in the tobacco heartland, 9 percent of all coal miners, 8.5 percent of all iron and steel workers. Beyond percentages, black workers were located strategically in the industrial centers of the Midwest and South; they constituted 68 percent of basic iron and steel workers in Alabama.[19]

In late 1935 and early 1936 the upstart industrial unions began to take up the cudgels for racially inclusive unionism. John L. Lewis had sought to crush Communist-led rank-and-file opponents during the coal strikes of the late 1920s, but he understood that the Communists had some of the most dogged and fearless organizers. The revolutionary unions, it turned out, had been a minor league of sorts for the CIO, providing scores of organizers for the most difficult assignments; most of those organizers brought with them an acute sensitivity to the need to win black workers to the new unions.[20]

On the West Coast, Harry Bridges's Longshore Union declared that the color bar on the docks had ended with the union hiring hall; the union would fight any employer who turned away black dockers. The Steel Workers Organizing Committee was determined to enroll black workers, having learned the lessons of the 1919 steel strike in which racial tensions had split the workers and crippled the strike. Henry Johnson, a veteran of the TUUL and later executive secretary of the Chicago chapter of the National Negro Congress, led a successful drive to recruit twenty thousand black steelworkers to the Amalgamated Association of Iron, Steel, and Tin Workers. Johnson also formed a group of fellow black organizers to unionize black packinghouse workers. The United Mine Workers convention in 1936 pledged to fight every manifestation of discrimination in the mining industry. An Alabama mine organizer declared that before the UMW would establish a Jim Crow local, "we won't establish any!" The International Association of Machinists in March 1936 announced that it was extending its jurisdiction to include metal and transport workers, skilled and unskilled—thereby virtually ending its white craft-union status. In the fall of 1936 the CIO launched a major drive to unionize black tobacco workers. Before long, the United Federal Workers of America would form a Committee for the Organization of Negro Employees of the Federal Government, with John P. Davis as assistant chair. The Communists experienced a glow of satisfaction when seventeen workers at the *Amsterdam News* fought a lockout after they joined the fledgling American Newspaper Guild. Party members and supporters came from all over New York in the fall of 1935 to support the locked-out workers of a newspaper that had been a major critic and adversary of the CP.[21]

The Seventh Comintern Congress in the summer of 1935 put the imprimatur of the highest body of world communism upon the popular front. The Party's Negro work would be deeply affected, resulting in the end of the League of Struggle for Negro Rights, the termination of the *Negro Liberator,* the merger of the National Scottsboro-Herndon Action Committee into a new liberal-led Scottsboro Defense Committee, the unification of the Unemployed Councils with other jobless organizations, the absorption of the tenants and small farmers of the Share Croppers' Union into the National Farmers' Union, and the inclusion of agricultural workers of the SCU in the CIO-affiliated United Cannery, Agricultural, Packing, and Allied Workers.[22]

Alabama and the Popular Front

The Extraordinary National Conference in 1933, called to reenergize the Party, heard a report by Al Murphy on the SCU. He recounted the experiences of the union in its first year: the unimaginably hard circumstances of black croppers and farmers, the small victories, the efforts to form alliances with national farmers' organizations, even the clandestine meeting that passed a resolution protesting the arrest of the German Communist leader Ernst Thaelmann. He also acknowledged that "the Negro masses in the Black Belt do not know what the right of self-determination means." But he criticized the Party for not explaining the concept clearly enough. He was convinced that the land hunger of the rural black population would ultimately turn them toward the Party and toward a conscious embrace of self-determination.[23]

In January 1934 the Central Committee criticized the Alabama comrades for not paying sufficient attention to organizing industrial workers. The national leaders insisted that the Party's experience in industry had shown that black and white workers could be unified on the basis of a growing understanding among the whites that racism undermined their own interests. Also, the success of the struggles in the rural areas to build the SCU depended in large measure upon support from workers in the industrial centers. The Party had to be built in the shops, mines, and mills of the steel, coal, machine, and railroad industries. Nat Ross admitted that the CP's trade union activists in the Birmingham area had not raised the Negro question forcefully until the strike wave in the spring of 1934, when they were able to show that NRA wage discrimination against blacks was also passed on to white workers.[24]

When the CIO came to the South, Party shop activists plunged into its member unions. Some of the most effective black Communists became local officers or full-time organizers, especially in the Steel Workers Organizing Committee and the United Mine Workers. Some left the Party with the belief that the labor movement was now a more effective arena as well as a promising opportunity for careers in the labor movement. For a larger number, work in the CIO offered the acceptability, strength, and security that the Party could not provide. Ironically, the arrival of the CIO in Alabama led to a decline in black involvement in the Party as the new federation absorbed black organizers' time and energies.[25]

In mid-1935 Murphy was exhausted from the tension of rural organizing. The Party had continued its criticism of the SCU for its failure to enlist white farmers. Murphy had always made a distinction between short-term, racially separate locals, which would facilitate organizing white farmers, and the fundamental goal of an integrated SCU. "At no time did we suggest separatism" as a guiding doctrine, he claimed. In December 1934 Murphy's desire to be relieved and the Party's desire to quickly cultivate an interracial SCU led to his replacement by Clyde Johnson. Murphy became one of a large and impressive group of black delegates to the Seventh Comintern Congress in Moscow. Whatever his disagreements with what he viewed as the Party's hesitant and unenthusiastic promotion of self-determination, he lived his final years in Charleston, Missouri, and until his death in 1977 remained a staunch defender of the Party and its record on black liberation.[26]

When Clyde Johnson took over as SCU secretary, he discovered a robust organization despite acute repression. The Bankhead Cotton Control Act had legislated mandatory acreage reductions, which resulted in large-scale removal of tenants and ensuing starvation conditions. The SCU dealt with this crisis by fighting evictions and turning its attention to the federal government. It agitated as best it could for fair representation of croppers and tenants on AAA committees and for direct payment of checks to tenants in compensation for reduced production.[27]

An SCU cotton pickers' strike in the spring of 1934 had been weakened by word from government relief agencies that pickers risked losing federal assistance if they refused to work. Landlords launched a campaign of terror — robbing cabins, arresting strikers, and getting them sentenced to heavy fines and long prison sentences on trumped-up charges. When Johnson took over, he executed Murphy's plan for a larger follow-up strike of cotton choppers to demand a daily wage of one dollar. The choppers won most of their objectives where the union had strength (Tallapoosa, Lee, and Chambers Counties). But in Lowndes, Montgomery, and Dallas Counties, landlords and local police answered the strikers with night rides, kidnappings, beatings, abandonment in dark woods, and murder. The disappearance of John "Willie" Foster; the murder of Joe Spinner Johnson; the beatings of Saul Davis, Robert Washington, Boris Israel, and Henry "Red" Johnson; the arrests of sixteen strikers in Dallas County alone: All were stark testament to the extent of repression. Remarkably, some partial victories boosted the union's membership to nearly ten thousand by the summer of 1935.[28]

With the popular front now enshrined, the SCU sought to fortify itself against the violence by joining with broader forces. The most likely candidate for merger was the Southern Tenant Farmers' Union, which had been formed in Arkansas in 1934 by Socialists Henry Clay East and H. L. Mitchell. But the STFU, itself a fragile coalition, avoided ideology, particularly notions of class warfare. It also had a paternalistic attitude toward its black members. Nevertheless, in November 1934 the SCU proposed to Mitchell that the two organizations unite to promote the Party-sponsored Farmers' Emergency Relief Bill to ban evictions, end the AAA, and institute a farmer-controlled relief plan. In December 1934 Socialists and Communists joined to sponsor an All-Southern Conference for Civil and Trade Union Rights in Chattanooga which included the SCU, STFU, the Highlander Folk School, and union, community, and religious organizations. At the JCNR's Howard University conference in May 1935, representatives of the SCU and the STFU again met to discuss unity and possible merger.[29]

Although they felt the pressure to talk, STFU leaders could not shed their suspicions of Communists. Moreover, the STFU was a predominantly white organization with little regard for the leadership of blacks. Mitchell could not conceive that the overwhelmingly black SCU was capable of developing and sustaining its own activists; it had to be the Communist Party in disguise. A visit by Mitchell to the area around Montgomery in the summer of 1935 yielded "no evidence of any sort of organization among the sharecroppers." It evidently never occurred to him that local blacks would be reluctant to talk about the union with a strange white man. He went away still believing that the Share Croppers' Union was indistinguishable from the Party and unwilling to amalgamate with the CP. Mitchell dismissed Johnson's courage and concern for security as self-caricature: Johnson "moved around very dramatically... unnaturally you know"; he was "to [sic] much the actor, always dramatizing himself, the leader, who goes on wild organizing sprees gets shot at and so on." Although the STFU board favored a merger, Mitchell successfully froze the project.[30]

Despite the disappointment, the SCU decided to go ahead with a large-scale cotton pickers' walkout to demand one dollar per hundred pounds of picked cotton, a moratorium on evictions, and wage equality. Johnson and his comrades did as best they could in the absence of merger with the STFU to get financial help from the AFL and the STFU (little was forthcoming). They pressured federal authorities not to use relief workers to break the strike.[31]

J. A. Bell awoke on August 19, 1935, to discover that no one was working his cotton field. He contacted Haynesville sheriff R. E. Woodruff, who demanded that SCU organizer Willie Witcher call off the strike. When Witcher declined, the sheriff shot him and then threw him into jail with untreated wounds. Simon Lacy, a Bell striker, was whipped viciously as deputies sought to extract the names of union members. Reverend G. Smith Watkins, a preacher and SCU activist, was captured by the vigilantes, who ripped open his stomach, filled his body with bullets, and threw it into a swamp near Fort Deposit. Woodruff rounded up deputies and landlords to raid the homes of six workers, whom they beat into unconsciousness. On August 22 the vigilantes shot and wounded SCU member Jim Press Meriwether, questioned him for hours, and then riddled him with more bullets, claiming that he was shot "while trying to escape." His wife Annie Mae was in her brother-in-law's home when the vigilantes broke in. They stripped her, beat her, and hanged her two feet off the floor from a wooden beam until eventually they released her unconscious. On September 2 a mob led by Deputy Sheriff Ed Arant of Fort Deposit broke into the home in Hope Hull of Ed Bracy, the leading local SCU activist, shooting him nineteen times. The toll from the two cotton strikes was at least four SCU leaders killed, scores arrested and beaten, and an uncounted number of striking croppers who hid in the woods and were possibly murdered. No indictments were ever forthcoming, despite formal protests by a delegation to Washington led by Clyde Johnson and Annie Mae Meriwether.[32]

The strike registered gains in Tallapoosa and Lee Counties, where union workers on several plantations won from seventy-five cents to one dollar per hundred pounds of cotton. However, the violence in Lowndes County virtually crushed the walkout there, forcing union members back to plantations for a pittance.[33]

At the same time, the SCU's reputation was spreading beyond Alabama and into Louisiana where membership was growing—suggesting the need for a strong regional organization capable of effective coalition politics to win concessions from a somewhat more responsive New Deal government. It was time for the SCU to shed its armed, underground status and emerge into daylight as part of a legitimate farm labor union. The Party's farm theoretician, Lem Harris, noted that the left-wing rank-and-file was gaining strength in the National Farmers' Union, an organization representing small and middle-sized farms. Attention had to be paid. Clyde Johnson built a solid relationship with the heads of the Alabama Farmers' Union, among whose ranks were many farm families with roots in the mines and mills, and who brought a trade union culture to the AFU. The prospect for merger of the AFU and SCU seemed promising.[34]

Johnson argued successfully with the Party's Central Committee that the NFU was the preferred route for rural radicalism. The first national convention of the SCU, held in New Orleans in 1936, endorsed a merger with the NFU; the Alabama affiliate of the NFU voted enthusiastically to support merger with the Share Croppers' Union. The entry of black small-scale farmers and tenants into an all-white organization moved its political dynamic to the left; the AFU adopted a civil rights plank and a program to define and systematize the economic relationships between tenants and landlords.[35]

A major problem remained: Technological changes wrought by the mechanical cotton picker and the government's agricultural policies had reduced large numbers of small-scale farmers and tenants to agricultural wage laborers. Farm laborers needed to be in an agricultural wage laborers' union. In 1936 the wage workers were released from the AFU and absorbed into the AFL-chartered Farm Laborers and Cotton Field Workers Union. When the CIO formally split from the AFL, the wage workers transferred to the CIO's

UCAPAWA, under the leadership of Donald Henderson. UCAPAWA struggled on with little support from the CIO, principally fighting for Farm Security Administration loans to tenants and launching initiatives to secure voting rights. Meanwhile, under left-wing leadership, the Alabama Farmers' Union became a robust defender of labor and civil rights. The UCAPAWA, on the other hand, was virtually extinct in Alabama by 1940, a victim of changing economic and social conditions, as well as of the marginal support of the CIO and AFU.[36]

The SCU did not perish because a rural revolutionary movement was sacrificed to the exigencies of the popular front. Nor was the Party's decision in November 1935 to strip self-determination of its organizational and agitational aspects a major factor. Rather, SCU's demise was foretold by economic and social changes in rural agriculture and by increased migration to jobs in the North as war loomed. Those changes were pushing sharecropping and tenantry to the edge of extinction — breaking up any vestige of a homogeneous Black Belt rural economy upon which self-determination was based. The growing phenomenon of agricultural wage labor heightened the need for ties with the CIO and the building of a political force with clout far beyond the Party's. The SCU's two-pronged merger with the AFU and the UCAPAWA was seen as a way to better defend its members against the truculence and brutality of the landlords. However, there was no serious discussion about maintaining the rural base of the SCU as a political, social, and cultural organization — flexible enough to have its members participate in the AFU and the agricultural workers' union, cohesive enough to maintain a radical and independent home for the croppers and tenants who were not fully satisfied with their new organizations.[37]

THE HERNDON AND SCOTTSBORO CASES

In September 1934 the Georgia Supreme Court rejected Angelo Herndon's appeal of his long sentence. On May 20, 1935, Whitney North Seymour, who had served in the solicitor general's office, argued Herndon's appeal before the U.S. Supreme Court. The Court said that it lacked jurisdiction because Herndon had failed to raise the First Amendment issue at the earliest opportunity; the core constitutional issue was thus dodged on a technicality. The ILD launched a campaign to obtain 2 million signatures on petitions for Herndon's freedom — while he toured the country with a replica of the standard cage used to house chain gang prisoners. In September six liberal and left groups formed the Joint Committee to Aid the Herndon Defense. On October 14 the Supreme

Court denied Herndon's request for a rehearing; with the Party's new willingness to play by the legal rules, Herndon prepared to return to prison. An influential group of liberals worked feverishly for executive clemency, but to no avail. On the eve of Herndon's departure for Georgia, the Joint Committee sponsored a rally at New York's Metropolitan Opera House, at which twenty-five hundred people raised their clenched fists and pledged not to rest until Herndon was free. On November 12 at the Fulton County Courthouse, Judge Hugh M. Dorsey heard a challenge to the insurrection statute through a petition for a writ of habeas corpus. Three weeks later, to nearly everyone's surprise, the judge ruled the statute to be unconstitutional. He released Herndon on reduced bail and gave the state twenty days to appeal.[38]

In mid-1936 the Georgia Supreme Court reversed Judge Dorsey's decision. This triggered outrage from a vastly strengthened labor movement, from liberals, and from a growing left. The AFL called for the law's repeal and for Herndon's release; the NAACP moved closer to committing itself fully to the Herndon defense movement; legal, fraternal, and community organizations joined the chorus demanding freedom for Herndon. The ILD, always intrepid, kept up the pressure through its patented mass actions. In early 1937 Herndon joined six youth leaders of the American Youth Congress for a brief meeting with Franklin D. Roosevelt. The president asked each delegate to offer an opinion of his plan to reorganize the Supreme Court. Herndon responded that it depended on how the Court would decide his case. "I am Angelo Herndon," he told the puzzled president.[39]

Later the Supreme Court, on a vote of five to four, threw out Herndon's conviction. A five-year struggle that had raised an obscure youth to a symbol for millions of aspirations for constitutional rights for black liberation was finally won.[40]

The Supreme Court also took action in the Scottsboro case. On April 1, 1935, the Court invalidated Clarence Norris's conviction, also effectively nullifying Patterson's conviction, on grounds of the systematic barring of blacks from grand and petit juries in Jackson County, Alabama. Communist leaders hailed the decision as a confirmation of the might of mass pressure; Leibowitz interpreted it as a "triumph for American justice." The Patterson and Norris cases were remanded to Alabama for further action — or no action. In November the Jackson County grand jury, with one black man on it, reindicted the defendants.[41]

In the meantime, the politics of the Scottsboro defense was changing dramatically. Robert Minor, acting at the behest of the Party's political bureau, telephoned Walter White, with whom he was personally cordial, to suggest that if White drafted a call for united action in the Scottsboro case, the Party would support it "in toto." The Communists were persuaded that Alabama would find a black grand juror, reindict the boys, and again sentence them to death. With legal and financial exhaustion looming, unity was required. White replied that Minor's confidence was at variance with past Communist practices; further, the NAACP board had specified only raising funds for the defense, and the secretary had no authority to exceed that limit. The prominent attorney Morris Ernst met with White to tell him that he too had been approached by "influential but unpublicized" Communists to form a united front. Ernst had already asked the Garland Fund for $5,000 to be expended on the case by a new group in an entirely ethical manner (so as not repeat the alleged bribery problems of the previous year). He strongly supported a united front "if fascism is to be checked in the United States." White expressed his distrust of the Communists and their "sabotage attacks, lying, and other tactics of that sort." Ernst persisted. White agreed to call a meeting of Norman Thomas, Minor, George Haynes, Roy Wilkins, Charles Houston and others "as individuals" to "explore the possibilities of effective action for the defense."[42]

The meeting took place in Ernst's office on October 9, 1935. Minor chose to ignore the charges that the Party had squandered Scottsboro funds on "propaganda." He stressed the need for every organization to commit fully to a detailed agreement covering the disbursement of funds, the hiring of lawyers, and the conduct of the case. That, Minor said, was the bedrock of mutual trust. The Communists were prepared to go forward, if need be, with their two-pronged legal defense and mass action. That would probably mean a continuing tug-of-war for control of the case, a herculean effort to find new grounds for anticipated appeals, and a painful new round of fund raising. These were strong reasons for pursuing a united front. But, above all, the CP was now deeply committed to the concept and practice of unity of all democratic forces. So much so, that it was prepared to commit to organizing principles that would effectively push it into the background.[43]

On December 19, 1936, the NAACP, ILD, ACLU, League for Industrial Democracy, and Methodist Federation for Social Service formed the Scottsboro Defense Committee, replacing the other Scottsboro coalitions. Thirty-eight-year-old Allan Knight Chalmers, pastor of the Broadway Tabernacle Congregational Church in New York, was selected to chair the new committee. Liberals were now in the forefront of the effort to free the Scottsboro boys.[44]

The fourth trial of Haywood Patterson ended in a fourth conviction. However, the young jury foreman held out for seventy-five years' imprisonment instead of the death penalty. He was convinced that the white boys started the fight because "a nigger's gonna stay in his place as long as you leave him alone." In July 1937 Clarence Norris was convicted for the third time and sentenced to death. The Scottsboro Defense Committee had promoted mass meetings around the country, but the cries of "they shall not die!" faded as Chalmers shifted to back-door maneuvering with southern "moderates" and Alabama officials. That frustrating exercise at least did not reverse Alabama's fading passion for execution. In July 1937 Andy Wright was convicted for the second time and sentenced to ninety-five years; Charlie Weems was convicted and sentenced to seventy-five years; Ozie Powell pleaded guilty to assaulting a sheriff and got twenty years. Alabama sought to finally end the sullying of its name around the world by dropping charges against Olen Montgomery, Willie Roberson, Eugene Williams, and Roy Wright. Governor Bibb Graves in 1938 commuted Norris's sentence to life imprisonment. The pardons process dragged on for years. Clarence Norris, the last of the remaining prisoners, was released in 1976.[45]

Earl Browder addressed the Seventh Comintern Congress in August 1935. It was a moment for pride. He announced that in five years, the Party's black membership had grown from fewer than a hundred to more than twenty-five hundred. The campaigns for Scottsboro and Herndon, he said, had now reached into every corner of the globe and had roused millions to the struggle for Negro rights.[46]

The impact of the Scottsboro and Herndon cases on the struggle for racial justice and on the nation's history was profound. The cases ended in victory for the right to legal representation, the right to be tried by a jury of one's peers, equal protection of the laws, and free speech. The movement to free the Scottsboro boys and Herndon achieved far more than survival for the defendants, as remarkable as that was. It bared the inner rot of racism that pervaded the nation's institutions; it raised the issues of freedom and justice to a new plateau; it sparked the black community's inherent resistance to injustice. In the darkest of times, it linked the fortunes of every American to black liberation, and in many ways helped set the stage for the next wave of struggle for racial equality in the postwar years. For all the pettiness, cynicism, manipulation, and self-serving behavior attributed to the Communists, their efforts left an indelible signpost on the long road to freedom.

A National Negro Congress

The vision of uniting black organizations into a single federation went back to Cyril Briggs's concept of a World Negro Congress and the Comintern's vision of a mighty global gathering of all the forces for Negro liberation. It echoed in the ANLC's aspiration to unite the black working class as a basis for broader cooperation among African Americans. The National Negro Congress, which was launched in Chicago in February 1936, was the capstone of the Party's growing determination to seek united action. That determination had been manifested in March 1933, when the CP appealed to the Socialists and the AFL for a unified campaign to free the Scottsboro boys. In early 1934 discussions had begun in the Party's Negro Commission (combined with the Harlem Section Committee) concerning the LSNR's inability to unite black mass organizations around a minimum program.[47]

Those discussions concluded that the disparate programs of the major Negro organizations — the NAACP, the NUL, the Garvey movement, the churches and fraternities — had been unable to meet the Depression's exigencies. However, masses of blacks remained in those movements; it was possible, according to James Ford, to "utilize these organizations and bring them into a program around the immediate demands of the Negro people." In a prearranged move, Ford spoke of the need for a National Negro Congress in a debate with Frank Crosswaith in January 1935. The JCNR's Washington, D.C., conference on the economic status of the Negro under the New Deal was envisioned as a starting point. Party representatives met with John P. Davis to explore ways to advance the idea of a congress at the Washington meeting. Davis had also been developing the idea after his participation in the Unemployment and Social Insurance Congress in early 1935. Invitations to the Washington conference were designed to assure the involvement of workers, sharecroppers, students, intellectuals, New Deal officials, and representatives of black mass organizations.

The conference, held on May 18, 1935, was perhaps the largest gathering of black leaders and white supporters to date. Du Bois jousted with sharecroppers over the question of violence; New Dealers pressed the merits of government programs; middle-class participants observed at close quarters the rising voice of working-class blacks; everyone debated overarching strategies for progress and freedom. Ford, claiming that the Communists sought to avoid "mechanically dominating" the conference, allotted himself only five minutes to address the meeting. After the two hundred fifty conferees from twenty-two organizations heard grim reports of the catastrophic conditions of blacks, of the intractable racism of the AFL, and of the negative consequences of the NRA, a consensus arose: An initiating committee of sixty people, including A. Philip Randolph, Sterling Brown, Nannie Burroughs, Reverend Thomas Harten, Charles Houston, Reverend W. H. Jernagin, and others, was approved to call a National Negro Congress. John P. Davis was to be the organizer. Among other things, this spelled an end to the JCNR.[48]

Organizing began. Five hundred black leaders around the country received copies of an article by Davis on the proposed Congress, published in the May 1935 issue of *Crisis*. A major push was on to enlist unions, farmers' organizations, churches, lodges, student and youth groups, nationalists, Socialists, Communists, even representatives from the Democratic and Republican Parties. Endorsements from newspapers, religious leaders, and black fraternities and sororities began to flow into Davis's office. Many blacks with conservative views shrugged off red baiting and willingly joined with radicals to form the Congress — as long as no political organization dominated it. Kelly Miller said that this was the one time he could agree with the Communist Party.

Not everything went smoothly. The Urban League was divided on the Congress, and the NAACP was lukewarm. Abram Harris, politically inclined toward Trotskyism, was opposed to a congress that included churches and fraternities; the churchman J. E. Dorsey did not want J. Finley Wilson and his black Elks in the new alliance, while Ford believed that Wilson's endorsement would open the door to the Elks' rank and file.

The CP's priority of building a working-class foundation for the congress was to be achieved by forming a Negro Labor Conference within the initiating committee to galvanize working-class support. The question of white participation in the congress was never mentioned in the meetings of the Negro Commission during the months preceding the congress. It was assumed throughout that it would be a multiracial organization under black leadership, working to build a Negro-labor alliance and advance civil rights on a wide front. That perspective assumed that whites would be invited to participate.

The program of the Congress, Ford said, should be based on minimum standards (perhaps a new, expanded bill of rights to expound economic rights and reflect the gathering's devotion to the nation's democratic traditions): the right of blacks to decent jobs, decent wages, and union membership; relief and security for every Negro family; assistance to tenants and sharecroppers; an end to lynching and police brutality; educational and work opportunities for youth; equality for women, including equal pay for equal work and the right to organize as consumers; opposition to war and fascism. Those issues would reflect the NNC's three-pronged foundation: a labor-Negro alliance, a broad front of struggle for civil rights, and internationalist solidarity with antifascism.[49]

What of the future of the LSNR? It could only be expected to do its best to garner support for the congress. Ben Davis pleaded that the league was now broader than many other predominantly black organizations. However, he acknowledged that if the congress proved to be an effective coalition, the LSNR could be absorbed into it.[50]

As in its earlier quarrels with Cyril Briggs and Richard B. Moore, the Party acted hastily to dissolve the *Negro Liberator* and mute the creative tension between national consciousness and working-class solidarity. But the NNC would register remarkable gains in consolidating the black-labor alliance, in cultivating a new generation of militant black youth, and in advancing the struggle for civil rights.[51]

On November 18, 1935, John P. Davis walked into the citadel of the Party's Negro policies—the Central Committee's Negro Commission. The language and content of his report to that body suggest that he had been a CP member for longer than generally believed. Davis began with a greeting to "Comrade Chairman and Comrades." He characterized the building of a broad NNC as "a paramount task of the Party." The project was a step toward carrying out the Seventh World Congress's decision to build a united front against war and fascism. Davis took on the issue of Communist control of the congress: "We are not afraid of 'control' of it. It is not a matter of maneuvering and getting Communists in as officers...but to do real Bolshevik work to bring these broadest groups of Negro people, white and Negro intellectuals, etc. in this mass movement for Negro rights in this country." Davis was offering an interesting formulation that might have seemed contradictory in any other period than the popular front: The Party would "control" the NNC to guarantee its breadth and democratic character.[52]

Davis confirmed that in March 1935, after consultation with Party leaders, plans had been made to use the JCNR economic conference as a springboard for the NNC. From that point, support for the movement had spread through women's clubs, the Elks, and church groups. An October tour by Davis had solidified large sponsoring committees in Chicago and Detroit that were endorsed by well-attended public meetings. With such an outpouring of the petty-bourgeois stratum, Davis said, the Party "could only be sure that we can control the Congress if truly proletarian elements are represented." That would happen not by a coup d'état, but by hard work at the grassroots—not by capturing offices, but by providing leadership. After reviewing progress among women, youth, trade unionists, and small-town residents, Davis turned his attention to the thorny question of the "open" participation of Communists in the congress. He took a hard line, insisting that "we must change sectarian timidity into bolshevik boldness"; "liberal front[s]" were not needed to approach liberals. He agreed that the great effort being undertaken required the involvement of people who were not labeled as reds, but stated that it was "equally important to begin now in the name of the Party" to build the congress.[53]

The National Negro Congress convened in Chicago on February 14–16, 1936. Over 800 delegates from 551 organizations representing over 3 million people attended. A. Philip Randolph was elected president; Marian Cuthbert, treasurer; and John P. Davis, national secretary. At the same time, the Communist Party's standing and acceptance among African Americans of all classes had reached unprecedented heights.

The Legacy

The NNC was a culmination of the labors of Communists and their allies to win a base in the black community and to forge an alliance between African Americans and the working-class movement. The proceedings echoed and filtered a range of thought and experience over two tumultuous decades: Cyril Briggs's pioneering search for a merger of nationalism and socialism; Robert Minor's troubled musings on the vast chasm between blacks and whites that had produced Garvey's movement; the painful birth and short, troubled life of the American Negro Labor Congress; the pivotal debate on the Negro question at the Sixth Comintern Congress; the searing and relentless struggles in the streets, factories, and farms in the 1930s to eradicate racial injustice, shatter the racial divide, and win the nation's working-class majority to the cause of equality.

By 1936 a profound change in racial thinking had taken place among significant sectors of American life. For the hundreds of blacks and whites who gathered in Chicago—and for the millions whom they represented—the quest for racial justice had become an integral part of struggle for economic, political, and social progress. Not since the founding of the NAACP had the Negro question become such an essential element of a broad progressive agenda. Many currents that flowed into the congress fully accepted the belief that racial oppression had been a function of the nation's economic and social system, that it had facilitated immense capital accumulation through superexploitation of black labor, and that it had been used to foment deadly antagonism within the nation's work force. Thus, the generative force of antiracist struggle was a belief that the elimination of discrimination was a preeminent self-interest for labor and its allies and a vital catalyst for wide-ranging political change.

The Communists had little use for discussions about "race" and "race relations," where fundamental issues of social structure and power were reduced to equal responsibility, pleas for reciprocal tolerance, and bogus "color-blindness." In the Communist view, all that obfuscated the reality of racial and national oppression and led to immersion in a quagmire of sentimentality and evasion. The racial divide was not sustained fundamentally by mutual misunderstanding and cultural estrangement. Rather, it was supported by the white chauvinism that held back progress and had to be fought with unprecedented vigor.

Communists stridently rejected—within their own ranks and within the larger society—stress upon ghetto pathology and the alleged need for blacks to modify their behavior. Whites who carped upon African American deficiencies were seen as derogating the reality of special oppression and justifying the myth of black inferiority. The inner dynamics of black life, in the Communist view, were generally shaped both by oppression from the larger society and by the growing assertiveness of the black community's working-class majority. National oppression had nurtured an identifiable culture of resistance; blacks were seen not as passive victims, but as active participants in seeking their own liberation. While a majority of the larger society embraced images of black docility, venality, and ignorance, the Party pressed the view that black aspirations and struggles constituted a supremely valuable and indispensable source of support for social change.

The path to reconciliation, cooperation, and unity among the dispossessed of both races had to be cleared by hard, relentless battle in the real world of institutional racism. Scottsboro became the most dramatic example of wide-ranging combat against legal inequality. The fight for access to jobs, union membership, adequate relief, an end to evictions, decent health care, and the rights of sharecroppers and tenants constituted the inescapable core responsibility of Communists and the movements they influenced. Achievement of those goals would bring greater security to all sectors of the working population and cultivate greater interracial understanding and cooperation.

By 1936 the concept of Black Belt self-determination had become little more than an echo of the departed Third Period. What remained, however, was substantial and had promise for at least mitigating the old contradiction between separation and assimilation. With the popular front, the notion of black solidarity as a foundation for alliances with whites was actually somewhat strengthened by growing Communist support for all-class African American unity. In turn, that unity, nurtured by common historic experience, would permit blacks to enter into alliances with whites based upon their own choices and without the sacrifice of identity and self-definition. The struggle for liberation would then break out of the narrow separatist ideology with its cramped ghetto prospects and its isolation from the economic and social mainstream. At the point where race, class, and nationality converged in the larger arena of politics and industry, blacks would join their white allies in battle for a just share of the truly significant wealth and power that undergirded the nation. At the same time, progressive whites would be obliged to demonstrate their trustworthiness by resolutely working for equality and liberation. Those concepts, though not always applied consistently and unwaveringly by the Communists, remain vital and worthy of exploration.

The Communists and non-Party Marxists made important contributions to extending the reach of African American culture, both within black communities and in the nation as a whole. At times black culture was promoted by the left with a mechanical imposition of self-defined proletarian standards (thereby weakening the organic character of black art). But the Communists and their allies worked to advance African American culture shorn of the intrusive, racist influence of the dominant commercial cultural market. Whatever the discordant and unpersuasive notes struck by metallic themes borrowed from dogma, the convergence of the Marxist sensibility with black literature, painting, and drama opened the door to exploration of neglected and suppressed experiences of black militancy and resistance. There is no credible evidence that "European" Marxism hijacked black culture. Whatever the problems, the rich radical cultural life of the 1930s helped build a larger arena for authentic black art and influenced broader liberal currents.

The Communists never won a decisive and steadfast white working-class majority to support black liberation. They were not always successful in balancing the need to take special steps to advance black labor with the need to sustain the support of white labor. That, along with their relative powerlessness and their pariah status, explains why they were not able to convince a black majority to fully embrace their revolutionary vision. However, the basic strategy that was always implicit in the Communist position on the Negro question did largely materialize: the establishment of a substantial Negro-labor alliance that would become the cornerstone of the struggle for progress and against reaction in coming years — and to this day.

In 1940 the National Negro Congress was shaken when the Communists and some of their allies sought to make it "the broad expression of anti-war and anti-imperialist struggle," in line with the shift of policy ushered in by the Nazi-Soviet nonaggression pact. Clinging to their cooperation with the increasingly anti-Roosevelt and isolationist John L. Lewis, the Communists also seemed to be violating the NNC's nonpartisanship by reacting warmly to Lewis's call for an alliance between the congress and the labor movement to create a new political force. A. Philip Randolph, always protective of his establishment ties and adept at making use of nationalism to checkmate the Communists, accused them of scuttling the "racial integrity" of the NNC in the interests of a higher allegiance to the Soviets (and now also to the CIO). Randolph, dreading what he perceived to be a dangerously sectarian turn in the NNC, embraced a quasi-nationalist agenda, excoriated the Communists for being "fundamentally [un]concerned about the Negro," and withdrew from the presidency of the congress. The old issues that in the past had hindered Communist aspirations in the black community had not gone away.[54]

Events marched on. The entry of African American workers into the shops and factories of the North accelerated with World War II, ushering in the dynamic growth of postwar black participation in the labor movement. The ideological imperatives of the war against fascism broadened the movement for racial equality, and the Cold War, with its ideological competition, obliged the government and society to be responsive to the demands of the growing civil rights movement. But that often came at the price of relentless red baiting, aimed in part at holding the movement within the Cold War's ideological and political poles. Through the late 1930s and 1940s commitment to racial justice had spread from the Communists to the liberal mainstream. But with the Cold War hovering, liberals sought to cut the radical heart out of the struggle that unfolded in the 1950s. "Integration" into a political order that would only trim the outer edges of racism without attacking its inner institutional core or its global ramifications often became the price of liberal support for civil rights. Martin Luther King saw a part of his liberal patronage evaporate after he spoke out against the Vietnam War and sought to galvanize the impoverished of all races with his Poor People's March. In reaction to liberal backsliding, part of a new generation of militant young blacks veered toward separatist solutions. That development reflected in part the diminution of radical influences that might have offered a third way, through a two-part program built on black self-determination combined with broader interracial alliances.

The connection between the events of the 1930s and the movement of the 1960s, however, was not severed. When two young white researchers appeared at Ned Cobb's door in 1969 to learn more about the Share Croppers' Union, Cobb knew immediately who they were. He had seen many who looked like them on television — working on voter registration, marching from Selma to Montgomery, riding the freedom buses. "This was his movement and he knew a lot about it; he had been active in it before we were born. Raising his right hand to God, he swore there was no 'get-back' in him: he was standing where he stood in '32."[55]

Today, despite the impressive growth of the African American middle class, institutional racism remains a tenacious factor in American society. It is underscored repeatedly by statistical comparisons between blacks and whites. From infant mortality to the impoverishment of children to disparities in employment, health care, housing, net financial assets, and prison populations, the oppressive effects of discrimination against African Americans are manifest and continue to constitute the foundation for all forms of racial, ethnic, and national discrimination.

The global economy and the accompanying restructuring of production in the United States has had a particularly devastating impact upon African American youth. The global "race to the bottom" in search of cheap labor, combined with the dismantling of the old industries, has left black youth, among many others, at the lowest rungs of nonunion employment — serving food, pumping gas, washing dishes — or entirely out of the labor market, often left to survive in an insulated shadow economy beyond the law. That isolation has engendered among many black working-class youth a discontinuity with the political consciousness that swept over much of black America from the 1930s through the struggles of the 1960s and beyond. Such a situation only deepens the need to make known the historical record of the 1930s and lay it before new generations.

The long road to freedom of African Americans today is dotted with literally thousands of initiatives to combat the consequences of racism and discrimination. And within the marrow of that continuing struggle is the legacy of the interface of blacks and reds in the 1930s: the scores killed and wounded in anti-eviction protests, strikes, and demonstrations; the "disappeared" sharecroppers; the struggles to build an interracial foundation for a new labor movement; the campaigns for justice from the courts. Of greatest importance, perhaps, is the living legacy of black women and men who seized upon the proffer from the left to act upon their own militant instincts, to build their own organizations, and to solidify the democratic content of their struggles, which ultimately depended upon their own resources and upon the initiatives of ordinary working people.

Whatever the short-term advantages of privilege derived by whites from discrimination, the Communists' case for the long-term fatal damage of racial injustice to white working-class interests still resonates. The existence of a low-wage (or no-wage) population at the bottom rungs of the economic ladder creates a downward pull on the economic fortunes of all workers at a time of dissolving industrial jobs and lingering wage stagnation. The siren song of racial resentment is played, often deafeningly, by conservatives to gain political advantage, which they then use to broadly undermine progressive values. The division of working people and the poor along racial lines continues to be the most serious barrier to a resurgent movement for a more equitable and democratic distribution of wealth and power.

We are left, finally, with two images that symbolize the passionate beliefs that constitute the heart of this story. One is the image of Rose Chernin as she was interviewed by the author in a nearly bare office in Los Angeles in 1973. Small, pencil-thin, with large glowing eyes, she relived, with a rare fusion of serenity and fire, that moment in 1932 when a Party leader warned that white Communists were only "treading water" without the Negro people and must be ready to sacrifice their lives if necessary to build solidarity. The other image is of Claude Lightfoot, sitting in a small house in the shadow of a closed steel plant in Gary, Indiana, in 1974. He told of the legendary black organizer Henry Johnson, who faced a hostile crowd of white packinghouse workers in Amarillo, Texas, in the mid-1930s. Johnson pressed on, talking union. Lightfoot lowered his voice to capture the drama of Johnson's final gambit: Over and over the organizer intoned, food on the table for black babies and white babies, black babies and white babies, black babies and white babies. Lightfoot's admiring laugh expressed his undying awe at an organizer's skills and perhaps reflected his own wonder about the multitude of struggles that had been fought on a long, and continuing, journey to liberation. The fight was not over — and the craving and the cry for unity were not extinguished.

Abbreviations

AAA	Agricultural Adjustment Act
ABB	African Blood Brotherhood
ACLU	American Civil Liberties Union
AFL	American Federation of Labor
AFU	Alabama Farmers' Union
ANLC	American Negro Labor Congress
CBP	Claude Barnett Papers, Chicago Historical Society
CEC	Central Executive Committee (CP)
CFL	Chicago Federation of Labor
CFWU	Croppers' and Farm Workers' Union
CHS	Chicago Historical Society
CI	Communist International (Comintern or Third International)
CIC	Commission on Interracial Cooperation
CIO	Congress of Industrial Organizations
CMA	Colored Merchants Association
Comintern	Communist International (CI, or Third International)
CP	Communist Party, USA
CWA	Civil Works Administration
DJ-FBI	Department of Justice — Federal Bureau of Investigation

DW	*Daily Worker*
ECCI	Executive Committee Communist International
FLCFWU	Farm Laborers and Cotton Field Workers Union
HKP	Henry Kraus Papers, Archive of Labor History and Urban Affairs, WSU
HL	*Harlem Liberator*
ILA	International Longshoremen's Association
ILD	International Labor Defense
Inprecorr	*International Press Correspondence* (CI)
ITUCNW	International Trade Union Committee of Negro Workers
IWO	International Workers Order
IWW	Industrial Workers of the World
JCNR	Joint Committee on National Recovery
KKK	Ku Klux Klan
KUTV	University of the Toilers of the East, Moscow
LAI	League against Imperialism and for National Independence
LC	Library of Congress, Washington, D.C.
LD	*Labor Defender*
LSNR	League of Struggle for Negro Rights
LU	*Labor Unity*
MHVP	Mary Heaton Vorse Papers, Archive of Labor History and Urban Affairs, WSU
NA	National Archives, Washington, D.C.
NAACP	National Association for the Advancement of Colored People
NAACP Papers	Papers of the NAACP, LC
NERL	National Equal Rights League
NFU	National Farmers' Union
NIRA	National Industrial Recovery Act
NL	*Negro Liberator*
NM	*New Masses*
NMU	National Miners Union
NNC	National Negro Congress
NPT	Negro People's Theater
NR	*New Republic*
NRA	National Recovery Act

NTWIU	Needle Trades Workers' Industrial Union
NTWU	National Textile Workers Union
NUL	National Urban League
NYPL	New York Public Library
NYT	*New York Times*
NYU	New York University
OHAL	Oral History of the American Left, Tamiment Institute, Bobst Library, NYU
PolCom	Political Committee (Communist Party)
Profintern	Red International of Labor Unions (RILU)
RILU	Red International of Labor Unions (also called Profintern)
RKC	Robert Kaufman Collection, Tamiment Institute, Bobst Library, NYU
RMP	Robert Minor Papers, Butler Library, Columbia University, New York
RTsKhIDNI	Russian Center for the Preservation and Study of Documents of Contemporary History, Moscow
RTsKhIDNI 495	Fond for Executive Committee of the Communist International, RTsKhIDNI
RTsKhIDNI 515	Fond for the Communist Party USA, RTsKhIDNI
RTsKhIDNI 534	Fond for the Red International of Labor Unions (also Profintern), RTsKhIDNI
SACP	South African Communist Party
SCRL	Southern California Research Library, Los Angeles
SCU	Share Croppers' Union
SLC	Stockyards Labor Council
STFU	Southern Tenant Farmers' Union
STFU Papers	Papers of the STFU, Southern Historical Collection, University of North Carolina, Chapel Hill
SWOC	Steel Workers Organizing Committee
TC	*The Crusader*
TDC	Theodore Draper Collection, Woodruff Library, Emory University, Atlanta
TL	*The Liberator*
TUCONW	Trade Union Committee for Organizing Negro Workers
TUEL	Trade Union Educational League

TUUL	Trade Union Unity League
UCs	Unemployed Councils
UCAPAWA	United Cannery, Agricultural, Packing and Allied Workers of America
UCP	United Communist Party
UMW	United Mine Workers
UNIA	Universal Negro Improvement Association
WESL	Workers' Ex-Servicemen's League
WP	Workers Party (USA)
WPA	Works Progress Administration
WSU	Wayne State University, Detroit
YCI	Young Communist International
YCL	Young Communist League

Notes

INTRODUCTION

1. For example, Stephan and Abigail Thernstrom, *America in Black and White: One Nation, Indivisible* (New York, 1997).

2. "The American Negro problem is a problem in the heart of the American. It is there that the interracial tension has its focus. It is there that the decisive struggle goes on" (Gunnar Myrdal, *An American Dilemma* [New York, 1944], xlvii).

3. Markus Wolf, *Man without a Face: The Autobiography of Communism's Greatest Spymaster* (New York, 1997), xii.

4. See Harvey Klehr and John Earl Haynes et al., *The Secret World of American Communism* (New Haven, 1995).

5. Draper wrote, "When we get to the really major decisions, we have to leave the area of the American movement altogether. These were inextricably bound up with problems and forces of international proportions, and international decisions originated in Moscow, not in New York" (Theodore Draper, *The Roots of American Communism* [New York, 1957], 8).

6. See *New York Review of Books*, 9 May 1985, 30 May 1985. Some of the books on American communism that rejected Draper's framework are Maurice Isserman, *Which Side Were You On: The American Communist Party during the Second World War* (Middletown, Conn., 1982); Roger Keeran, *The Communist Party and the Auto Workers Union* (Bloomington, Ind., 1980); Mark Naison, *Communists in Harlem during the Depression* (Urbana, Ill., 1983); Steve Nelson, James R. Barrett, and Rob Ruck, *Steve Nelson: American Radical* (Pittsburgh, 1981). A compilation of essays

that challenge Draper's view is Michael Brown, Frank Rosengarten, Randy Martin, and George Snedeker, eds., *New Studies in the Culture and History of U.S. Communism* (New York, 1993).

7. Draper, in *New York Review of Books,* 15 August 1985, 44.

8. Naison, *Communists in Harlem during the Depression,* 289.

CHAPTER 1: THE PIONEER BLACK COMMUNISTS

1. Most accounts of the early black presence in the Communist Party claim that Huiswoud and Hendricks both attended the National Left Wing Conference and were charter members of the Party. See Robert A. Hill, "Racial and Radical: Cyril V. Briggs, *The Crusader* Magazine, and the African Blood Brotherhood, 1988–1922," introduction, in Robert A. Hill, ed., *The Crusader: A Facsimile of the Periodical,* 3 vols. (New York, 1987), 1:xxvi, lvi n. 106. However, Huiswoud's widow, Hermina Huiswoud, has written an extensive, detailed memorandum: "Re: Otto Eduard Huiswoud" (n.d.) (in author's possession). I am indebted to Mary Licht for providing me with a copy of this important document. The memorandum gives precise dates of major events in Huiswoud's life and is emphatic about Hendricks's fate. His disappearance from the emerging Communist scene had never been explained until the discovery of the memorandum. Also the long-held contention that no blacks were present at the CP founding convention is refuted by the memorandum. That claim, reported in Theodore Draper, *American Communism and Soviet Russia* (reprint, New York, 1986), 325–26, and repeated by many historians, was based on Joseph Zack Kornfeder's contention that he saw no blacks at the 1 September 1919 meeting. Perhaps Kornfeder did not realize that the light-complexioned Huiswoud was a Negro.

2. Charlotte Todes, *William Sylvis and the National Labor Union* (New York, 1942), 73–79; Philip S. Foner, *American Socialism and Black Americans: From the Age of Jackson to World War II* (Westport, Conn., 1977), 94–115.

3. W. Burghardt Turner and Joyce Moore Turner, eds., *Richard B. Moore, Caribbean Militant in Harlem: Collected Writings, 1920–1972* (Bloomington, Ind., 1988), 1–44.

4. Turner and Turner, *Richard B. Moore,* 27–31; Hubert H. Harrison, "Socialism and the Negro," *International Socialist Review* (July 1912): 65–68; Harrison obituary, *New York Amsterdam News,* 21 December 1927; Theodore Draper, interview with W. A. Domingo, 18 January 1958, New York City, box 21, item 9, TDC.

5. Interview with Charlene Mitchell, Boston, 17 June 1995. Mitchell, a former leader of the Communist Party, grew up in Los Angeles and was friendly with Briggs during his later years in the 1950s and 1960s. Hill, *The Crusader,* 1:v–lxvi. George W. Harris, editor and publisher of the *New York Amsterdam News,* coined the description "Angry Blond Negro." From notes for an autobiography, in Briggs Papers, SCRL. I am grateful to Robert A. Hill for providing this material.

6. A federal agent shadowing Briggs commented that he was "very nervous and his stammering is quite noticeable" (DJ-FBI, Report of Special Agent Edward J. Brennan, 19 October 1923, file 6700, case file 61-23, in Theodore Kornweibel, ed., *Federal Surveillance of Afro-Americans [1917–1925]: The First World War, the Red Scare, and the Garvey Movement* [Frederick, Md., 1985]). All DJ-FBI documents cited in these notes are drawn from this collection, unless otherwise noted.

7. Herbert Shapiro, *White Violence and Black Response: From Reconstruction to Montgomery* (Amherst, Mass., 1988), 107–11.

8. *New York Amsterdam News,* 5 September 1917.

9. Hill, *The Crusader,* 1:xiv; Briggs to Draper, 7 March 1958, TDC, series 3.3, reel 8.

10. Hill, *The Crusader,* 1: xvii. Among the radical black publications were Hubert Harrison's *Voice,* which began publishing in July 1917; W. A. Domingo's *Emancipator,* Garvey's *Negro World,* which at times took radical positions, especially when edited by Domingo; William Bridges's *Challenge;* and Owen and Randolph's *Messenger.*

11. *TC* 1, no. 1 (September 1918): 1–5, 8, 10; 1, no. 3 (November 1918): 6–7. The "Catechism" called for unqualified sacrifice to attain the greatness in arms, commerce, and the arts that would finally bring respect and security to a great, besieged global mass of blacks. For a discussion of the "Catechism," see Theodore Vincent, *Marcus Garvey and the Black Power Movement* (Berkeley, Calif., 1971), 46–47, 79.

12. Parker had written the impassioned booklet *Children of the Sun,* a neglected landmark in the literature of black nationalism. *TC* 1, no. 4 (December 1918): 22; Hill, *The Crusader,* 1:xx–xxi.

13. *TC* 1, no. 6 (February 1919): 6–7; 1, no. 8 (April 1919): 8–9.

14. *TC* 1, no. 8 (April 1919): 10, 23; 1, no. 9 (May 1919): 4; 1, no. 10 (June 1919): 7; 1, no. 11 (July 1919): 6.

15. Hill, *The Crusader,* 1:xxv; *New York Amsterdam News,* 12 March 1919; *NYT,* 26 January 1919.

16. *TC* 1, no. 7 (June 1919): 7; 1, no. 11 (July 1919): 4, 6; 1, no. 12 (August 1919): 4; 2, no. 2 (October 1919): 9. The July issue carried a notice of Briggs's voluntary departure from the *New York Amsterdam News.*

17. *TC* 1, no. 12 (August 1919): 6; 2, no. 2 (October 1919): 9, 13.

18. McKay to Kalaroff, 23 December 1922, RTsKhIDNI 515/1/93/88–89; Briggs to Draper, 17 March 1958, box 31, TDC; RTsKhIDNI 515/1/93/89; Draper, *American Communism and Soviet Russia,* 22. Briggs left the erroneous impression that Minor and Stokes were from competing factions that vied for his allegiance. Briggs to Draper, 17 March 1958, box 31, TDC. Both were members of the Goose Caucus. Arthur and Pearl Zipser, *Fire and Grace: The Life of Rose Pastor Stokes* (Athens, Ga., 1989), 236. Minor's association with McKay through their co-editorship of the *Liberator* had given Minor an effective gateway to the black radical intelligentsia.

19. Briggs to Sheridan W. Johns III, Briggs Papers, SCRL.

20. *TC* 2, no. 2 (October 1919): 27; Turner and Turner, *Richard B. Moore*, 34–35.
21. Draper, *American Communism and Soviet Russia*, 326; Hill, *The Crusader*, 1:xxviii. Hill effectively challenged Draper's neglect of early Communist influences in the ABB. However, Hill's claim that the ABB was an early "black auxiliary" of the CP must be qualified.
22. Biographical data on Otto Huiswoud are drawn from Hermina Huiswoud, "Re: Otto Eduard Huiswoud."
23. Hill, *The Crusader*, 1:xxviii; Harry Haywood, *Black Bolshevik, Autobiography of an Afro-American Communist* (Chicago, 1978), 189; Philip S. Foner and James S. Allen, *American Communism and Black Americans: A Doumentary History, 1919–1929* (Philadelphia, 1987), ix, 17, 203–4; DJ-FBI, file 0051 GI-23. Robert A. Hill's biography of Huiswoud is in Bernard Johnpoll and Harvey Klehr, *Biographical Dictionary of the American Left* (Westport, Conn., 1986), 219–21.
24. *TC* 3, no. 6 (February 1921): 5; 4, no. 1 (March 1921): 9–10. A detailed description of ABB structure and ritual was published in *TC* 2, no. 10 (June 1920): 7, 22. The "blood brotherhood" aspect was drawn from a vague connection with tribal rituals in which fraternity was sealed by the ceremonial drawing of blood (but no survivor could recall witnessing such a ceremony). See Theodore Burrell's article on blood rituals, *TC* 5, no. 3 (November 1921): 6, 32. The federal undercover agent reported that the oath "puts ABB before everything but the redemption of Africa. To break this oath, your own blood shall be on your hands, whatever that means" (DJ-FBI, file 61-8-26, Agent 800 to Ruch, 7 October 1921).
25. *TC* 2, no. 5 (January 1920): 5; 2, no. 10 (June 1920): 12–13.
26. Hill, *The Crusader*, 1:xxviii; "ABB Program," *Communist Review* (London) 2 (1922): 488–54.
27. *TC* 2, no. 10 (June 1920): 19. Lowe was not a blatant anti-Semite; his attitude toward Jews can best be described as grudging ambivalence. The Hamiticists claimed no innate evil in Judaism, but complained about its failure to recognize its Africanist, non-Caucasian roots. *TC* 2, no. 11 (July 1920): 19.
28. *TC* 3, no. 6 (February 1921): 9–10.
29. *TC* 3, no. 2 (October 1920): 8.
30. *TC* 4, no. 2 (April 1921): 8–11.
31. *TC* 4, no. 4 (June 1921): 9; 4, no. 6 (August 1921): 12; 5, no. 2 (October 1921): 8.
32. App. 1, "Cyril V. Briggs," in Robert A. Hill, ed., *The Marcus Garvey and Universal Negro Improvement Association Papers*, 7 vols. (Berkeley, Calif., 1983–90), 1:523; Hill, *The Crusader*, 1:xxxviii; Haywood, *Black Bolshevik*, 122; Agent 800 to Ruch, 23 September 1921, DJ-FBI, file 61-826. There may at various times have been about fifty posts throughout the country — with a few in the South and an occasional post in the West Indies. Briggs, Offord interview, Federal Writers Project, 27 July 1939, Schomburg Center for Research in Black Culture, NYPL. An informer noted

wryly that "Briggs has always tried to make me believe that his organization is very strong when I know that it is only on paper" (Report of Agent 800, DJ-FBI, file 61-826-X18, no. 19140). Government agents in 1921 reported that the ABB's bank balance never went above $75–$100 (DJ-FBI, file 61-444-6).

33. *Chicago Defender,* 4 and 25 June 1921, 5 November 1921; *TC* 4, no. 5 (July 1921): 5–6; *NYT,* 4 June 1921. The quote is in Scott Ellsworth, *Death in a Promised Land: The Tulsa Race Riot of* 1921 (Baton Rouge, La., 1982), 136.

34. Briggs had suspiciously used words very similar to those of the Tulsa "commander." *TC* 4, no. 5. (July 1921): 5–6, 8, 10; Hill, ed., *The Marcus Garvey and UNIA Papers,* 3:667–68.

35. *TC* 4, no. 4 (June 1921): 21–23; 4, no. 5 (July 1921): 12–14; 5, no. 3 (November 1921): 15–16, 23; 6, no. 1 (January–February 1922): 6; Hill, *The Crusader,* 1:xxxv–xxxvi.

36. E. T. Allison, "The Economic Basis of the Tulsa Race Riot," *Toiler,* 18 June 1921; *TC* 4, no. 4 (July 1921): 8.

37. *TC* 4, no. 5 (July 1921): 8–9.

38. Three months before the founding of the U.S. Communist Party, Briggs ruminated about the greed and arrogance of Harlem landlords and noted that when the Negro "makes common cause with the Bolsheviki of the world then the grabbing landlords may be interested" (*TC* 1, no. 9 [May 1919]: 4); also see *TC* 1, no. 11 (July 1919): 6; 2, no. 4 (December 1919): 9–10; 2, no. 6 (February 1920): 5–6.

39. *TC* 4, no. 4 (June 1921): 8–9; 4, no. 5 (July 1921): 8–9; 5, no. 3 (November 1921): 15.

40. Theodore Draper, *The Roots of American Communism* (New York 1957), 192; "Manifesto and Program of the Communist Party of America," reprinted in *Communist* 1, no. 1 (27 September 1919): 10–11.

41. William Z. Foster, *History of the Communist Party of the United States* (New York 1953), 173.

42. Foster, *History of the CPUSA,* 173, 177–78; Foner and Allen, *American Communism and Black Americans,* 3; Hill, *The Crusader,* 1:xxxviii. Lenin's alleged letter "demanded action and a report on [the Negro] question" (Kornfeder to Draper, box 18, no. 5a, TDC). William Weinstone, a charter member of the CP, denied the letter's existence (Weinstone to Solomon, 3 March 1974, in author's possession. I am indebted to Drs. Galina Khartulary and Valery Klokov in Moscow for their invaluable assistance in investigating the "Lenin letter."

43. Hill, *The Crusader,* 1:xxxviii; "Financial Statement and Trial Balance for the Period from July 1921 to July 31, 1922," account 107, exhibit 20, file 61-443-642, Documents Seized at Bridgman, Michigan, DJ-FBI; app. 3, "The Comintern and American Blacks, 1919–1943," in Hill, ed., *The Marcus Garvey and the UNIA Papers,* 5:841–54; RTsKhIDNI 515/1/93/89.

44. Hill, *The Crusader,* 1:lxix. "The Program of the American Arm of the Communist International," *Toiler,* February 1921, 2.

45. Draper, *American Communism and Soviet Russia,* 25–26; Foster, *History of the CPUSA,* 181; "The UCP and the CP United," *Communist* 1, no. 1 (July 1921): 3.

46. John Bruce and J. P. Collins, "The Party and the Negro Struggle," *Communist* 1, no. 4 (October 1921): 18–20. Kornfeder claimed that he had used the Collins pseudonym, but never explicitly claimed credit for the article. He was hazy on the identity of Bruce, but the second part of this article revealingly changed John Bruce to Robt. Bruce, a gaffe that suggests Robert Minor was probably a co-author. See "The Party and the Negro Struggle" (continuation), *Communist* 1, no. 5 (November 1921): 15, 17.

47. "The Party and the Negro Struggle," *Communist* 1, no. 4 (October 1921): 19; 1, no. 5 (November 1921): 17.

48. "Report of the CEC on Its Activities during Amalgamation," DJ-FBI, Documents Seized at Bridgman Convention, document no. 77, file 61-443-642, 22 August 1922. (That date refers to government processing. The actual date of formulation of the document is unknown, but judging from its content it was most likely produced in the late summer or fall of 1921.) I am indebted to Harvey Klehr for making the document available. Foster, *History of the CPUSA,* 187; Hill, *The Crusader,* 1:xxxvii, xl; *TC* 6, no. 1 (January–February 1922): 15–16; McKay to Wallungus, 28 November 1922, RTsKhIDNI 515/1/93/77; McKay to Kalaroff, 23 December 1922, RTsKhIDNI 515/1/93/88.

49. Workers Party of America, *Program and Constitution* (New York, 1921); Foner and Allen, *American Communism and Black Americans,* 9. William Z. Foster, while criticizing the document for its failure to characterize the Negro question as a national question, said that "this was the most advanced resolution on the matter ever adopted by any Marxist party in the United States up to that time" (Foster, *History of the CPUSA,* 193).

CHAPTER 2: LOOKING FOR THE BLACK UNITED FRONT

1. *TC* 6, no. 1 (January–February 1922): 15.

2. Vincent, *Black Power and the Garvey Movement,* 270–71; *TC* 2, no. 6 (February 1920): 8; 2, no. 7 (March 1920): 5; 2, no. 8 (April 1920): 5.

3. Jervis Anderson, *This Was Harlem: 1900–1950* (New York, 1981), 121–27; Judith Stein, *The World of Marcus Garvey: Race and Class in Modern Society* (Baton Rouge, La., 1986), 61–88.

4. *TC* 2, no. 9 (May 1920): 5; 2, no. 11 (July 1920): 8; 3, no. 1 (September 1920): 6, 8; 3, no. 2 (October 1920): 11; Vincent, *Black Power,* 81; Stein, *The World of Marcus Garvey,* 142.

5. *TC* 4, no. 4 (June 1921): 4.

6. Stokes's most moving (and least sectarian) words were her descriptions of the "rewards" of antediluvian prejudice and racist violence bestowed upon blacks returning from the Great War and her defense of armed black resistance. *Negro World,* 27 August 1921; Hill, ed., *The Marcus Garvey and UNIA Papers,* 3:675–81.

7. Hill, ed., *The Marcus Garvey and UNIA Papers*, 3:637–39; Hill, *The Crusader*, 1:xli. Kornfeder in his informer years claimed that Briggs's bulletin was "dressed up" to make it appear to be an official organ of the convention. "Subversion in Racial Unrest, Part I," public hearings of the state of Louisiana Joint Legislative Committee, Baton Rouge, 6 March 1957, 18, 39.

8. Hill, ed., *The Marcus Garvey and UNIA Papers*, 4:xlii, 23–25, 289, 5:928–29; Edmund David Cronon, *Black Moses: The Story of Marcus Garvey and the Universal Negro Improvement Association* (Madison, Wis., 1955), 73–102.

9. *TC* 5, no. 2 (October 1921): 8; Briggs to Sheridan Johns III, 10 April 1961, Briggs Papers, SCRL; Hill, *The Crusader*, 1:xii. The UCP in February 1921 had called on its black cadre to "expose reactionary leaders" who dominated Negro institutions. "The Program of the American Arm of the Communist International," *Toiler*, 12 February 1921, 2.

10. Hill, *The Crusader*, 1:xii; "The Program of the American Arm of the Communist International," *Toiler*, 12 February 1921, 2.

11. DJ-FBI, 61-826, in Hill, ed., *The Marcus Garvey and UNIA Papers*, 4:74–77; *TC* 5, no. 2 (October 1921): 23–24; C. B. Valentine (Briggs), "The Negro Convention," *Toiler*, 1 October 1921, 13; William H. Ferris, editorial, *Negro World*, 21 November 1921.

12. "Report of the CEC on Its Activities during Amalgamation," DJ-FBI, Bridgman Convention documents, document no. 77, 22 August 1922, file 61-443-642; Foster, *History of the CPUSA*, 181–82; C. B. Valentine (Briggs), "The Negro Convention," *Toiler*, 1 October 1921, 13.

13. *TC* 5, no. 2 (October 1921): 8–15, 23–26; *Negro World*, 8 October 1921, 3; J. Edgar Hoover to George F. Ruch, 17 November 1921, DJ-FBI, file 61, in Hill, ed., *The Marcus Garvey and UNIA Papers*, 4:196; *TC* 5, no. 3 (November 1921): 14, 17; *New York Amsterdam News*, 15 November 1921; Chicago *Defender*, 19 November 1921; *Negro World*, 3 December 1921. Garvey also slapped Briggs with a libel suit for implying that Garvey had been forced to depart London for "having raped a white girl in a friend's office." Garvey had Briggs held for Special Sessions in $500 bond. The case apparently never came to trial. See Hill, ed., *The Marcus Garvey and UNIA Papers*, 4:217–18, 232.

14. "Confidential Informant 800 to George F. Ruch," DJ-FBI, file 61-820-826-X9; DJ-FBI, file 61-826, in Hill, ed., *The Marcus Garvey and UNIA Papers*, 4:220, 5:192, 219.

15. Briggs to Sheridan Johns, 7 June 1961, Briggs Papers, SCRL; John Bruce and J. P. Collins, "The Party and the Negro Struggle," *Toiler* 1, no. 4 (October 1921): 19; "Report by Special Agent Mortimer J. Davis, Nov. 18, 1921," in Hill, ed., *The Marcus Garvey and UNIA Papers*, 4:197, 355–56. Briggs in the 1950s said that he had steadfastly refused to release any information to the government before publication in *The Crusader* or release by his Crusader News Service, which he and W. A. Domingo operated after the demise of the magazine. Hill, *The Crusader*, 1:xlv. However, Agent

800 claimed that Briggs had told him that he had furnished the Post Office Department with affidavits from people in Philadelphia, Norfolk, New York City, and other places who bought tickets on the *Phyllis Wheatley,* but never got passage (Agent 800 to Ruch, 20 December 1921, DJ-FBI, case file G1-826-X15, 19144).

16. *TC* 5, no. 4 (December 1921): 5, 20–23, 34; 6, no. 1 (January–February 1922): 3, 18–23. McGuire, former UNIA chaplain, was installed as head of the ABB's Department of Religion and Education. Hill, *The Crusader,* 1:xliii. Crichlow claimed that he was owed $1,300 in back salary for his service as Garvey's "resident commissioner" in Liberia. "George F. Ruch to W. W. Grimes, Bureaus of Investigation," DJ-FBI, file 61-826. McKay's communication is RTsKhIDNI 515/1/93/88.

17. *TC* 5, no. 2 (October 1921): 16. In 1922 the ABB produced an updated version of its short nine-point program, originally promulgated in 1920. The updated document made a more direct assault on capitalism. For example, point 1 of the 1922 program changed liberation from "exploitation" to liberation from "capitalism." Other changes were in a similar vein. See Hill, *The Crusader,* 1:lxvii–lxx.

18. Henry Williams, *Black Response to the American Left: 1917–1929,* Princeton Undergraduate Studies in History (Princeton, N.J., 1973), 29, 32, 34, 36–39, 41.

19. *TC* 6, no. 1 (January–February 1922): 5; Hill, ed., *The Marcus Garvey and UNIA Papers,* 3:app. 1, p. 525. On the Crusader News Agency, see J. G. Tucker, "Special Report," 25 February and 25 March 1922, DJ-FBI, case file 61-23 0057. On Huiswoud's tour, see Report of Special Agent J. G. Tucker, 18 August 1923, DJ-FBI, case file 61-23 0064. The process of absorption of the ABB into the WP did not entail any financial assistance from the Party. See ibid.; also *The Worker,* 15 July and 5 August 1922.

20. Hill, ed., *The Marcus Garvey and UNIA Papers,* 2:app. 1, p. 525; DJ-FBI, case file 61-23 0064. The Brotherhood's letterhead in spring 1923 claimed that its activities included calisthenics, consumers' cooperatives, forums, a press service, and a "Sick and Death Benefit Department — 25c. per month."

21. Turner and Turner, *Richard B. Moore,* 49, 51–52; Report of Agent Earl E. Titus, DJ-FBI, case file 61-23 0050. A sole ABB delegate was registered from Montgomery, West Virginia, at the founding convention of the ANLC in the last week of October 1925.

22. Dr. M.A.N. Shaw to Moorfield Storey and James W. Johnson, 29 December 1922, NAACP Papers; Sanhedrin file, RKC.

23. Hill, ed., *The Marcus Garvey and UNIA Papers,* 4:558; "Call Issued for All-Race Conference or 'Negro Sanhedrin,'" Crusader News Service, n.d., Sanhedrin file, RKC; Kelly Miller, *The Negro Sanhedrin: A Call to Conference,* undated pamphlet, Sanhedrin file, RKC; *New York Amsterdam News,* 21 January 1923. A memorandum from James Weldon Johnson to Robert Bagnall regarding the NAACP's participation in a follow-up meeting of the United Front Conference Committee (always held at the home of Grace Campbell) advised that the association not become "so

close as to make ourselves responsible for its probable failure" (confidential memorandum, Johnson to Mr. Bagnall and Miss Randolph, 19 July 1923, Sanhedrin file, RKC).

24. Crusader News Service, 24 March 1923; Miller, *The Negro Sanhedrin: A Call to Conference,* 5–6.

25. Cyril Briggs to *Pittsburgh Courier,* 28 June 1923; Miller to Briggs, 25 July 1923; Briggs to Miller, 26 July 1923; all in Sanhedrin file, RKC.

26. "Minutes of the Third Assembly of the Permanent 'United Front' Conference, June 16, 1933" and "Program of the First Meeting of the Negro Sanhedrin All Race Conference," both in Sanhedrin file, RKC; Hill, ed., *The Marcus Garvey and UNIA Papers,* 4:559.

27. The all-black contingent was composed of former members of the virtually defunct Chicago Pushkin Post of the ABB and the veteran of the Harlem Socialist club, Lovett Fort-Whiteman, who was soon to become head of the Party's Negro work. Box 13, folder "Negro-Sanhedrin, 1924," RMP; *DW,* 11 February 1924. Federal agents monitored Fort-Whiteman as early as 1919. Fort-Whiteman was a pioneer member of the 21st AD Socialist Party club, a Rand School student, IWW member, organizer for the Communist Labor Party, and a former actor and critic who wrote at various times for Randolph's *Messenger.* After study in Russia in 1924, he walked the streets of New York and Chicago wearing a *rabochka* (a long belted peasant blouse worn to the knees) with Bohemian aplomb. Scholars and writers have been taken with this sectarian image to the extent that his contributions have received virtually no attention. U.S. Military Intelligence Reports: Surveillance of Radicals in the United States, 1917–1941," reel 1: Reports of Special Agents Lewis Loebl and A.L. Rodau, DJ-FBI, 11 October 1919; "Resolutions Proposed by Delegates Representing the Workers Party of America at the Negro Sanhedrin," box 13, RMP.

28. *DW,* 11, 12, 14, 15, 16 February 1924; Miller, *The Negro Sanhedrin: A Call to Conference,* 6. Robert Minor noted that the Sanhedrin's leadership was a repressed petty bourgeoisie, which wavered between the bourgeoisie and the working class and was excluded by racial oppression from full equality in a white-dominated nation. Robert Minor, "The Black Ten Millions," *The Liberator,* March 1924.

29. *DW,* 11 February 1924.

30. "Resolutions Proposed by the Delegates," box 13, folder "Negro-Sanhedrin, 1924," RMP; *Inprecorr* 3, no. 2 (1923): 22.

31. Fort-Whiteman used the panel "Physical Stamina of the Race" (geared to physicians) to blame capitalism's systemic racism for the high mortality and disease rates among blacks. Miller was obliged to place Fort-Whiteman on the assembly's Labor Commission. *DW,* 13 February 1924.

32. The *Pittsburgh Courier,* 23 February 1924, commented that "the Sanhedrin has prepared its legislative program! Those attending with the expectation of radical or hurried decisions on the part of the conference must have been disappointed." A

Daily Worker editorial the following month continued the attack on the "ambitious and sleek rich men of the race" (*DW*, 22 March 1924). Israel Amter, *Mirovoe Osboboditel'noe Dvishenie Negrov* (Moscow, 1925), 3.

33. Briggs to Sheridan H. Johns III, 7 June 1961, Briggs Papers, SCRL.

34. *New York Amsterdam News*, 20 June 1923; Cronon, *Black Moses*, 103–37; *DW*, 9 August 1924; *Inprecorr* 3, no. 2 (1923): 15–16.

35. Foner and Allen, *American Communism and Black Americans*, 45; Joseph North, *Robert Minor, Artist and Crusader: An Informal Biography* (New York, 1956); Harvey Klehr, *The Heyday of American Communism: The Depression Decade* (New York, 1984), 19; Haywood, *Black Bolshevik*, 139–40.

36. Minor to William Z. Foster, 13 November 1952, box 5, folder "Correspondence," RMP; *DW*, 13 August 1924.

37. *DW*, 29 July 1924. Minor (in his letter to Foster, 13 November 1952) saw the reference to India and China in 1924 as prescient. The first letter is in *DW*, 5 August 1924; the second in *DW*, 23 August 1924.

38. *DW*, 2 and 23 August 1924; Hill, ed., *The Marcus Garvey and UNIA Papers*, 4:738–39. Garvey believed that the KKK's influence could be useful to the "Back to Africa" campaign. He had been insisting that the Klan acted out what 90 percent of whites believed, but would not admit: "I love the straightforward white man, and that is why I have great respect for the members of the Ku Klux Klan." *Negro World*, 20 and 27 October 1923, 12 July 1924.

39. *DW*, 23 August 1924.

40. Hill, ed., *The Marcus Garvey and UNIA Papers*, 4:769.

41. Ibid., 4:770–71.

42. *DW*, 5 August 1924.

43. Haywood, *Black Bolshevik*, 101–14.

44. *DW*, 11 and 23 August 1924.

45. *DW*, 18, 20, 30 August 1924; Robert Minor, "Death, Or a Program," *Workers Monthly* (April 1925): 270.

46. *DW*, 5 July 1924.

47. Undated memorandum, box 12, RMP.

48. Ibid.

CHAPTER 3: THE COMINTERN'S VISION

1. William Z. Foster, *History of the Three Internationals* (New York, 1955), 200–203.

2. J. Stalin, *Foundations of Leninism* (New York, 1939), 15–19, 36.

3. V. I. Lenin, *Imperialism: The Highest Stage of Capitalism* (New York, 1939), 88–128; "Further Extracts from Lenin's Writings: On the Connection of the Russian Revolution with the Liberation Movement of the People of the East," *Communist International*, n.s. 2 (1924): 14.

4. V. I. Lenin, "Capitalism and Agriculture in the United States," in *Capitalism in Agriculture* (New York, 1946), 18–21.

5. Reed to Zinoviev, 25 February 1919, RTsKhIDNI 495/155/1.

6. Foner and Allen, *American Communism and Black Americans*, 5–8.

7. V. I. Lenin, "Preliminary Draft Theses on the National and Colonial Questions," in *Collected Works*, vol. 31 (Moscow, 1966), 144–51. The Indian Communist, M. N. Roy, assisted Lenin in preparing the Colonial Theses at the Second Congress. But he challenged Lenin's contention that Communists should support bourgeois national movements that led the fight for liberation in colonies and dependent countries. Roy argued that the national bourgeoisie often temporized with imperialism; he stressed the organized pressure of workers and peasants in the colonial revolutionary process. That concept probably had some indirect influence upon the American Party's emphasis on working-class leadership of the black liberation movement. In the mid-1920s Roy was head of the CI's Anglo-American Secretariat. But by the time of the pivotal Sixth Congress, he was ensnared in the fervor against Comintern head Nikolai Bukharin and was soon expelled from the Comintern (despite his own "leftist sectarian" history). Thus, he was not a factor in the pivotal debates of 1928. Draper, *American Communism and Soviet Russia*, 406; John Haithcox, *Communism and Nationalism in India: M. N. Roy and Comintern Policy, 1920–1939* (Princeton, N.J., 1971), 10–15.

8. Jane T. Degras, ed., *The Communist International: Documents, 1923–28*, vol. 2 (London, 1956–65), 552–53.

9. Foner and Allen, *American Communism and Black Americans*, 28–30; Claude McKay, *A Long Way from Home* (New York, 1970), 140; McKay, *The Negro In America*, ed. Alan L. McLeod (Port Washington, N.Y., 1979), 88; Wayne F. Cooper, *Claude McKay: Rebel Sojourner in the Harlem Renaissance* (Baton Rouge, La., 1987), 168–69; Turner and Turner, *Richard B. Moore*, 47.

10. McKay to Wallungus, 28 November 1922, RTsKhIDNI 515/1/93/77; Cooper, *Claude McKay*, 177. McKay's determination to speak to the liberal mainstream led to articles in Du Bois's *Crisis*. Claude McKay, "Soviet Russia and the Negro," *Crisis* 27 (December 1923): 61–65; RTsKhIDNI 515/1/93/77–78. The State Department listening post in Riga, Latvia, was a trove of misinformation, reporting that the CI Negro Commission would begin recruiting "special Negro detachments" in the United States for the Red Army. The reports also had McKay remaining in Russia "as President of the Negro Section of the Executive Committee of the Third International," or heading home to organize a "colored Soviet," or recovering from a "wicked venereal disease." W. Hurley, State Dept., to William J. Burns, 11 January 1923, file 6700, case file 61-23; Report from U.S. Legation, Riga, 4 December 1922, file 6700, item 138; Hurley to Burns, 17 March 1923, file 6700, item 143; all in *Federal Surveillance of Afro-Americans* (1917–1925).

11. McKay, *A Long Way from Home,* 174. Katayama was among the founders of *Revolutionary Age,* sponsored by the Communist Labor Party. U.S. Military Intelligence Report (agent 66), document 10110-1146 (agent 66), 5 September 1919, in Randolph Boehm, ed., *U.S. Military Intelligence Reports: Surveillance of Radicals in the United States* (Frederick, Md., 1984).

12. McKay's criticism of the Party appeared to be confirmed by a report of the Workers Party's Second Convention, which he read about in the *New York Times* while he was in Russia. The Party's resolution on the Negro question again pledged to "fight for economic, political, and educational equality." According to the *Times,* a motion to add "and for social equality" was overwhelmingly defeated. McKay, *A Long Way from Home,* 174; Foner and Allen, *American Communism and Black Americans,* 28; McKay, *The Negroes in America,* 37.

13. Huiswoud's address is in Communist Party of Great Britain, 4th Congress of the Communist International: Abridged Report of the Meetings held at Petrograd and Moscow, Nov. 7–Dec. 3, 1922 (London, n.d.), 257–60.

14. Rose Pastor Stokes, "The Communist International and the Negro," *The Worker,* 10 March 1923; Roger E. Kanet, "The Comintern and the 'Negro Question': Communist Policy in the U.S. and Africa, 1921–41," *Survey* 19, no. 4 (Autumn 1973): 91–93; Woodford McClellan, "Africans and Black Americans in the Comintern Schools, 1925–34," *International Journal of African Historical Studies* 26, no. 2 (May 1993): 372–73; Foner and Allen, *American Communism and Black Americans,* 28–30.

15. McKay's animus toward Huiswoud was manifest fifteen years later when he derisively identified the light-skinned Huiswoud as "the mulatto delegate" (*A Long Way from Home,* 173). Susan Campbell, "'Black Bolsheviks' and Self-Determination," *Science and Society* 58, no. 4 (Winter 1994–95): 449; St. Clair Drake, foreword to 1970 edition, in Mckay, *A Long Way from Home,* xiv.

16. Foster, *History of the CPUSA,* 215. The name often used in this period was Workers (Communist) Party.

17. Interview with Gilbert Green, New York City, 29 April 1974.

18. Haywood, *Black Bolshevik,* 131–40.

19. *DW,* 6 and 18 March 1924.

20. *DW,* 1 and 22 March, 2 April 1924; Haywood, *Black Bolshevik,* 141.

21. Workers (Communist) Party, *Proceedings of the Fourth National Convention* (New York, 1925), 119. The Third Congress of the Comintern's Red International of Labor Unions told the TUEL to pay attention to the "politically and industrially disfranchised negroes" and to demand for them "the same social, political, and industrial rights as whites" (*Labor Herald* [organ of the TUEL] 3 [July 1924]: 152).

22. Edward P. Johanningsmeier, *Forging American Communism: The Life of William Z. Foster* (Princeton, N.J., 1994), 97–99. The SLC pamphlet said in part that race hatred was "the basis of poverty, ignorance and job competition that underlies all

serious race antagonism. Unity here will clear the social atmosphere as lightning clears the heavens.... The menace of race riots, of poverty-stricken wage slavery... will become a nightmare of an ignorant barbaric past" (Stockyards Labor Council, *Chicago Race Riots* [Chicago, 1919], 30). Foster, *History of the CPUSA*, 230–31. The unionizing drive among black stockyard workers brought twenty thousand Negroes out of two hundred thousand into the packinghouse unions. Earl Browder, "Experiences in Organizing Negro Workers," *Communist* 9 (January 1930): 35–41.

23. William Z. Foster, *The Great Steel Strike*, quoted in Mckay, *The Negroes in America*, 28–30; Johanningsmeier, *Forging American Communism*, 91–93, 96, 144; *DW*, 21 June 1924; RTsKhIDNI 495/155/42/1.

24. William F. Dunne, "Negroes in American Industry," *Workers Monthly*, March 1925, 206–27; April 1925, 257–60. Dunne's "Negroes as an Oppressed People," *Workers Monthly*, July 1925, 395–98, deals with the situation of African Americans within a global imperial context.

25. RTsKhIDNI 495/155/5.

26. Secretariat of the Executive Committee of the Communist International to the Central Committee of the Workers Party of America, 25 February 1923, RTsKhIDNI 495/155/16; Kuusinen to Central Committee of Workers Party of America, RTsKhIDNI 515/1/164.

27. RTsKhIDNI 495/155/37/42-43.

28. RTsKhIDNI 495/155/37/43. An undated memorandum from the U.S. Party's Negro Commission (sometimes called CEC Negro Subcommittee) said that it "has been initiating and carrying through under the authority of the CEC all of the Party policies in the Negro field for the past year and a half, and which now sees its work about to bear fruit in the Negro Labor Congress, *the proposal of which was originated with this committee*" (Minutes of CEC Negro Subcommittee, 18 January 1925, RTsKhIDNI 515/1/183/23; emphasis added). A handwritten notation on the document dates it to 18 January 1923. Since the minutes deal with very advanced planning for the American Negro Labor Congress, the document must be incorrectly dated.

29. Foner and Allen, *American Communism and Black Americans*, 69–70; James Jackson (pseud.), "The Negro in America" *Communist International* 8 (February 1925): 50–52.

30. *Communist International* 8 (February 1925): 52. The *Communist International* was responding to the spoken and written versions of Fort-Whiteman's address, which were essentially the same.

31. Foner and Allen, *American Communism and Black Americans*, 69–70; RTsKhIDNI 495/155/30/1.

32. RTsKhIDNI 495/155/30, 155/19. The meeting requested a progress report from the Workers Party, and a suggestion to the WP to campaign for support of the ANLC

among white union members and white organizations. RTsKhIDNI 495/155/29/2. The same people were present at a second meeting, now constituted as a Negro Commission of the ECCI. RTsKhIDNI 495/155/30.

33. RTsKhIDNI 495/155/32. My thanks to Russian research associates for suggesting the notion of a "Negrotern."

34. Draper, *American Communism and Soviet Russia*, 139–46; Haywood, *Black Bolshevik*, 142; "Resolution of the Parity Commission," in Foner and Allen, *American Communism and Black Americans*, 99–103.

35. Briggs later said that he urged ABB members to transfer their allegiance to the ANLC, "but while a substantial number accepted my advice, the majority did not." Briggs's memory on the matter may not have been accurate. In the same communication, he admits that the ABB was defunct by 1925. It is doubtful that a significant "membership" existed to resist absorption into the new organization. Briggs to Sheridan H. Johns III, 12 May 1961, Briggs Papers, SCRL.

36. Haywood, *Black Bolshevik*, 130–40; Mark Naison, *Communists in Harlem during the Depression*, 12–13. Haywood in Chicago described warm interracial relationships anchored not in insular "cells," but in district and city-wide functions. But in Harlem, the predominantly black West Side Harlem unit under Bolshevization was merged with largely white groups into a consolidated Harlem branch. This caused tensions as blacks expressed a sharp sensitivity to slights and insults from white comrades. The post-Bolshevization experience of Claude Lightfoot and William Patterson was closer to Haywood's description. Interviews with Claude A. Lightfoot, Chicago, 25 April 1974, and William L. Patterson, New York City, 28 June 1974. Bolshevization was mainly a political football between two factions, each accusing the other of promoting "fake Bolshevization."

37. RTsKhIDNI 495/155/33. Fort-Whiteman noted that the students were "sincere, energetic, and unquestionably devoted to the cause." Yelena Khanga's grandfather, J. O. Golden, was one of the first group of students (Yelena Khanga, *Soul to Soul* [New York, 1992], 51–54). The selection process did not avoid disappointment. In July 1926 Henry V. Phillips wrote to Ruthenberg, pointing out that in the previous fall the plan had been to send six students to Moscow. Because of financial exigencies, only five went, while Phillips was left behind. The letter implied that it was time for Phillips to make the journey. RTsKhIDNI 515/1/720.

Chapter 4: The American Negro Labor Congress

1. Untitled document by "The National Negro Committee (Committee of Seven)," box 12, folder "Negro 1924–25," RMP; "Outline of Party Speakers on the Subject: The American Negro Labor Congress and Its Background," box 11, RMP.

2. Richard B. Moore, Otto E. Huiswoud, Aubrey C. Bailey, and August Warren to CEC, 31 May 1925, RTsKhIDNI 515/1/504.

3. *DW,* 16 September 1925; Cleveland *Herald,* 14 August 1925; ANLC press release 331.83A, October 1925, ANLC file, RKC.

4. *NYT,* 10 August and 8 October 1925; *Literary Digest,* 21 November 1925. Minor noted that the entrance of the Metropolitan Community Center, which housed the congress sessions, was crowded every day with "a score of Mr. Coolidge's federal dicks" (Minor, "The First Negro Workers' Congress," *Workers Monthly* [December 1925]: 71).

5. Baltimore *Afro-American,* 7 November 1925; *NYT,* 17 January 1926; Du Bois, "The Black Man and Labor," *Crisis* 31 (December 1925): 60; Abram L. Harris, Jr., "Lenin Casts His Shadow over Africa," *Crisis* 33 (April 1926): 272–78.

6. Theodore Kornweibel Jr., *No Crystal Stair: Black Life and the Messenger,* 1917–1928 (Westport, Conn., 1975), 186–87.

7. A. Philip Randolph, "The Menace of Negro Communists," *Messenger,* August 1923, 195–97; Earl Ofari Hutchinson, *Blacks and Reds: Race and Class in Conflict,* 1919–1990 (East Lansing, Mich., 1995), 33.

8. Irving Bernstein, *The Lean Years: A History of the American Worker,* 1920–1933 (Boston, 1960), passim.

9. There was also considerable padding, with various Workers Party members registering as members of paper organizations or local organizing committees. ANLC press release 331.88A.

10. *DW,* 31 October 1935; Haywood, *Black Bolshevik,* 144–45; ANLC press release 331-88A; Hutchinson, *Blacks and Reds,* 31.

11. "Constitution and Program of the American Negro Labor Congress," n.d., ANLC file, RKC; Hutchinson, *Blacks and Reds,* 31–32.

12. *DW,* 2 November 1925; "Constitution and Program," 40. Bertha Lomax, leader of a Howard Uiversity strike in May 1925 against military training classes, was the only student and woman elected to the ANLC national committee. Otto Huiswoud and Richard Moore were members of an executive board of twenty-five, which was established later. *DW,* 12 June and 2 November 1925.

13. Draper, *American Communism and Soviet Russia,* 332; "Report of the Committee on Negro Work," 24 February 1927, RTsKhIDNI 515/1/1108; *DW,* 16 November 1926; Edgar Owens, "Report for the Negro Committee of the CEC," 14 April 1926, RTsKhIDNI 515/1/819/30–31.

14. *DW,* 5, 9, 18, 19, 23 October 1926.

15. *NYT,* 3 May 1926; *DW,* 30 September 1926, 19 March 1927; *New York Amsterdam News,* 26 September and 6 October 1926

16. Harold Cruse, *Crisis of the Negro Intellectual* (New York, 1967), 75; *New York Amsterdam News,* 6 October 1926.

17. "Directions for the Party Fraction in the National Executive Committee of the American Negro Labor Congress," RTsKhIDNI 495/155/39; "Report of the Committee on Negro Work" (of the WP), 24 February 1927, RTsKhIDNI 515/1/1108.

18. Moore, Huiswoud, and Charles Henry led demands for Fort-Whiteman's removal. RTsKhIDNI 495/155/32; RTsKhIDNI 515/1/720/3. On Fort-Whiteman, see *DW*, 31 May 1928; Hutchinson, *Reds and Blacks*, 54; RTsKhIDNI 495/155/56/96, 495/155/66/6. Fort-Whiteman was reportedly jailed for a time during Stalin's purges in the late 1930s. Alan Culison, "How Stalin Repaid the Support of Americans," *Washington Times*, 9 November 1997.

19. "Report and Recommendations on the Conference of the Party Fraction in the General Executive Board of the American Negro Labor Congress, submitted to the PolCom by Alex Bittelman, Secretary of the CEC Sub-Committee on Negro Work," RTsKhIDNI 495/155/1/3. The fraction response is in RTsKhIDNI 495/155/1/6.

20. Hill, ed., *The Marcus Garvey and UNIA Papers*, 3:app. 1, 525; Haywood, *Black Bolshevik*, 189; Turner and Turner, *Richard B. Moore*, 52–55.

21. The resolution reflected Moore's self-taught erudition. It depicted the cultural and political attainments of the neglected African empires of antiquity and blamed slavery and modern imperialism for the poverty and oppression into which Africa had sunk. Turner and Turner, *Richard B. Moore*, 53–54; "Proceedings of the Congress of the League against Imperialism and for National Independence" (Berlin, 1927), 126–30.

22. Coverage of Huiswoud's Caribbean activity is in the *Liberator*, 7 December 1929.

23. "On the RILU International Bureau of Negro Workers," RTsKhIDNI 495/155/53/1. The conference was originally to convene in Berlin no later than October 1929 with the largest delegation coming from the United States; South Africa would be the second largest group, with three delegates. RTsKhIDNI 495/155/53/3. I am indebted to Harvey Klehr for identifying "Carlstone" or "Carleton" as the young Chicago Communist Henry V. Phillips.

24. A letter from the Comintern urged the Party to try to undercut Pickens, who objected to the "Negro Resolution," written largely by Ford. The resolution attacked the British Labor Party, characterized Kadalie in South Africa and Randolph in the United States as reformists, and designated the USSR as "the fatherland of workers and oppressed people." "Report on the Negro Question at the League against Imperialism Congress," RTSKhIDNI 534/3.450/50; "Draft Letter to the CP of the United States," RTsKhIDNI 495/155/80/13.

25. "Report of James W. Ford, to the First International Conference of Negro Workers, Hamburg, Germany, July 1930," box 12, folder "1931," RMP; "Report on the Negro Question at the League against Imperialism Congress," RTsKhIDNI 534/3/450/50.

26. James R. Hooker, *Black Revolutionary: George Padmore's Path from Communism to Pan-Africanism* (London, 1967), 17–18. The RILU instructed the ITUCNW to operate under the direction of the European Secretariat of the RILU. RTsKhIDNI 495/155/87/432. Another confidential document called upon the committee to organize unions in Africa, the West Indies, "and such other countries where no sections of the RILU exist" (RTsKhIDNI 495/155/96/10–13). The program stressed equal pay

for equal work; an eight-hour day; social insurance; protection of women and youth; the right to organize; opposition to lynching; improved housing and social conditions in industrial centers; protection for agricultural workers; opposition to seizure of peasant lands; universal education; self-determination for blacks in South Africa, the West Indies, and the American South; opposition to bourgeois and church influences; and defense of the USSR. International Propaganda and Action Committee of Transport Workers, "The ITUCNW of RILU Trade Union Program for Negro Workers" (London, n.d.), 1–14.

27. Hooker, *Black Revolutionary,* 17–38.
28. Turner and Turner, *Richard B. Moore,* 55–56.
29. *DW,* 17, 18, 21 November 1921; Hutchinson, *Blacks and Reds,* 36.
30. *DW,* 12 January 1928; Johanningsmeier, *Forging American Communism,* 238–43.
31. *DW,* 12 January and 7 May 1928; Martin Abern, "The Fighting Miners," *LD* 5 (November 1929): 218; Johanningsmeier, *Forging American Communism,* 240–41; *Pittsburgh Courier,* 12 May 1928.
32. Mark Solomon, *Red and Black: Communism and Afro-Americans,* 1929–1935 (New York, 1987), 494–96; Abern, "The Fighting Miners," 218; Arthur G. McDowell, "Negro Labor and the Miners Revolt," *Opportunity* 9 (August 1931): 236.
33. William H. Harris, *Keeping the Faith: A. Philip Randolph, Milton P. Webster, and the Brotherhood of Sleeping Car Porters,* 1925–1937 (Urbana, Ill., 1977), 93, 111–13; Sterling D. Spero and Abram L. Harris, *The Black Worker: The Negro and the Labor Movement* (New York, 1968 [1931]), 449; Richard B. Moore, "An Open Letter to Mr. A. Philip Randolph," *The Negro Champion,* 8 August 1928, 1.
34. Spero and Harris, *The Black Worker,* 455.
35. Jay Lovestone, "The Great Negro Migration," *Workers Monthly* (February 1926): 179–84; *DW,* 23 April 1927, 31 March 1928.
36. RTxKhIDNI 495/155/64/1–7.
37. In the transcript of Comintern debate on the Negro question (see chapter 5), Harry Haywood and the Siberian Nasanov, in advocating Black Belt self-determination, specifically attacked the Fort-Whiteman–Phillips document. RTsKhIDNI 495/155/56/54.
38. "Policies on Work among the Negroes," adopted by the April 30, 1928, meeting of the Political Committee of the Workers (Communist) Party. RTsKhIDNI 495/155/64/8–10.
39. *DW,* 2 February and 7 September 1929.
40. *DW,* 9 and 11 March 1929; RTsKhIDNI 495/155/1/3.
41. Klehr, *Heyday of American Communism,* 11–13; Foster, *History of the Three Internationals* (New York, 1955), 367–69.
42. *Program of the American Negro Labor Congress* (New York, n.d.), 2–3. With the onset of the Depression, one final attempt was made to resurrect the ANLC through a tour by Huiswoud in January 1930. He claimed to have recruited two hundred new members, especially industrial workers and miners. But meetings were poorly

attended, no meetings were arranged in Chicago and Pittsburgh, and the Chicago leadership showed an interest in liquidating the ANLC. Otto E. Huiswoud, "Report on ANLC Tour," 4 February 1930, RTsKhIDNI 515/1/2024.

43. Writing on the history of black labor and unionism in 1938, Charles H. Wesley located the ANLC in the continuum of struggle against the AFL's "crime against the working class" in refusing to integrate and democratize organized labor. Charles H. Wesley, "Organized Labor's Divided Front," *Crisis* 46 (July 1938): 224.

CHAPTER 5: A NATION WITHIN A NATION

1. Moore to Ford, 28 June 1928, RTsKhIDNI 495/155/66/5.
2. Haywood, *Black Bolshevik,* 5–148; Draper, *American Communism and Soviet Russia,* 332–35.
3. Haywood, *Black Bolshevik,* 218. Nasanov is variously listed as "N. Nasanov," "Nasanoff," or "Nasanov" without initials. However, I am informed by Samuel Adams Darcy, who knew him well as a fellow "rep" of the YCI, that he was called "Charlie." Darcy to Solomon, 27 June 1974 (in author's possession).
4. Interview with Haywood, Detroit, 13 April 1974; Haywood, *Black Bolshevik,* 221, 231–34; "Black Nation in the South: How the Line Was Developed," *National Guardian,* 8 August 1973.
5. Haywood, *Black Bolshevik,* 234.
6. Draper, *American Communism and Soviet Russia,* 168; RTsKhIDNI 495/155/56/42–46.
7. Haywood claimed that the Haywood-Nasanov document summarized "our position in support of the self-determination thesis," suggesting a far more definitive thesis than the document warranted. Haywood, *Black Bolshevik,* 261; RTsKhIDNI 495/155/56/59–63.
8. RTsKhIDNI 495/155/56/59. The balance of the thesis covers familiar ground: principal focus of work among the new black proletariat, strengthening of the ANLC, approval of the Negro Miners' Relief Committee and the Harlem Tenants' League (the only essentially successful Party efforts among blacks), and so forth. The document made one new concrete proposal: the opening of a Party office in Birmingham, Alabama (and the launching of work among Negro tenant farmers).
9. RTsKhIDNI 495/155/56/46, 61–62.
10. Years later, Darcy wrote the author claiming that he was the only white comrade to openly resist the Haywood-Nasanov thesis (Darcy to Solomon, 2 June 1974, in author's possession). Haywood makes the same claim (*Black Bolshevik,* 262, 265). The memories of both men were far from accurate on this point. Wolfe wanted to appoint a subcommission of the U.S. delegation with the addition of some Negro students to produce a more comprehensive document. RTsKhIDNI 495/155/56/48.
11. RTsKhIDNI 495/155/56/50.
12. RTsKhIDNI 495/155/56/52–53.

13. RTsKhIDNI 495/155/56/54–55. Ford's grandfather, according to a biography in the ITUCNW's *Negro Worker,* had been lynched in Gainsville for allegedly "getting fresh with a white woman." When Ford's father drew his first paycheck from the Tennessee Coal, Iron and Railroad Company, his pay envelope said "Ford." When he protested, the foreman said, "Keep that name. It don't matter about a nigger's name nohow." "Negro Worker Nominated for Vice President," *Negro Worker* 2, no. 6 (June 1932): 25–27; Klehr, *The Heyday of American Communism,* 330.

14. RTsKhIDNI 495/155/56/55.

15. Ibid., 88.

16. Ibid., 91; *Inprecorr* (13 August 1928): 856–57.

17. RTsKhIDNI 495/155/65/10/12; William L. Patterson, *The Man Who Cried Genocide* (New York, 1971), 91–94. Patterson saw a troubling connection between the execution of the immigrant Italian anarchists and the lynching of blacks — perhaps exacerbated by the fact that he had been clubbed during a Sacco-Vanzetti demonstration in Boston. His embrace of communism began when Briggs gave him a copy of *The Communist Manifesto.*

18. RTsKhIDNI 495/155/56/93.

19. Ibid., 82–85.

20. Ibid., 24–25.

21. Ibid., 83.

22. Eight were nominated. Haywood received nine votes, Nasanov and Petrovsky got seven each, Ford and Patterson received six votes each. The losers were Engdahl with three votes, Mahoney with four, and Otto Hall, who received only one vote. RTsKhIDNI 495/155/56/84; Haywood, *Black Bolshevik,* 268; *Inprecorr* 8, no. 80 (12 December 1928): 1506–7; "Resolution of the Communist International," 26 October 1928, in CPUSA, *The Communist Position on the Negro Question* (New York, 1934), 56–64. As an indication of how tightly the original six-point resolution was hewn to Petrovsky, Wolfe's "may" had crept in between "which lead" in the typed copy in the Comintern files and was penciled out vigorously. RTsKhIDNI 495/155/56/95.

23. RTsKhIDNI 495/155/56/100–101.

24. RTsKhIDNI 495/155/58/90.

25. RTsKhIDNI 495/155/56/102–3.

26. Haywood and Ford were elected over Otto Hall, Patterson, Phillips, and Mahoney. RTsKhIDNI 495/155/56/103.

27. Kanet, "The Comintern and the 'Negro Question,'" 18, 22, 23; Sidney P. Bunting, "The Labour Movement of South Africa," *Inprecorr* 2, no. 98 (1922): 787–88; Haywood, *Black Bolshevik,* 269–72; RTsKhIDNI 495/155/56/112.

28. The French and British colonial situations were postponed pending the accumulation of additional materials. RTsKhIDNI 495/155/56/112. Commission members attending the meeting were Petrovsky, Mikhailov, Nasanov, Haywood, Roux, Jones

(Otto Hall), Phillips, Lazerey of France, "Douglass," Fort-Whiteman, "Adams" (probably Darcy), Wicks, Patterson, Rivers, Bunting, Mrs. Bunting (the only woman), Jacquemot, Mahoney, Pepper, and "Don." Ibid., 113.

29. Ibid., 114. Mikhailov moved to insert the phrase, "to the point of separation and organization of a separate state," after self-determination. This passed with only two negative votes, but failed to survive editing. Ibid.; "The Communist International Resolution on the Negro Question"; Foner and Allen, *American Communism and Black Americans*, 192.

30. RTsKhIDNI 495/155/56/115.

31. Ibid., 116. No records have been located on the work of the editorial committee or on any additional tinkering that may have gone on in the ECCI before publication of the resolution on October 26, 1928. However, it appears that alterations were minor. Haywood, *Black Bolshevik*, 268–69.

32. *DW*, 12 November 1928; Otto Huiswoud, "World Aspects of the Negro Question," *Communist* 9 (February 1930): 132–47.

33. John Pepper, "Amerikanische Negerprobleme," *Die Kommunistische Internationale* (Berlin), 15 September 1928, 2245–52; James Ford and William Wilson (Patterson), "Zur Frage der Arbeit der amerikanischen Kommunistischen Partei unter den Negern," *Die Kommunistische Internationale* (Berlin), 29 August 1928, 2132–46; Harry Haywood, "Das Neger-problem und die Aufgaben der K.P. der Vereinigten Staaten," *Die Kommunistische Internationale* (Berlin), 5 September 1928, 2253–62.

34. Haywood, *Black Bolshevik*, 216, 254–55; Andre Sik, "The Comintern Programme and the Racial Problem," *Communist International* 5, no. 16 (15 August 1928), 407–9.

35. N. Nasanov, "Against Liberalism in the American Negro Question," *Communist* 9 (April 1930): 304–6; Earl Browder, "For National Liberation of the Negroes! War against White Chauvinism," in *Communism in the United States* (New York, 1935), 303; Harry Haywood, "The Theoretical Defenders of White Chauvinism in the Labor Movement," in CPUSA, *The Communist Position on the Negro Question* (New York, 1934), 35. Ford's view is in *DW*, 15 September 1930.

36. Memo to Kuusinen (unsigned), 18 May 1929, RTsKhIDNI 495/155/30/24.

37. RTsKhIDNI 495/155/80/78. A letter from Haywood's Negro Section in December 1929 noted that although there were definite improvements in the Party's Negro work since the Sixth Congress, there was a continuing underestimation of the self-determination slogan, festering white chauvinism, and no discernible progress on work among southern rural blacks. RTsKhIDNI 495/155/80/161–65.

38. Browder, Ford, Dunne, Weinstone, Patterson, Haywood, Nasanov, Mingulin (now head of the Anglo-American Secretariat), Mikhailov, and some African American students participated. "Resolution of the Communist International, October 1930," in *The Communist Position on the Negro Question*, 41–56; Harry Haywood, "Bour-

geois Liberal Distortion of Leninism on the Negro Question in the United States," *Communist* 9, no. 8 (August 1930), 694; "The Theoretical Defenders of White Chauvinism," 38.

39. "Resolution ... October, 1930," 44–45, 49, 54–55. Self-determination has been routinely confused with separation. Dan Carter's book on Scottsboro mistakenly says the CP's solution to the race problem "was the secession of all black people from the United States" (Dan T. Carter, *Scottsboro: A Tragedy of the American South* [New York, 1971], 64).

40. V. I. Lenin, *Collected Works*, vol. 41 (Moscow, n.d.), 314; Institute of Marxism-Leninism, *Leninism and the National Question* (Moscow, 1977), 19–40; V. I. Lenin, *Statistics and Sociology*, in *Collected Works*, 23:275–76.

41. "Resolution ... October, 1930," 46.

42. Allen was undeterred by signs that the Black Belt was losing its black majority. That was not the only criterion for a future Black Belt republic, he claimed. Other factors, such as history, economy, and "the status of the revolution" in the region, were of equal importance. James S. Allen, "The Black Belt: Area of Negro Majority," *Communist* 13, no. 6 (June 1934): 581–83, 594; "Lenin and the American Negro," *Communist* 30, no. 1 (January 1934): 53–61.

43. James E. Jackson, "Some Aspects of the Negro Question in the United States," *World Marxist Review* 2, no. 7 (July 1959): 16–24.

44. Draper's characterization, in *American Communism and Soviet Russia*, 354–56.

45. "The Theoretical Defenders of White Chauvinism," 31. See Harry Haywood and Milton Howard, *Lynching: A Weapon of National Oppression* (New York, 1934); James S. Allen, *Smash the Scottsboro Lynch Verdict* (New York, 1933); *The American Negro* (New York, 1934); *Negro Liberation* (New York, 1932); *Reconstruction: The Battle for Democracy* (New York, 1937); George Padmore, *The Life and Struggle of Negro Toilers under Imperialism* (London, 1931).

46. Richard Wright, *Native Son* (reprint, New York, 1966), 358, 364.

47. James S. Allen, *Negro Liberation*, quoted in *DW*, 18 November 1932.

48. In writing to Cyril Briggs for assistance, Theodore Draper told him that he sought to drive the canard of Stalin's authorship of self-determination in the Black Belt out of existence. He did the opposite. Draper to Briggs, 11 March 1958, Briggs Papers, SCRL; Draper, *American Communism and Soviet Russia*, 349–50.

49. RTsKhIDNI 495/155/65/10, 495/155/54/6.

50. RTsKhIDNI 495/64/44, 515/1/1620/826.

51. RTsKhIDNI 495/155/65/2. Some researchers have claimed that the black students were treated as "honored guests," getting preferential treatment in terms of board, room, paid vacations, special tutors, clothing, and "fairly easy access to high officials." This is at best only a partial description of the conditions that the students had to cope with. McClellan, "Africans and Blacks in Comintern Schools," 376.

52. Patterson complained to the Workers Party that the bulk of KUTV studies were too abstract; he wanted more concrete analysis of "western capitalist conditions" (RTsKhIDNI 495/155/65/10).

53. Alison Blakely, *Russia and the Negro: Blacks in Russian History and Thought* (Washington, D.C., 1986), 88. Black students at the Lenin School were enrolled in the Soviet Communist Party and "the act of addressing themselves to the CPSU" was considered appropriate. "Resolution of the Situation in the American Lander Group of the ILS," 3 October 1932, RTsKhIDNI 515/2602/44–47; McClellan, "Africans and Black in Comintern Schools," 376–77, 387; RTsKhIDNI 532/1/441/2.

CHAPTER 6: THE TURN

1. Gordon B. Hancock, "When the Manna Faileth," *Opportunity* 6 (May 1928): 133; Jesse O. Thomas, "Cotton No Longer King," *Opportunity* 7 (May 1929): 157. On changes in industrial employment, see Charles S. Johnson, "Present Trends in the Employment of Negro Labor," *Opportunity* 7 (May 1929): 146; editorial, *Opportunity* 6 (April 1928): 99.

2. *Pittsburgh Courier,* 9 February and 8 June 1929.

3. *DW,* 17 January and 7 February 1930; Harvey Klehr, *Communist Cadre* (Stanford, Calif., 1978), 37–52; Klehr, *The Heyday of American Communism,* 161–65.

4. Turner and Turner, *Richard B. Moore,* 57. It is not clear if Fort-Whiteman was actually in the United States to campaign. He most likely was in Moscow. *DW,* 15 and 22 October, 8 and 10 November 1928.

5. *New York Age,* 22 November 1930; National Urban League, Department of Industrial Relations, *Unemployment Status of Negroes: A Compilation of Facts and Figures respecting Unemployment among Negroes in One Hundred and Six Cities* (New York, 1931). The Comintern's Resolution on the Negro question singled out the Negro Miners Relief Committee and the Harlem Tenants League "as examples of joint organizations of action which may serve as a means of drawing the Negro masses into struggle" (Resolution . . . October 1930," 63). Turner and Turner, *Richard B. Moore,* 53–54, 56; Foster, *History of the CPUSA,* 268; Cyril Briggs, "Our Negro Work," *Communist* 8 (September 1929): 497; *New York Amsterdam News,* 12, 19, 26 December 1928, 9 January 1930; *NYT,* 3 February 1928.

6. *DW,* 9 and 11 March 1929.

7. Draper, *American Communism and Soviet Russia,* 417–23; Haywood, *Black Bolshevik,* 91, 304–5, 307; *DW,* 25 April, 8, 9, 10, 16, 23 May 1929; Naison, *Communists in Harlem,* 19.

8. *DW,* 25 April, 30 May, 8 June 1929.

9. *DW,* 8, 10, 13, 16, 19, 25 April 1929.

10. *New York Amsterdam News,* 5 June 1929. Solomon Harper, the indefatigable Harlem Party activist, complained about press reports of the crowd's size, claiming that Briggs had photos showing between five hundred and one thousand demonstrators. *DW,* 3 June 1929.

11. *DW,* 6 and 8 June, 4 July, 10 August, 24 November 1929.

12. *TL,* 7 December 1929; *New York Amsterdam News,* 8 January 1930; Naison, *Communists in Harlem,* 28; *DW,* 11 September and 30 October 1929; *Revolutionary Age,* 1 November 1929.

13. *DW,* 11 July, 15 and 19 August, 6 and 14 September 1929; Otto Hall, "Gastonia and the Negro," *LD* 5 (August 1929): 153, 164.

14. *DW,* 5 and 27 June 1929; *New York Amsterdam News,* 18 September 1929. Williams's claim is in letters to the Baltimore *Afro-American,* 21 and 28 September 1929.

15. The police denied complicity in Luro's death, claiming that he was accidentally struck by a "block of wood" that fell from a Lenox Avenue building. *Pittsburgh Courier,* 12 July 1930; Baltimore *Afro-American,* 12 July 1930; *NYT,* 1 July 1930. Roger N. Baldwin of the American Civil Liberties Union denounced the Gonzalez shooting and insisted that it "could not have occurred if it were not for the present policy of breaking up meetings" (*NYT,* 2 July 1930). Cyril Briggs, returning to a favorite target, blamed UNIA leader S. William Wellington Grant for the murder of Luro. *Inprecorr* 11, no. 21 (1931): 407–8. The *New York Amsterdam News* estimated the multiracial crowd in the Gonzalez procession at over two thousand (9 July 1930).

16. *DW,* 14 September 1929. George S. Schuyler, after the Chicago anti-eviction deaths: "I said as far back as 1923, that [Communist] tactics would only result in the slaughter of a whole lot of Negroes. My prediction is being justified. To the burden of being black amid a populace raised from the breast on rabid color prejudice, the Communists would add 'Redness' to the Negroes' load" ("News and Reviews," *Pittsburgh Courier,* 28 August 1931).

17. TUUL endorsed full equality and "right of national self-determination." Carl Reeve, "American Labor's New Center," *LD* 5 (October 1929): 197; William Z. Foster, "The Convention of the Trade Union Unity League," *Inprecorr* 9, no. 54 (1929): 1168–69. Foster said that "it was far and away the best Negro delegation ever developed at any left wing convention in the United States" (*Program of the Trade Union Unity League* [New York, 1929], 24).

18. James Green, *The World of the Worker: Labor in Twentieth Century America* (New York, 1980), 100–102.

19. William F. Dunne, "The Struggle of the American Coal Miners," *Inprecorr* 8, no. 36 (1928): 611–12.

20. Charles Fulp was beaten and then arrested for "assaulting an officer." Martin Abern, "The Fighting Miners," *LD* 5 (November 1929): 217–18; Philip S. Foner, *Organized Labor and the Black Worker: 1619–1973* (New York, 1974), 192.

21. On Ford, *DW,* 14 December 1929; A. Mills, "Achievements and Weaknesses in Work Among Negroes in the Miners' Strike," *DW,* 17 November 1931. Klehr, *Heyday of American Communism,* 45. Haywood, *Black Bolshevik,* 368.

22. Anne Braden, Ken Lawrence, and Eileen Whalen, "Where Are the Black Workers?" *Southern Patriot* (November 1973): 5.

23. Charles S. Johnson, "The New Frontier of Negro Labor," *Opportunity* 9 (June 1931): 173; Arthur G. McDowell, "Negro Labor and the Miners' Revolt" (part 1), *Opportunity* 9 (August 1931): 236; (part 2) *Opportunity* 9 (September 1931): 275; W.E.B. Du Bois, "Postscript," *Crisis* 38 (March 1931): 94.

24. CPUSA, "Some Lessons of the Miners Strike in the Work among the Negroes" (n.d.), box 11, folder "Negro-mining," RMP.

25. Rosemond was severely beaten in a major strike of the NTWIU in February 1929. *DW,* 6 February 1930.

26. Interview with Maude White Katz, 4 April 1974, New York City.

27. White pointed out that most of the workers in the system were women who had done back-breaking labor in laundries and dry cleaners and who were hired as pressers in the belief that they would perform high-speed labor for low wages. Maude White, "Special Negro Demands," *LU* 6 (May 1931): 10–11; White, "Fighting Discrimination," *LU* 7 (November 1932): 27–28; J. A. Bosse, "Strike of American Needle Workers Begins," *Inprecorr* 9, no. 13 (1929): 230.

28. *Auto Workers News* 1, no. 12 (March 1928); 3, no. 5 (20 August 1929); 3, no. 9 (December–January 1930); *LU* 7 (May 1932): 5; "Constitution of the Auto Workers Union," box 1, HKP, WSU; "The Tasks of the TUUL," Resolution Adopted by the Eighth Session of the RILU (Profintern) Central Council, *LU* 7 (June 1932): 9.

29. Anne Burlak Timpson said that an organizer in the 1930s would think nothing of bedding down on a park bench, living on doughnuts, going for days or weeks without bathing, surviving on borrowed nickels and dimes. That was possible and "socially acceptable," she said, because it really was not too much out of line with the way millions were then living. Interview with Anne Burlak Timpson, Boston, 22 August 1987.

30. Tom Johnson, "International Workers Order in the South," *DW* 30 November 1930.

31. Irving Keith, "Organizing in Virginia, *DW,* 6 May, 2 December 1929; *TL,* 7 December 1929, 1 February 1930; Sol Auerbach, "Breaking Barriers," *LD* 5 (January 1930): 8.

32. Mary Heaton Vorse, untitled article, box 122, MHVP, WSU.

33. Tom Tippet, *When Southern Labor Stirs: The Strike at Gastonia* (Huntington, W.Va., 1972), 76, 108.

34. *DW,* 4 October, 19 September, 29 November 1929; William Z. Foster, "The Historic Southern Conferences," *LD* 5 (December 1929): 223; Baltimore *Afro-American,* 19 October 1929.

35. Foner, *Organized Labor and the Black Worker,* 187–91; Liston Pope, *Millhands and Preachers,* 4th ed. (New Haven, Conn., 1958), 245. Klehr quotes a Gastonia organizer as stating that there were no blacks in the Gastonia mill (*The Heyday of American Communism,* 29). However, Carl Reeve had a vivid memory of the black workers in the waste mill (interview, Philadelphia, 21 March 1974). The 1972 reprint

of Tom Tippet's *When Southern Labor Stirs* has a photograph of striking Gastonia workers on the inside cover. One striker, at least, appears to be African American.

36. ILD press release, 30 July 1929, box 155, MHVP, WSU; William F. Dunne, *Gastonia: Citadel of the Class Struggle in the New South* (New York, 1929), 27; *DW*, 27 August, 26 September 1929. The "workers' jury" was composed of ten whites along with black ANLC members Solomon Harper and Charles Frank (probably Charles Alexander).

37. Klehr, *The Heyday of American Communism*, 420 n.2.

38. Cyril Briggs, "The Negro Question in the Southern Textile Strikes," *Communist* 8 (June 1929), 327.

39. Mary Heaton Vorse quotes a strike organizer: "You'll find [the Party's] Negro organizer. You may be in time to see him lynched" (untitled article, box 122, MHVP, WSU). Briggs, "Further Notes on the Negro Question in the Southern Textile Strikes," *Communist* 8 (July 1929) 392; *DW*, 22 August, 7 September, 9 November 1929; Baltimore *Afro-American*, 24 August 1929.

40. Baltimore *Afro-American*, 3 and 17 August 1929; Tippett, *When Southern Labor Stirs*, 108.

41. *DW*, 31 December 1929.

CHAPTER 7: THE COMMUNIST PARTY IN THE DEEP SOUTH

1. A confidential letter (dated 29 December 1929), sent to the CP by the CI's Negro Section (essentially KUTV students) and approved by the Anglo-American Secretariat, castigated the Party for continuing to underestimate the significance of self-determination. RTsKhIDNI 495/155/80/161–65. CP, "Draft Resolution on Negro Work: The Immediate Task of Drawing the Masses into the Struggle against the Increasing Wave of Terror against Negroes," box 13, folder "1931," RMP; "Extract from Draft Thesis for Party Convention (CPUSA), Work in the South," 3 March 1930, RTsKhIDNI 495/155/83.

2. Klehr, *The Heyday of American Communism*, 273.

3. Robin D.G. Kelley, *Hammer and Hoe: Alabama Communists during the Great Depression* (Chapel Hill, N.C., 1990), 1–10; Horace Davis to Mark Solomon, 31 May 1967 (in author's possession); interview with James S. Allen, 24 March 1974, New York City; NUL, "Unemployment Status of Negroes," 11.

4. Al Murphy fondly recalled Jackson as fearless, but a merciless critic who made little or no effort to account for a recruit's inexperience when leveling criticism (interview, Charleston, Mo., 22–23 April 1974).

5. Horace Davis to Mark Solomon, 31 May 1967; interview with James S. Allen, New York City, 24 March 1974; Kelley, *Hammer and Hoe*, 10–14.

6. Charles Martin, *The Angelo Herndon Case and Southern Justice* (Baton Rouge, La., 1976), 5–9; Angelo Herndon, *Let Me Live* (New York, 1969), 76–77; Kelley, *Hammer and Hoe*, 15.

7. Interview with James S. Allen, New York City, 24 March 1974; Kelley, *Hammer and Hoe,* 16–17. In 1930 the Party ran black candidates deliberately in the face of Jim Crow and disenfranchisement. In Maryland, for example, the Party nominated Samuel Parker, a twenty-six-year-old, for governor. Baltimore *Afro-American,* 5 July 1930.

8. U.S. Congress, House of Representatives, Special Committee on Communist Activities in the United States, 71st Cong., 2d sess., *Investigation of Communist Propaganda,* vol. 1, pt. 6 (Washington, D.C., 1930), 150–99; interview with James S. Allen, New York City, 24 March 1974; Kelley, *Hammer and Hoe,* 19.

9. By November 80 percent of the work force at Tennessee Coal and Iron in Ensley was out of work. *Southern Worker,* 8 November, 27 December 1930; interview with Herbert Benjamin, Silver Spring, Md., 7 April 1974. See also "Draft Resolution: TUUL National Committee" (n.d.), box 14, folder "Trade Unions," RMP; *DW,* 22 December 1930; Kelley, *Hammer and Hoe,* 18–19.

10. Kelley, *Hammer and Hoe,* 21–22.

11. Ibid., 23–24; interview with Al Murphy, Charleston, Mo., 22–23 April 1974; Nell Irvin Painter, *The Narrative of Hosea Hudson* (Cambridge, Mass., 1980), 13–14.

12. Interview with Hosea Hudson, Atlantic City, N.J., 14 December 1974; Kelley, *Hammer and Hoe,* 24; Painter, *The Narrative of Hosea Hudson,* 14.

13. Interview with Hosea Hudson, Atlantic City, N.J., 14 December 1974; extracts from a manuscript by Nell Painter (in author's possession); Painter, *The Narrative of Hosea Hudson,* 2–13, 81–82.

14. Hosea Hudson, "On Some of the Early Party Organization in the South, Potickly in Birmingham and Ala.," unpublished manuscript (in author's possession).

15. Hudson, "On Some of the Early Party Organization," 2; interview with Hosea Hudson, Atlantic City, N.J., 14 December 1974. Simms was murdered on February 10, 1932, in the Harlan, Kentucky, strike. Klehr, *The Heyday of American Communism,* 46–47. Angelo Herndon, from the Fulton Tower jail, shared his memories of the eager, courageous teenager who had come to Birmingham to assist in organizing. Angelo Herndon, "In Memory of Harry Simms," *LD* 9 (February 1934): 17.

16. Hudson, "On Some of the Early Party Organization," 1–3.

17. Kelley, *Hammer and Hoe,* 25–26. Johnson left Birmingham in 1931 because of health problems; Jackson led the district from Chattanooga. However, the arrival of Ross and another New Yorker, Ted Wellman, signaled a tightening of the structure of District 17. Hudson, "On Some of the Early Party Organization," 3–4.

18. Kelley, *Hammer and Hoe,* 95; Painter, *The Narrative of Hosea Hudson,* 21. Here, West is identified as "Jim Gray."

19. The Central Committee sent Allen and his wife Isabel to Chattanooga to launch a paper in a city with a bit more breathing space for Communists than repressive Birmingham. Interview with James S. Allen, New York City, 24 March 1974; Kelley, *Hammer and Hoe,* 16. The place of publication on the masthead of the *Southern*

Worker was listed as Birmingham—a ruse to throw the authorities off the trail. "Draft Program for Negro Farmers in the Southern States" and "Draft Program for the Negro Laborers in the Southern States," *Communist* 9 (March 1930): 246–55; James S. Allen, "Some Rural Aspects of the Struggle for the Right to Self-Determination," *Communist* 10 (March 1931): 254–55.

20. Horace B. Davis to Mark Solomon, 31 May 1967 (in author's possession); Kelley, *Hammer and Hoe*, 38.

21. Kelley, *Hammer and Hoe*, 34–37; Katherine Du Pre Lumpkin, *The South in Progress* (New York, 1940), 127–32; John Beecher, "The Share Croppers' Union in Alabama," *Social Forces* 13 (October 1934): 124–31; *Southern Worker*, 11 October 1930.

22. Interview with Al Murphy, Charleston, Mo., 22–23 April 1974; Kelley, *Hammer and Hoe*, 38; *TL*, 14 March 1931; Art Shields, "Chattel Slavery," *LD* 7 (February 1931): 32; Harrison George, "Slavery—1931 Style," *LD* 7 (June 1931): 111; Jane Dillon, "Fighting for Bread in Dixie," *LD* 7 (October 1931): 188; "A Sharecropper Tells His Story," *LD* 7 (September 1931): 169; "A Negro Worker, 'From Peonage to Struggle,'" *LD* 6 (April 1930): 73; "'American Democracy' in the South," *Working Woman* 1, no. 9 (June 1930): 1.

23. Klehr, *The Heyday of American Communism*, 136–52; Kelley, *Hammer and Hoe*, 38–39; *TL*, 25 July 1931.

24. Kelley, *Hammer and Hoe*, 40; *TL*, 25 July 1931.

25. *TL*, 25 July 1931, 15 December 1932; Carter, *Scottsboro*, 123–24; Kelley, *Hammer and Hoe*, 40. Kelley notes that Coad was illiterate. Nevertheless, the Party ran him for municipal judge in Chattanooga, before his return to Alabama to work for the Croppers' Union.

26. Melvin P. Levy, "Camp Hill—Slavery That Is Legal," *LD* 7 (January 1932): 13.

27. Kelley, *Hammer and Hoe*, 41; William Nowell, "Why Camp Hill?" *LD* 6 (September 1931): 167; Carter, *Scottsboro*, 124–25; *DW*, 11 August 1931; Lowell Wakefield, "A Sharecropper Tells the Story," *LD* 6 (September 1931), 169; *DW*, 18 July 1931; *NYT*, 18 July 1931. There are minor variations in the recounting of events. Gray's brother said that Ralph was murdered in his bed. Lowell Wakefield of the ILD said that Gray was dragged from his bed and murdered on the way to jail. The *New York Times* said that Gray was wounded in the exchange of fire at his house and died en route to jail. The same scenario was reported by the *Birmingham Age-Herald* (20 July 1931), which stated that Gray was left for dead on the road because Sheriff Young was "losing blood and had to be rushed to a hospital."

28. *Birmingham News*, 17 July 1931; *Birmingham Post*, 18 July 1931. The *Post* reported that police knew of "a Chattanooga, Tenn. negro" who was an organizer and led thirty-five "ringleaders." *Montgomery Advertiser*, 18 July 1931; James Goodman, *Stories of Scottsboro* (New York, 1994), 71.

29. "Day Letter" from Walter White and "Walter White Sees Trick," Associated Negro Press dispatches, both in Camp Hill File, RKC. Harris Gilbert (Lem Harris), writ-

ing in the *Daily Worker,* admitted that cropper organization moved faster than the Party anticipated; the launching of a "mass meeting" on July 15 was something of a surprise and a contravention of advice "to hold only small meetings and to work closely and carefully" (*DW,* 11 August 1931). *NYT,* 19 July 1931; *TL,* 8 August 1931; *Crisis* 38 (September 1931): 314.

30. Kelley, *Hammer and Hoe,* 43; Eugene Gordon, "Camp Hill," *DW,* 28 July 1931; "Camp Hill Cropper Free, Tells Story," *Southern Worker,* 29 August 1931; *Opportunity* 9 (August 1931): 234–35.

31. Kelley, *Hammer and Hoe,* 43–44; interview with Al Murphy, Charleston, Mo., 22–23 April 1974; CPUSA, "Draft Resolution on Negro Work — The Immediate Task."

32. Interview with Al Murphy, Charleston, Mo., 22–23 April, 1974; Kelley, *Hammer and Hoe,* 48–49; Haywood, *Black Bolshevik,* 402–3.

33. On February 10, 1931, a rally against hunger and evictions landed Mary Dalton (one of the "Atlanta Six"), historian Elizabeth Lawson, and Harry German in jail for vagrancy and inciting to riot. By August the Chattanooga Unemployed Council was matching the actions of its counterparts in the North by moving the furniture of evicted tenants, mainly blacks, back into their homes. Interview with James S. Allen, New York City, 24 March 1974; *Southern Worker,* 31 January, 7 and 14 February, 14 and 28 March, 30 May, and 15 August 1931; Horace Davis to Solomon, 31 May 1967; *NYT,* 8 June 1930.

34. Organized Party units in the cities mentioned were determined by the listings of sales and subscription targets by the *Southern Worker,* 1 November 1930.

35. C. Clark to Harold Preece, 29 June 1941 (date on postmark), Sharecroppers file, RKC.

36. Martin, *The Angelo Herndon Case,* 5–6; Herndon, "In Memory of Harry Simms," 17.

37. Acting director, NAACP, to Will W. Alexander, Commission on Interracial Cooperation, 27 May 1930, NAACP Papers; Atlanta Six file, RKC; Martin, *The Angelo Herndon Case,* 19, 21; ILD, *Death Penalty!* (New York, 1930), 4–5, 7–8; John Dos Passos, "Back to Red Hysteria," *NR* 68 (July 1930): 161–62; "Fulton Superior Court, Criminal Division, Grand Jury for May Term, 1930, State of Georgia, County of Fulton," Atlanta Six file, RKC.

38. Will W. Alexander to Walter White, 27 June 1930, NAACP Papers; Atlanta Six file, RKC; interview with Anne Burlak Timpson, Boston, 24 June 1987.

39. Interview with Anne Burlak Timpson, Boston, 24 June 1987. In 1930 the Communists in Atlanta netted eighty-three black recruits; not a single white seems to have joined. *TL,* 8 March 1930.

40. *Southern Worker,* 6 and 20 December 1930, 18 and 25 April, 18 and 25 July 1931.

41. "Report of Comrade Clara Holden on Work in the South," RTsKhIDNI 534/7/500/ 23/27; Erwin D. Hoffman, "The Genesis of the Modern Movement for Equal Rights

in South Carolina, 1930–39," in Bernard Sternsher, ed., *The Negro in Depression and War* (Chicago, 1969), 203–6.

42. "Organizational Experience in the South," *Party Organizer* (April 1931): 14–15. In 1934 all of District 16 had a hundred dues-paying members, half in Richmond and Norfolk. Klehr, *The Heyday of American Communism*, 273; Kelley, *Hammer and Hoe*, 28.

CHAPTER 8: WIPE OUT THE STENCH OF THE SLAVE MARKET

1. RTsKhIDNI 495/155/80/61. Mary Heaton Vorse claimed that Owens had put in a brief appearance in Gastonia, but had left quickly when confronted with potential KKK provocation (untitled manuscript on Gastonia, box 122, MHVP, WSU).

2. RTsKhIDNI 495/155/80/59–60. The other signatories were Elizabeth L. Griffin, Charles Henry, and Edward L. Doty.

3. RTsKhIDNI 495/155/43/14–15. The Party preferred the term *chauvinism* to *racism* or *white supremacy*. Chauvinism was considered a precise ideological manifestation of national superiority. The term was derived from the legendary nineteenth-century French soldier, Nicholas Chauvin, who was zealous in his advocacy of French national supremacy. "The Communist International Resolution on the Negro Question in the United States," 193–94; Louis Koves, "For Negro and White Workers' Unity," *DW*, 23 December 1930.

4. Sadie Van Veen, "Lily White and Pure," *DW*, 31 March 1931; Harry Haywood, "The Struggle for the Leninist Position on the Negro Question in the USA," *Communist* 12 (September 1933): 889.

5. Earl Browder, "For National Liberation of the Negroes! War against White Chauvinism!" in *The Communist Position on the Negro Question* (New York, 1934), 11–12.

6. Harry Haywood, "Lenin and the Negro Question in the United States," *DW*, 14 January 1933.

7. "The Communist International Resolution on the Negro Question in the United States," 195; "Resolution . . . October, 1930," 45.

8. Cyril Briggs, "Our Negro Work," *Communist* 8 (September 1929): 494–95.

9. Ibid., 496–97. Briggs acknowledged that since the Sixth Congress "the instructions of the Communist International to push the Negro comrades to the front in Party work have been carried out on a large scale."

10. Ibid., 498; Baltimore *Afro-American*, 2 November 1929.

11. "On Fighting White Chauvinism," *Party Organizer* (May 1931): 14–16.

12. Briggs, "Our Negro Work," 500; Vera Saunders, "Negro Workers Will Come into Our Party," *DW*, 26 February 1931; "Resolution of the Central Committee, USA on Negro Work," *DW*, 23 March 1931.

13. Saunders, "Negro Workers Will Come into Our Party."

14. "Resolution of the District Bureau, CPUSA, District 2, on the Struggle against Chauvinism," *DW*, 19 February 1931. More than 40 percent of the Party's membership was unemployed in 1932. Klehr, *The Heyday of American Communism*, 161.

15. The Central Committee is quoted in "Resolution of the District 2 Bureau, CPUSA, on the Struggle against Chauvinism."

16. Interview with Rose Chernin, Los Angeles, 3 January 1973.

17. *DW*, 7 January 1932. Washington, a segregated city in the 1930s (and through early postwar years), was the scene of repeated instances of racist behavior at social events in the Party's orbit. The district leadership refused to accept the excuse that such conduct reflected larger societal influences. Such a rationalization was attacked as an expression of "anti–working-class" bias. Roy Peltz, "White Chauvinism in Washington," *DW*, 9 September 1931; *Pittsburgh Courier*, 27 August 1932; Robert Woods, "White Chauvinism and the Right Danger," *DW*, 5 and 19 December 1929; *Pittsburgh Courier*, 27 August 1932.

18. *DW*, 7 January 1931.

19. *DW*, 11 February 1931.

20. *TL*, 28 March, 16 May 1921; "Vets Rebuke Cause of Anti-Negro Prejudice," *DW*, 28 September 1932.

21. In response to my observation that the trials were contrived, Haywood said wryly, "Of course they were contrived. They were not bourgeois courts; they were designed to make an unmistakable political point" (interview with Harry Haywood, Detroit, 12 April 1974). Ethel Stevens, "Buffalo White Chauvinist to Face Workers," *DW*, 11 October 1932.

22. In the dawning popular front period (1935), the Party still reported that it had registered 11,298 native-born and 17,570 foreign-born members, a 40–60 percent split. Jack Stachel, "Organizational Problems of the Party," *Communist* 10 (July 1935): 267.

23. *TL*, 18 January 1930; *DW*, 20 December 1930.

24. *DW*, 10 and 20 December 1930, 23 July 1931. The Chicago Lithuanian situation even caught the attention of Solomon Lozovsky, secretary of the RILU, who said, "I hold that an incident like this is a crying disgrace and blot upon the revolutionary labor movement" (quoted in Maude White, "Against White Chauvinism in the Philadelphia Needle Trades," *DW*, 28 January 1931).

25. Harold Cruse has argued that not only did the Party break the ethnic cooperatives, but also it denied to blacks "important indoctrination along economic cooperative lines which, in the long run would have proved more beneficial ... than the formation of trade unions" (Cruse, *Crisis of the Negro Intellectual*, 138). However, in his analysis Cruse ignored the steady growth of the black working class — notwithstanding the wishes of Communists or cooperationists. In the 1930s African Americans made economic progress through jobs in industry — and industrial unionism became their weapon. Cruse also ignored the marginal impact of cooperative ventures in general and especially of George S. Schuyler's failing Young Negroes' Cooperative League of 1931.

26. Interview with Maude White Katz, New York City, 2 March 1974.

27. *DW,* 16 February 1931; *TL,* 21 February 1931.

28. *DW,* 16, 21, 24 February, 3 March 1931; *NYT,* 28 February and 2 March 1931; *TL,* 14 March 1931; Foster, *History of the CPUSA,* 288; *Chicago Defender,* 7 March 1931; CPUSA, *Race Hatred on Trial* (New York, 1931), 32.

29. *Chicago Defender,* 7 March 1931.

30. *DW,* 3 and 4 March 1931; Haywood, "The Struggle for a Leninist Position," 498; Browder, "For the National Liberation of the Negroes!" 5; *DW,* 11 January 1933.

31. *Chicago Defender,* 14 January 1933.

32. Antichauvinist pressure on the ethnics began before the Yokinen trial. Louis Koves, "For Negro and White Workers' Unity," *DW,* 23 December 1930.

33. *DW,* 28 February, 3 March 1931; *NYT,* 3, 4, 5 March 1931; *TL,* 14 and 28 March, 21 February 1931.

34. "Resolution of the Central Committee, CPUSA, on Negro Work," 16 March 1931, box 12, folder "1931," RMP. The Negro Section of the Anglo-American Secretariat of the CI sent a letter in January 1930 sharply criticizing the alleged fobbing of Negro work to blacks and to the LSNR. RTsKhIDNI 495/155/90/30–33.

35. Maude White, "Against White Chauvinism in the Philadelphia Needle Trades," *DW,* 28 January 1931.

36. "For a Sharper Fight on White Chauvinism in the Revolutionary Unions," *DW,* 5 and 9 February 1932.

37. Ibid.; *Pittsburgh Courier,* 13 February 1932.

38. Haywood, "The Struggle for a Leninist Position," 899; Browder, "For the National Liberation of Negroes," 16–17.

39. Briggs, "The Negro Question in the Southern Textile Strikes," 324–28; Briggs, "Further Notes on the Negro Question in the Southern Textile Strikes," 393–94; George Rivera, "The Communist Party and the Negro Question: 1919–1945," honors thesis, Department of African American Studies, Harvard University, April 1977, 29; Horace Cayton and George S. Mitchell, *Black Workers and the New Unions* (New York, 1938), 85–87, 114–18, 337–41.

40. An Aunt Jemima expulsion took place in Greenville, South Carolina, in 1931. Interview with Anne Burlak Timpson, Brookline, Mass., 11 September 1995.

41. *TL,* 18 April, 5 August 1931. With typical puffery, the Party claimed that revivals of *Birth of a Nation* were directed at its own efforts to build black-white unity. *DW,* 30 March, 21 July 1931; *TL,* 15 August 1932.

Chapter 9: Fighting Hunger and Eviction

1. Edmund Wilson, *An American Earthquake* (Garden City, N.Y., 1938), 463–64.

2. "Negroes and the Relief of Unemployment," *Crisis* 38 (December 1931): 414–15; 39 (February 1932): 47.

3. CP, *Unemployment Relief and Social Insurance: The Communist Party Program against the Capitalist Program of Starvation* (New York, 1931), 2; Klehr, *The Heyday of American Communism*, 50–51.

4. Foster, *History of the CPUSA*, 281; Klehr, *The Heyday of American Communism*, 49–68; interview with Carl Winter, New York City, 23 May 1980.

5. Baltimore *Afro-American*, 1 March 1930; *NYT*, 30 January 1930.

6. On February 26, 1930, Chicago police arrested four hundred black and white demonstrators who were actually seated in the Musicians' Hall listening to a procession of speakers. The initial charge was "exhorting." *NYT*, 22, 27, 28 February 1930; *TL*, 8 March 1930.

7. The Unemployed Councils claimed that one and a quarter million marchers hit the streets in more than a dozen cities. Foster, *History of the CPUSA*, 282. Police estimates of the crowds were typically lower. The American Civil Liberties Union reported that twenty-two demonstrations were prohibited, broken up, or marred by clashes between demonstrators and police. Two hundred fifty-six people were arrested in twenty-two cities. *NYT*, 7 and 27 March 1930.

8. *TL*, 15, 22 March 1930.

9. *TL*, 8, 15, 22 February 1930.

10. From August 10, 1930, to December 8, 1932, the *New York Times* reported forty-seven significant demonstrations and hunger marches conducted by the Unemployed Councils and cooperating groups.

11. *NYT*, 17 October 1930, 11 February 1931. On the same day as the Capitol Hill event, demonstrations were held around the country, as warm-ups for National Unemployment Insurance Day on February 25, 1931.

12. *TL*, 19 September 1931, 4 November 1932.

13. Herndon, *Let Me Live*, 83–86, 93–94; Kelley, *Hammer and Hoe*, 30–31; *DW*, 9 November 1932.

14. *TL*, 25 April, 5 September 1931.

15. Vern Smith, "Unity of Negro and White in Hunger," *TL*, 30 May 1931.

16. James S. Allen, "The Scottsboro Struggle," *Communist* 12 (May 1933): 437–48; interview with Carl Winter, New York City, 24 June 1980; interview with Herbert Benjamin, Silver Spring, Maryland, 7 April 1974.

17. *NYT*, 12 July 1932; *TL*, 1 August 1932.

18. Local public hearings organized in conjunction with the marches singled out the particular hardships of blacks. The councils claimed that specific outrages were curbed as a result of the hearings. *TL*, 14 and 21 November 1931; *NYT*, 30 November 1931; interview with Herbert Benjamin, Silver Spring, Maryland, 7 April 1974.

19. *Pittsburgh Courier*, 12 December 1931; *NYT*, 7 December 1931; *TL*, 19 December 1931; *Opportunity* 10 (January 1932): 28.

20. The Chicago group was broken up in Hammond, Indiana, by local police. Skirmishes also took place in Tonawanda, New York, Boston, Hartford, and a few other cities. *NYT,* 30 November and 8 December 1931; *TL,* 19 November and 19 December 1931.

21. Horace R. Cayton, "The Black Bugs," *Nation* 133, no. 3453 (9 September 1931): 255–256.

22. Michael Gold, "The Negro Reds of Chicago," *DW,* 4 October 1932.

23. Interview with Claude Lightfoot, Gary, Indiana, 26 April 1974.

24. *DW,* 20 September, 4 October 1932. Radical actions against evictions had become so commonplace that it was not unusual "when eviction notices arrived . . . for a mother to shout to the children, 'run quick and find the reds!'" St. Clair Drake and Horace Cayton, *Black Metropolis* (New York, 1945), 87.

25. In Detroit five hundred blacks and whites fought two hundred police when the UC attempted to move back the furniture of an evicted Negro. In fall 1932, in the Brownsville section of Brooklyn, the Herzl Street Block Committee gathered five hundred people to demonstrate at the home of a landlord, protesting the alleged charging of higher rents to blacks than whites. The demonstration convinced the landlord to equalize rents. *TL,* 16 June, 4 November, 15 December 1932; *NYT,* 7 December 1932.

26. John Williamson, "The Lessons of August 3 in Chicago and the Next Tasks," *DW,* 19 August 1931.

27. *Chicago Whip,* 1 August 1931; *Chicago Defender,* 3 August 1931; *DW,* 19 August 1931.

28. Harold F. Gosnell, *Negro Politicians: The Rise of Negro Politics in Chicago* (Chicago, 1967), 330; *Pittsburgh Courier,* 8 August 1931; *Chicago Defender,* 1 and 8 August 1931; *Chicago Tribune,* 4 and 6 August 1931; *Chicago Herald and Examiner,* 5 August 1931; *Chicago American,* 4 August 1931; *DW,* 4 and 5 August 1931. When Armstrong did not come home on the night of the riot, his wife went to the city morgue, but was shown Grey's body. Her husband had already been identified as "Thomas Page." The mistake was corrected when the body was being prepared for burial and someone recognized it as Armstrong. *Chicago Defender,* 15 August 1931; *DW,* 10 August 1931; *Hunger Fighter* 2 (4 March 1933).

29. *Chicago Tribune,* 6 and 7 August 1931; *Pittsburgh Courier,* 8 August 1931; Bill Gebert, "The Chicago Massacre," *DW,* 8 August 1931.

30. *Chicago Tribune,* 7 August 1931; *Chicago Bee,* 16 August 1931; *Chicago Whip,* 15 and 22 August 1931.

31. *Chicago Herald and Examiner,* 5 August 1931; *Chicago Daily News,* 5 August 1931; *DW,* 7 August and 28 September 1931.

32. *DW,* 9 November 1931.

33. Frank Armstrong's wife refused to let the Unemployed Councils take charge of her husband's body. *Chicago Defender,* 15 August 1931; *DW,* 7 August 1931.

34. The leaflet offered a nineteen-point program from uemployment insurance to "not a penny for imperialist war." Leaflet in Chicago 1931 file, RKC.
35. The ILD estimated that sixty thousand people, including twenty thousand whites, marched in the biggest demonstration in the city's history. The local black press claimed around fifteen thousand marchers and thousands more who watched. All observers agreed that around one-fourth of the mourners were white. *Chicago Whip*, 15 August 1931; *Chicago Bee*, 16 August 1931.
36. Gosnell, *Negro Politicians*, 332; *DW*, 31 May 1933.
37. Klehr, *The Heyday of American Communism*, 153–54; interview with Claude Lightfoot, Gary, Indiana, 25 April 1974.
38. Kelley, *Hammer and Hoe*, 92–95; interview with Ishmael Flory, Chicago, 27 April 1974.
39. Lightfoot could not recall the precise charges against Poindexter. Interview with Claude Lightfoot, Gary, Indiana, 25–26 April 1974.
40. *TL*, 15 July, 1 October 1931, 14 November 1932; *NYT*, 3 September 1932.
41. *Chicago Defender*, 3 December 1932.
42. *NYT*, 28 December 1932; interview with Carl Winter, New York City, 24 June 1980.
43. *Pittsburgh Courier*, 7 January 1933.

CHAPTER 10: NATIONALISTS AND REFORMISTS;LT/;MT

1. Earl Browder was nettled at the idea of "two nationalisms" — one bourgeois, the other proletarian — that was popular in the Party. To link the two phenomena in any way would somehow suggest that they were not contradictory. Browder, "For National Liberation of the Negroes!" 17.
2. Robert Minor expounded that "social fascism tends to concentrate in the effort to head off the rising movement of the Negro masses under the lash of the economic crisis and the race persecution that goes with it" (Minor, "The Negro and His Judases," *Communist* 10 [July 1931]: 639).
3. Joseph Stalin, *Marxism and the National Question* (New York, 1942), 20.
4. Browder, "For National Liberation of the Negroes!" 13; Briggs, "Further Notes on the Negro Question in the Southern Textile Strikes," 395; District 2, CP, "Resolution of the district Bureau, CPUSA, District 2 on the Struggle against Chauvinism," *DW*, 19 February 1931.
5. *TL*, 18 January 1930.
6. *TL*, 25 January 1930; Hill, *The Crusader*, 1:xlviii.
7. "Minutes of Meeting of Negro Commission," 3 January 1929, RTsKhIDNI 515/1/1685/6.
8. Harry Haywood, *The Road to Negro Liberation* (New York, 1934), 52–53, 58.
9. *Pittsburgh Courier*, 7 and 14 March 1931; *Opportunity* 7 (July 1929): 210; 9 (May 1931): 154; Du Bois in *Crisis* 38 (March 1931); "Along the Color Line," *Crisis* 10 (May 1932): 162; "Progress," *Crisis* 39 (October 1932): 323.
10. *TL*, 28 March and 6 June 1931.

11. *TL*, 6 June 1931; *DW*, 3 December 1931.

12. The black press itself in the early 1930s was laden with criticism of the conservatism of much of the middle class. See *Chicago Whip*, 15 August 1931; Baltimore *Afro-American*, 19 March 1932.

13. T. Arnold Hill, "Interracial Business," *Opportunity* 9 (March 1931): 86, 91.

14. Loren Miller, "The Plight of the Negro Professional Man," *Opportunity* 9 (August 1931): 239–41.

15. Eugene Gordon, "Black Capitalists in America," *NM* (January 1932): 23–24.

16. On the collapse of the Binga and Douglass banks, see Du Bois, *Crisis* 37 (December 1930): 425. On insolvencies of black-owned banks and insurance companies, see the Baltimore *Afro-American*, 10 May 1931, 23 April and 14 May 1932; *Crisis* 38 (September 1931): 289. On CMA, see the Baltimore *Afro-American*, 17 December 1932; also *Pittsburgh Courier*, 5 August 1933. John Nail was quoted in the *Pittsburgh Courier*, 11 April 1931. Occomy's comment in *Business Review* was quoted in the *Pittsburgh Courier*, 8 August 1931.

17. *HL*, 26 August 1933.

18. Undated document, "Memorandum on Negro Business — the Negro Bourgeoisie" (in author's possession); *HL*, 17 June 1933.

19. *TL*, 26 April 1930, 10 October 1931; *DW*, 28 and 30 July 1930. The vitriol in the Party press against the black bourgeoisie in the early 1930s was seemingly endless. For example, William L. Patterson, "The Agents of the Bosses Attack Us," *LD* 13 (January 1933); Harry Haywood, "The NAACP Prepares New Betrayals of the Negro Masses," *DW*, 30 May 1932.

20. *TL*, 19, 25 April, 6, 13, 20 June 1931.

21. *TL*, 21 December 1929, 25 January 1930, 21 November 1931.

22. Haywood, "The NAACP Prepares New Betrayals of the Negro Masses"; Walter White, "The Negro and the Communists," *Harper's Magazine* 164 (December 1931): 62–72.

23. *DW*, 12, 25 May, 18 December 1931; *TL*, 13 June 1931.

24. *DW*, 28, 30 May 1932.

25. W.E.B. Du Bois, "Programs of Emancipation," *Crisis* 37 (April 1930): 137. This piece was based on a long analysis of the ANLC programs prepared for Walter White. NAACP file, RKC.

26. *TL*, 29 March, 30 April 1930.

27. *TL*, 25 April 1931.

28. Cyril Briggs, "Our Approach to the Garveyites," *TL*, 23 September 1933. The article was a response to criticism that Briggs had failed to differentiate sufficiently the leadership and the rank and file of the UNIA. See chapter 14.

29. Garvey's attack on communism is quoted in Amy Jacques Garvey, *Garvey and Garveyism*, 93. *TL*, 13 June 1931; William L. Patterson, "Does Russia Love the Negro?" *LD* 7 (November 1931): 215.

30. W.E.B. Du Bois, "As the Crow Flies," *Crisis* 37 (March 1930): 77; 37 (October 1930): 343; 38 (June 1931): 188. "The Camera," *Pittsburgh Courier,* 16 and 23 August 1930, 15 August, 5 September 1931; *TL,* 21 February 1931. By the mid-1930s the black media were paying more attention to the small African American community in Moscow. I.D.W. Talmadge, "Mother Emma," *Opportunity* 11 (August 1933): 245–47; Langston Hughes, "Going South in Russia," *Crisis* 41 (June 1934): 162–63; Baltimore *Afro-American,* 7, 12, 28 September 1935, 12 June, 22 August, 24 November 1936.

31. *Chicago Defender,* 6 October 1934.

32. Interview with Louise Thompson Patterson by the author, New York City, 28 June 1974; interview with Patterson by Ruth Prager for the OHAL Project, 17 October 1981.

33. Thompson fashioned a committee of diverse leftists that included W. A. Domingo, Malcolm Cowley, Rose McClendon, John Henry Hammond, and Waldo Frank. Jack El-Hai, "Black and White and Red," *American Heritage* (May–June 1991): 84; Arnold Rampersad, *The Life of Langston Hughes: I Too Sing America,* vol. 1: 1902–41 (New York 1986), 243–44.

34. El-Hai, "Black and White and Red," 87; interview with Louise Thompson Patterson, New York City, 28 June 1974; Rampersad, *The Life of Langston Hughes,* 1:247; *Crisis* 39 (August 1932): 261.

35. Interview with Thompson Patterson, New York City, 28 June 1974; Rampersad, *The Life of Langston Hughes,* 1:250–51; McClellan, "Africans and Blacks in the Comintern Schools," 383; Allison Blakely, *Russia and the Negro: Blacks in Russian History and Thought* (Washington, D.C., 1986), 93–96.

36. Rampersad, *The Life of Langston Hughes,* 1:250–52; El-Hai, "Black and White and Red," 88.

37. *Crisis* 39 (September 1932): 294; Baltimore *Afro-American,* 8 October 1932; *Pittsburgh Courier,* 3 September 1932. Calvin added that James W. Ford, who was running for vice president in 1932 on the Communist ticket, would be forced to "bow his head in shame" because "twenty-two of his own brothers and sisters are stranded 4,000 miles from home on the avowed grounds of bowing to race prejudice" (*Pittsburgh Courier,* 8 October 1932).

38. *Crisis* 40 (February 1933): 37; *DW,* 8 and 24 September, 15 October 1932; *Chicago Defender,* 1 October 1932; RTsKhIDNI 532/1/441/13.

39. *Pittsburgh Courier,* 3 September 1932.

40. Hooker, *Black Revolutionary,* 13–15.

41. Ibid., 15–16; RTsKhIDNI 534/3/450/1–3.

42. Hooker, *Black Revolutionary,* 19–22. The first two issues of the monthly (January and February 1931) were called the *International Negro Workers' Review.* The purpose of the publication was neither to be "theoretical" nor to serve as an organ of opinion. Rather, it was to be a journal of analysis of the "day to day problems" of

black workers the world over and a mobilizer of action. *International Negro Workers' Review* 1, no. 1 (January 1931): 2–3.

43. Hooker, *Black Revolutionary*, 22–23.

44. Ibid., 25.

45. Ibid., 30.

46. Padmore claimed that he refused to accept the invitation unless suitable security was provided and his trip was given wide publicity. Ibid., 31. But in an article written in early 1934 and published in *Crisis* in October 1935, Padmore complained that the CI refused to discuss any matters bearing upon the "liquidation of the Negro Committee and the suppression of the *Negro Worker*" (Padmore, "An Open Letter to Earl Browder," *Crisis* 42 [October 1935]: 302). Editorial, "Au Revoir," *Negro Worker* 4, nos. 8–9 (August–September 1933): 18. The announcement of Padmore's expulsion appeared in *Negro Worker* 4, no. 2 (June 1934): 14.

47. Hooker, *Black Revolutionary*, 32. Padmore's biographer confused the Woodson-Huiswoud identity, believing that they were separate individuals. Woodson, he claimed, was "an undistinguished man" who "soon gave way" to Huiswoud. Robert A. Hill's short biography of Huiswoud can be found in Johnpoll and Klehr, *Biographical Dictionary of the American Left*, 219–21. RTsKhIDNI 534/3/1055/42.

48. "Greenwood," "A Betrayer of the Negro Liberation Struggle," *Inprecorr* 37 (1934): 968; RTsKhIDNI 534/3/1055/42. The first edition of the reconstituted *Negro Worker* declared that "we are backing the struggle for freedom and complete emancipation of the Negro toiling masses from the barbarous exploitation and slave oppression of world imperialism" (*Negro Worker* 4, no. 1 [May 1934]: 1).

49. Hooker, *Black Revolutionary*, 16. Padmore claimed that the Comintern left him with only Japan to attack as a colonialist power—something that he found particularly distasteful. But the *Negro Worker*'s lead editorial in its August 1934 edition castigated "British, American and Belgian imperialists," without mentioning Japan (*Negro Worker* 4, no. 4 [August 1934]: 1).

50. "A Betrayer of the Negro Liberation Struggle," 968; "Expulsion of George Padmore from the Revolutionary Movement," *Negro Worker* 4, no. 2 (June 1934): 14; HL, 29 September 1934. Padmore took umbrage in particular at an article in the June 1934 *Negro Worker*, which alleged that he had given the names of black seamen to the police. He threatened to sue, declaring that "when you accuse me of being a police agent this is going beyond all sense of decency and fair play" (Padmore, "Open Letter to Earl Browder," 315). Browder backed away from the charge that Padmore had given names to the police. Instead, he said that Negro seamen who had distributed the *Negro Worker* had "unaccountably" fallen into the hands of the police. He added that "there is not the slightest doubt that this was caused, if not by Padmore directly, then by his new associates" (*Crisis* 42 [December 1935]: 372).

51. Helen Davis, "The Rise and Fall of George Padmore as a Revolutionary Fighter," *Negro Worker* 4, no. 4 (August 1934): 15–18.
52. "A Betrayer of the Negro Liberation Struggle," 968; Padmore, "An Open Letter to Earl Browder," 302.
53. Hooker, *Black Revolutionary,* 19–22; Arnold Ward to William L. Patterson, 14 November 1933, RTsKhIDNI 534/3/895/122.
54. I am indebted to Azinna Nwafor for discussions of this interpretation of Padmore's pan-Africanism. See Nwafor's introduction to Padmore's *Pan-Africanism or Communism* (New York, 1972), xxx–xli.
55. Ibid., xxxvi–xxxvii.
56. Hooker, *Black Revolutionary,* 35.
57. Interview with William L. Patterson, New York City, 19 April 1973. Angelo Herndon, who came to symbolize the persecution of black Communists in the South, wrote that in Marxism he found "a realistic recognition of the world and a rational plan of scientific socialism with which to create order and harmony out of human chaos" (Herndon, *Let Me Live,* 88).
58. Julian Mayfield in the Howard University Oral History Collection, quoted in Alan Wald, "Marxist Literary Resistance to the Cold War," *Prospects: An Annual of American Cultural Studies* 20 (1995): 487.
59. One of many examples is Herbert Aptheker's master's thesis, written in 1937: *Nat Turner's Slave Rebellion: The Environment, the Event, the Effects* (reprint, New York, 1966). *The Liberator,* under Briggs's editorship, regularly featured historical and cultural pieces.
60. Painter, *The Narrative of Hosea Hudson,* 21.

CHAPTER 11: DEATH TO THE LYNCHERS

1. New York *World,* 8 February 1931; Arthur F. Raper, *The Mob Still Rides: A Review of the Lynching Record,* 1931–35 (Atlanta, 1936), 5, 23–24.
2. Raper, *The Mob Still Rides,* 24.
3. Harry Haywood and Milton Howard, *Lynching,* International Pamphlets 25 (New York, 1931), 5–6.
4. *Pittsburgh Courier,* 6 and 13 September 1930; *TL,* 11 January, 22 March, 19 April, 11 October 1930, 19 December 1931, 23 February 1932; A. Jakira, organization secretary, ILD, to district organizers, 21 May 1930, Antilynch file, RKC.
5. J. Louis Engdahl, "The ILD after Four Years," *LD* 6 (February 1930): 23; A. Jakira, "Toward a Firmer Basis," *LD* 6 (February 1930): 37; Gilbert Lewis, "In Action against Jim Crow," *LD* 6 (February 1930): 33; *Pittsburgh Courier,* 11 January 1930; Baltimore *Afro-American,* 4 January 1930.
6. The NAACP's lynching records for 1930 and 1931 showed twenty-five lynchings in 1930, more than double the number in 1929 (NAACP, "Lynching Records for 1930

and 1931," Antilynch file, RKC; Patterson, "Manifesto to the Negro People," *LD* 8 (November 1932): 208; *Southern Worker,* 27 September 1930; *Pittsburgh Courier,* 26 April 1930; *TL,* 21 December 1929; George Maurer, "The Tasks of the ILD," *LD* 6 (March 1930): 56.

7. Editorial, "At the Basis of Lynching," *Southern Worker,* 27 September 1930; Otto Huiswoud, "Unity against Boss Terror," *LD* 6 (August 1930): 162; Cecil S. Hope, "The Flames of Lynch Law Spread," *LD* 6 (December 1931): 237; William L. Patterson, "Maryland Gets a Jolt," *LD* 7 (September 1931): 167.

8. *TL,* 17 October, 5 December 1931; Baltimore *Afro-American,* 4 November 1933; *DW,* 6 July 1932.

9. Interview with James S. Allen, New York City, 24 March 1974; interview with Al Murphy, Charleston, Missouri, 23 April 1974.

10. *TL,* 7 and 28 December 1929, 11 January, 15 February, 3 May 1930, 14 and 28 March 1931; *Pittsburgh Courier,* 26 April, 29 May 1930. Laura Wood (sometimes identified as "Weed") was found hanging by a plow chain from a tree. Joseph North to City Editors, 18 February 1930, RKC; *NYT,* 8 June 1930, 12, 13, 14, 15 March 1931; "Fight against Growing Lynch Terror and Persecution of Negroes in USA," *Inprecorr* 11, no. 55 (1931): 1001. For the Newton quote, see *LD* 6 (December 1930): 291.

11. Nora West, "Fascism — Southern Style," *LD* 6 (November 1930): 220; John Hammond Moore, "Communists and Fascists in a Southern City: Atlanta, 1930," *South Atlantic Quarterly* 67 (Summer 1968): 441, 451–54; editorial, *Pittsburgh Courier,* 13 September 1930; NAACP Memo, "American Fascist Association or Black Shirts," 14 February 1931, and Press Service of the Commission on Interracial Cooperation, "All The Starch Taken Out of the Black Shirts," both in American Fascisti file, RKC; *Time,* 8 September 1930, 17.

12. *DW,* 9 October 1931; *Pittsburgh Courier,* 13 September 1930, 2 June 1931.

13. "Draft Resolution on Negro Work," 2–3, box 12, folder "1931," RMP.

14. *DW,* 1 and 4 October 1930; *Southern Worker,* 1 November 1930; *Chicago Defender,* 11 October 1930; *Pittsburgh Courier,* 19 July 1930. For criticism of sectarian tactics in that period, see James W. Ford, *The Negro and the Democratic Front* (New York, 1938), 81–83.

15. RTsKhIDNI 495/155/80/161–65.

16. *LD* 6 (December 1930): 257; *Pittsburgh Courier,* 8 November 1930; *DW,* 4, 5, 25 November 1930; "Draft Program of the League of Struggle for Negro Rights," box 12, folder "1931," RMP.

17. "The IRA Surveys the ILD," *LD* 7 (July 1931): 141; "Work among the Negro Masses (Examples of How Not to Work)," *Party Organizer* (March 1931): 19–20; "How the League of Struggle for Negro Rights Is Being Built," *Party Organizer* (April 1931): 15–16.

18. "Decision of the Polcommission on the LSNR and Other Negro Matters," 12 May 1931, RTsKhIDNI 495/155/96/31–32; RTsKhIDNI 515/1/2214/10–11.

19. "The IRA Surveys the ILD," *LD* 7 (July 1931): 141.

20. Carter, *Scottsboro*, 51; *NYT*, 26 March 1931; James S. Allen, "Scottsboro — A Proclamation of Freedom," *LD* 11 (June 1935): 14; *DW*, 2 April 1931; Edmund Wilson, "The Freight-Car Case," *NR* 68 (26 August 1931): 40. There are differing versions of how the Communists responded to Scottsboro. Carter (*Scottsboro*, 51) has Charles Dirba reading about the case in the *New York Times* and wiring Wakefield to investigate. John Hammond claimed that Wakefield, who "happened to be in the vicinity," telegraphed New York for lawyers (John Henry Hammond Jr., letter, 24 September 1932, box 4, Scottsboro Case Correspondence, ILD Papers). Allen's version is the only firsthand and precise account. It is doubtful that the Chattanooga Communists had to wait for a wire from New York to learn about the case.

21. *DW*, 2 April 1931; Louis Berg, "Scottsboro, Ala.," *LD* 7 (October 1932): 183.

22. "Scottsboro — A Proclamation of Freedom," 14; Carter, *Scottsboro*, 57–58.

23. Scottsboro materials cited in this discussion are from series D, legal files, Scottsboro Record Group, NAACP Papers, LC. Unsigned document, "Report on Steve Roddy," 26 April 1931 (copy, 28 April 1931), and Stephen R. Roddy, "To the Friends and Relatives of the Nine Negro Boys Charged with Rape, In Jackson County, Alabama," 11 April 1931, both in D-68, NAACP Papers.

24. Dr. P. A. Stephens to Walter White, 2 April 1931, and Walter T. Andrews to Stephens, 7 April 1931, both in D-68, NAACP Papers.

25. *Birmingham Age Herald*, 15 April 1931; Milton Howard, "Some Facts on the Scottsboro Case" (prepared for the Labor Research Association, 19 January 1932), 23, D-71, NAACP Papers; Brodsky, telegram to Darrow, Scottsboro Case Correspondence, box 4, ILD Papers; White to Darrow, 10 April 1931, D-68, NAACP Papers; *DW*, 24 April 1931.

26. Jeanne Scott to Walter White, 17 April 1931, and Wilkins to White, 15 May 1931, both in D-68, NAACP Papers; *Chicago Defender*, 9 May 1931. The *Daily Worker* on May 8 singled out the *Chicago Defender, Boston Guardian, Florida Booster*, and other papers for giving strong support to the ILD.

27. White to Jeanne Scott, 20 April 1931, and "Memorandum to Dr. P. A. Stephens and the Interdenominational Ministers Alliance of Chattanooga on Points to Be Included in *Written* Contract, Letter or Other Memorandum with Messrs. S. R. Roddy and Milo Moody, Of Chattanooga and Scottsboro Respectively," 2 May 1931, both in D-68, NAACP Papers. Herbert Seligmann, the NAACP director of publicity, wrote to the *New Republic* during the same period, stating that "[the NAACP] took up their cases at their very inception" (*NR* 67 [27 May 1931], 47).

28. Carter, *Scottsboro*, 59. The meeting at which Janie Patterson spoke ended in a march down Lenox Avenue and an inevitable confrontation with police. *NYT*, 2 May 1931; "Almanac of Protest," *LD* 6 (October 1931): 188; *NL*, 6 and 13 August 1934. Josephine Herbst offered a moving portrait of Ada Wright's life in "Lynching in the Quiet

Manner," *NM* 7 (July 1931): 11. The linkage of women's potential with the Scottsboro mothers was in *Working Woman* (June 1931).

29. Investigating the scope of activities to free the Scottsboro boys would try the patience of the most indefatigable researcher. The first reports of protests appeared in the *Daily Worker,* 21 April, 18 and 27 May 1931. Wright's remark is in *Inter-State Tattler,* 3 June 1931.

30. Baltimore *Afro-American,* 11 June 1931.

31. Carter, *Scottsboro,* 122; Padmore to Negro Department, TUUL, RTsKhIDNI 534/6/140/41; Mogul, "Experience in Organizing a Block Committee for Scottsboro Defense," *Party Organizer* (June 1931): 16–18.

32. *New York Amsterdam News,* 1 July 1931, reported a demonstration of a 3,500-member "red army," which it called the largest protest ever staged in Harlem. By 1932 concerts and dances featuring leading African American artists, such as W. C. Handy, Rose McClendon, Alberta Hunter, and Cab Calloway, had become fairly commonplace. *Boston Guardian,* 11 May 1932; *New York Amsterdam News,* 5 October 1932; Pickens to White, 15 May 1931, D-68, NAACP Papers; interview with Herbert Benjamin, Silver Spring, Maryland, 7 April 1974.

33. *DW,* 27 April 1931; *Chattanooga Times,* 6 June 1931; *Dayton Times,* 11 July 1931; James W. Ford, "Scottsboro before the World," *LD* 8 (April 1932): 64–66; *NYT,* 1 July 1931; *Crisis* 39 (June 1931): 192; Baltimore *Afro-American,* 4 July 1931.

34. Dr. P. A. Stephens to Walter White, 24 April 1931, D-68, NAACP Papers; Howard, "Some Facts on the Scottsboro Case," 6–7; memorandum, "Points to Be Emphasized by Walter White, Secretary of the NAACP in Talking with Scottsboro Defendants at Kilby Prison," special correspondence, D-68, NAACP Papers.

35. Memorandum from Walter White to NAACP national office, 3 May 1931, and White to Dr. Herbert A. Turner, 11 May 1931, both in D-68, NAACP Papers. White's comment on the parents' trust of white men was repeated in a number of letters. Also McPherson to White, 28 July 1931, D-70, NAACP Papers.

36. James S. Allen, "The Scottsboro Struggle," *Communist* 12, no. 5 (May 1933): 438–39.

37. "Memorandum re Telephone Conversation with Mr. Beddow," 5 August 1931, and White to Robert R. Moton, 19 August 1931, both in D-70, NAACP Papers.

38. White to Turner, 11 May 1931, and White to Pickens, 27 May 1931, both in D-69, NAACP Papers. The Williams Wilcox quote is in Carter, *Scottsboro,* 91. Carter describes the "condescension" of White and Pickens in dealing with the parents as "a grave tactical error." In light of the repetition and intensity of their contempt for the parents, it was hardly a tactical error; rather, they ultimately were unable to conceal their class bias.

39. Du Bois wrote, "If [Camp Hill] was instigated by Communists it is too despicable for words." Du Bois, "Postscript," *Crisis* 38 (September 1931): 314. Pickens's speech was reported in Chattanooga *Daily Times,* 8 June 1931; *Pittsburgh Courier,* 20 June

1931; White to William L. Patterson, 14 June 1933, D-73, NAACP Papers; *DW,* 12 May 1931.

40. "The Battle of Scottsboro," *Crisis* 41 (December 1934): 364; Guy B. Johnson, "Negro Racial Movements and Leadership in the United States," *American Journal of Sociology* 43 (1937): 71; Du Bois, "Postscript," 315.

41. Schuyler in *Pittsburgh Courier,* 3 June 1933.

42. Eugene Gordon in *Pittsburgh Courier,* 27 May 1933.

43. William L. Patterson, "How We Organize: The International Labor Defense and Courtroom Technicians," *LD* 9 (May 1933): 54.

44. Allen, "The Scottsboro Struggle," 437; Pickens to White, 6 June 1931, D-69, NAACP Papers; White to Beddow, 19 August 1931, D-70, NAACP Papers; White to Beddow, Fort, and Ray, 2 September 1931, D-70, NAACP Papers.

45. Carter, *Scottsboro,* 96, 101–2; White to Weems and Roberson (misspelled as "Robinson"), 4 January 1932 (incorrectly typed as "1931"), D-71, NAACP Papers.

46. "Meeting of the Buro of the Negro Dept. CC Held January 4, 1932" (in author's possession).

47. *NYT,* 8 November 1932.

48. *NYT,* 8 and 13 November 1932; Hugh T. Murray, "The NAACP versus the Communist Party: The Scottsboro Rape Cases, 1931–1932," *Phylon* 28 (1967): 285–86. White pressed on, telling the *New York Times* that "we are especially gratified that the decision reaffirms the principle and precedent established in . . . the Arkansas riot cases . . . carried to the Supreme Court by this association." The Court's majority, in fact, went out of their way to observe that "it does not sufficiently appear that the defendants were seriously threatened with, or that they were actually in danger of mob violence" (ibid.).

49. Harry Haywood, "Scottsboro and Beyond," *LD* 8 (June 1932): 103.

50. The Amis telegram is in Howard, "Some Facts on the Scottsboro Case," D-68, NAACP Papers. The Urban League's *Opportunity* worried that the telegrams would inflame people more against the Communists than against the injustice of the case: "opposition to communism may blind well-meaning citizens to the gravity of the Negro's plight and lead to condemnation of the valiant efforts which Negroes are making to secure their rights guaranteed by the Constitution" (editorial, "Scottsboro," *Opportunity* 11 [May 1933]: 134).

51. William L. Patterson, "The Scottsboro Decision: An Analysis," *LD* 9 (January 1933): 229; Goodman, *Stories of Scottsboro,* 341–44.

52. Patterson, "The Scottsboro Decision," 229. The liberal legal scholar Morris Ernst also bemoaned the fact that the Court evaded rulings on a fair trial and jury exclusion. Carter, *Scottsboro,* 163–64.

53. Editorial, "The Scottsboro Case," *Revolutionary Age,* 18 July 1931. Walter White, "The Negro and the Communists," *Harper's Magazine* 164 (December 1931): 71,

quoted the editorial extensively and approvingly, incorrectly identifying it as "sharp criticism from within their [the Communists'] own party."

54. Goodman, *Stories of Scottsboro*, 311–13.

55. The comment on Negro students and Scottsboro is in Lawrence D. Reddick, "What Does the Younger Negro Think?" *Opportunity* 11 (October 1933): 312. Also Roger N. Baldwin, "Negro Rights and the Class Struggle," *Opportunity* 12 (September 1934): 265. On student activity, see Hugh T. Murray Jr., "Aspects of the Scottsboro Campaign," *Science and Society* 35 (summer 1971): 180. Also "Negro Editors on Communism: A Symposium of the American Negro Press," *Crisis* 39 (April 1932): 118, 156; Asbury Smith, "What Can the Negro Expect from Communism?" *Opportunity* 11 (June 1933): 211.

Chapter 12: The Search for Unity and Breadth

1. *Chicago Defender,* 1 November 1930.

2. W.E.B. Du Bois, "Marxism and the Negro," *Crisis* 40 (May 1933): 104, 118.

3. Joe Benson and Fred Allen to Secretariat CC CPUSA, 19 November 1932, RTsKhIDNI 515/1/2224/233–38.

4. Interview with James Jackson, New York City, 11 September 1996.

5. A. H. Harfield to Weiner, 1 and 21 December 1931, RTsKhIDNI 515/1/2224/248–49, 265–66.

6. Dave Doran to District Committee 16 (with a copy to the Central Committee), 9 March 1933, RTsKhIDNI 515/1/3308/40–45. A. H. Harfield, the District 13 organizer, insisted that racial separation in Charlotte had ended by 1933. RTsKhIDNI 515/1/3308/124–25. Jim Mallory (Elizabeth Lawson), "On the Errors of the Party in the South on the Negro Question," *DW,* 31 May 1933.

7. "The Situation in District 17 and the Tasks of the Party," RTsKhIDNI 515/1/2225/77; Joan Barbour to Secretariat, CPUSA, 6 July 1932, RTsKhIDNI 515/1/2928/39–40. YCL member and LSNR organizer John Jefferson described the tense situation in the New Orleans Party organization (Jefferson to National Office, 11 October 1932, RTsKhIDNI 515/1/2829/31–32, and Jefferson to William Z. Foster, 2 January 1933, RTsKhIDNI 515/1/3311/2–4).

8. "Resolution on All-Southern Conference Adopted by District Bureau, District 17 of the ILD, October 15, 1932," RTsKhIDNI 515/2225/73; Kelley, *Hammer and Hoe,* 85–86.

9. The CPUSA file in the Russian archives contains a series of richly documented, carefully written reports by Murphy to the district and national leadership of the Party. The reports provide a breakdown of SCU membership, activities, work of the auxiliaries, and so forth. Murphy's comments on the changes wrought by the new organizational scheme are in RTsKhIDNI 515/2229/5–6, 98–103.

10. "To the Central Committee," 15 November 1932, RTsKhIDNI 515/1/2229/100.

11. "To the Central Committee," RTsKhIDNI 515/1/2229/101–2.

12. RTsKhIDNI 515/1/2229/102–3; "The Situation in District 17 and the Tasks of the Party," 76.

13. "Draft Resolution, TUUL National Committee" (in author's possession); Nathaniel Honig, "Miners Discuss Their Problems," *LU* 7, no. 4 (April 1932): 19–21; Jack Stachel, "Lessons of Two Recent Strikes," *Communist* 11, no. 6 (June 1932): 527–36; interview with Carl and Anne Reeve, Philadelphia, 6 April 1974.

14. "Lessons of Two Recent Strikes," 537–38; Earl Browder, "Smash Sectarianism — Penetrate the Factories," speech at Chicago Shop Conference, 1 January 1933, *Party Organizer* (February 1933): 84.

15. Robert W. Dunn, "Background of Ford Massacre," *LU* 7, no. 4 (April 1932): 10–11; "Young Workers in the Auto Industry," unsigned document, HKP, WSU.

16. *NYT*, 8, 12, 17 March 1932; *Chicago Defender*, 12 March 1932; *TL*, 18 March 1932; interview with David Moore, Detroit, 14 April 1981; "The Massacre of the Ford Hunger Marchers, by a Worker Who Was There," *New Force* (April–May 1932): 6–7; notes in HKP, WSU.

17. B. K. Gebert, "How the St. Louis Unemployed Victory Was Won," *Communist* 11, no. 9 (September 1932): 786–91; *St. Louis Post-Dispatch*, 9, 12, 13 July 1931.

18. Joseph L. Moss to Brown Squire, 23 November 1932; Wilfred S. Reynolds to Moss, 11 October 1932; "Attempted Demonstration at 109th St. and Michigan Avenue on September 14, 1932"; all in Cook County Bureau of Public Welfare files, CHS.

19. "Attempted Demonstration at 109th St. and Michigan Avenue on September 14, 1932"; interview with Herbert Benjamin, Silver Spring, Maryland, 7 April 1974; interview with Merrill C. Work, Detroit, 16 April 1974.

20. Klehr, *The Heyday of American Communism*, 60–61; Central Committee, CPUSA, "Lessons of the Bonus March," *Communist* 11, no. 9 (September 1932): 792–804.

21. Baltimore *Afro-American*, 15 October 1932; "Lessons of the Bonus March," 798; *TL*, 15 July 1932; *DW*, 21 September 1932.

22. Roy Wilkins, "The Bonuseers Ban Jim Crow," *Crisis* 39 (October 1932): 316.

23. *NYT*, 30 July 1932; *TL*, 15 August 1932. In addition to Ford, five black WESL activists were arrested. They were Erskine Brown of Chicago, Thomas W. Plunkett of New York, and William R. Powell, Orlando E. Hill, and Valdosta Price, all of Washington, D.C.

24. *Pittsburgh Courier*, 20 August 1932.

25. Naison, *Communists and Harlem*, 99. The portrait is also drawn from the author's own observations when Ford led Party work in the Bedford-Stuyvesant section of Brooklyn in the late 1940s.

26. Klehr, *Communist Cadre*, 57; Arthur Simson (Arthur Zipser), "The Communists and Black Liberation, 1930–31," *Political Affairs* 31 (February 1957): 7; Michael Gold, "The Communists Meet," *NR* 71 (15 June 1932): 117–19; Joseph North, "The

Communists Nominate," *NM* (July 1932): 3–7; *Pittsburgh Courier,* 4 June 1932. Hathaway was unaware that Frederick Douglass had been the vice presidential candidate on the Equal Rights ticket in 1872.

27. "The Communists Meet," 117–19; Baltimore *Afro-American,* 4 June 1932.

28. Press release, National Campaign Committee, CPUSA, "Equal Rights Committee Calls for Support of Communist Most Important Document since Civil War," 27 October 1932, Political file, CBP, CHS.

29. "Problems" (document circulated in Negro Department), 22 December 1932, RT-sKhIDNI 515/1/2910/88–90; "What's to Be Done," draft resolution presented to ILD convention, *LD* 7 (October 1932): 184; Frank Spector, "Keynotes of the Convention: Broaden the Base of the ILD," *LD* 8 (November 1932): 207; Frank Spector, "The Problems of United Front against Boss Terror," *LD* 9 (February 1933): 14.

30. The most successful regional campaigns were those of Claude Lightfoot, who won a sizable share of the vote in his quest for a seat in the Illinois State Assembly, and William Patterson, who won 24,222 votes in his New York mayoral candidacy. Black Communists ran for office in New York, Illinois, Tennessee, Minnesota, Wisconsin, Indiana, Texas, North Carolina, Maryland, Alabama, and other states, often as write-in candidates. Interview with Claude Lightfoot, Gary, Indiana, 25 April 1974; *TL,* 15 June, 15 August, 1 September, 4 November 1932; Baltimore *Afro-American,* 19 November 1932.

31. "Angelo Herndon's Story," *LD* 10 (May 1934): 19; Martin, *The Angelo Herndon Case,* 29–35.

32. Benjamin J. Davis, *Communist Councilman from Harlem* (New York, 1969), 31–55; Gerald Horne, *Black Liberation/Red Scare: Ben Davis and the Communist Party* (Newark, Delaware, 1994), 27–40.

33. Davis, *Communist Councilman,* 55–60; Martin, *The Angelo Herndon Case,* 34, 36–38. On the eve of the Herndon trial, the prosecution hastily added the names of two blacks for jury duty. They were empaneled for a larceny trial and quickly removed by peremptory challenges by defense lawyers. Nevertheless, the *Atlanta World* credited Davis and Geer for this small but significant advance in the struggle for equal legal rights.

34. Davis, *Communist Councilman,* 60–65; Martin, *The Angelo Herndon Case,* 50–55; "Herndon's Speech to the Jury," in Philip S. Foner and Herbert Shapiro, *American Communism and Black Americans: A Documentary History, 1930–1934* (Philadelphia, 1991), 324–29.

35. Martin, *The Angelo Herndon Case,* 56–61; Davis, *Communist Councilman,* 76–82.

36. *Atlanta Constitution,* 19 January 1933; *DW,* 19 January 1933; Herndon, *Let Me Live,* 351–54.

37. *NR* 69 (1 February 1933): 308–9; *Nation* (15 February 1933): 162; *DW,* 21 January 1933.

38. Walter White offered the NAACP's legal resources to the Herndon defense. However, he also asked A. T. Walden, president of the Atlanta office, to explore "the possibilities of the Association gaining exclusive control of the case." Some things never changed. Martin, *The Angelo Herndon Case,* 62–82.

39. White to Patterson, 13 and 29 April 1933, Patterson to White, 28 April 1933, all in D-73, NAACP Papers; Carter, *Scottsboro,* 248.

40. Carter, *Scottsboro,* 186–87, 228–33; Goodman, *Stories of Scottsboro,* 19–23.

41. Goodman, *Stories of Scottsboro,* 20–21; "Ruby Bates' Story of Her Life," *LD* 9 (October 1933): 65.

42. Goodman, *Stories of Scottsboro,* 154, 198–99, 202, 242; "Patterson Gives Assessment of Ruby Bates," *Pittsburgh Courier,* 24 June 1933; "My Dear Miss Ruby" (from Viola Montgomery), *LD* 8 (June 1933): 70.

43. Ada Wright, "I Go to Jail for the Scottsboro Boys," *LD* 8 (October 1932): 185; *DW,* 10 and 18 May, 9 and 24 June, 11 August, 8 October 1932; Carter, *Scottsboro,* 172; "Enlarged Minutes of Negro Buro," 14 July 1932, RTsKhIDNI 515/1/2734/69.

44. "Report on Agrarian Work in the South to Meeting of the Negro Department," 18 January 1932, RTsKhIDNI 515/1/2784/10–14.

45. Ibid., 16–17.

46. *Chicago Defender,* 24 December 1932; *TL,* 15 October 1932; Kelley, *Hammer and Hoe,* 48–49.

47. Dale Rosen, "The Alabama Share Croppers Union," undergraduate thesis in social studies, Radcliffe College, March 1969, 41.

48. "The Alabama Share Croppers Union," 42–44; Kelley, *Hammer and Hoe,* 49.

49. "The Alabama Share Croppers Union," 45; Kelley, *Hammer and Hoe,* 50; "Work, Waste, and Wealth," *Crisis* 40 (February 1933): 39; Benjamin Goldstein, "Tallapoosa Croppers on Trial," *LD* 9 (July 1933): 14.

50. "The Alabama Share Croppers Union," 46–49; *Pittsburgh Courier,* 31 December 1932; *Chicago Defender,* 24 December 1932; Carter, *Scottsboro,* 174–77; Lumpkin, *The South in Progress,* 129–30; John Beecher, "The Share Croppers' Union in Alabama," *Social Forces* 13 (October 1934): 128–29; Kelley, *Hammer and Hoe,* 50–51; *Montgomery Advertiser,* 20 December 1932.

51. "The Alabama Share Croppers Union," 49; "What Happened in Tallapoosa County?" *LD* 9 (February 1933): 3; Lumpkin, *The South in Progress,* 130; Kelley, *Hammer and Hoe,* 51. Mrs. James was quoted in the *Chicago Defender,* 14 January 1933. *Pittsburgh Courier,* 31 December 1933.

52. Kelley, *Hammer and Hoe,* 52; "The Alabama Share Croppers Union," 43; "What Happened in Tallapoosa County?" 4; Carter, *Scottsboro,* 177; "Tallapoosa Croppers on Trial," 14, 22.

53. *Chicago Defender,* 6 May 1933; "The Alabama Share Croppers Union," 33; Kelley, *Hammer and Hoe,* 52–53; "Tallapoosa Croppers on Trial," 14. Cobb was "Nate Shaw" in Theodore Rosengarten's monumental *All God's Dangers* (New York, 1974).

54. Kelley, *Hammer and Hoe*, 52–53.

55. *NYT*, 22 and 25 November, 1, 3, 4 December 1932; interview with Carl Winter, New York City, 6 October 1981; interview with Anne Burlak Timpson, Boston, 14 September 1995.

56. *NYT*, 1, 2, 7 December 1932; *Washington Tribune*, 9 December 1932; Baltimore *Afro-American*, 10 December 1932; *Pittsburgh Courier*, 10 December 1932.

57. Robert Minor, "Report of Comrade Minor on the Negro Question," RTsKhIDNI 515/1/2734/27–30 (noted in Russian archives as "CPUSA Departmental Matters, Negro Department, February 1932").

58. Minor, RTsKhIDNI 515/1/2734/32–35.

59. Ibid., 36.

60. Ibid., 37–38.

61. "Negro Editors on Communism: A Symposium of the American Negro Press," *Crisis* 39 (April 1932): 117–19, and (May 1932): 154–56. Similar views (especially the warning of Communist advances if the democratic promise was not fulfilled) were expressed in *Opportunity* 9 (August 1931): 234, and (May 1933): 134.

CHAPTER 13: NEW DEALS AND NEW DIRECTIONS

1. Central Committee, CPUSA, "Agitprop Outline for Speakers and Editors," box 12, folder "1931," RMP; "JL for the Eighth District Secretariat to the CC Organization Department," 10 November 1933, RTsKhIDNI 515/1/3265/284. A Crusader News Agency press release (prepared by Cyril Briggs) in October 1932 said Roosevelt fostered "a lifetime of Negro Oppression" (29 October 1932, CBP, CHS).

2. Raymond Wolters, *Negroes and the Great Depression: The Problem of Economic Recovery* (Westport, Conn., 1970), 93, 99, 102–3, 107, 113, 124; editorial, "Black Labor and the Codes," *Opportunity* 11 (August 1933): 231; Robert C. Weaver, "A Wage Differential Based on Race," *Crisis* 41 (August 1934): 236, 238; Eugene Kinckle Jones, "The Negro in Industry and in Urban Life," *Opportunity* 12 (May 1934): 141–44; John P. Davis, "What Price National Recovery?" *Crisis* 40 (December 1933): 271–72; W.E.B. Du Bois, "Postscript — NIRA and the Negro," *Crisis* 40 (September 1933): 21; editorial, "The Color Line and Recovery," *Opportunity* 11 (December 1933): 359.

3. Wolters, *Negroes and the Great Depression*, 41, 44–45, 78–79; Baltimore *Afro-American*, 25 July 1936; *Chicago Defender*, 14 April, 22, 29 September 1934.

4. Wolters, *Negroes and the Great Depression*, 110; Jonathan Scott Holloway, "Repositioning the Negro: John P. Davis and the New Black Activism," paper delivered at the Association for the Study of Afro-American Life and History, 5 October 1996.

5. Holloway, "Repositioning the Negro"; *Chicago Defender*, 7 and 21 October 1934.

6. Wolters, *Negroes and the Great Depression*, 140–41; *DW*, 2 December 1933.

7. John P. Davis, "Statement before the Complaint Hearing of the NRA," 28 February 1934, Record Group 183, NA.

8. *DW*, 2 December 1933.

9. *Pittsburgh Courier*, 23 September 1933; Holloway, "Repositioning the Negro"; Harvard Sitkoff, *A New Deal for Blacks: The Emergence of Civil Rights as a National Issue: The Depression Decade* (New York, 1978), 47–48. Among the sponsoring organizations were the Public Affairs Committee of the YWCA, the Race Relations Department of the Federal Council of Churches, the National Baptist Convention, the AME Zion Church, the Elks, and the National Negro Business League.

10. *Pittsburgh Courier*, 23 September 1933; Baltimore *Afro-American*, 7 July 1934; Wolters, *Negroes and the Great Depression*, 111–12; Sitkoff, *A New Deal for Blacks*, 48; confidential memorandum, "Summary of Work Accomplished and Suggested Next Steps in Program for the Joint Committee on National Recovery," 15 September 1933, JCNR file, RKC. Davis's "exposé" of the Recovery Board was reported in the *Afro-American*, 30 December 1933.

11. Holloway, "Repositioning the Negro"; Wolters, *Negroes and the Great Depression*, 110–12; Frances Williams to White, 1 January 1934, and White to William H. Hastie, 3 February 1934, both in JCNR file, RKC; Lawrence S. Wittner, "The National Negro Congress: A Reassessment," *American Quarterly* 22 (winter 1970): 884–85. White offered to publish JCNR research under the NAACP imprimatur in exchange for a $100 monthly subsidy, if other sponsoring groups guaranteed Davis's $140 monthly salary. Neither the subsidy nor the guarantees materialized.

12. Interview with Henry Winston, New York City, 13 December 1973.

13. The Party's line for public consumption in 1933 and 1934 remained resolutely opposed to the New Deal. In one of many examples, the LSNR charged that the "the eagle of the NRA has buried its claws with a firmer grip upon the body of Negro labor" ("Manifesto of the League of Struggle for Negro Rights," *HL*, 4 November 1933). Klehr, *The Heyday of American Communism*, 95; Central Committee, CPUSA, *An Open Letter to the Membership of the Communist Party* (New York, 1933).

14. Wolters, *Negroes and the Great Depression*, 56–57.

15. Interview with Ralph Turner, Chicago, 25 April 1974; interview with Merrill Work, Detroit, 20 April 1974; interview with William Crawford, Philadelphia, 3 April 1974; interview with Frank Sykes, Detroit, 19 April 1974.

16. Memorandum from Walter White to Roy Wilkins, 25 September 1933, and telegram from White to President Roosevelt, 19 October 1933, both in Anti-lynch file, RKC; *Chicago Defender*, 16 December 1933.

17. Walter White, "The Costigan-Wagner Bill," *Crisis* 42 (January 1935): 10–11; editorial, "The Meaning of the Costigan-Wagner Bill," *HL*, 24 February 1934; *HL*, 25 August, 15 December 1934. The LSNR proposed as a substitute a "Bill of Rights for the Negro People," which advocated a total ban on discrimination and demanded the death penalty for lynching.

18. William L. Patterson, "The ILD Faces the Future," *Communist* 13 (July 1934): 718–25; leaflet, "The Eastern Conference against Lynching," Anti-lynching file, RKC;

B. D. Amis, "The National Recovery Act Lynch Drive Calls for Mass Resistance," *Inprecorr* 14, no. 8 (1934): 225. When thirty-three young black leaders convened at Amenia, New York, and called for internal racial solidarity combined with a black-labor alliance, the CP deigned to take serious notice. "Findings of the Second Amenia Conference, August, 1933," Amenia file, RKC.

19. *LD* 9 (July 1933): 9; 10 (February 1934): 3; 11 (January 1935): 4–6.

20. Ibid.

21. A. G. Bosse, "Scottsboro Frame-up Crumbles," *Inprecorr* 13, no. 19 (1934): 431; Goodman, *Stories of Scottsboro*, 103–5; interview with William L. Patterson, New York City, 28 June 1974; Mary Heaton Vorse, "The Scottsboro Trial," *NR* 74 (19 April 1933): 276; New York *Daily News*, 9 January 1933.

22. Baltimore *Afro-American*, 10 November 1933; Carter, *Scottsboro*, 183–85, 192–242; Mary Heaton Vorse, "The Scottsboro Trial."

23. *New YorkAmsterdam News*, 12 and 19 April 1933; *DW*, 12 and 15 April 1933; *Pittsburgh Courier*, 15 April 1933. In a letter to members, Browder noted the upsurge in black militancy and warned of increased efforts to crush it. "Statement of Central Committee, CPSUA to All Members" (Earl Browder, signatory), 29 November 1933, RTsKhIDNI 515/1/3251/4.

24. *HL*, 15 April 1933.

25. Baltimore *Afro-American*, 29 April 1933; *Washington Times*, 8 May 1933; Central Committee, CPUSA, "Organize Meetings in Negro Neighborhoods for the Freedom of the Scottsboro Boys," RTsKhIDNI 515/1/3160. William Davis led a group to Washington that included J. Dalmus Steele, a leading Harlem figure, and Arthur A. Schomburg. *HL*, 5 May 1933; Minutes of Meeting of District 2 Bureau, 10 May 1933, RTsKhIDNI 515/1/3202/78.

26. The Gruening-Boardman article appeared in the *Nation* on June 27, 1934. Houston replied on July 4; additional correspondence appeared in the issues of July 18 and August 8. Houston denied a charge by Patterson that he had failed to produce black potential jurors in the jury challenge. Charles H. Houston to Douglass Freeman, 19 September 1934, D-53, NAACP Papers; *Chicago Defender*, 30 December 1933; Martha Gruening, "The Truth about the Crawford Case," *NM* (8 January 1935): 9–14. A pamphlet on the case by Gruening and Boardman was distributed to delegates at the NAACP national convention in 1935. A foreword was signed by twenty-four members of the association and five members of the Boston branch executive committee. *New York Amsterdam News*, 22 June 1935. Shortly before leaving the *Crisis*, Du Bois sharply criticized the handling of the case by NAACP lawyers. *New York Amsterdam News*, 28 April 1934.

27. Scottsboro Defense Committee, *The Scottsboro Case: Opinion of Judge James E. Horton* (New York, 1936), 7–36; "Scottsboro and Mr. Leibowitz," *HL*, 15 July 1933; Mary Heaton Vorse, "Judge Horton, the Most Unforgettable Character I Have Ever Known," manuscript in box 119, MHVP, WSU.

28. Sender Garlin, "Judge Horton's Verdict in the Scottsboro Case," *Inprecorr* 13, no. 32 (1933): 717; Joseph Brodsky, "Mass Action—Mass Protest—Mass Defense," *LD* 10 (November 1934): 4; Isadore Schneider, "Judge Horton's Decision," *LD* 9 (August 1933): 30. Louis Colman of the ILD argued, with a bit of vulgar Marxism, that Horton's move represented a win for the more sophisticated industrial exploiters of Alabama over the antediluvian plantation owners. Louis Colman, "Alabama's Underlying Forces," *NM* (13 February 1934): 22.

29. *Pittsburgh Courier,* 1 July 1933; *Chicago Defender,* 22 July 1934.

30. John Hammond Jr., "Due Process of Law in Alabama," *Nation* (20 December 1933): 701–2; Carter, *Scottsboro,* 274–302.

31. Carter, *Scottsboro,* 310–11.

32. On cross-examination, Price changed her story, admitting that she had first told Pearson that she wanted $500. Transcript of Pre-Trial Hearing, State of Alabama *vs.* Sol Kone, Daniel Swift, and J. T. Pearson, Legal Correspondence file, box 2, C6, ILD Papers; *Jackson County Sentinel,* 4 October 1934.

33. Carter, *Scottsboro,* 308–9; *NYT,* 2 October 1934; *New York Herald Tribune,* 1 October 1934.

34. *NYT,* 11 October 1934; *New York Amsterdam News,* 13 October 1934; Carter, *Scottsboro,* 312–13.

35. *NYT,* 11 October 1934. The *Chicago Defender* (13 October 1934) surveyed black voters and found them "expressing beliefs that the Scottsboro victims and Swift and Kone were 'framed.'"

36. On the stand, she told the prosecutor that "Swift" offered payment for her "life story" at $10 a copy. The Alabama attorney corrected her: "Wasn't it ten dollars a page, instead of a copy?" (Transcript of Pre-Trial Hearing, State of Alabama *vs.* Sol Kone, Daniel Swift, and J. T. Pearson, Legal Correspondence file, box 2, C6, ILD Papers).

37. Carter (*Scottsboro*) cites the *Chattanooga Daily Times* and *New York Times* (both on 2 October 1934) as the source for his claims that Kone and Schriftman were caught "red handed." The other versions are in the *Norfolk Journal and Guide,* 6 October 1934, and *New York Amsterdam News,* 6 October 1934. Also *Jackson County Sentinel,* 4 October 1934.

38. *New York Amsterdam News,* 1 June 1935. The International Juridical Association charged that Alabama officials violated the federal antikidnapping law by forcibly taking the attorneys from Tennessee in defiance of a writ of habeas corpus. *New York Daily News,* 7 October 1934; *New York Post,* 11 October 1934; *NYT,* 5 October 1934.

39. *New York Amsterdam News,* 17 November 1934, 7 September 1935; *Chicago Defender,* 26 January 1935.

40. Carter, *Scottsboro,* 313–15; *DW,* 15 October 1934.

41. Baltimore *Afro-American,* 20 October 1934; interview with William Weinstone, New York City, 18 June 1974.

42. *Norfolk Journal and Guide,* 1 December 1934; Carter, *Scottsboro,* 317–18; *New York Amsterdam News,* 13 October 1934.

43. Scottsboro-Herndon Action Committee to the American Scottsboro Committee, 27 November 1934, Scottsboro file, RKC.

44. *DW,* 28 November, 17 December 1934; *New York Amsterdam News,* 9 February 1935; Carter, *Scottsboro,* 319. In February 1933 the Comintern, responding to a plea from the Socialists for a united front, sent an open letter to Communist parties suggesting that they seek to form "a united front of struggle with Social-Democratic Parties." However, the message implied that Communists should still attempt to win rank-and-file Socialists and Social Democrats from their respective leaderships. By early 1935 that harsh qualification had weakened. See Klehr, *The Heyday of American Communism,* 98–99.

45. Martin, *The Angelo Herndon Case,* 98–105; *New York Amsterdam News,* 2 June 1934; *NM* 10 (27 March 1934): 4; Central Committee, CPUSA, in *DW,* 11 July 1934; Jesse Crawford, "Fulton Tower, Where Herndon Faces Death," *LD* 10 (March 1933): 25; Don West, "Georgia Officials Ape Hitler Terror," *LD* 10 (July 1934): 6. *Nation* (15 February 1933): 162; (2 May 1934): 508; (6 June 1934): 632–33; (1 August 1934): 127–28.

46. Martin, *The Angelo Herndon Case,* 112–13; *New York Amsterdam News,* 9 June 1936; Don West, "Georgia Wanted Me — Dead or Alive," *NM* (26 June 1934): 15–16.

47. Martin, *The Angelo Herndon Case,* 117–19. The most emotional report of Herndon's arrival at Penn Station was written by Ted Poston in the *New York Amsterdam News,* 11 August 1934. The *Norfolk Journal and Guide,* 18 August 1934, gave extensive coverage to the entire journey and a fulsome biography; the *Boston Chronicle,* 18 August 1934, ran an extended interview with Herndon, as did other black newspapers. Also see *New York Age,* 13 August 1934; *Chicago Defender,* 11 August 1934.

48. *NL,* 6 January 1934; "Statement of Ishmael P. Flory Re: His Dismissal from Fisk University," 8 March 1934, Flory file, RKC.

49. "Statement of Ishmael P. Flory"; interview with Ishmael Flory, Chicago, 25 April 1974.

50. Fisk University document, "The Facts in the Case of the Withdrawal of the Fisk University Singers from the Agreement to Appear at Loew's Theater in Nashville" (n.d.), C-292, NAACP Papers. Walter White to Thomas E. Jones, 13 March 1934; Jones to White, 16 March 1934; Jones, "Chapel Talk," 28 February 1934; all in C-292, NAACP Papers. Interview with Ishmael Flory, Chicago, 25 April 1974.

51. *HL,* 7 April 1934; Baltimore *Afro-American,* 28 September, 16 November 1935; *Chicago Defender,* 1 June 1935.

52. R. Shaw, "St. Louis' Biggest Strike," *LU* 8, no. 2 (March 1933): 8–11.

53. *HL,* 15 July 1933.

54. Joe Evans, "15,000 Cotton Pickers on Strike," *LU* 8, no. 9 (December 1933): 8–10.

55. *New York Amsterdam News,* 14, 21, 28 July, 4 August 1934. Donald Henderson, an economics instructor who was fired from Columbia University for "radical activi-

ties," and his wife were organizers at Seabrook for the cannery union. They were subjected to serious physical threats and arrests. The first president of the local was a Negro, Jerry Brown, who was forced to leave the area after being fired upon. The vice president during the July 1934 strike was Clifford White, a black who had served under Clarence Cain, a white farm worker, who was president of the local.

56. Klehr, *The Heyday of American Communism,* 118–34.

57. Jack Stachel, "Work in the Trade Unions," *Communist* 13 (March 1934): 289; J. Sefeld and J. Wilson, "The Strike Wave Begins in Auto," *LU* 10, no. 3 (March 1934): 9.

58. Foner, *Organized Labor and the Black Worker,* 204.

59. Kelley, *Hammer and Hoe,* 63; interview with Hosea Hudson, Atlantic City, New Jersey, 14 December 1974.

60. Vern Smith, "Victory Achieved in Alabama Coal Strike," *Inprecorr* 71 (28 December 1935): 748–49; *HL,* 12 May 1934.

61. Nat Ross, "Some Problems of the Class Struggle in the South," *Communist* 14 (January 1935): 65; Ross to Secretariat, Central Committee, 6 June 1933, RTsKhIDNI 515/1/3311/94.

62. Nat Ross, "The Next Steps in Alabama and the Lower South," *Communist* 14 (October 1935): 972; Ross to Secretariat, Central Committee, 6 June 1933, RTsKhIDNI 515/1/3311/94–96; John P. Davis, *The Negro in Labor Struggles since the New Deal* (Washington, D.C., 1935).

63. Kelley, *Hammer and Hoe,* 67–69; Jim Mallory [Elizabeth Lawson], "Class War in Alabama," *LU* 9, no. 5 (June 1934): 15.

64. H. Wickman, "With the Gulf Longshoremen," *LU* 8, no. 4 (May 1933): 29–31; Davis, *The Negro in Labor Struggles since the New Deal,* 2–3.

65. Interview with Claude Lightfoot, Gary, Indiana, 25 April 1974; Green, *The World of the Worker,* 163.

66. Davis, *The Negro in Labor Struggles since the New Deal,* 8; Baltimore *Afro-American,* 29 September 1934.

67. Davis, *The Negro in Labor Struggles since the New Deal,* 6; *NM* 11 (29 May 1934): 4–5. The *New Masses* of March 20, 1924, added to the list of black workers in strikes—and of black-white solidarity—Plymouth auto workers, as well as workers at Buick, Chevrolet, Fisher Body, and Ford (all in Michigan).

68. Kelley, *Hammer and Hoe,* 74.

Chapter 14: Harlem and the Popular Front

1. *HL,* 8 May 1933.

2. *HL,* 27 May, 8 and 22 July, 16 December 1933; Naison, *Communists in Harlem,* 78–79, 259; "Minutes of the Meeting of the District 2 Bureau," 10 May 1933, RTsKhIDNI 515/1/3202/80.

3. "Minutes . . . District 2 Bureau," 10 May 1933, 78.

4. Ibid., 79. Clarence Hathaway added testily that united front "maneuvers" should be conducted to expose misleaders, not welcome them.

5. Ibid., 81–87; H. Williams, "Statement of [LSNR] Activity in the New York District" (n.d.), RTsKhIDNI 515/1/3038/12–16.

6. Earl Browder, "Why an Open Letter to the Party Membership," *Communist* 12 (August 1933): 761–62, 767. In contrast to Harlem, Browder praised "Comrade M" (Al Murphy) for showing how the Black Belt sharecroppers had been "politicized" into "an integral, conscious part of the international revolutionary movement." Harry Haywood, *The Road to Negro Liberation*, Report to the Eighth Convention of the CPUSA (New York, 1934), 50–63.

7. Naison, *Communists in Harlem*, 99–100.

8. William Muraskin, "The Harlem Boycott of 1934: Black Nationalism and the Rise of Labor-Union Consciousness," *Labor History* 13 (summer 1972): 361–62. Figures on Harlem unemployment are drawn from a survey conducted by the Urban League in 1933, quoted in James W. Ford, "The Rosenwald Economic Conference," *HL*, 17 June 1933.

9. Naison, *Communists in Harlem*, 100–101; *HL*, 5 August 1933.

10. Interview with Merrill Work, Detroit, 20 April 1974; Naison, *Communists in Harlem*, 101.

11. Turner and Turner, *Richard B. Moore*, 63; Haywood, *The Road to Negro Liberation*, 54–58.

12. Haywood, *The Road to Negro Liberation*, 20–23, 50–51.

13. Ibid., 54–57.

14. Ibid., 53–54; Baltimore *Afro-American*, 17 March 1934; Naison, *Communists in Harlem*, 98.

15. Turner and Turner, *Richard B. Moore*, 63–65.

16. James W. Ford, "Report to the District on Harlem," 1 October 1933, RTsKhIDNI 515/2/3302/190; draft statement by Cyril Briggs in response to his removal from the *Harlem Liberator*, RTsKhIDNI 515/1/3160/24–29.

17. Draft statement by Briggs, RTsKhIDNI 515/1/3160/24–29.

18. Ibid., 26.

19. Naison, *Communists in Harlem*, 103; "Minutes . . . District 2 Bureau," 11 October 1933, RTsKhIDNI 515/1/3202/188.

20. The new generation of Communists was also distinctly youthful. Of the nearly thirty thousand members in 1935, over sixteen thousand were under forty. Alexander Bittelman, "Approaching the Seventh World Congress," *Communist* 14 (June 1935): 627.

21. Ibid.

22. *HL*, 27 May 1933, 1 December 1934.

23. Interview with Louise Thompson Patterson, New York City, 13 April 1973; interview with Thompson Patterson by Ruth Prager, 17 October 1981, OHAL.

24. *HL,* 17 and 24 June 1933, 21 April, 1 September 1934; Klehr, Haynes et al., *Secret World of American Communism,* 199. Burroughs returned to the United States in 1945. Her son Charles G. Burroughs was a cofounder of the DuSable Museum in Chicago.

25. Interview with Audley Moore by Mark Naison, 3 May 1974, OHAL.

26. On Bonita Williams, see *HL,* 8 July 1933.

27. Interview with William L. Patterson, New York City, 13 April 1973. By July 1934 the Harlem Workers School reported over five hundred students. *NL,* 7 July 1934.

28. Ford projected the "LSNR [as] the main organization for the centralizing of the [Party's] work" ("Minutes . . . District 2 Bureau," 11 October 1933, RTsKhIDNI 515/1/3202/190–93). Louis Sass, "Development of Work in the Harlem Section," *Communist* 14 (April 1935): 319; *HL,* 3 June 1933.

29. "Minutes . . . District 2 Bureau," 11 October 1933, RTsKhIDNI 515/1/3202/190–91; Naison, *Communists in Harlem,* 104–5.

30. Groucho was quoted as follows: "Look at the whole business down South. The Negroes have been submitting passively to abuse for almost a hundred years. Fighting is the only thing that can change the situation. Fight and protest" (*HL,* 26 May 1934). On the March riot, see *NYT,* 1 March 1934; "An Open Letter to Mayor La-Guardia," *New York Amsterdam News,* 15 September 1934.

31. Joseph North, "The Big May Day," *NM* (8 May 1934): 8–11.

32. Naison, *Communists in Harlem,* 105–7; *HL,* 3 and 10 February, 10 and 17 March, 21 April, 2 and 9 June 1934.

33. Muraskin, "The Harlem Boycott of 1934," 362–63.

34. Ibid., 363–64; *New York Age,* 4 and 11 August 1934; *NL,* 28 July 1934.

35. Muraskin, "The Harlem Boycott of 1934," 365–66. Adam Clayton Powell Jr. claimed that the color problem arose from a "distorted" photograph of some saleswomen in the *New York Age* (Powell, *Marching Blacks* [New York 1945], 81). However, Muraskin claims that there was considerable merit to the charge of color prejudice.

36. *HL,* 14 and 21 April, 8 and 15 September 1934. Ashford had led a successful market boycott in Detroit. Interview with Frank Sykes, Detroit, 16 April 1974; Naison, *Communists in Harlem,* 121–22.

37. Naison, *Communists in Harlem,* 107–8, 122–23; *HL,* 6 October 1934.

38. *HL,* 28 April, 19 May 1934; *NL,* 21 July, 1 September, 15 December 1934, 15 January 1935; interview with Claude Lightfoot, Gary, Indiana, 26 April 1974; interview with Thomas Walton, Los Angeles, 17 January 1973; Robert Weisbrot, *Father Divine: The Utopian Evangelist of the Depression Era Who Became an American Legend* (Boston, 1984), 148–52.

39. On the growing Comintern consensus on the popular front, see E. H. Carr, *Twilight of the Comintern: 1930–1935* (New York, 1982), 147–55; interview with Claude Lightfoot, Gary, Indiana, 26 April 1974. Lightfoot is the source for the observation

on the Wright-Haywood relationship. On Father Divine, see James W. Ford, "The United Front on Ethiopia," *Party Organizer* (July 1935): 16–18; and Earl Browder, "The Strategy of the United Front," *Communist* 13 (October 1934): 959.

40. James W. Ford, "The United Front in the Field of Negro Work," *Communist* 14 (February 1935): 169–73; Ford and Sass, "The Development of Work in the Harlem Section," 116.

41. Naison, *Communists in Harlem,* 134; Klehr, *Communist Cadre,* 57; Bittelman, "Approaching the Seventh World Congress," 627. On Hughes's elevation, see *HL,* 4 November 1933.

42. *DW,* 29 July, 10 and 19 December 1929; James W. Ford, "The Negro Workers Awaken," *LU* 7, no. 4 (April 1932): 7–9; *NM* (16 July 1935): 6; *HL,* 27 May, 3 June 1933; *NL,* 20 January, 22 September, 6 October 1934.

43. Joseph North, "U.S. Second Congress against War and Fascism," *Inprecorr* 14, no. 56 (1934): 1490–91.

44. James Ford, after his return from the Seventh Comintern Congress, disclaimed knowledge of Soviet shipments of war material to Italy. He countered with a description of his meeting in Geneva (on the way home from Moscow) with Tecia Hawariate, the Ethiopian delegate to the League of Nations, who expressed pleasure with Soviet foreign minister Maxim Litvinov's strong attack on Italy at the league. *New York Amsterdam News,* 28 September 1935. William Patterson, writing from Russia, was particularly sensitive to the "go to Abyssinia" slogan being raised in black communities. It was "utopian" and was no danger to Italy or other imperialist powers. Beneath the surface, Patterson was troubled by the exclusively racial focus of the rhetorical campaign to send only blacks to fight Mussolini. William L. Patterson, "The Abyssinian Situation and the Negro World," *Inprecorr* 15, no. 20 (1935): 542–43; *DW,* 24 and 29 June, 14 September 1935.

45. Joe Foster, "Harlem Discusses Ethiopia," *DW,* 2 August 1935.

46. Naison, *Communists in Harlem,* 138–39; James W. Ford, "The United Front on Ethiopia," *Party Organizer,* July 1935, 16–18.

47. *New York Amsterdam News,* 9 March, 13 and 27 July, 10 August, 7, 21, 28 September, 5 October 1935.

48. Naison, *Communists in Harlem,* 139; Baltimore *Afro-American,* 11 May, 28 September 1935; Charles H. Wesley, "The Significance of the Italo-Abyssinian Question," *Opportunity* (13 May 1935): 148–51.

49. Interview with Louise Thompson Patterson by Ruth Prager, 17 October 1981, OHAL; Naison, *Communists in Harlem,* 140–41; *The Complete Report of Mayor LaGuardia's Commission on the Harlem Riot of March* 19, 1935 (New York, 1969), 7–11; Sasha Small, "What Happened in Harlem," *LD* 11 (May 1935): 17.

50. *The Complete Report,* 10–11; *NL,* 1 April 1935; William L. Patterson, "Negro Harlem Awakes," *Negro Worker* 5, nos. 7–8 (July–August 1935): 26. Patterson, however, who

was far from the scene, also reverted to characteristic Third Period attacks on "misleaders."

51. James W. Ford, *Hunger and Terror in Harlem: The Causes and Remedies for the March 19th Outbreak in Harlem,* Testimony Prepared for the Mayor's Commission on Harlem (New York, 1935), 13–14; Naison, *Communists in Harlem,* 143; *DW,* 21 March 1935.

52. *New York Amsterdam News,* 30 March 1935; *NYT,* 22 March 1935. The *Times* featured a statement by Roy Wilkins warning that the authorities would be in grave error to attribute the riot to the Communists.

53. Interview with Louise Thompson Patterson by Ruth Prager, 17 October 1981, OHAL; interview with Thompson Patterson by author, New York City, 28 June 1974; Naison, *Communists in Harlem,* 144.

54. Naison, *Communists in Harlem,* 147–51.

55. *DW,* 3 June 1935; *NL,* 1 and 15 June 1935; *NYT,* 19 June 1935; interview with Audley Moore by Mark Naison, 3 May 1974, OHAL; Sitkoff, *A New Deal for Blacks,* 70–72.

56. *Report of Mayor LaGuardia's Commission,* 3.

57. Briggs's statement is drawn from a mimeographed program for a Harlem Section CP election rally held on September 30, 1933, at Rockland Palace in Harlem (in author's possession); Cyril Briggs, "Negro Revolutionary Hero — Toussaint L'Ouverture," *Communist* 13 (May 1929): 251.

58. Ford's comments are in Joseph North, "The Communists Nominate," *NM* (July 1932): 6. Michael Gold, "Drunk with Sunlight" (review of McKay's *Banjo),* *NM* (July 1929): 17. On Van Vechten, see *NM* (February 1930): 9.

59. Philip Schatz, "Songs of the Negro Worker," *NM* (May 1930): 6–7. There is evidence of considerable confusion in CP circles regarding Negro music. The Liberator Chorus, for example, was reported to have presented a curious mix of songs at Camp Unity, the workers' resort at Wingdale, New York. Among the songs were (in order of listing): "Water Boy," "Old Black Joe," "John Henry," "Carry Me Back to Ole Virginny," and "Proletarian Songs of Negro Origin" (*HL,* 15 July 1933).

60. V. J. Jerome (music by Lahn Adobmyan), "A Negro Mother to Her Child," in mimeographed program for a Harlem Section CP election rally on 30 September 1933 (in author's possession); Richard Frank, "Negro Revolutionary Music," *NM* (15 May 1934): 29.

61. Kelley, *Hammer and Hoe,* 105–8; Langston Hughes, "Good Morning Revolution," *NM* (September 1932): 8; Richard Wright, "I Have Seen Black Hands," *NM* (26 June 1934): 16.

62. Eugene Gordon, "Negro Novelists and the Negro Masses," *NM* (July 1933): 16–20.

63. Ibid.; Granville Hicks, "Revolutionary Literature in 1934," *NM* (1 January 1935); Walt Carmon, "Away from Harlem," *NM* (October 1930): 17. The *New York Amsterdam News* (7 July 1934) noted that Hughes's short stories were "intensely racial"

and were concerned more with the "tragedy of the individual rebelling against white dominance than the class system which perpetuates that dominance."

64. Gordon, "Negro Novelists," 19–20.

65. Letter from Lawrence Gellert, *NM* (20 November, 11 December 1934): 22.

66. For an example of the concept of "people's culture," see Sidney Finkelstein, *Jazz: A People's Music* (New York, 1948). Also see Ernest Kaiser, "In Defense of the People's Black and White History and Culture," in *Freedomways* (New York, 1970), 2–65.

67. John Lyman, "Stevedores and Saints," *Opportunity* 12 (May 1934), 148–50; Michael Gold, "Stevedore," *NM* (1 May 1934): 24.

68. *New York Amsterdam News*, 5 and 26 May 1934; George Streator, "'A Nigger Did It,'" *Crisis* 41 (July 1934): 216–17; Gold, "Stevedore," 29. Many blacks still had reservations about the fidelity of white workers to support for black workers. Ralph Matthews, writing in 1936 about the Federal Theater Project's production of *Turpentine* by J. A. Smith and Peter Morel, said that the play's notion of poor whites in the turpentine woods teaming up with blacks "smacks more of Union Square than Dixie realism" (Baltimore *Afro-American*, 4 July 1936).

69. *NYT*, 2 February 1934; Baltimore *Afro-American*, 3 March 1934; review by George Streator in *Crisis* 41 (April 1934): 104; Roy Wilkins, memo, 24 February 1934, C-303, NAACP Papers; *New York Amsterdam News*, 28 February, 14 April 1934. Criticisms of *They Shall Not Die* are in *NM* (13 March 1934): 22; (26 June 1934): 26. *Scottsboro, Limited* is in *NM* (November 1931): 17.

70. *HL*, 24 June 1933; *DW*, 28 July 1935.

71. *NM* (4 June 1935): 28; (11 June 1935): 27. *New York Amsterdam News*, 8 June 1935; Baltimore *Afro-American*, 8 June 1935; Naison, *Communists in Harlem*, 152–53.

72. Baltimore *Afro-American*, 8 June 1935; Hollace Ransdell, "The Soap Box Theater," *Crisis* 42 (April 1935): 122, 124–25.

73. Claude McKay, "Negroes of New York: The Harlem Artists' Guild," WPA Writers' Project, Schomburg Center, New York City; *New York Amsterdam News*, 24 November 1934. Preceding the formation of the guild, radical artists staged a groundbreaking exhibition at the ACA Gallery in New York entitled "The Struggle for Negro Rights," where the works of black artists were shown with paintings by white artists from around the world. *NM* (19 March 1935): 29.

74. Orrick Johns, "The John Reed Clubs Meet," *NM* (30 October 1934): 25.

75. Interview with Ishmael Flory, Chicago, 25 April 1974.

76. Interview with Louise Thompson Patterson, New York City, 13 April 1973; interview with Thompson Patterson by Ruth Prager, 17 October 1981, OHAL; interview with Merrill Work, Detroit, 20 April 1974; interview with Frank Sykes, Detroit, 19 April 1974; interview with Henry Winston, New York City, 13 December 1973.

77. Interview with Audley Moore by Mark Naison, 3 May 1974, OHAL; *New York Amsterdam News*, 9 February 1935; Naison, *Communists in Harlem*, 137.

78. Interview with Louise Thompson Patterson by Ruth Prager, 17 October 1981, OHAL; interview with Al Murphy by author, Charleston, Missouri, 23 April 1974.

79. Stuckey, *Going through the Storm*, 187–227; Martin B. Duberman, *Paul Robeson* (New York 1994), 184–214.

CHAPTER 15: TOWARD A NATIONAL NEGRO CONGRESS

1. T. Arnold Hill, "The Negro's Need for Unemployment Insurance," in *Unemployment Insurance Review* (New York, n.d.), 9; Israel Amter, "National Social Insurance Congress, USA," *Inprecorr* 63 (15 December 1934): 1687–88.

2. *Chicago Defender*, 21 July 1934; Baltimore *Afro-American*, 28 July, 4 August 1934; Jesse O. Thomas, "Negro Workers and Organized Labor," *Opportunity* 12 (September 1934): 277.

3. Baltimore *Afro-American*, 14 April 1934.

4. *Chicago Defender*, 12 and 26 October 1934. The NAACP's San Francisco branch participated in the picketing of the convention. *Crisis* 42 (November 1934): 342; Foner, *Organized Labor*, 205–7; *Opportunity* 12 (October 1934): 299; 12 (December 1934): 384–85.

5. *New York Amsterdam News*, 13 July 1935; Foner, *Organized Labor*, 208. The committee was led by John Brophy of the UMW. He was the only member of the group who was sympathetic to the demands of black workers.

6. *New York Amsterdam News*, 12 October 1935. Abram Harris also led a "swing to the left" at the annual conference of the NAACP in 1935, calling for a pervasive "union of white and black labor." *Chicago Defender*, 15 June 1935.

7. *NL*, 15 July 1935; *New York Amsterdam News*, 9 March, 27 July 1935. All was not sweet between Communists and Socialists in 1935. Crosswaith held a "trade union solidarity" rally at Rockland Palace at the start of the year. Communists in the audience tried to get the floor for Scottsboro mother Ida Norris. When James Ford and Ben Davis brought Mrs. Norris to the platform, Crosswaith adjourned the meeting. Fighting broke out between YCL members and Socialist youth. The police cleared the hall. *New York Amsterdam News*, 12 January 1935.

8. Foner, *Organized Labor*, 209.

9. American Social History Project, Joshua Freeman et al., *Who Built America? Working People and the Nation's Economy, Politics, Culture, and Society* (New York, 1992), 406–7; Foner, *Organized Labor*, 211–12; Baltimore *Afro-American*, 26 October 1935.

10. Horace R. Cayton and George Mitchell, *Black Workers and the New Unions* (Chapel Hill, N.C., 1939), 342–68.

11. Robert C. Weaver, "The New Deal and the Negro," *Opportunity* 13 (July 1935): 200; Nancy J. Weiss, *Farewell to the Party of Lincoln: Black Politics in the Age of FDR* (Princeton, N.J., 1983), 209–35; Loren Miller, "One Way Out — Communism," *Op-*

portunity 12 (July 1934): 216; Lester Granger, "Industrial Unionism and the Negro, *Opportunity* 14 (January 1936): 30; Leon P. Miller, "The Negro and the 'Closed Shop,'" *Opportunity* 13 (June 1935): 168; Baltimore *Afro-American*, 15 July, 9 September 1933; "The Rosenwald Conference," *Crisis* 40 (July 1933): 156–57. The *Crisis* said that it was "self evident to minority groups in this country that the best insurance against the destruction of their liberties is joint action" against fascist reaction (editorial, *Crisis* 42 [January 1936]: 17).

12. Lester B. Granger, "Negro Workers and Recovery," *Opportunity* 12 (May 1934): 153; T. Arnold Hill, "Workers to Lead the Way Out," *Opportunity* 12 (June 1934): 183; Hill, "The Urban League and Negro Labor: Yesterday, Today, and Tomorrow," *Opportunity* 13 (November 1935): 340–42, 349.

13. Lester B. Granger, "Leaders Wanted—1934 Model," *Opportunity* 12 (October 1934): 311.

14. *New York Amsterdam News*, 6 July 1935.

15. Baltimore *Afro-American*, 6 July 1935.

16. *Chicago Defender*, 7 December 1935; Baltimore *Afro-American*, 30 November, 21 December 1935.

17. Central Committee, CPUSA, TUUL Bureau, Manning Johnson, "Report on Negro TU Work in New York," December 1934, RTsKhIDNI 534/7/520/60.

18. Ibid.

19. Foner, *Organized Labor*, 213.

20. Cayton and Mitchell, *Black Workers*, 82–87, 111–22, 132, 138–40, 257, 262, 337–41; Klehr, *The Heyday of American Communism*, 223–51.

21. Interviews with William Allen and Irene Marinovich, Detroit, 18 April 1974; *Chicago Defender*, 8 August, 12 September 1936; Baltimore *Afro-American*, 15 February, 17 October 1936; interview with Claude Lightfoot, Gary, Indiana, 25–26 April 1974; interview with Nate Sharpe, Chicago, 24 April 1974; *New York Amsterdam News*, 13 July 1935, 8 February, 14 March 1936.

22. The most authentic exposition of the united front (unity of all sectors of the working class) and the "people's" or "popular" front (multiclass antifascist unity led by the proletariat) is Georgi Dimitroff's main report to the Seventh Congress of the Comintern: Dimitroff, "The Fascist Offensive and the Tasks of the Communist International," in *The United Front: Problems of Working Class Unity and the People's Front in the Struggle against Fascism and War* (New York, 1938), 9–93. Also Kelley, *Hammer and Hoe*, 173.

23. "Comrade M.," "Achievements and Tasks of the Share Croppers' Union," in *Proceedings of the Extraordinary Conference of the Communist Party, July 7–10, 1933* (New York, 1933), 39–48.

24. Nat Ross, "Some Problems of the Class Struggle in the South," *Communist* 14 (October 1935): 968–69; Ross, "Next Steps in Alabama and the Lower South," *Communist* 14 (October 1935): 976.

25. Kelley, *Hammer and Hoe*, 151; interview with Hosea Hudson, Atlantic City, New Jersey, 14 December 1974.

26. Al Murphy to Mark Solomon, 8 July 1974 (in author's possession); interview with Al Murphy in Charleston, Missouri, 22–23 April 1974; Kelley, *Hammer and Hoe*, 159–60; Haywood, *Black Bolshevik*, 447.

27. Rosen, "The Alabama Share Croppers' Union," 59.

28. Al Murphy, "The Share Croppers' Union Grows and Fights," *Party Organizer* (May–June 1934): 44–48; *DW*, 15, 20, 25 May 1935; Kelley, *Hammer and Hoe*, 163; Ross, "Next Steps in the South," 973–74; SCU leaflet, "The Cotton Choppers Strike Has Been Won!" STFU Papers; editorial, "Death in the Black Belt," *NM* (10 September 1935): 5; "Labor in Action Again" (24 September 1935): 9; *NL*, 1 September 1934; Robert Wood (Charles Sherill), *To Live and Die in Dixie* (New York, n.d,), 27.

29. Ross, "The Next Steps in Alabama and the Lower South," 974; Kelley, *Hammer and Hoe*, 164. E. B. McKinney, a black organizer in the STFU, was expelled in 1939, in part for attempting to organize a Negro caucus within the union. Rosen, "Alabama Share Croppers Union," 104.

30. H. L. Mitchell to Gardner Jackson, 23 September 1936, STFU Papers.

31. Kelley, *Hammer and Hoe*, 165.

32. Wood, "To Live and Die in Dixie," 27–28; "Three Lynch Affidavits," *NM* (22 October 1935): 16–18; Rosen, "Alabama Share Croppers Union," 69–70; Kelley, *Hammer and Hoe*, 166. The names of some croppers are spelled differently in varied accounts. For example, "Meriwether" is often spelled "Meriweather," or "Merriweather." I have chosen the spelling that appears in the affidavits.

33. Kelley, *Hammer and Hoe*, 169–70.

34. Rosen, "Alabama Share Croppers Union," 105–9.

35. Kelley, *Hammer and Hoe*, 171–72; Rosen, "Alabama Share Croppers Union," 109–13.

36. Harold M. Ware, "A Revolution in Cotton," *NM* (8 October 1935): 11–16; Rosen, "Alabama Share Croppers Union," 112–17.

37. Rosen, "Alabama Share Croppers Union," 92; Kelley, *Hammer and Hoe*, 174–75.

38. Martin, *The Angelo Herndon Case*, 140–67; *New York Amsterdam News*, 26 October 1935; "A Message from Angelo Herndon," *LD* 11 (November 1935): 12.

39. Martin, *The Angelo Herndon Case*, 169–74; memo by Charles H. Houston, 20 July 1936, D-59, NAACP Papers; *NYT*, 23 February 1937.

40. "Angelo Herndon Is Free," *Negro Worker* 2, no. 6 (June 1937): 3.

41. Goodman, *Stories of Scottsboro*, 395; Anna Damon, "Scottsboro Victory Rocks the South," *LD* 11 (May 1935): 7; Osmond K. Fraenkel, "The Legal Status of the Scottsboro Case," *LD* 11 (July 1935): 11.

42. Memorandum by Walter White, 14 October 1935, D-74, NAACP Papers; Carter, *Scottsboro*, 333.

43. Central Committee, CPUSA, "Re: Scottsboro Joint Committee," 9 October 1935, RTsKhIDNI 515/1/3933/17; memorandum by Walter White, 14 October 1935, D-74,

NAACP Papers. Leibowitz turned out to be the major stumbling block for the ACLU and the NAACP, but not necessarily for the CP. Roger Baldwin reported that the ACLU board unanimously wished Leibowitz to withdraw because it believed that the boys would never be freed as long as the Brooklyn lawyer headed the defense. After delicate negotiations, Leibowitz agreed to move into the background at the next trial, allowing a southern lawyer to take over in the courtroom.

44. Carter, *Scottsboro*, 334–35.

45. Goodman, *Stories of Scottsboro*, 278–397; *Crisis* 42 (March 1936): 88.

46. *Inprecorr* 15, no. 45 (1934): 1061.

47. James W. Ford, "The United Front in the Field of Negro Work," *Communist* 14 (February 1935): 165; report of James W. Ford on the National Negro Congress, "Special Meeting of the Negro Commission of the Central Executive Committee and the Harlem Section," 13 June 1935, RTsKhIDNI 515/1/3775/19. Ford's report provides the basis for the discussion in the following paragraphs.

48. Eleanor Ryan, "Toward a National Negro Congress," *NM* (4 June 1935): 14, 46.

49. Ford's proposal for an economic bill of rights predated Franklin D. Roosevelt's similar idea by eight years. Ford, "Special Meeting," RTsKhIDNI 515/1/3775/23; James W. Ford, "The Coming National Negro Congress," *Communist* 15 (February 1936): 140–41.

50. Later Ford offered an unflattering comparison between the LSNR and the NNC. Of the eighty-six members of the LSNR National Council, sixty-two were Communists. Of the seventy-five members of the NNC Council, fewer than ten were Party members. Ford, "Special Report," RTsKhIDNI 515/1/3775/23; James W. Ford, "Build the National Negro Congress Movement," *Communist* 15 (June 1936): 560.

51. Lawrence S. Wittner, "The National Negro Congress: A Reassessment," *American Quarterly* 12 (winter 1970): 883–97.

52. "Meeting of Negro Commission, CC and Harlem Section Committee," 18 November 1935, RTsKhIDNI 515/1/3775/31. The transcript of Davis's report was unsigned, but his authorship is indisputable. He refers specifically to "an article in May in the *Crisis* under my name in which the conference is projected." The article is John P. Davis, "A Black Inventory of the New Deal," *Crisis* 42 (May 1935): 55. The report also contained a wealth of detailed information on Davis's travels and meetings that only Davis himself could provide.

53. "Meeting of Negro Commission, CC and Harlem Section Committee," 18 November 1935, RTsKhIDNI 515/1/3775/34–35. The breadth of Davis's contacts before the congress is summarized in the *New York Amsterdam News*, 1 June 1935.

54. Wittner, "The National Negro Congress," 897–901.

55. Rosengarten, *All God's Dangers*, xiv.

Bibliographical Essay

Historians who have sought to write about the history of the American Communist Party have often complained of an absence of coherent records and reliable accounts of the Party's decision — making processes. Many have griped about a netherworld of hidden motives and agendas, and about a mountain of verbiage and self-congratulation that threatened to unhinge the most intrepid researcher. Justified or not, a good deal of that disquiet has been negated by the opening of files relating to American communism in the Russian Center for the Preservation and Study of Documents of Contemporary History (RTsKhIDNI), in Moscow. Other major developments, such as the discovery of a complete set of Cyril Briggs's pioneering *Crusader,* have lightened the historian's task and have opened the door to realization of fuller and more balanced studies of American communism.

The task of deciphering communism is also eased for the period under study by the Party's practice of merciless self-criticism, which obliged its members to bare publicly their shortcomings, disappointments, and outright failures — even as they exalted their revolutionary leadership. Mixed with garish claims like that of being the "party of the Negro people," the Communists in the 1920s and 1930s compiled largely accurate, often self-deflating figures on black membership and the scope of work in black communities. Endless exhumations of the causes of weaknesses, along with manifest achievements, also provide the historian insight into the problems inherent in the sought-after black-red fusion.

The responses of African Americans to the reds in their midst are reflected in the pervasive interest in and animated exploration of radicalism to be found in black newspapers, magazines, and journals; the files of leading organizations; and personal collections. These vast primary sources from black life, along with the documents of the Russian archives, the papers of prominent American Communists and others, and interviews with dozens of participants in the events under study, provide this book's foundation.

Following is a description of the key sources used in this study. Additional materials are cited in the notes.

Manuscript Collections and Other Primary Sources

The papers of the Russian Center for Preservation and Study of Documents of Contemporary History (RTsKhIDNI) in Moscow are divided into scores of "fonds" (collections) representing discrete organizational structures that existed in modern Russia, principally in the Soviet period. Research for this book concentrated on three deposits: the massive Fond 495, documents of the Executive Committee of the Communist International; Fond 515, documents of the Communist Party USA; Fond 532, documents of the University of the Toilers of the East (KUTV); and Fond 534, documents of the Red International of Labor Unions. This by no means exhausts the research possibilities in RTsKhIDNI for the study of American Communists and black Americans. However, the most important and revealing documents are in these deposits. The papers of the ECCI (Fond 495), for example, run the gamut from John Reed's reflections on the Negro question in the United States, to Claude McKay's personal letters to Comintern officials in the formative days of the CI, to Comintern correspondence regarding the founding of the American Negro Labor Congress, the League of Struggle for Negro Rights, and other groups. Perhaps the most important document in Fond 495 is the virtually complete set of transcripts of the pivotal debate on the Negro question at the Sixth Congress. These transcripts follow the discussion from its beginning in the Anglo-American secretariat to its completion in the larger Colonial Commission. Fond 515 contains extensive minutes of meetings of leading bodies of the American Communist Party, including various minutes of the Party's Negro Commission. Fond 534 holds a large correspondence between American Communists and the RILU on racial issues in the trade unions. The most helpful guide to understanding and using RTsKhIDNI is J. Arch Getty and V. P. Kozlov, eds., *Russian Center for Preservation and Study of Documents of Contempory History: A Research Guide* (Moscow, 1993).

The multivolume *Marcus Garvey and Universal Negro Improvement Association Papers,* edited by Robert A. Hill (Berkeley, Calif., 1983–), ranges widely into the vibrant culture of the New Negro Crowd in the early 1920s and captures a trove of material on Briggs, *The Crusader,* and federal surveillance of black radicals.

Various government documents also illuminate relentless monitoring of post–World War I black radicals and provide a sketch of the daily lives of the pioneer black Communists. The richest source of such material is Theodore Kornweibel, ed., *Federal Surveillance of Afro-Americans (1917–1925): The First World War, the Red Scare, and the Garvey Movement* (Frederick, Md., 1985). The microfilm collection of U.S. Military Intelligence reports, *Surveillance of Radicals in the United States,* 1917–1941, edited by Randolph Boehm (Frederick, Md., 1984), has some interesting material on the involvement of African Americans in the Socialist and early Communist movements as well as in the Comintern. However, since they relied on raw, unsubstantiated data filtered through the U.S. legation in Riga, Latvia, these reports at times were a poisoned well of bizarre misinformation. The congressional investigation of Communist activities among blacks by the Fish Committee in 1930 is in U.S. Congress, Special Committee on Communist Activities, *Investigation of Communist Propaganda in the United States,* 71st Cong., 2d sess. (Washington, D.C., 1930).

Two major collections were crucial for this study. The Library of Congress is the repository of the papers of the National Association for the Advancement of Colored People, which were indispensable in exploring Scottsboro and the general relationship between black middle-class leaders and the Communists. The papers of the International Labor Defense at the Schomburg Center for Research in Black Culture in New York portrayed the exhaustive labors of Communists and their allies against "lynch justice." Those two collections, so different in ideological and political perspective, had a symbiotic relationship that underscored both clashing outlooks and grudging movement toward common ground.

The Robert Minor Papers at Columbia University, New York, include an extensive collection of CP position papers and resolutions, as well as Minor's own assessments of the Party's "Negro Work" and his often penetrating thoughts on the Negro question.

Among the most useful manuscript sources was the well-mined Theodore Draper Collection at Emory University, Atlanta, which contains materials gathered by Draper for his chapter in *American Communism and Soviet Russia* (Vintage paperback edition, New York, 1986) on the Negro question. Draper's correspondence with Briggs, Joseph Kornfeder, and others presents a vivid picture of the sources of many of his influential (though open to challenge) assertions. The Southern California Research Library in Los Angeles holds some of Briggs's correspondence as well as a substantial collection of radical pamphlets. The Henry Kraus Papers at the Archive of Labor History and Urban Affairs at Wayne State University in Detroit contain valuable material on the fight for racial equality in the auto industry and on the Ford Hunger March. The papers of the journalist Mary Heaton Vorse in the same archive contain notes and observations on the Gastonia strike and on other episodes in the fight to bring racial justice to the South. The papers of the influential black journalist and editor, Claude Barnett, at the Chicago Historical Society contain useful material on Communist electoral activities among blacks. The CHS also has a substantial file of materials relating to the Unemployed Councils and Communist battles with relief agencies in the black community.

Robert Kaufman was an indefatigable researcher who died tragically at a young age while preparing a doctoral dissertation on radical black labor. He had accumulated vast amounts of material on a range of personalities, issues, and organizations. Unfortunately, he did not leave precise notations for a mountain of letters and documents culled from the NAACP and ILD papers and from journals, newspapers, and other sources. However, the material is broken down topically into files (such as "The Sanhedrin," "Scottsboro," "Anti-Lynch," "Black Labor," etc.) and has been deposited with the Tamiment Institute, Bobst Library, New York University, where scholars will have access to it. Mary Licht of the Communist Party's history commission located Hermina Huiswoud's memorandum on Otto Huiswoud's role in founding the Communist Party.

The Oral History of the American Left project of the Tamiment Institute was a valuable supplement to my interviews with Louise Thompson Patterson and Maude White Katz, and also contained a useful interview with Audley Moore. The New York Public Library provided microfilmed copies of *The Liberator*, various left-wing labor publications, and scattered copies of *The Crusader* before publication of the full set. The Papers of the Southern Tenant Farmers' Union at the University of North Carolina, Chapel Hill, contain revealing documents on the STFU's shaky relationship with the Share Croppers' Union.

NEWSPAPERS AND PERIODICALS

Publication of the complete file of *The Crusader* in three volumes under the editorship of Robert A. Hill (New York, 1987) made it possible to explore in depth Cyril Briggs's ideological development, the evolution of the African Blood Brotherhood, and the impact of Briggs and the Brotherhood upon the CP's first approaches to black America. Hill's introductory essay in volume 1 is a model of impeccable scholarship and incisive thinking—and an indispensable guide to study of the emergence of revolutionary socialism in the black community.

A major source for Communist perspectives on the Negro question is *The Liberator,* the Party-sponsored weekly under Cyril Briggs's editorship from 1929 to 1933 and at various times the organ of the American Negro Labor Congress and the League of Struggle for Negro Rights. After Briggs's departure, the paper lingered as the *Harlem Liberator* and the *Negro Liberator.* Attacked often within the Party as turgid, narrow, and formalistic, *The Liberator,* nevertheless, was a fount of information on CP activities in the black community, and despite reflecting primarily Briggs's distinct interpretations of CP policy, it was also a mirror of the Party's evolving viewpoint on black liberation.

The *Daily Worker* provided a steady stream of reportage and commentary on the Communists' work among blacks. Although the accuracy of its reports on such things as the size and scope of radical demonstrative activities have to be carefully scrutinized, the Party's official paper carried opinion pieces, commentary, and self-critical articles from correspondents in the field that offer a graphic picture of the Party's labors. The *Southern Worker* was an indispensable tool for surveying Communist activity in the South, assessing the Party's strength in the area, and getting a picture of the problems inherent in southern organizing. The New York Public Library provided a few surviving copies of ANLC's *Negro Champion* and the *Hunger Fighter,* which gave a picture of the scope of the work among the jobless done by the CP and the Unemployed Councils.

The ILD's *Labor Defender* covered the battle for defense of blacks in the legal system and against lynching. *Labor Unity,* the publication of the Trade Union Unity League, articulated the TUUL's egalitarian aspirations and the frustrating resistance to equal rights in its own ranks and in the labor movement in general. *Workers' Monthly* carried occasional theoretical pieces on the Negro question in the formative 1920s. *The Communist,* the Party's theoretical organ published during the period under study, printed scores of articles on the Communist position on the Negro question. The *Party Organizer* was the vehicle of grassroots activists, often vividly describing both the small victories and the shortcomings in daily political work for Negro rights. *New Masses,* the Marxist cultural organ, opened its pages to explorations of black culture and to debates on the relationship between politics and esthetics. International publications, such as *Communist International, Inprecorr* (International Press Correspondence of the Comintern), and *The Negro Worker,* contained edgy, tendentious, but also at times penetrating articles on the movement for black freedom in the United States and the liberation battles of nonwhite populations in the colonies and semi-colonies.

The African American press and black periodicals constituted a remarkable running commentary, collective diary, and multifaceted dialogue on black life in the United States and in the world. Despite middle-class control of black media, they expressed a wide variety of views on the meaning and importance of Communist work among blacks. The Baltimore *Afro-American's* coverage of Party-generated activities was lavish and generally approving. The *Pittsburgh Courier* also reported heavily on Communists from a largely critical point of view. The *Chicago Defender* always surprised its readers with a mixture of awe, admiration, disquiet, and disapproval for the reds. The *Norfolk Journal and Guide* similarly mixed censure with recognition of the leverage upon the larger society offered by the Communists. The *Chicago Whip* provided the most comprehensive coverage in the black press of Chicago's unemployed workers' demonstrations and the bloodshed in August 1931. The *New York Amsterdam News* was consistently hostile to the Party, but thorough in its coverage of its activities, particularly in Harlem. In the 1920s, UNIA's *Negro World* was an authentic barometer of Garvey's views on the Communists. The ILD's huge clipping file (in the ILD Papers) on Scottsboro in the Negro press offered partial, but useful, insights into the views of smaller, more localized African American papers.

Among the magazines and journals, Du Bois's *Crisis* was the most trenchant critic of the Communists — particularly of their tactics in the Scottsboro case — and of the applicability of Marxism to the black experience. The National Urban League's *Opportunity* contained many probing pieces on black labor and in that connection dealt sympathetically (and surprisingly) with radical efforts to forge a Negro-labor alliance.

The *New York Times* regularly covered Scottsboro, unemployed workers' demonstrations, the Herndon case, and other issues relating to Communist efforts among blacks. The *Chicago Daily News* and the *Chicago Tribune* had extensive reportage on their city's South Side upheavals. The *Birmingham Age-Herald*, the *Birmingham Post*, the *Birmingham News*, and the *Montgomery Advertiser* were particularly useful in plotting Communist activities in rural Alabama and the South in general. Among the journals, *The Nation* and the *New Republic* paid attention rather consistently to black-red issues, with the latter taking a more critical stance.

INTERVIEWS

Given understandable human lapses of memory regarding past events, interviews with participants were less useful than documents in verifying specific happenings. However, the importance of interviews to this study was in a far more significant area: giving human voice and sensibility to occurrences and ideas whose complexity and emotional force could never be satisfactorily inferred from documents. Two days spent with Al Murphy, for example, confirmed his inner strength as well as the pain in his eyes, which refracted the horrors faced by Black Belt organizers decades earlier. Louise Patterson's ebullience, Maude White's icy calm, Harry Haywood's irrepressible contentiousness, Claude Lightfoot's expansiveness, William Patterson's reflectiveness, Herbert Benjamin's reawakened feistiness as he mulled the tactical lessons of organizing the unemployed: All these gave life to this study of Communist political activity in the black community, and also a feel for the reality of it all that could be not attained in any other way. Every person interviewed (including those whose interviews are not used here) contributed in that respect. Interviews were conducted with the following individuals:

James S. Allen, New York City, 24 March 1974
William Allen, Detroit, 18 April 1974
Christopher Alston, Detroit, 21 April 1974
B. D. Amis, Philadelphia, 19 and 20 March 1974
Herbert Benjamin, Silver Spring, Maryland, 7 April 1974
Lloyd Brown, New York City, 2 February 1974
Rose Chernin, Los Angeles, 3 January 1973
William Crawford, Philadelphia, 3 April 1974
Ishmael Flory, Chicago, 25 and 27 April 1974
Harry Haywood, Detroit, 12 and 13 April 1974

Hosea Hudson, Atlantic City, New Jersey, 14 December 1974
James Jackson, New York City (by phone), 11 September 1996
Maude White Katz, New York City, 2 March and 4 April 1974
Jack Kling, Chicago, 25 April 1974
Claude Lightfoot, Chicago and Gary, Indiana, 25 and 26 April 1974
Irene Marinovich, Detroit, 18 April 1974
Francis Meli, Moscow and New Delhi, 30 November and 1 December 1974
David Moore, Detroit (by phone), 14 April 1981
Charlene Mitchell, Boston, 17 June 1995
Al Murphy, Charleston, Missouri, 22 and 23 April 1974
Louise Thompson Patterson, New York City, 13 April 1973 and 28 June
    1974
William L. Patterson, New York City, 13 and 19 April 1973, 28 June 1974
Carl Reeve, Philadelphia, 21 March and 6 April 1974
Anne Reeve, Philadelphia, 21 March and 6 April 1974
Nate Sharpe, Chicago, 24 April 1974
Frank Sykes, Detroit, 16 and 19 April 1974
William Taylor, Los Angeles, 7 and 9 January 1973
Anne B. Timpson, Boston, 24 June and 22 August 1987, 11 and 14
    September 1995
Ralph Turner, Chicago, 25 April 1974
Thomas "Ace" Walton, Los Angeles, 17 January 1973
William Weinstone, New York City, 18 June and 11 August 1974
Don Wheeldin, Los Angeles, 5 and 6 January 1973
Frank Whitley, Los Angeles, 14 January 1973
Henry Winston, New York City, 13 December 1973
Carl Winter, New York City, 23 May and 24 June 1980, 6 October 1981
Merrill Work, Detroit, 16 and 20 April 1974

In addition, there was written correspondence with Samuel A. Darcy, Horace
B. Davis, Theodore Draper, and William Weinstone.

SECONDARY GENERAL SOURCES AND BIOGRAPHICAL ACCOUNTS

Among the small number of books on reds and blacks left over from the Cold
War, only Harold Cruse's *Crisis of the Negro Intellectual* (New York, 1967) remains worthy of a serious response. Theodore Draper's *American Communism and Soviet Russia* (Vintage paperback edition, New York, 1986) provides

reliable background material on the early years of American communism. His interpretation of the CP position on the Negro question also compels a response. William Z. Foster's *History of the Communist Party of the United States* (New York, 1952) presents an "official" portrait of CP history—eliminating figures consigned to oblivion while stressing Foster's own quasi-syndicalist viewpoint to the detriment of political probing. At the same time, the book presents a record of concrete struggle absent from Draper's work. Harvey Klehr's *Heyday of American Communism: The Depression Decade* (New York, 1984) is a heavily researched and factually reliable account of the Party's efforts in the active Depression years. Although Klehr is drawn to the Moscow-first line inherited from Draper and is preoccupied with factional intrigues and a steady tatoo of failure, he does not ignore effective mass campaigns. Klehr's *Communist Cadre* (Stanford, Calif., 1978) contains valuable information on Party membership and demographics. Two useful compilations of materials from the public record are Philip S. Foner and James S. Allen, *American Communism and Black Americans: A Documentary History, 1919–1929* (Philadelphia, 1987), and Philip S. Foner and Herbert Shapiro, *American Communism and Black Americans: A Documentary History, 1930–1934* (Philadelphia, 1991). The scattered writings on the Negro question in V. I. Lenin's *Collected Works* (Moscow, 1966) were valuable for grasping the evolution of Comintern policy regarding American blacks. The most authoritative compilation of Comintern documents before opening of the archive remains Jane Degras, ed., *The Communist International, 1919–1943: Documents*, 3 vols. (London, 1956–65).

Among the biographies and autobiographies, the ones most useful to this study were Claude McKay, *A Long Way from Home* (New York, 1970); Wayne F. Cooper, *Claude McKay: Rebel Sojourner in the Harlem Renaissance* (Baton Rouge, La., 1987); Claude McKay, *The Negroes in America*, edited by Alan L. McLeod (Port Washington, N.Y., 1979); Joyce Moore Turner's excellent biography of Richard B. Moore in W. Burghardt Turner and Joyce Moore Turner, *Richard B. Moore, Caribbean Militant in Harlem: Collected Writings, 1920–1972* (Bloomington, Ind., 1988); Harry Haywood, *Black Bolshevik: Autobiography of an Afro-American Communist* (Chicago, 1978); Edward P. Johanningsmeier, *Forging American Communism: The Life of William Z. Foster* (Princeton, N.J., 1994); James R. Hooker, *Black Revolutionary: George Padmore's Path from Communism to Pan-Africanism* (London, 1967); Nell Irvin Painter, *The Narrative of Hosea Hudson: His Life as a Negro Communist in the South* (Cambridge, Mass., 1980); Arnold Rampersad, *The Life of Langston Hughes: I Too Sing America*, vol. 1:

1902–1941 (New York, 1986): Angelo Herndon, *Let Me Live* (Arno Press reprint edition, New York, 1969).

Many works by other historians contributed to this study. The most important were the two outstanding regional studies that have appeared in recent years: Mark Naison, *Communists in Harlem during the Depression* (Urbana, Ill., 1983); and Robin D.G. Kelley, *Hammer and Hoe: Alabama Communists during the Great Depression* (Chapel Hill, N.C., 1990). Those two books considerably eased the burden of preparing this study. Other useful works were Charles Martin, *The Angelo Herndon Case and Southern Justice* (Baton Rouge, La., 1976); Theodore Kornweibel Jr., *No Crystal Stair: Black Life and the Messenger, 1917–1928* (Westport, Conn., 1975); Scott Ellsworth, *Death in a Promised Land: The Tulsa Riot of 1921* (Baton Rouge, La., 1982); Allison Blakely, *Russia and the Negro: Blacks in Russian History and Thought* (Washington, D.C., 1986); Philip S. Foner, *Organized Labor and the Black Worker: 1619–1973* (New York, 1974); and Tom Tippet, *When Southern Labor Stirs: The Strike at Gastonia* (Huntington, W.Va., 1972). Although one may question Dan T. Carter's understanding of Communist motives and tactics, the narrative clarity of his *Scottsboro: A Tragedy of the American South* (New York, 1971) makes it an essential work for grasping that complex case. James Goodman's *Stories of Scottsboro* (New York, 1994) is a brilliant kaleidoscope of the sharply diverging social and ideological viewpoints that raged around the case.

Two works on blacks and the Great Depression provided helpful background: Raymond Wolters, *Negroes and the Great Depression: The Problem of Economic Recovery* (Westport, Conn., 1970); and Harvard Sitkoff, *A New Deal for Blacks: The Emergence of Civil Rights as a National Issue, The Depression Decade* (New York, 1978).

Of scores of journal articles, the following were the most pertinent: William Muraskin, "The Harlem Boycott of 1934: Black Nationalism and the Rise of Labor Union Consciousness," *Labor History* 13 (Summer 1972); Woodford Mc-Clellan, "Africans and Black Americans in the Comintern Schools, 1925–34," *International Journal of African Historical Studies* 36, no. 2 (May 1993); Roger E. Kanet, "The Comintern and the 'Negro Question': Communist Policy in the U.S. and Africa," *Survey* 19, no. 4 (Autumn 1973); Hugh T. Murray Jr., "The NAACP versus the Communist Party: The Scottsboro Rape Cases, 1931–1932," *Phylon* 28 (1967); Hugh T. Murray Jr., "Aspects of the Scottsboro Campaign," *Science and Society* 35 (Summer 1971). I offer my apologies to scholars whose works are not cited here, due to space constraints.

Index